CHAUCER ILLUSTRATED

Five Hundred Years of The Canterbury Tales in Pictures

"And what is the use of a book," thought Alice,
"without pictures or conversations?"

- Alice in Wonderland, ch. 1

Drawn by Mortimer.   Engraved by Hogg.

DEPARTURE of the CANTERBURY PILGRIMES. *Prologue.* Canterbury Tale. Chaucer

London Published Feb.y 2.th 1787 by I. R. Smith, N.o 31 King Street Covent Garden.

Mortimer, Departure of the Canterbury Pilgrims

CHAUCER ILLUSTRATED
Five Hundred Years of The Canterbury Tales in Pictures

WILLIAM K. FINLEY & JOSEPH ROSENBLUM

OAK KNOLL PRESS &
THE BRITISH LIBRARY

2003

First Edition, 2003

Published by **Oak Knoll Press**
310 Delaware Street, New Castle, Delaware, USA
Web:http://www.oakknoll.com
and **The British Library**
96 Euston Road, St. Pancras, London, NWI 2DB, UK

ISBN: 1-58456-102-5 (USA)
ISBN: 0-7123-4816-6 (UK)

Title: Chaucer Illustrated: Five Hundred Years of The Canterbury Tales in Pictures
Editors: William K. Finley & Joseph Rosenblum
Typography: Adam Koster
Illustration reproduction: Spearhead Worldwide Inc.
Cover design by Adam Koster & Michael Hohne Designs
Publishing Director: J. Lewis von Hoelle

Library of Congress Cataloging-in-Publication Data

Chaucer illustrated : five hundred years of the Canterbury tales in pictures / edited
   by William K. Finley and Joseph Rosenblum.
        p. cm.
   Includes bibliographical references and index.
   ISBN 1-58456-102-5
     1. Chaucer, Geoffery, d 1400. Canterbury tales--Illustrations. 2. Christian pil-
grims and pilgrimages in art. 3. Tales, Medieval--Illustrations. I. Finley, William
Kirkland, 1947- II. Rosenblum, Joseph.

   PR1874.C48 2003
   821'.1--dc21

                                                                    2003040585

British Library Cataloguing-in-Publication Data
A CIP Record is available from The British Library

This work was printed in the United States of America on 60# & 80#
archival, acid-free paper meeting the requirements of the American
Standard for Permanence of Paper for Printed Library Materials.

CONTENTS

(Color plates follow page 206)

LIST OF ILLUSTRATIONS

PLEASE NOTE: Figures refer to the black and white illustrations accompanying each chapter. Color plates refer to the portfolio of color images that appear following p. 206.

168 of unknown work, bound into a copy of *The Works of Geoffrey Chaucer*, ed. John Urry (London, 1721), fEC. C3932.C/721 W, facing page 27. 15.5 cm. x 21 cm. The Houghton Library, Harvard University

Figure 9. *Miller of Trompington and Two Scholars*. Drawn by John Hamilton Mortimer (before 1779), engraved by William Sharp (1787). Leaf intended for volume 2, page 193 of unknown work, bound into a copy of *The Works of Geoffrey Chaucer*, ed. John Urry (London, 1721), fEC. C3932.C/72 I W) facing page 32. 15.5 cm. x 21 cm. The Houghton Library, Harvard University

Figure 10. *The Coke and Perkin*. Drawn by John Hamilton Mortimer (before 1779), engraved by Edward Williams (1787). Leaf intended for volume 2, page 212 of unknown work, bound into a copy of *The Works of Geoffrey Chaucer*, ed. John Urry (London, 1721), fEC. C3932.C/721 W, facing page 35. 15.5 cm. x 21 cm. The Houghton Library, Harvard University

Figure 11. *The Sompnour, Devil, and Old Woman*. Drawn by John Hamilton Mortimer (before 1779), engraved by Jacob Hogg (1787). Leaf intended for volume 3, page 71/72 of unknown work, bound into a copy of *The Works of Geoffrey Chaucer*, ed. John Urry (London, 1721), fEC. C3932.C/721 W, facing page 88. 15.5 cm. x 21 cm. The Houghton Library, Harvard University

Figure 12. *The Frere and Thomas*. Drawn by John Hamilton Mortimer (before 1779), engraved by Jacob Hogg (1787). Leaf intended for volume 3, page 93 of unknown work, bound into a copy of *The Works of Geoffrey Chaucer*, ed. John Urry (London, 1721) fEC. C3932.C/721 W, facing page 94. 15.5 cm. x 21 cm. The Houghton Library, Harvard University

Figure 13. Scene from the Second Nun's Tale, citing VIII:222-23. Drawn by Thomas Stothard, engraved by James Heath. Frontispiece to volume 5 of *The Poets of Great Britian*, ed. John Bell (London, 1782-83, rpt. 1807). 6.4 cm. x 6.4 cm. Rare Book Department, The Free Library of Philadelphia

Figure 14. Scene from the Shipman's Tale, citing VI:156-57. Drawn by Thomas Stothard, engraved by James Heath. Frontispiece to volume 4 of *The Poets of Great Britian*, ed. John Bell (London, 1782-83, rpt. 1807). 6.4 cm. x 6.4 cm. Rare Book Department, The Free Library of Philadelphia

Figure 15. The Friar. Drawn by James Jefferys (1781), no engraver credited. 27.5 cm. x 33 cm. Department of Printing and Graphic Arts, The Houghton Library, Harvard University

Figure 16. The Manciple. Drawn by James Jefferys (1781). 27.5 cm. x 36 cm. Department of Printing and Graphic Arts, The Houghton Library, Harvard University

Figure 17. The Cook. Drawn by James Jefferys (1781). 27.5 cm. x 36 cm. Department of Printing and Graphic Arts, The Houghton Library, Harvard University

Figure 18. The Five Citizens. Drawn by James Jefferys (1781). 27.5 cm. x 36 cm. Department of Printing and Graphic Arts, The Houghton Library, Harvard University

Figure 19. The Franklin. Drawn by James Jefferys (1781). 27.5 cm. x 36 cm. Department of Printing and Graphic Arts, The Houghton Library, Harvard University

Appendix 3
Figures 1-3 reproduce Robert van Vorst Sewell's murals executed for George
    Gould's Georgian Court, Lakeside, New Jersey. Reproduced courtesy of M.
    Christina Geis and Georgian Court College

ACKNOWLEDGMENTS

The editors wish to thank first of all the University of North Carolina at Greensboro for its generous financial support of our efforts. Without a university grant, we would have produced a much-diminished volume. We also wish to thank the many individuals and institutions that kindly supplied images for this volume and allowed us to reproduce these pictures. They are noted in the list of illustrations. The interlibrary loan department of Walter Clinton Jackson Library of the University of North Carolina at Greensboro secured many needed items in a timely fashion, and the university's computer staff was invariably helpful. Creative Services of the Teaching and Learning Center, UNCG, produced many of the lovely black-and-white and color prints that grace this volume.

Without the hard work of our contributors, this volume would have been impossible. They responded promptly and with good humor to all our requests.

We are grateful to Robert D. Fleck and John von Hoelle of Oak Knoll Press for agreeing to publish this volume and for allowing us a free hand in choosing so many images despite the cost these added to the production of this book. Adam Koster did yeoman's work in typesetting this volume.

Notes on Contributors

Mark Allen is Professor of English at the University of Texas at San Antonio. He is Bibliographer for the New Chaucer Society, and he moderates the Chaucer Online Bibliography. He is author of articles in *Studies in the Age of Chaucer, South Central Review*, and elsewhere. He is currently co-editing the Variorum edition of *The Wife of Bath's Prologue and Tale*.

Betsy Bowden is Professor of English at Rutgers University, Camden. Currently at work on the Wife of Bath during the "long eighteenth century," she has published three books on Chaucer and one on Bob Dylan. Articles cover a range of topics including but not limited to medieval Latin pedagogy (especially in relation to proverbs and Ovidiana), folklore, horses, Mark Twain, Shakespeare, Dante, puns, punctuation, the implications of orality, and visual/verbal interpretations of Chaucer's work between the late sixteenth and early nineteenth centuries.

David R. Carlson is Professor in the Department of English and Adjunct Professor in the Graduate Program in Classical Studies of the University of Ottawa. His recent work includes "Printed Superior Figures in Nicholas Jenson's Lawbooks, 1478-80," *Papers of the Bibliographical Society of America* 96 (2002): 4-22, and "The 'Opicius' Poems (British Library, Cotton Vespasian B.iv) and the Humanist Anti-Literature in Early Tudor England," *Renaissance Quarterly* 55 (2002): 2-35.

Judith L. Fisher is Associate Professor of English at Trinity University in San Antonio, Texas. Her specialty is nineteenth-century British literature, particularly prose fiction and the relation between the verbal and visual arts. She has published articles in journals such as *Victorian Studies, Nineteenth Century Literature*, and the *Victorian Periodicals Review*. She is co-editor and contributor to *When They Weren't Doing Shakespeare*, a collection of essays on Victorian drama. Her most recent publication is *Thackeray's Skeptical Narrative and the "Perilous Trade" of Authorship*, a study of William Makepeace Thackeray's narrative techniques.

Phillipa Hardman, BA, BLitt, was educated at the University of East Anglia and Somerville College, Oxford. She is a Lecturer in the School of English and American Literature at the University of Reading. Her main teaching and research interests are in the field of late medieval English literature. She has published articles on Chaucer, the *Gawain*-poet, Lydgate, medieval romance, and manuscript studies, and has recently edited a facsimile of *The Heege MS* (MS Nat. Lib.Scot, 19.3.1), and a collection of essays: *The Matter of Identity in Medieval Romance*. Among current projects, she is a member of the team working with Dr. K. L. Scott on *An Index of Images in English Manuscripts from the Time of Chaucer to Henry VIII*.

Peter Holliday (MA, MSc) is an art historian with special interests in the fields of typography, printing history, and the technologies of art. He was formerly a senior lecturer at Ravensbourne College of Art and Design in London, and an Assistant to the Curator at Ditchling Museum, the spiritual home of Eric Gill. Holliday has published on Eric Gill, and a study on Edward Johnston is in preparation.

Maria McGarrity is an Assistant Professor of English at Long Island University in Brooklyn, New York. She is a former managing editor of the *James Joyce Literary Supplement*. Her work has previously appeared in the *James Joyce Quarterly*. She works primarily on Irish and Caribbean literary and cultural formations. Her current project charts the relation among Ireland, the Caribbean, and the Atlantic World.

Mary C. Olson received her B.A. from the University of Illinois (Springfield, IL) and her M.A. from Southern Illinois University (Edwardsville, IL). Her Ph.D. is from Purdue University. She is the author of *Fair and Varied Forms: Visual Textuality in Medieval Illuminated Manuscripts*. She teaches in the English Department at Tuskegee University.

Dennis M. Read is associate professor of English at Denison University, Granville, Ohio, where he teaches courses in English Romantic literature, nonfiction, and literary biography. He has published articles on numerous figures of English and American literature, including William Blake, Hart Crane, and William Carlos Williams. A particular interest has been the engraver and editor R. H. Cromek.

Duncan Robinson is the Director of the Fitzwilliam Museum and the Master of Magdalene College, Cambridge University. Formerly he was the Director of the Yale Center for British Art, New Haven, Connecticut.

Warren Stevenson has degrees from Bishop's, McGill, and Northwestern Universities and has taught at the Universities of Saskatchewan, Manitoba, and British Columbia. He has published three books of poetry and six of criticism, including *Romanticism and the Androgynous Sublime* and *A Study of Coleridge's Three Great Poems*. He lives in retirement in Vancouver, B.C.

Jake Milgram Wien (A.B., Stanford; M.Phil, Oxford; J.D., University of California at Berkeley) is a cultural historian and free-lance curator of American art. His articles on Rockwell Kent have been published by Archives of American Art *Journal* (Winter 2002), *Print Quarterly* (September 2001), the Monhegan Museum (July 1998), and the Columbia *Library Columns* (Autumn 1997). He is curating the forthcoming traveling exhibition "Rockwell Kent: The Mythic and the Modern" organized by the Portland (Maine) Museum of Art. In 1995 he curated and wrote the exhibition catalogue for "The Vanishing American Frontier," which surveyed the historical lithographs of Bernarda Bryson Shahn.

INTRODUCTION

The essays in *Chaucer Illustrated* examine pictorial renditions of the *Canterbury Tales* from the early 15th-century Ellesmere manuscript (c. 1410) to the 20th-century images created by Rockwell Kent and Eric Gill. The contributors to this volume address two separate but overlapping concerns. The essays examine the way these pictures illuminate the history of book production, marketing, and readership, and they also consider how the illustrations interpret Chaucer's text. Accompanying the ten original works of scholarship that make up this book are some forty color and well over a hundred black and white illustrations, including many that have rarely if ever been published previously. The first appendix presents William Blake's description of his *Canterbury Pilgrims*. This text is readily available but will prove convenient here. Far less accessible is William Paulet Carey's discussion of Thomas Stothard's painting of the same subject. Carey's *Critical Description* is here reprinted for the first time since 1818, and Maria McGarrity's annotations enhance its accessibility for the modern reader. The final appendix treats a fascinating rendition of Chaucer's pilgrims, Robert van Vorst Sewell's mural in the mansion built by George Gould in Lakewood, New Jersey and now part of Georgian Court College.

Mary C. Olson's opening essay considers what are probably the best known images of Chaucer's pilgrims, images perhaps more familiar than Chaucer's own descriptions. That the two—text and illustration—do not necessarily correspond, is one of Olson's points. She observes that medieval manuscript illustration relies heavily on types, or schemata, rather than necessarily trying to provide a faithful artistic translation of text. Indeed, as Olson notes, the artists who created the Ellesmere miniatures probably did not read the *Canterbury Tales*. Instead they relied on instructions from the supervisor, instructions they supplemented with conventional imagery when necessary.

The Ellesmere illustrations enhance the beauty of the manuscript, which was certainly commissioned by a rich bibliophile. As Olson points out, by Chaucer's time manuscript production was no longer the exclusive or even predominant province of the monastery or university. Lay scribes and artists had assumed a prominent role in the making of books, and one such atelier created the Ellesmere Chaucer as a showpiece, the early 15th-century equivalent of the coffee-table book. But the pictures were functional as well as decorative. Appearing in the margin at the beginning of the tales, they allowed a reader to find a particular story quickly. In addition, they would remind the reader of Chaucer's account of the tellers that he presented in his General Prologue.

The illustrations thus serve as rubrics and mnemonics. They also emphasize the fictional orality of the tales. The stories in the *Canterbury Tales* are of course not really told by various pilgrims traveling in southern England in 1387 but rather were written over a period of years by Geoffrey Chaucer. But the placing of the supposed tellers in the margin helps foster the illusion that these fictional figures are the narrators.

The images serve a further function in helping the reader visualize and judge the characters. Even though the illustrations rely heavily on schemata, they reflect a new interest in individual portraits: portrait painting was introduced to England during the reign of Richard II (1377-1399). Thus, the facial features and coloration of the Shipman, Summoner, and Miller mark them as unsavory. The Franklin, Prioress, and Squire enjoy a higher moral status than these other three, as one can see by comparing their respective pictures. Perhaps the most interesting image in the Ellesmere manuscript is that of Chaucer himself, which may be one of the earliest examples of authentic portraiture in England. Whether the miniature exhibits the real or the idealized Chaucer, its placement seems curious. The pilgrim Chaucer tells two tales, that of "Sir Thopas" and that of "Melibee." The first fails so badly that the Host interrupts it, forcing Chaucer to offer the second. It may be that the Ellesmere artist or supervisor put Chaucer's miniature next to "Melibee" rather than "Sir Thopas" to emphasize the seriousness of "Melibee" and to distance Chaucer from the unsuccessful fragment of "Sir Thopas."

Although the Ellesmere is the best known of the *Canterbury Tales* manuscripts, it is but one of eighty-four, though many of these are only fragments. Fully a third of these manuscripts (twenty-eight) contain illumination of some sort, but only seven include pictures. Four of these (Lansdowne 851, Bodley 686, Devonshire, and Rawlinson Poetry 223) contain historiated initials, two ("Oxford" Fragments and Cambridge University Library MS Gg.4.27) have oblong figures in the text, and in one, the Ellesmere, the portraits appear in the margins. Phillipa Hardman's essay examines the pictorial representations in the manuscripts other than the Ellesmere. Hardman discusses, inter alia, the various ways that the author is presented in the historiated initials of the different manuscripts and how these distinctions relate to the mixture of orality and literacy of the text.

Hardman comments on a curious feature of the Rawlinson Poetry 223 manuscript: the presence of historiated initials at the beginning of "Melibee" and the Friar's Tale. The first of these probably represents Chaucer, at least as generic author, to show that this tale belongs to him. Since Chaucer had just been telling a different story, readers might otherwise think that "Melibee" belonged to another narrator. Regarding the second historiated letter, because the Summoner tells a tale about a friar, as the Friar recounts the misadventures of a summoner, the designer of the manuscript may have feared confusion over which of these stories "belonged" to the Friar. A generic image of a friar introducing the pilgrim Friar's tale clarifies the situation.

Neither the "Oxford" Fragments nor the Cambridge manuscript any longer contains a full program of illustrations, but the portraits that survive indicate that the pictures were intended to serve not only as rubrics but also as commentary. Thus, the posture and coloring of the Monk in the Cambridge manuscript indicate melancholy, a mood consistent with the tragic tone of his tale. Only three miniatures survive in the "Oxford" manuscript, but even these show the artist as interpreter. Hardman points out that the Man of Law's superior status is reflected in the fine steed he rides and the horse's lavish appointments. The Cook's horse and equipage are good, but not as impressive as those of the Man of Law. The Miller rides a lowly mule with a rope halter and with sacks of flour for a saddle. Hardman adds that such images inform the reader's approach to the individual tales. The Man of Law's tale, for example, would then be read as much more formal than the story related by the lowly Miller.

The invention of printing from individual letters in the mid 15th-century did not instantly end the manuscript era. Shakespeare's sonnets and John Donne's poems circulated in manuscript for years in the late 16th and early 17th centuries. And hand illumination often adorned printed books. While modern purists object to hand-colored woodblocks, many bibliophiles of the incunabular period apparently preferred such embellishment, if one may judge from surviving copies of books like the *Nuremberg Chronicle* with their tinted illustrations.

Despite this endurance of the hand-made and hand-decorated book, the tradition of Chaucerian illustration shifted to the woodcut once William Caxton introduced the art of printing into England. A lover of his fellow Kentishman Chaucer, Caxton in about 1478 produced the first printed text of the *Canterbury Tales*. This edition appeared without illustrations. Some five years later, Caxton issued a second edition, claiming in its preface that he had secured a more accurate text. Whether he actually believed this claim or whether it was merely a marketing ploy, Caxton added forty-seven illustrations, probably derived, as David Carlson points out, from the "Oxford" Fragments, to enhance the salability of this publication. These woodcuts served the same functions as the hand-painted illustrations, acting as rubrics and mnemonics, connecting the descriptions in the General Prologue to the tales and allowing the reader to locate quickly a particular story. Olson observes that the shared aspects of the Ellesmere pictures – all in the margins, all the characters on horseback – help to unify what might otherwise appear to be merely a collection of tales. Caxton's woodcuts of the pilgrims serve this unifying function as well.

As attempts at interpretation the woodcuts are more problematic. Caxton's forty-seven images were made from twenty-three woodblocks. Some of the duplication results from the repetition of images in the General Prologue and then with the individual tales. But Caxton also used the same picture for different pilgrims. This practice was common. Hartmann Schedel's 1493 *Nuremberg Chronicle* employed the same woodblocks to illustrate diverse scenes. Adrian Wilson's *The Making of the Nuremberg Chronicle* (Amsterdam: Nico Israel, 1976) observes, "Two different blocks are used to represent the many ecclesiastical councils. One of them is repeated thirteen times in the Latin and ten times in the German edition. . . . The other ecclesiastical cut is used eight times in the Latin and eleven times in the German edition" (187). The same woodcut would depict supposedly different cities or different kings. In Raphael Holinshed's *Chronicles of England, Scotlande, and Ireland* (1577), the same image can illustrate as many as ten different rulers. Ruth Sampson Luborsky, in "Connections and Disconnections between Images and Texts: The Case of Secular Tudor Book Illustration," *Word and Image* 3 (1987): 74-85, distinguishes three types of illustration. The first is decorative, intended to be purely ornamental. The second is general, meaning that the picture is suitable for the book but not specific to the text. Direct illustration, the third category, actually seeks to depict part of the text.

Carlson argues that Caxton's illustrations and the entire woodblock tradition of the *Canterbury Tales* over the next two hundred years, which sprang from Caxton's c. 1483 edition, was at best general but not

direct.   Thus, the same woodblock image serves Caxton for both
Shipman and Canon's Yeoman; another depicts the Merchant, Franklin,
and Summoner.   They are stock figures, lacking for the most part the
individual traits seen in the Ellesmere portraits.   The repetition of the
same figure within an edition and from edition to edition did not apparently trouble readers.   The familiarity may in fact have proved com-
forting.   To draw a fairly modern parallel, for many readers the John
Tenniel illustrations are the quintessential images of Lewis Carroll's
Alice books and the only ones they want. Publishers in the 15th and
16th centuries would have reused woodblocks as long as they could to
save money, but if purchasers had rebelled, the practice certainly would
have ceased.   On the contrary, Luborsky found that in romances of the
16th century, publishers repeated the same or similar images in the
same pattern from edition to edition.   Perhaps the repetitive pattern of
woodblock illustration in the *Canterbury Tales* suggests that it, too,
was read as a collection of romances.   Or it may be that readers of the
period did not draw such nice distinctions among decorative, general,
and direct illustration.

By the beginning of the 17th century the illustrative program for the
Canterbury Tales had been reduced to showing only the Knight.
Economy may have been a factor.   Another reason for the disappearance of illustration may have been increasing literacy.   Running heads
and other textual markers now served the functions previously performed by pictures, such as facilitating the locating of a particular text.
Also, the fiction of orality had vanished.   The first (1598) Speght edition includes a biography of Chaucer and an imagined coat of arms for
the author, whose image appears on the woodcut title page.   Chaucer,
not the pilgrim narrators, has become the focus of the tales, which are
acknowledged the product of a literate creator.   The picture of the
Knight served to link the tales to the Middle Ages as well as to suggest
that these tales were genteel; Chaucer's coat of arms served this same
function. Even as the spelling was modernized in the Speght editions,
the typeface remained black letter, another attempt to suggest the
archaic nature of the work.

The first roman letter edition of the *Canterbury Tales* appeared in
1721.   Arguably the worst edition of Chaucer ever produced from a textual point of view, its illustrations both looked back to the manuscript
tradition, drawing particularly from Cambridge University Library MS
Gg.4.27, and forward to a new type of image that offered scenes of
action.   Caxton had shown the pilgrims eating at the Tabard Inn on the

night before they set out for Canterbury. The picture appears just above the lines "Gret chere made our ost to us everychon/And a soupere sette he us anon" (f. c iiii). It is the first group portrait of Chaucer's characters and includes twenty-four pilgrims. Some of them can be identified specifically, such as the Squire with his feather or the Prioress, while others, especially those with their backs to the viewer, remain generic pilgrims. The 1721 Urry edition, named for the man who would have edited the text had he not died several years before its appearance, provides the first illustration of the pilgrims' progress from the gates of the Tabard Inn. As such, it is the progenitor of the frontispieces designed by Thomas Stothard for the Bell edition of Chaucer's poems (1782-1783), for the paintings by William Blake and Thomas Stothard that are the subjects of chapters 5 and 6 of this work, and for the mural discussed in this volume's third appendix.

The Urry edition also reflects Chaucer's classical status by 1700, or at least the attempt to bestow such status upon him. This edition, published by Bernard Lintot, resembles English translations of Virgil (1696) and Ovid (1717) published by Jacob Tonson, also embellished with fine engravings and containing lives of the authors. Betsy Bowden observes that in England and on the continent intellectuals were debating the relative merits of Greek and Latin authors on the one hand and more recent vernacular writers on the other. John Milton, Matthew Prior, and Chaucer were afforded the same deluxe editions as Homer and Virgil.

Bowden examines the various 18th-century copperplate images of the *Canterbury Tales*. One might note in passing that the diverse processes used to create the Chaucerian illustrations, from hand-painting in manuscripts to woodblocks to copperplate engravings and beyond, reveal in miniature the changes in book illustration over the period this book covers. Bowden suggests that John Mortimer may have planned an edition of Chaucer even more sumptuous than Urry's, and with a reliable text as well. Historical painting was valued above portraiture in 18th-century English aesthetics, and Mortimer's drawings are consistent with that view. Rather than depicting pilgrims, he actually illustrates scenes from the tales. Such depictions also are consistent with the treatment of the tales as literary sites to serve as the basis of artwork, not as oral tales whose supposed tellers are to be given life-like reality. Thomas Stothard and Lady Diana Beauclerk similarly drew inspiration from Chaucer's stories.

These images do more than reproduce episodes from the text. Bowden shows how the pictures serve as commentary. For example, in the Reeve's Tale Mortimer makes the daughter of the miller no larger than the goose she is about to cook. Mortimer thus suggests that to the students in the tale the feelings of woman and bird are equally unimportant. Thomas Stothard's design based on the Shipman's Tale highlights the sensuality of the monk and merchant's wife.

Bowden also looks at a series of pilgrim portraits created by James Jeffreys, pictures long thought to have been lost. Bowden links Jeffreys' portraits to the antiquarian interest of the period; his pictures illustrate context as well as text. For example, Chaucer does not describe the five Guildsmen who have hired the Cook to accompany them. Jeffreys draws them in attire appropriate to the period. He also endows each pilgrim with a distinct personality, even when he uses the same model for more than one character.

As Bowden observes at the end of her article, Blake, despite his insistence on his originality, took much from Stothard and other 18th-century predecessors when he painted and then engraved his *Canterbury Pilgrims*. Nonetheless, Warren Stevenson shows in his examination of this picture how it remains distinctly Blakean. In the tradition of Chaucerian illustration going back to the Ellesmere manuscript, Blake combines the particular with the type, even though, as Stevenson points out, Blake rejected generalization.

The particular details in Blake's picture sometimes draw on Chaucer's text. The Pardoner's long, lank hair and jewel-encrusted cross derive from the General Prologue. The Prioress wears the brooch that Chaucer gives her, and she is accompanied by the hounds mentioned in the General Prologue, though Chaucer does not specify that she has brought them along on this journey. The Squire's bright attire is also consistent with his description in the *Canterbury Tales*. The Wife of Bath's sharp spurs of the General Prologue are evident in her portrait.

Overall, though, Blake seeks to make Chaucer Blakean rather than making himself Chaucerian. One of the most fascinating ways in which Blake imposes himself on the picture appears in the faces of some of the pilgrims. The Ploughman serves as a self-portrait, and Stevenson maintains that in the Second Nun Blake painted his wife. The unsavory Pardoner and Summoner bear the visages of William Pitt and Fox, two prominent politicians of the period whom Blake disliked.

Blake also added details consistent with the mythology he was developing in the prophetic books written at the same time he was painting the *Canterbury Pilgrims*. Stevenson points for example to the four black ravens and five white doves in the picture, suggesting Blake's ravens of dawn in *The Marriage of Heaven and Hell* and the five senses mentioned in *Europe*. Blake was to criticize Stothard's painting for leading the pilgrims in the wrong direction, but he himself shows them heading west rather than southeast (the direction Canterbury lies from London) because for Blake westward lies "the current of/ Creation" (*Jerusalem* 77). Stevenson shows that Blake's painting of the pilgrims serves as a Blakean commentary on religion, sex, politics, war, the creative process, and human nature.

Blake claimed that Thomas Stothard's idea for *The Pilgrimage to Canterbury* was stolen from him. Dennis M. Read traces the evolution of Stothard's picture, which in the 19th century enjoyed far more pop-ularity than Blake's. Whatever the truth of Blake's accusation, Read demonstrates that the two artists chose diametrically opposed approaches to illustrating Chaucer. Unlike Blake, Stothard pursued no prophetic program. Rather, he sought to recreate faithfully a medieval procession. Read quotes Stothard's biographer Anna Eliza Bray's statement about the artist's pouring over medieval manuscripts and monument effigies for images of 14th-century dress and of Stothard's surveying the Surrey Hills along the road that Chaucer's pilgrims would have taken from London to Canterbury.

Still, Read points out how Stothard took liberties with details. In some instances Stothard was merely exercising his artistic license, but Read observes that Stothard was also creating an image of medieval England that would accord with that of his audience. Stothard therefore rejected all sense of hierarchy in the procession to emphasize a sense of equality. His characters also accord well with the view of "merrie olde England." The Wife of Bath, for example, appears young and genial, not the domineering middle-aged woman Chaucer describes. The Friar and Monk are similarly jovial. The pilgrims in this painting lack somewhat of the "ful devout corage" that Chaucer mentions (I. 22). They would, however, be a pleasant group with whom to travel. Read quotes Robert Hartley Cromek, who encouraged and promoted Stothard's painting. Cromek described the overall impression of the procession as "*a pleasurable Tour, sanctified by the name of Pilgrimage.*"

Both Blake and Stothard intended their pictures as free-standing works, not as illustrations to accompany a text. Judith L. Fisher and Mark Allen examine a variety of 19th-century artwork specifically created to appear alongside Chaucer's words, though they discuss some free-standing paintings, too. The Victorian era was the golden age of book illustration, as is evident to anyone looking at the portfolio of color pictures included in this volume. Like Stothard, the Victorian artists whom Fisher and Allen discuss sought a measure of historical fidelity, but they reproduced a medieval England that coincided with the 19th-century's image of that period. The Gothic revival had begun in the 18th century as signaled by Horace Walople's building of Strawberry Hill in the 1750s, Walpole's Gothic novel *The Castle of Otranto* (1764), Thomas Percy's *Reliques of Ancient English Poetry* (1765), and the popularity of James Macpherson's and Thomas Chatterton's medieval forgeries. The Victorian era marked the heyday of what Mark Girouard has called *The Return to Camelot* (New Haven: Yale University Press, 1981).

For many in the flux of the 19th century, the Middle Ages represented stability. Fisher and Allen observe that Robert Buss grouped Chaucer's pilgrims by class, gender, and vocation, placing together the Wife of Bath and Prioress, for example, or the Man of Law and Physician, violating the order of the General Prologue to emphasize notions of hierarchy. Images of the Monk, Friar, Summoner, and Pardoner reflect the 19th-century Protestant view of Catholic clerics.

The 19th-century's love of narrative art also is reflected in Chaucerian illustration. Caxton had shown the pilgrims eating. The 1721 Urry edition had shown them riding, and some of Stothard's frontispieces to the late 18th-century Bell edition of Chaucer had illustrated scenes from the tales. But until the Victorian era, the pilgrims themselves rather than the characters in their tales had been the focus of the images inspired by Chaucer's text. One of the most popular stories was that of patient Griselda, told by the Clerk. Fisher and Allen find some twenty versions of scenes from this tale. And the two favorite moments were the marriage and the first trial, when Griselda meekly submits to her husband's decision to kill their first child. These are moments of high drama, certainly, but, as Fisher and Allen comment, their popularity derives from their re-presenting the Victorian ideal of female subservience. Fisher and Allen write that the courtship and marriage of Arveragus and Dorigen that begins the Franklin's Tale is never painted in the 19th century because it shows a man subservient to a woman and that man's being elevated in status through this marriage. Such gender role reversal did not accord with Victorian sensibilities. Emily of the Knight's Tale, on the other hand, was sometimes illustrated, though not as often as Griselda, because she, too, surrenders her wish to remain single and yields to the demand of Theseus to marry one of her suitors.

For all the Victorian fascination with Chaucer's pilgrims and their stories, the author remains primary. Edward Henry Corbould's *Canterbury Pilgrims Assembled in the Yard of the Tabard Hostelry* (1872) shows Chaucer holding a book and looking towards the characters he has created. This picture recalls to this viewer Robert Buss's unfinished *Dickens's Dream*, also from 1872, in which the sleeping or dead Dickens (who was indeed dead by 1872) is seated in his study that is filled with characters from his fiction. Ford Madox Brown's *Chaucer Reading the 'Legend of Custace' to Edward III, and His Court* . . . similarly emphasizes Chaucer's role as author. Fisher and Allen describe the earliest version of this painting, *The Seeds and Fruits of English Poetry*, as "an altarpiece to English literary heritage."

In its final form this picture epitomizes the Victorian ideas about Chaucer. According to Brown, the picture captures Chaucer as he is reading from the Man of Law's Tale about the beleaguered Custace as she is protecting her child. The scene thus appeals to Victorian sentimentality and notions of motherhood. The figures are shown in authentic medieval attire, and even though there is no evidence that Chaucer ever read this or any other Canterbury Tale to the court, Brown describes in detail the historical moment in which the event he paints supposedly occurred. His account was good enough to prompt the *Illustrated London News* to agree that Brown's painting was probably an accurate portrait of the event. The picture furthermore highlights the (con)fusion of the Middle Ages and the 19th century because, as Fisher and Allen state, Brown placed his friends in Edward III's court. Chaucer's face is actually that of Pre-Raphaelite painter and poet Dante Gabriel Rossetti. The Fair Maid of Kent is Brown's fiancée.

In the book arts, William Morris' 1896 Kelmscott Chaucer, the subject of Dunacn Robinson's essay, marks the epitome of the 19th-century fascination with the Middle Ages. Robinson recounts how impressed Morris was by John Ruskin's essays on the Pre-Raphaelite movement and "The Nature of Gothic" (1853). After leaving Oxford, Edward Burne-Jones, who would illustrate the Kelmscott Chaucer, apprenticed himself to Dante Gabriel Rossetti, and Morris went to work for George Edmund Street, an architect drawn to Gothic forms. When Morris and Burne-Jones became roommates in 1856, their furnishings reflected their love for the medieval. The Victoria and Albert Museum houses their wardrobe, which Burne-Jones decorated with a scene from Chaucer's Prioress' Tale. Morris throughout his life would create illuminated manuscripts, and the home furnishings produced by William Morris and Company draw heavily on medieval motifs.

This same love of the Middle Ages is evident in the books issued by Morris' Kelmscott Press (1891-1896). Robinson notes that to emphasize his links with this period Morris intended his first book to be William Caxton's translation of Jacobus de Voragine's *Golden Legend*, which appeared in 1892, as did a new edition of Caxton's first book in English, *The Recuyell of the Historyes of Troy*.

The Kelmscott Chaucer, too, links Morris to Caxton, though the text he used derives from the best 19th-century scholarship. The Burne-Jones illustrations were printed from woodblocks, just as Caxton's had been, though again Morris used the latest technology to produce those blocks. The decorative program that embellishes the book derives from the vinets characteristic of late medieval illuminated manuscripts.

Still, Burne-Jones's pictures reflect the Victorian world. The depiction of scenes from Chaucer's works is consistent with the period's love of narrative art. And the scenes that Burne-Jones drew emphasize the courtly and chivalric. At least half of the *Canterbury Tales* consists of bawdy stories, none of which Burne-Jones illustrated. Conversely, the most heavily illustrated tale in the Kelmscott Chaucer is the most chivalric and the one told by the highest-ranking pilgrim, the Knight's Tale. Robinson notes further than Burne-Jones applied 19th-century rationalism to the magical story of the Squire by making the metal horse look like a mechanical toy. The edifice made of twigs that Chaucer describes in *The House of Fame* is likewise stripped of its exoticism: Robinson rightly says that Burne-Jones's picture looks like a lobster-pot.

Chaucer himself appears on the first page of the *Works*. He is standing in a garden, holding a quill in one hand, a book in the other. The fiction of orality is long vanished, but this picture suggests another fiction – Chaucer, like Shakespeare, warbling his wood-notes, or at least garden-notes wild rather than drawing on the corpus of classical and medieval literature (as in fact both did) to create his works. As in Ford Madox Brown's picture, Chaucer is shown as the founder rather than the heir of a literary tradition, working in a fresh, natural medieval world unburdened by the academicism shunned by the Pre-Raphaelites.

William Morris deeply influenced Rockwell Kent, who produced one of the most important examples of 20th-century Chaucerian illustration. In his chapter on Kent's pictures Jake Wein observes that Kent was an ardent bibliophile concerned with all aspects of book production. Like Morris, he cared about paper, typography, and layout, not just the illustrations.

Kent's designs for the *Canterbury Tales* harken back to the Ellesmere, Cambridge, and "Oxford" manuscripts in the sense that they depict the pilgrims rather than scenes from their tales. Kent's portraits also resemble those of medieval manuscripts in their placement at the beginning of the subjects' respective tales in the original 1930 limited edition. Interestingly, Kent drew images of only two characters from the tales themselves, Sir Thopas and Melibius, and in the trade edition the latter is renamed Chaucer. Like the medieval illuminators, then, Kent suggests through his images that the prose tale of Melibee more accurately reflects Chaucer's narrative skills than the interrupted poetic tale and that the tale of Melibee is meant to be taken more seriously than that of Sir Thopas.

In other ways, Kent broke with tradition. For example, Wein notes that Kent abandoned his effort to depict the characters in the costumes of the period after the chief librarian at Copenhagen told him that pictures of 14th-century English dress were scarce. Kent also eliminated the pilgrims' steeds, perhaps because, as Betsy Bowden observes in her essay, horses are so hard to draw. Perhaps, too, Kent wanted to focus on the pilgrims themselves. The featureless background offers no distraction, either. While to some extent Kent follows Chaucer's descriptions in the General Prologue, his images reflect the influence of Freud and the 20th century's fascination with psychology, because he attempts through gesture, posture, and facial expression to capture the personality of each pilgrim. Another 20th-century influence that Wein finds in Kent's pictures is that of the movies. Kent never achieved the success in Hollywood that he sought, but in his *Canterbury Tales* and portraits of Greenlanders from this same period he reveals a cinematic eye.

Wein notes that Kent admired William Blake, but Kent's pilgrims have not embarked on either a Blakean or religious quest. Seen individually and without horses, they are decidedly secular figures. According to Wein, Kent sometimes used diagonal lines to lend a spiritual dimension to his pictures. No such rays appear in the pilgrim portraits. Instead, Kent presents them as literally and figuratively earthbound.

Eric Gill's illustrations for the *Canterbury Tales*, like those of his contemporary Rockwell Kent, are endebted to William Morris. In one sense Gill is, as Peter Holliday indicates, very much the modern. Holiday quotes Gill's statement, "I am not a learned antiquarian." Holliday also links Gill's views on illustration with those of Beatrice Warde and Jan Tschichold about typography. All three sought a modern, chaste presentation of the page that did not distract from the text.

Still, Holliday describes Gill's modernism as conservative. Like Morris, Gill rejected the commercialism and mechanization of the modern era. Wood engraving appealed to him, as it did to other members of the Arts and Crafts movement, because this technique recalled the age of the craftsman. Gill admired the work of Thomas Bewick (1753-1828) and studied with Edward Johnston, who revived calligraphy in England by teaching how medieval scribes worked.

Gill's illustrations for the *Canterbury Tales* recall medieval manuscripts with his decorative vinets, though Gill's examples are two-dimensional and typographical. In creating a title-page for each tale, Gill, like Kent, echoes the mise-en-page of the Ellesmere, Cambridge, and "Oxford" manuscripts. Gill's woodcuts recall the Caxton and Pynson editions not only in technique but also in their generality. Just as David Carlson argues that Caxton and his successors used woodcuts for commercial far more than for interpretive purposes, so Holliday maintains that Gill regarded the *Canterbury Tales* commission as just another job. Indeed, as in the 15th- and 16th-century editions of Chaucer, the Golden Cockerell version uses the same images in different places in the text, indicating that Gill was not trying to illustrate specific scenes or characters. Holliday notes that Gill may not even have read Chaucer's entire text, thus unconsciously forging another link with medieval illuminators and their woodcutting successors.

All good books must end (as must all bad ones as well), and this one concludes with Gill. The illustrative tradition of the *Canterbury Tales* did not, of course, die in 1931. Arthur Szyk's colorful vision of the departure for Canterbury that serves as frontispiece to the 1946 Heritage Club edition of the *Tales* and Ronald King's abstract designs of various Pilgrims for the General Prologue to the *Tales* (Guildford, England: Circle Press, 1978) are but two examples of the ongoing appeal of Chaucer's work for artists as well as readers. Perhaps the present volume may inspire scholars to examine other 20th-century renditions of the *Canterbury Tales* as well as to revisit earlier portrayals.

Here taketh the editors of this book their leve. Now preye we to hem alle that herkne this tretys or rede, that if ther be any thing in it that liketh hem, that therof they thanken the contributors, of whom procedeth al wit and al goodnesse. And if ther be any thing that displese hem, we preye hem also that they arrette it to the defaute of the editors unkonnynge and nat to oure wyl, that wold ful fayn have sayd better if we had konnynge. For oure book seith, "Al that is written is written for oure doctrine," and that is oure entente.

The Editors

Chapter 1

Marginal Portraits and the Fiction of Orality: The Ellesmere Manuscript

Mary C. Olson

"Turne over the leef," says Chaucer, "and chese [choose] another tale" (I.3177),[1] providing one of the few verbal references within the *Canterbury Tales* to the fact that the work is written; most of the work emphasizes a fictional orality - the pretense that the pilgrims tell their tales to one another as they ride. The preponderance of the "bookish" character of the work comes from the physical manuscript itself, not only in the fact that it is a written artifact, but in the characteristics of each individual manuscript. Each manuscript of the *Canterbury Tales* is a unique version of the text whose page layout and size, use of initials, rubrics, glosses, illustrations, and the character of the hand produce an interpretation of the verbal material that is different from every other. Much more than a representation of the sounds of the words that make up the text, each manuscript is also a visual reading of the text reflecting the responses of the scribe, illustrator, and anyone else who may have had a hand in its production. For this reason, Martin Stevens calls for a new definition of authorship: "Chaucer is . . . construed not so much as the single originating poet, but as a voice constructed both from his own work and its redaction. In short, the editor is embraced in the term 'authorship.' This is why, I believe, the appropriate name for the poet we read in *The Riverside Chaucer* is the 'Ellesmere Chaucer' (with the qualification that at times, when good subjective judgment by a later team of editors dictates, other manuscript voices are substituted for the readings of the exemplars" ("Introduction" 22). To carry this idea further, the Chaucer of the Ellesmere Manuscript is not the same author as the Chaucer of the *Riverside Chaucer*. A reading of the Ellesmere Manuscript as a unique

textual product will be different from a reading of the Hengwrt manuscript, a later printed version such as the Riverside, or Chaucer's own
(still undiscovered) holograph.

The producers of the Ellesmere manuscript have heightened the
interaction between telling and writing which is present throughout the
text, but particularly noticeable in the two tales told by Geoffrey the
narrator. The portrait of Chaucer which accompanies these two tales
adds to the tension because of the way the illustrator has presented the
author who, although bumbling and inept in Chaucer's representation
of his narrator persona, is venerable in his portrait. The illustrator who
produced most of the pilgrim portraits contributes to the visual emphasis on telling with an unusual degree of variation in the facial features
that highlights the variety of the tellers and is highly unusual for a
manuscript of this period An examination of the Ellesmere manuscript
and its mode of production will provide a background for a reading of
this unique text which focuses on the play between ideas of writing
and telling.

The Manuscript

Arguably the most familiar of the *Canterbury Tales* manuscripts
because of the portrait miniatures, the Ellesmere manuscript,
Huntington Library, San Marino, CA MS EL 26 C9 is one of the earliest versions, made around 1410 according to the reckoning of most
scholars, although Kathleen Scott suggests an earlier date of 1400-1405
based on her examination of other manuscripts whose borders she
believes were produced by the same limners (103-106). The Hengwrt
manuscript (National Library of Wales, Aberystwyth, MS. Peniarth
392), usually considered to be slightly earlier than the Ellesmere, may
have been copied by the same scribe (Doyle 49), but orders the tales
differently. It has some decorated initials, but no illustrations, and it
lacks the extensive glosses of the Ellesmere. Only the opening page
approaches the level of the Ellesmere decoration. The Ellesmere manuscript was undoubtedly made as a commercial endeavor, but for whom is
not known. Though it lacks the elaborate full-page illustrations of a manuscript like the *Très Riches Heures* of the Duke of Berry (Chantilly, Musée
Condé), it is still elaborate and expensive with its portrait miniatures and
extensive bookish apparatus of running heads, glosses, and rubrics which
surround the central tale text. Such features suggest a wealthy owner or
owners, possibly the DeVere family (Manly and Rickert I.1588-59).[2]

Manuscript illustration in this period is still characterized by the use of schemata[3] and by the emphasis on the conceptual, although the time is not too distant when the emphasis will shift to the perceptual.[4] The Ellesmere portraits, like their counterparts in the verbal text, present depictions that are as much types as individuals. While the artists provide details particular to the described person, the bases for the portraits are as schematically derived as those of their eleventh-century counterparts. V.A. Kolve describes the process for the typical illustration program for this period:

> Most often, the picture cycle was simply copied from one manuscript to the next, with only changes in costume, setting, or painting style to indicate updating. The 'new' response is as likely to be to the picture cycle itself as to the text it illustrates. The hand of tradition lay heavy on the productions of the ateliers. On almost every artistic level, sometimes including the highest, it was an age of the pattern book and the copy recopied. (66)

However, in the Ellesmere manuscript, we can see the beginnings of a new kind of illustration. In the first place, the relationship between the pictorial and verbal texts presents somewhat different problems from those where the text has an iconic tradition. Here the verbal text is a recent production (even though it incorporates a lot of older material), and the pictorial text is the product of a reaction to that text on the part of persons who may have been acquainted with the poet. Where there is no tradition of accompanying illustration as in this manuscript, the artist may use patterns (the manuscript shows some evidence of this),[5] but adapt standard iconography and schemata to the particularities of the text at hand. But also, like Chaucer's verbal portraits, the illustrations go beyond the expected stereotypes to suggest individuals.

At first glance, the illustrations seem to accord well with the verbal text; but if we study them closely, we see that they agree only in some particulars, as Richard Emmerson has pointed out (154).[6] In particular, there is tension between Chaucer's portrait and his presentation of himself in the verbal text. The illustrator's choice of portraits of the tale-tellers rather than narrative illustrations strongly emphasizes the fiction of the orality of the tales, and the role of Chaucer as a participant rather than controlling creator. The only comparable work is Boccaccio's *Decameron,* and illustrated manuscripts of that work depict scenes from the tales, so the choice of the project supervisor to illustrate the speakers is probably an innovation. [7]

The Making of Texts in the Fourteenth Century

Once almost entirely under the control of monasteries, by Chaucer's time book production had become increasingly commercialized. Books may have been produced in small family-owned shops where the man and wife divided the labor between them (Camille 147-48), although Doyle and Parks claim that there were no shops until later in the 15th century, all of the work being contracted to individual scribes and illustrators ("Production of Copies"). A natural result of the shift toward commercial production would have been a change in the ways in which the scribe and illustrator understood their goals. Although Anglo-Saxon monastics had produced manuscripts for patrons, their primary allegiance was to God and to the glorification of holy scripture. But in Chaucer's time, a wealthy patron might request a manuscript, even of a religious text, with his or her own glorification in mind. Lavish visual displays using gold leaf or expensive blue pigment of ground lapis lazuli, plus depictions of the owner and the family arms, redirected the attention from God to the patron. Less wealthy patrons would have commissioned or purchased plainer manuscripts. In any case, the patron was the one whose tastes and needs dictated the form the page would take, the one who must be satisfied with the result. Certainly, by the late 14th century monastic scriptoria continued to turn out manuscripts, but they had lost their almost exclusive control of book production.

Not only did manuscript production change, but ways of reading changed as well. The influence of orality was still operative, but in different ways. In the words of Ward Parks, "Literacy was spreading and interacting with orality in many complex modalities" (156). According to Paul Saenger, one practice which had profound influence was that of word separation. In classical and early medieval texts, words on the page were representative of spoken words - connected to one another, with pauses (spaces) only at breathing points. Developing through the ninth, tenth, and eleventh centuries, word separation made silent reading easier (378).[8] Techniques of textual division which had been used to a limited extent since the seventh century became more common.[9] Ivan Illich refers to the development of the "bookish text," (115) which is characterized by a new kind of page layout, alphabetization, indices, concordances, and other apparatuses. "Alphabetic indexes," writes Walter Ong, "show strikingly the disengagement of words from discourse and their embedding in typographic space" (124). Illich sees the shift to a more bookish kind of text, which took place in the twelfth century, as constituting as profound a change as that produced by the invention of the printing press. He writes:

> Before [Hugh of St. Victor's] generation [c.1130], the book is a record of the author's speech or dictation. After Hugh, increasingly it becomes a repertory of the author's thought, a screen onto which one projects still unvoiced intentions. . . . During the next four centuries, [people] no longer read with the tongue and ear. They were trained in new ways: the shapes on the pages for them became less triggers for sound patterns than visual symbols of concepts. (95)

Saenger points out that illustrations, especially gospel portraits, reflect this shift. In earlier manuscripts, an angel or other being dictates the words to the writer. In later illustrations, the author often copies from a scroll (383). These changes coincide with the rise of the universities, the rediscovery of Aristotle, and scholasticism. Illich claims, "The page became a bookish text, this latter shaped the scholastic mind, and the text-mind relationship was as necessary a foundation for print culture as alphabetic recording had been for the culture of literature and philosophy in ancient Greece" (116). Saenger, on the other hand, claims that silent reading developed as a result of scholasticism's complex ideas and arguments which are more difficult to follow when read aloud (383). Changes in page layout accommodated silent reading techniques, and alphabetizing and indexing freed the text from its sound-related linearity. Instead of a succession of ideas or events, the text could now function as a group of simultaneous parts. Glosses move from between the lines to the margins. The difference is not absolute; older texts such as biblical texts also could be read randomly, and the practice of allegorical exegesis provides a sense of correspondence that approaches simultaneity.

The pilgrim portraits of the Ellesmere manuscript exhibit the characteristic kind of participation in the multivalent manuscript page. In the Old English period, elements alternated on the page: words with pictures, primary text with gloss. By Chaucer's time, the margins of the page have become the site for commentary, decoration, and a kind of playful anti-reading of the central text. This central text is often introduced with a historiated initial as rubric and illustration. Michael Camille sees this development as part of the shift to bookish text:

> This extra-textual space only developed into a site of artistic elaboration as
> the idea of the text as written document superseded the idea of the text as a
> cue for speech. . . . Now it was the physical materiality of writing as a sys-
> tem of visual signs that was stressed. This shift, from speaking words to see-
> ing words, is fundamental to the development of marginal imagery, because
> once the letter had to be recognizable as part of a scanned system of visual
> units, possibilities for its deformation and play became limited. No longer
> forming the letter, representations either enter its frame to form what is
> known as the historiated or pictured initial common in Gothic manuscripts,
> or they are exiled into the unruled empty space of the margins - the tradi-
> tional site of the gloss. (18-20)

The kinds of elaboration which proliferated in the margins of
Gothic manuscripts included babewyns (grotesque figures), carniva-
lesque scenes featuring inversion, and people and animals engaging in
nonsensical or sexual/scatological activities. These illustrations often
appear in sacred texts such as Books of Hours, suggesting that even
these are not immune to the simultaneous and legitimized presence of
inverse readings. In particular, Camille points out that while women in
central illustrations are the idolized ladies of courtly love, those in the
margins are "clearly the victims of a deep misogyny . . . which seals
them into oppressive simulations of their social position" (127). At the
same time, glosses constitute another kind of simultaneous, parallel
text which could underscore authoritative claims. Instead of the alter-
nating texts common to the earlier period, two or more texts inhabit the
page simultaneously. These changes have profound ramifications for
the study of the Ellesmere manuscript illustrations.

The layout of the Ellesmere manuscript places the main text centrally on the page, as one would expect, but the area is narrow enough
to allow for a column for glosses. The diagrams below show the
approximate layout of the pages with running heads at the top, glosses
on the outside and rubrics interrupting the column of the main text.
Often the column for glosses is empty, and the borders and miniatures
are fit into that space or between it and the main text. Since most of
the main text is verse, the varied length of the lines allows for some leeway in the placing of decorative images.

Richard Emmerson provides a plausible scenario for the production
of the manuscript. According to his hypothesis, a supervisor planned
the layout of the pages, made the decision to illustrate the tale-tellers
rather than the tales, and assigned work to various limners, three illustrators, and a scribe (151). Alexander believes that the supervisor "is

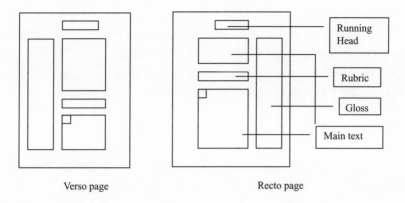

Verso page   Recto page

surely Chaucer's self-proclaimed disciple, Thomas Hoccleve" ("Art History" 18). The artists may have worked in the same room or separately, but they do not seem to have worked from the verbal text. Emmerson suggests that the supervisor, thoroughly familiar with Chaucer's descriptions, gave the artists some of the information to work from. The artist who made the portrait of Chaucer may have followed an exemplar, since it is so similar to the portrait in *The Regiment of Princes*. Of course, that portrait may have been copied from this one (153). The descriptions of the other pilgrims may have varied between general and particular. This procedure would explain why the illustrations sometimes reflect textual details and sometimes do not. But, in addition to providing a reaction to the text on the part of the supervisor, they also provide the artists' interpretations of the Pilgrims as types.

The variety of people who populate the *Canterbury Tales* reinforces its status as a compendium of material of different genres. Doyle and Parkes call the tales "repositories of *auctoritas* [authority] - *sententiae* [wise sayings], and aphorisms on different topics which are indicated by marginal headings" ("Production of Copies" 190), and the variety of the portraits call attention to the variety of the tales. However, the ways in which they are alike - all on horseback, in similar positions on the page, for example - have a unifying effect, as does the uniformity of the page layout. Also, the borders are all three-sided, and they differ only in small details. Martin Stevens has pointed out that the portraits, many of whose textual details are taken from the descriptions in the General Prologue, function to recall the Prologue and provide another unifying factor ("Ellesmere Miniatures" 113).

The choice of subject matter for the illustrations and their positioning in the margins profoundly affect critical response to the material. These choices emphasize the fictional orality of the tales, calling attention to the context rather than the content of the story-telling. The marginal position ensures the simultaneity of verbal and pictorial texts; the pilgrims exist alongside the beginnings of their stories, to be held in the mind of the reader as the tale unfolds, until another portrait appears to signal a new teller. The arrangement recalls the iconography of speech scrolls placed next to the speaker, especially near the mouth, which may or may not contain words, but in either case indicate that the individual is speaking. Earlier, the iconography of scrolls and books had a purely metonymic function, but in Chaucer's time, they were more likely to contain a text; in the Ellesmere manuscript, the scroll is absent, but the words are still placed as though coming from the speaker.[10] However, a tension is at work in this arrangement in several ways. For one thing, the bookish apparatus, self-reflexively literary, operates in conjunction with the marking of fictional orality. While the pilgrim portraits emphasize orality, the rest of the contents of the graphic field emphasizes the fact that the orality is fiction. In addition, their marginal positioning figures the waning role of orality in a culture that is becoming progressively more bookish. Additional tension results from the portraits' function as rubrics. They are so visible that they allow a reader to find easily any tale to read at random. The means of marking the orality is also the means for escaping from the linearity inherent in that orality.

Chaucer's and the pilgrims' portraits, as we have seen, may have been painted by artists who had not read the verbal text, but relied on the directions and description of the supervisor to provide specifics. For example, the Miller (color plate 1) has a bagpipe and red beard, the Wife of Bath (color plate 2) wears a wide hat, wimple, "foot mantel" and spurs, the Prioress (color plate 3) has a bracelet of beads, and the Summoner (color plate 4) has a garland on his head, all details which derive from the General Prologue.[11] But the Reeve (color plate 5) does not have the kind of cropped haircut described by the narrator, although he does wear a long blue surcote. The supervisor evidently did not list every textual detail used to describe a particular person. Nor, probably, did he or she dictate the details which we see in the portraits that were not provided by the verbal text. The illustrations represent a response to the text on the part of the supervisor, combined with a response on the part of the artists to the supervisor's prompting, and the collective image pool available.[12] These could have come from a pattern book, from the artists' memories of or access to other manuscript illustrations, or from commonly accepted stereotypes. For example, a friar must have a habit with a hood and a tonsure. Such characteristics are cultural clichés, and easily recognizable. The Man of Law's coif (color plate 6), the Physician's urinal (color plate 7), and the Cook's meat hook (color plate 8) are all schematic attributes which would not necessarily represent the way a pilgrim would look in any particular situation. Emmerson comments that this apparent inconsistency is a problem "only if we assume that the General Prologue is the locus of the 'real' - that the miniatures should illustrate that 'reality' - and that the only authorized variation from the text should be to represent dramatic characters in a dramatic activity, that is, riding along the road to Canterbury" (157). By "real," Emmerson seems to mean not only the historically real, but particularly the perceptual or visible. Such is not the agenda of the illustrations. In spite of the individual details that match the verbal descriptions, the artists present concepts of persons in different professions as well as individuals.

The great majority of the pilgrims who populate the *Canterbury Tales* come neither from the aristocracy nor the peasant classes. With the exception of the Knight and the Plowman, they are drawn from that large body of people in between, people of Chaucer's own background. Jill Mann remarks that "it is a cliché of Chaucer criticism that the Canterbury pilgrims are both individuals and types" (187). As such, they would be the products of a combination of tradition, imagination, and personal experience. In responding to Chaucer's characters, Chaucer's audience could have called upon their own knowledge of traditions and their own experiences. Some of the characters seem to accord closely with what we know of medieval stereotypes. The Friar (color plate 9), for example, seems to be a character from anti-fraternal satire come to life. The idealized Clerk (color plate 10), on the other hand, seems to be less stereotypical than another clerk, "Hende" Nicholas of the Miller's Tale. For some pilgrims, their relation to a type constitutes part of the mechanism of interaction between tale and teller, such as the Wife and her prologue and tale, where she embodies the kinds of misogynistic literature she attacks. For others, like the Parson, where Chaucer uses the stereotype as a kind of anti-definition, the ways in which they diverge from the type is significant. For both, a strong connection to a recognizable type provides a set of expectations to be reinforced or subverted. The Cook, for example, exemplifies the popular negative stereotype. The narrator-Chaucer praises the Cook's professional expertise in the General Prologue, but remarks, "But greet harm was it, as it thoughte me, / That on his shyne a mormal hadde he" (I.385-86). In the Cook's Prologue, however, we get a clearer idea of his character from the Host:

> For many a pastee hastow laten blood,
> And many a Jakke of Dovere hastow soold
> That hath been twies hoot and twies coold.
> Of many a pilgrym hastow Cristes curs,
> For of thy percely [parsley] yet they fare the wors,
> That they han eten with thy stubbel goos,
> For in thy shoppe is many a flye loos.
>   (I.4346-52)

In his study of the Cook, Kolve compares another portrait, that found in Cambridge, Univ. Lib. MS. Gg.iv.27, fol. 193v (color plate 24) to the Ellesmere portrait. The Cambridge portrait, he feels, better represents the type of cook that Chaucer's particular group of London guildsmen would have hired. He is more presentable, better dressed, and more appealing to a group of men conscious of their social status than the Ellesmere Cook, whose mormal is clearly visible, even enhanced with a grimy bandage and bright red pustules. Kolve calls attention to the medieval connections between cooks and demons. The latter are often pictured with flesh hooks, and their work associates them with flames, gluttony, and lechery (260-61). At least, the mormal suggests the unsound, the diseased, and the corrupt. It is obvious that the two illustrators are presenting different Cook-concepts; but the later Cambridge portrait seems more particularized, in spite of the fact that the Ellesmere portrait is closer in many ways to the verbal description. It shows the Cook not just as a type, but as the kind of cook appropriate for the particular group he accompanies. The Ellesmere portrait is closer to other representations of cooks, who are often depicted as somewhat demonic, standing before a fire, wearing an apron and short tunic, and holding a flesh hook.

The Squire's portrait (color plate 11) closely matches his verbal description in the General Prologue:

> A lovyere [lover] and a lusty bacheler,
> With lokkes crulle [curled] as they were leyd in presse.

Of twenty yeer of age he was, I gesse.
Of his stature he was of evene lengthe,
And wonderly delyvere [agile], and of greet strengthe.

Embrouded [embroidered] was he, as it were a meede
Al ful of fresshe floures, whyte and reede.

Short was his gowne, with sleves longe and wyde.
Wel koude he sitte on hors and faire ryde.
                                        (I. 80-84, 89-90, 93-94)

His portrait shows his youth, his curly hair, his embroidered tunic with long, wide sleeves, and his rearing horse. It is highly reminiscent of young men in other manuscript illustrations such as the young man pictured on f. 7 of the Rohan Hours (Paris Bib. Nat. MS lat. 9471) or the young men in the hunting party depicted in the *Très Riches Heures* (f. 8v). In contrast, two portraits, those of the Knight (color plate 12) and the Parson (color plate 13), do not wear the clothing that one customarily finds in illustrations of such characters. Most show priests in liturgical vestments and knights in armor. Neither of these would be appropriate dress for a pilgrimage, and perhaps their incongruity would apparently be greater than that of the urinal or the flesh hook. Both the knight's and the priest's portraits employ more general schemata. Evidently, the portraits need only be recognizable types to satisfy the requirements of a commercial production, and there is enough schematization to identify the pilgrims as types: the profession of the Cook, for example, would not have had to be labeled by anything other than his apron and meat hook. However, in most cases, there is also enough particularization to identify the pilgrims as Chaucer's pilgrims. The Cook is not just an identifiable cook, but the particular Cook of the *Canterbury Tales* who has a mormal on his shin. However, the Ellesmere patron may have had specific requests as to how the manuscript was to be executed, and these, of course, would have to be met. After that, there was probably a lot of leeway in what might be done in the execution, including flexibility in the way the pilgrims were portrayed. This manuscript seems to be fairly conservative in terms of imaginative marginalia. There is only one babewyn, for example, which occurs on the opening page (f. 1r), and that is rather small.

Schemata always show an artist's individual idiosyncrasies, as well as adherence to a common iconographic code. Of the artists who painted the portraits, there are generally thought to be three. The illustrator who is responsible for the portraits of the Nun's Priest, Second Nun, Monk, Canon's Yeoman (color plate 14), and Manciple (color plate 15) has a set of personal schematic characteristics that differs slightly from that of the others but is quite consistent for this artist. The grassy base on which these figures are placed is a common feature. Another is the proportions of the figures, which vary somewhat from that of the other illustrators. And all have round, shiny faces with comparatively small features (with the possible exception of the Monk, whose face is so smeared that the features are unreadable). This artist's heads are larger in proportion to the bodies than the others. Faces are rounder, horses stockier. Another illustrator painted only Chaucer's portrait, and the others are considered to be the work of a third person.

Facial Variation among Portraits

The portraits of this third illustrator show a surprising variety in the representation of facial features, much more than is usual for the period. The size and shape of eyes, noses, and mouths vary to the extent that each pilgrim appears to have an individual personality. This illustrator is called Artist 1 by Emmerson and Hand Three by Margaret Rickert (I shall use Emmerson's term). This artist painted seventeen of the twenty-three portraits, so it is possible to study their characteristics in some detail. There are several possible explanations for this individualization of facial features. The first, and least likely to my mind, is that the artist may have anticipated the shift to perceptual representation which became prevalent in the Renaissance, and made the portraits resemble actual individuals. The second is that, as Margaret Rickert (596) and Herbert Schulz (3) have speculated, there may have been a fourth illustrator, but this explanation accounts for only some of the variations. The third is that the features are still schematic, but the schematic unit is smaller in this case - individual features rather than the whole figure.

While the portraits appear to have some individuality, I do not believe that the artist wanted to represent visual perceptions. While monumental art was beginning to show attempts to depict mimetic representations of actual persons, textual illustration was still largely schematic, and usually these schemata are quite consistent within the work of any one illustrator, varying only in the view - profile, three-quarter, or frontal-but variations are not unheard of. I think it unlikely that the portraits in question are mimetic; the monument art that was mimetic sought to depict a deceased individual, whereas the Ellesmere illustrations present fictional characters, all of whom are stereotypical in some aspects. Moreover, they do not show the same kinds of individuality that appear on tomb portraits. Janet Backhouse does make a claim for the presence of mimetic portraits at this time:

> Portraits within manuscripts already had a long history. . . . True likenesses are found with increasing frequency from the late fourteenth century onward, the many recognizable miniatures of Charles V and his brother Jean de Berry providing excellent and early examples. ("French Manuscript Illustration" 173)

Annabel Patterson bases her argument for the "true likeness" of Chaucer's portrait partly on this claim (see the discussion below), but Backhouse cites no English examples, and most of her examples are later than the Ellesmere manuscript. In any case, there is no evidence in this period for mimesis where portraits do not depict a particular individual. The variation one sees among the portraits of Artist 1 may be a portent of change to come, but is not the thing itself.

I consider it likely that a fourth artist painted the Franklin and the Reeve, not because they are significantly different from the others, but because their features are alike. They resemble each other more than any other two in the group by Artist 1, and if they did not differ in size, they could have been traced from the same pattern. The other portraits share a mouth, eye or nose schema with one or more others and seem to constitute a spectrum from large to small features with the Summoner (Figure 1) at one extreme, the Wife (Figure 2) or Man of Law (Figure 3) at the other, and the Parson (Figure 4) in the middle. However, the Knight and Reeve are the only two with their particular configuration, differing from the other illustrations especially in the eyes and mouth. Their

Fig. 1 - Detail of Summoner

position in the manuscript neither confirms nor denies a fourth artist. The manuscript is made up of twenty-nine quires, fourteen of which have only one portrait, and four of which have two. Of those which have two, quire 26 has two portraits by Artist 3, and quires 18 and 11 have portraits by Artist 1. Chaucer's portrait is the only one in quire 20, and the Knight's portrait is alone in quire 2; the Reeve shares quire

6 with the Cook. While it seems unlikely that two artists worked on quire 6, it is possible that some unknown circumstance could have made it necessary, especially if the illustrators were working in the

Fig. 2,3,4 - Detail of the Wife of Bath, The Man of Law, and The Parson

same location. Artist 3 (of the grassy bases) shares a quire with the first artist-quire 29 has both the Manciple and the Parson by Artists 3 and 1 respectively, although all of the third artist's portraits are together at the end, and the Parson's portrait (by Artist 1) follows them as the last illustration in the manuscript. If there was indeed a fourth artist, however, the variation among the remaining portraits by Artist 1 still needs an explanation.

There is some precedent for variation in facial features within the work of an individual artist. However, marked variation is usually applied to types of base or evil characters and is especially seen in depictions of marginalized types such as Jews, Saracens, peasants, or otherwise denigrated people, and is often consistent for types.[13] Skin color is often gray or brown, and features distorted:

> Distortions, deformities, and stereotyped racial and ethnic features were exhibited preeminently by the face - especially eyes, nose, and mouth. We find eyes that are enlarged, bulging, slant, crossed, squint, and red; noses hooked, oversize, broken, porcine, bulbous, flattened and turned up; mouths very large, very small, twisted, sunken, opened wide, or tightly closed; lips enlarged, fleshy, or very thin; chins that project or recede; and teeth that are huge, projecting, clenched, or missing. (Melinkoff 1.121).

These are common throughout European, including English, manuscripts of the period.[14] One of the most common scenes which uses denigrating schemata is the Flagellation of Christ. Commonly, dark-skinned Jews with large hooked noses and wide mouths contrast with a Christ whose features are smaller and more regular, and whose body is pale and slender.[15] Hair also has a signifying role. Lower class characters are shown with short hair. Red hair denotes ugliness, and it is sometimes combined with distorted noses, dark skin, or warts to show the depravity of the individual (Mellinkoff 1.150).

Such practices confirm the presence of schemata, even as they provide variety of character. Another place where one can find schematization of individual features is in literature, especially lyrics and romances. Here also, the writer points either to the ideal or the base. Women especially are characterized by individual features. One example is the following poem that praises the beauty of the beloved's features-brows, nose, mouth, lips, teeth, neck, breasts, and waist:

> Heo hath browes bend and heh,
> Whit bitwene and nout too neh;
> Lussum lif heo ledes;
> Hire neose is set as it well semeth;
> I deye for deth that me demeth;
>
> Heo hath a mury mouth to mele
> With lefly rede lippes lele,
> Romaunce for to rede;
> Hire teth aren white as bon of whal,
> Evene set and atled all,
> Ase hende mowe taken hede;
> Swannes swire swithe well isette,
> A sponne lengore then I mette,
>
> Hir tittes aren anunder bis
> As apples two of parays,
> Youself ye mowen seo.
>
> Heo hath a mete middel small
> Body and brest well mad all
> Ase feines without fere.
>   (Luria and Hoffman #29)

The language is typical. The same metaphors for the same features and body parts figure in other descriptions of beautiful women. A parody of this kind of lyric, the following also calls attention to individual features, head, brow, breasts, nose, nostrils, shoulders, belly, feet, and back:

> Remembering your grete hede and your forhed round,
> With staring eyen, visage large and huge,
> And either of youre pappes like a water-bowge.
>
> Your camused nose, with nose-thrilles brode,
> Unto the chirch a noble instrument
> To quench tapers brenning afore the roode,
>
> Your babir lippes of color ded and wan,
> With suche mouth like to Jacobes brother,
> And yellow tethe not like to the swan-
> Set wide asunder, as eche cursed other;
>
> Youre body is formed all in proporcion,
> With hanging shuldres waving with every winde,
> Small in the belly as a wine toune,
> With froward fete, and crooked bak behinde.
> (Luria and Hoffman #73)[16]

Men are not immune to such parodies, but the body receives a greater share of attention than the face (although the nose is not neglected in this selection):

> Youre manly visage, shortly to declare,
> Your forehed, mouth, and nose so flatte,
> In short conclusion, best likened to an hare
> Of alle living things, save only a catte;
>
> Your thighes misgrowen, youre shankes much worse;
> Whoso beholde youre knees so crooked-
> As ech of hem bad oder Cristes curse,
> So go they outward; youre hammes ben hooked;
> Such a peire chaumbes I never on looked!
> So ungoodly youre heles ye lifte,
> And youre feet ben crooked with evil thrifte.
> (Luria and Hoffman #72)

While none of the Ellesmere portraits has such exaggeration of negative features, these examples, like the manuscript illustrations, call

attention to the fact that people of Chaucer's time were used to thinking in terms of individual features to indicate types. The *Canterbury
Tales* itself is a good example. The General Prologue describes the features of many of the pilgrims. Thus, Chaucer writes that the Miller was
"a stout carl for the nones;"

> Ful byg he was of brawn, and eek of bones.
> That proved wel, for over al ther he cam,
> At wrastlynge he wolde have alwey the ram.
> He was short-sholdred, brood, a thikke knarre;
> Ther was no dore that he nolde heve of harre,
> Or breke it at a rennyng with his heed.
> His berd as any sowe or fox was reed,
> And therto brood, as though it were a spade.
> Upon the cop right of his nose he hade
> A werte, and theron stood a toft of herys,
> Reed as the brustles of a sowes erys;
> His nosethirles blake were and wyde.
> A swerd and a bokeler bar he by his syde.
> His mouth as greet was as a greet forneys [furnace].
>   (I.545-59)

While the artist does not seem to follow the books on physiognomy
in any specific way, it is possible that he or she may have been familiar with the general ideas supplied by such books as the *Secretum
Secretorum*[17] in which we find the general idea that features which are
neither too large nor too small are the ideal:

> Þat man es euenest and best tempred whilk acordes in meneté. þat es to say
> noþer to longe ne to schorte, noþer to thyk ne to thynne, noþer to brode ne
> to narowe, noþer to mykel ne to litel, noþer to white ne to blak ne to rede,
> bot faire broune rody, with blak eyghne, blak heres and roundenes of visage,
> euenes of stature, with holnes of body, whose wordes are selden bot when
> nede askes, mediocrité of voyce, þat es to say noþer to smalle ne to grete,
> mediocrité also of of heuede whose culour es lufly white rody broune. Haue
> þat man with þe and trust to him for he es trewe. (11)

Features that are large often indicate a person of low character - lying
or lecherous:

> Whose nose holes has grete openyng, he es hard and wrathfull; and when þe
> nose es brode in þe mydell and goyng to heght, þat man is wordefull and
> lufyng to lye and lyenge. Þat man es euenest and best, whose nose is
> medioker in length, and medioker in brede at the ende, and þe holes are noght
> to mykel. (12)

On the other hand, features which are too small are also often indications of character faults:

"A litell mouthe is womannyssh, and his cheres and inwit accordeth with them." (105)

Fig. 5, 6, 7 - Detail of The Squire, The Prioress, and The Cook

Let us turn now to the portraits in question. The size of eyes, noses, and mouths of the first artist's faces vary a great deal in relation to the size of the face, and there are several combinations of feature types. The Man of Law and the Wife of Bath have small noses and mouths with eyes whose whites are clearly visible. The Squire (Figure 5) and the Prioress (Figure 6) are similar with slightly larger noses and mouths. The Pardoner has a small mouth with large nose and protruding eyes, as does the Parson. The Cook (Figure 7), Miller (Figure 8), Summoner, and Shipman all appear to follow the same schema with large eyes, nose and mouth. The Friar, Physician, and Clerk are depicted using a profile

Fig. 8 - Detail of The Miller

schema which shows no variations. In the differing facial types, there is no sense that the illustrator was following his or her visual perceptions to produce realistic, individualized portraits of living persons, but rather that the schematic elements are smaller in these illustrations than in others - separate features rather than faces. The Reeve, one of the more despicable characters, resembles the idealized Knight more than any other pilgrim. The Parson, another idealized character, looks most like the Shipman whose kind, according to Jill Mann, are thieves and murderers (170). The Shipman, the Summoner and

Fig. 9 - Detail of The Knight   *Fig. 10 - Detail of The Reeve*

the Miller have the darkest skin color of the group painted by Artist 1. The Knight (Figure 9) and Reeve (Figure 10) have medium-sized mouths and noses, and the whites of their eyes are not visible. If they are the product of Artist 1, they would fit somewhere in the middle of the spectrum, which might be another reason to suspect a fourth artist with a consistent schema, since we would expect Artist 1 to place them in different social categories.

If the supervisor provided only a few details for the artist to follow for each portrait, he or she probably did not provide information about character, but only about clothing or other obvious physical features such as the mormal on the Cook's shin. The artist, then, would have had to supply missing details, and we have seen how this was done with attributes such as the Physician's urinal, the Clerk's book, and the Cook's apron and meat hook. This artist decided to represent the pilgrims with facial attributes as well, and perhaps the results are based on the kinds of popular stereotypes we have seen, in conjunction with the individual artist's personal experience or idiosyncratic conceptions of people in these social positions.

Martin Stevens writes that illustrators who offer original details are "the first interpreters and critics of Chaucer's text, and they clearly must be taken seriously" ("Ellesmere Miniatures" 123). Artistic expression was moving toward a more individualistic mode of representation, and the work of this artist is in keeping with that trend. If we categorize the pilgrims according to the features the artist gives them, the Cook, Miller, and Shipman would not surprisingly be placed in the category of characters of lower social and/or moral status, although the Summoner's inclusion is less expected. In this scheme, for the artist, the Pardoner would be a somewhat more positive character than the

Summoner. If the illustrator has not read the text, he or she may be more influenced by satirical representations of parsons than by Chaucer's idealized description, and made him, along with the Pardoner, a kind of in-between character. The Franklin, the Prioress, and the Squire are similar to one another and also represent a kind of medial position. While the first artist's portraits draw heavily on the practice of schematization and the stereotypes that practice provides, they nevertheless represent something new in manuscript illustration - a reduction of the schematic unit for portraying familiar types that allows for much greater variation among those in the group.

Metonymic Focus on Orality

In the illustrations, schematic representations are also metonymic (that is, they represent something more than their literal referent, an individual and particular pilgrim), and the construction of types through the means described above contributes to their symbolic func-tion. The supervisor's decision to illustrate the tale-tellers rather than the tales has, as we have seen, two effects: the first is to emphasize the teller rather than the tale; the second is to focus on the fiction of the orality of the tales.[18]   Chaucer's audience were probably willing accomplices in the fiction that twenty-nine or so people could share stories which would be audible to all, as they rode their horses to Canterbury. The author has only to be sure that the reader "hears" the tale for the fiction to be satisfactory. The concept of the contest is more important than the plausibility of its execution. Positioned at the begin-ning of the tales, the portraits function as metonyms of oral telling. Each pilgrim portrait introduces his or her tale, and also reminds the reader that the tale is more than the narrative itself. The portrait repre-sents the personality of the teller, with whom it is linked in a bond that is legitimized by the presence of the teller's physical likeness with it on the page. The metonymic function is in operation even when the por-traits do not coincide precisely with the verbal text. Once again, they must be recognizable representations of types.

The portrait of Chaucer (color plate16) is especially significant. As Alan Gaylord has pointed out, it represents him as a man older than he would have been at the time of the pilgrimage, and therefore more authoritative ("Portrait" 133). The emphasis on Chaucer the poet would, as Alfred David notes, enhance the prestige of the patron (310). Gaylord sees the portrait as part of the iconic tradition of depicting authors with their work - either sitting at a desk writing, or presenting a book. But this particular portrait differs from most others: the indications of age correspond iconographically to another tradition, that of the wise old man, also found in the portrait of Chaucer in Hoccleve's *Regiment of Princes* (Harley 4866, f. 88r.) The two portraits are so similar that they must have come from a common exemplar, or one must have been copied from the other. Gaylord claims that they do not represent any attempt to produce a true likeness. Annabel Patterson challenges this claim, partly on the basis that the Ellesmere portrait is not as venerable as Gaylord sees it:

> It [Gaylord's reading] misreads the Ellesmere portrait by subsuming its characteristics under those of the Hoccleve portrait, which *could* be described in the terms that Gaylord uses for both of them. The Hoccleve portrait is older, whiter-haired, not so obviously portly or particular....It is also conservatively religious in its substitution of the beads for the bridle. (171)

Patterson argues that the Hoccleve portrait apologizes for the less serious Ellesmere portrait by refiguring the poet's persona. This argument assumes that the Hoccleve portrait followed the Ellesmere portrait, although that has by no means been proven. While it is true that the Hoccleve portrait shows an older and perhaps more serious man, nevertheless, the venerability of the Ellesmere portrait does not suffer by comparison. And even if it were shown conclusively that the features resembled Chaucer's, the portrait would still present a concept of the author as a particular type of person. Ultimately, the patron who commissioned the manuscript would have to be satisfied with the result. If this were in fact Thomas Chaucer, he would no doubt want his late father shown in the best light possible.

Because the Ellesmere portrait portrays the poet's pilgrim persona, its metonymic function is doubled. However, the pictorial image of Chaucer does not completely accord with the way he presents himself in the text. In Chaucer's prologue, as is often his habit when he places himself in a narrator persona, he presents himself as inept.[19] His two Canterbury tales are not the most entertaining, the Host calls his poetry "drasty" (i.e., worthless), and he is accused of keeping too much to himself. However, as Benson notes, his persona in the General Prologue is rather different. He makes the acquaintance of the other pilgrims, and seems to have an intelligent appreciation of the genuinely good characteristics of the Parson, the Clerk, and the Plowman (63).

His inept (verbal) persona, however, is spatially congruent with his authoritative (visual) poet portrait. The illustrator conflates Chaucer, the author of the *Canterbury Tales,* with Chaucer the narrator. The problem confronting the artist and/or supervisor was deciding which of the poet's personas to put in the illustration and where to put it. Because the portrait is positioned at the head of the tale, with the teller gesturing toward it, the image constitutes a metonymic representation of the pilgrim Chaucer telling his *Tale of Melibee* orally; but because it is larger than the others, and shows the poet as a venerable old man, it is also a metonym for Chaucer the public figure, poet to kings and dukes, and of everything else associated with his career, reputation and public life. The commerciality of the project encourages a representation of Chaucer as a prestigious author which is in contrast to the way he represents himself in the work.

Another aspect of the portrait which has concerned observers is what is seen as the disproportion of the figure. The head and torso are very large in proportion to the figure's legs and to the horse. The responses have ranged from literalism (Chaucer was short and disfigured) to criticism of the artist's skill. Gaylord suggests that the artist copied an existing portrait of a standing figure "with more attention to the top than the bottom of the figure" ("Portrait" 124), but except for the proportion, the bottom of the figure shows as much detail and care as the top. No one seems particularly concerned that several of the other figures have bodies that are almost as disproportional to their legs (for example, the Merchant, Physician, Franklin, and Pardoner) and that all of the figures are disproportionate to some degree.

One of the salient features of medieval art is that because it is little concerned with representing a particular version of visual perceptions, but rather with representing concepts, the size of objects often corresponds to the artist's understanding of their importance. This is particularly noticeable in medieval illustrations of cities, where the people are very large in proportion to the buildings and walls. Heads are usually unrealistically large in proportion to the body, compared to actual measurements. In fact, the disproportion in Chaucer's portrait, and in all of the other portraits as well, is between the body and horse, the horse being the less important element. Because Chaucer's upper body is drawn very large to express the perceived importance of the poet, the artist had either to accommodate the lower body to the size of the horse by shortening his legs, or to allow his legs to drag on the ground. In addition, the artist was constrained by the planned space, which was the same size as that allowed for the other pilgrims. The horse fills up its space, even crowding the initial somewhat. It is approximately the same size as the largest of the other horses. Below is a silhouette of a horse and rider taken from a photograph next to silhouettes of the Ellesmere illustrations of Chaucer, the Franklin, and the Canon's Yeoman where the horses are approximately the same size. The comparison demonstrates that each of the artists made figures which are large in proportion to their horses.[20] The people are more important than the horses, and Chaucer is the most important; therefore he is larger in proportion to his horse than the others. What seems to be a distortion is no more than the conceptual representation of Chaucer's role as a famed poet and public figure.

Actual proportions   *Chaucer*   *Franklin*   *Canon's Yeoman*
of man and horse
from photo

Because the illustrations portray the pilgrims, the Ellesmere version of the *Canterbury Tales* is a graphic production that celebrates the spoken word. It is a compendium of people, as well as a compendium of stories. Diversity is an inherent quality of the didascalic genre of the text.[21] Most didascalic works depend on overall structure to give them coherence, and the *Canterbury Tales* is no exception; the frame structure of the tale-telling contest provides that structure. But the manuscript also holds the tales and characters together in its similarity of page layout and portrait treatment. While the illustrations emphasize the tellers, it is not possible to separate the tellers from the tales. In some cases, the figure is doubled in another pilgrim's tale, as is the case with the Friar and the Miller, so that there is constant cross reference between and among "fictional" and "real" characters. The pilgrim Friar becomes conflated with Friar John of the Summoner's Tale, and the portrait attains a secondary metonymic function.

The Tales of *Thopas* and *Melibee*

Geoffrey the narrator's two tales exemplify opposite approaches to the practice of tale-telling, and so will serve to demonstrate how, within the verbal text itself and in the page layout, the oral and the literate exist in tension. Also, the juxtaposition of the Chaucer portrait with the *Tale of Melibee* signals an interpretation on the part of the Ellesmere manuscript's supervisor of both the tale and the author. Both tales are part of Fragment VII, which Gaylord characterizes as dealing with "the art of storytelling" ("Sentence and Solaas" 226). In reference to their different treatment of this broadly designated topos, Seth Lerer writes, *"Sir Thopas* is the supreme moment in the *Canterbury Tales* that actively engages the phenomenon of voice. . . .By contrast the *Melibee* is (perhaps second only to the *Parson's Tale*) a text that actively disengages the phenomenon of voice. This sort of text is about other texts" (183).

Lee Patterson argues that in the *Tale of Sir Thopas*, Chaucer draws upon the tradition of minstrel performance as a means of situating his own work outside the traditions of both courtly romance and classical epic (123-25). One of the characteristics of minstrelsy is its orality, which includes the use of stock phrases and type scenes. In *Sir Thopas*, this takes the form of parodic imitations of popular romance literature. "Hackneyed stereotyping . . .," write Ruth Waterhouse and Gwen Griffiths, "is an important part of the 'game' of the tale" (I. 348). The meter is iambic tetrameter, in a style mocked by the Host as "drasty speche" (VII.923).

The opening lines of *Sir Thopas* are typical in their appeal for the audience's aural attention: "Listeth, lordes, in good entent, / And I wol telle verrayment / Of myrthe and of solas [pleasure]*"* (VII.712-14). The word "doughty" is one of the commonest that romance writers use to describe their heroes. "Sir Thopas wax a doghty swayn," writes Chaucer (VII.724), and the tale of *Sir Degrevant* reports that its hero "dowghty was of dede" (l. 12). The term serves to identify Sir Thopas as a romance hero. The humor of Chaucer's parody is that he begins with a stock phrase which, in successive lines, descends into inanity. For example, after calling Thopas "a doghty swayn," Chaucer describes him in feminine terms: "Whit was his face as payndemayn [white bread], / His lippes rede as rose; /His rode is lyk scarlet in grayn," and then concludes with a filler line and a banal observation:

"And I yow telle in good certayn / He hadde a semely nose" (VII.725-29).
The same kind of play occurs in the description of Sir Thopas's armor
as he prepares to fight the giant:

> His spere was of fyn ciprees,
> That bodeth werre, and nothyng pees,
>   The heed ful sharpe ygrounde;
> His steede was al dappull gray,
> It gooth an ambil in the way
>   Full softely and rounde
>   In londe.
>   (VII.881-87)

The cypress spear with its sharply ground point is reminiscent of
other romance terminology, but in the easy, ambling gait of his horse
(the kind of horse ridden by the Wife of Bath), he again becomes fem-
inized; and again, the stanza ends in a vacuous phrase, "in londe."
Chaucer calls upon his audience's familiarity with the stock phrases
and scenes of popular romance to establish expectations which are
thwarted when they are surprised by a switch to the unexpected. He
uses schematic (oral) elements, but he applies them wrongly by giving
characteristics of an idealized romance heroine to Sir Thopas with
comic effect.

In contrast to the highly oral nature of the verbal text, the page layout is set apart from that of the other tales by a particular visual feature.
The tale is written in tail-rhyme stanzas with several irregularly placed
bob lines. The rhymed lines are set in columns and connected with
brackets, so that the *a* lines are in one column, the *b* lines in another,
and the bob lines in a third. Tail-rhyme is not uncommon for romances
(especially incompetent ones, according to Judith Tschann [7]), and
brackets are sometimes found in rhymed works, although not necessarily in tail-rhyme romances. These brackets provide a spatial patterning
which corresponds to the aural patterning of the spoken word. The
Hengwrt scribe brackets the *Thopas* rhymes, but they are arranged in
only two columns; the bob lines do not have a separate column. For
Sir Thopas, they set this tale apart graphically from the others, a mark
of distinction which may have originated with Chaucer or with the
project supervisor. Tschann calls attention to the fact that the progressive
inanity of the lines such as "his name / was Sir Thopas" and "he hadde a
semely nose," is emphasized by their being placed in columns (7).

The stanza type, the "progressive diminution" of the fit length (to use A.J. Burrow's term) (57), the vacuous end lines, and the insubstantiality of the content all contribute to the humor of the poem. The overdetermination of the joke by the visual doubling adds to the humor, and again emphasizes the literate nature of a fictionally oral phenomenon.

After the Host derides Geoffrey for his ineptitude in *Sir Thopas*, he begins again with the *Tale of Melibee*, a work as different in tone from *Sir Thopas* as it can be. While *Sir Thopas* exemplifies an oral style of story telling, *Melibee* exemplifies a literate one, and Chaucer again goes to extremes. Waterhouse and Griffiths have remarked that the discourse obscures the story in *Melibee*, as opposed to the discourse of *Sir Thopas*, which emphasizes it (I. 342). *Melibee* is all *sentence*, and the *Sir Thopas* is all *solaas* (I. 344).[22] Neither is effective storytelling. The preponderance of material is didactic quotation. Aphorisms, adages, sage advice from biblical, patristic, and classical sources pile up in an avalanche that overwhelms the modern reader. The sheer volume of so many aphorisms becomes deadening. Daniel Kempton remarks, "I would call the 'little thing in prose' Chaucer's 'grete clobbed stave'" (271). On the surface, the tone is unrelentingly serious. However, Waterhouse and Griffiths argue convincingly that for one who is familiar with the source material, the quotations must be taken as ironic. To give only one example, Prudence's first quotation from Ovid calls the comforter a fool who tries to prevent a mother from weeping for her child (VII.976-77). However, she then does just that to Melibee, calling *him* a fool for weeping too much: "Allas, my lord, . . .why make ye youreself for to be lyk a fool? For sothe it aperteneth nat to a wys man to maken swich a sorwe?" (VII.980-81). Prudence has also produced a role reversal, taking the part of the male comforter in the Ovid citation, and placing Melibee in the role of the weeping mother (Waterhouse and Griffiths, II. 53).

The tale appears to be an allegory, although to call it strictly an allegory would be to misrepresent it. Something else is going on in the tale which subverts attempts at traditional interpretation. Certainly the characters' names - Melibee, Prudence, and Sophia - alert the reader at once to look for an allegorical inclination. Prudence herself portrays the event of the attack on Sophia by three enemies as allegorical:

> Thy name is Melibee; this is to seyn, 'a man that drynketh hony.' Thou hast
> ydronke so muchel hony of sweete temporeel richesses, and delices and hon-
> ours of this world that thou art dronken and hast forgeten Jhesu Crist thy
> creatour... Thou hast doon synne agayn oure Lord Crist, for certes, the three

enemys of mankynde - that is to seyn, the flessh, the feend, and the world -
thou hast suffred hem entre in to thyn herte wilfully by the wyndowes of thy
body, and hast nat defended thyself suffisantly agayns hire assautes and hire
temptaciouns, so that they han wounded thy soule in fyve places; this is to
seyn, the deedly synnes that been entred into thyn herte by thy fyve wittes.
And in the same manere oure Lord Crist hath woold and suffred that thy
three enemys been entred into thyn house by the wyndowes and han
ywounded thy doghter in the forseyde manere. (VII.1409-12, 1419-26)

Some have found inconsistencies in the allegory, pointing out, for
one thing, that Prudence urges Melibee, against all Christian teaching,
to be reconciled to his enemies: the world, the flesh, and the devil
(Waterhouse and Griffiths 1.346). Also, Sophia, the personification of
Wisdom, disappears early from the plot, without ever having contributed to the allegorical fabric. The very inconsistencies in the allegorical material subvert a reading that is completely literal. But
Melibee is so overcome by Prudence's great flood of words that he
does not question the conflict between the conciliating direction of her
advice and the warning about the world, the flesh, and the devil. And
once she assures him that his daughter will eventually recover, he forgets about Sophia completely, so caught up is he in the intricacies of
Prudence's argument. When, at last, the enemies agree that they have
acted wrongly, and place themselves under Melibee's judgment, we
find that he seems to have missed the point after all. His plan is "to
desherite hem of al that evere they han and for to putte hem in exil for
evere" (VII.1835). However, if these enemies truly symbolize the
world, the flesh and the devil, his sentence is appropriate. Either
Melibee is following the metaphor to its logical conclusion, or he is a
complete dolt. But the allegorical reading of the situation is not
allowed to direct the result, because Prudence insists on treating the
enemies like people rather than symbols. Chaucer, the bumbling pilgrim, lacks a sense of moderation. Just as *Sir Thopas,* Chaucer's example of oral telling, parodies the romance, so *Melibee* parodies bookish
and servile appeals to *auctoritas.*

Not everyone agrees that *Melibee* is a parody. Carolyn Colette
places it in a body of female courtesy literature which features the
woman's responsibility to mitigate the behavior of her husband by subtle application of advice and correction (416-33). Others have seen in
it a reflection of the political scene, pointing to Richard's choice of
counselors, the war with France, or the involvement of women such as
Joan of Kent in England's political affairs.[23]

In the contention over the question of the nature of the *Tale of Melibee,* critics have assumed that all medieval readers either took it at face value or read it ironically. The third, and to me most likely, possibility is that they did not all read it in the same way. We have seen that there is good reason to believe that readers who were familiar with Chaucer's source material would have interpreted it ironically. On the other hand, if we look at the illustration of the poet that accompanies the tale, we must come to the conclusion that the manuscript supervisor probably took it seriously. If there was a joke, the supervisor either didn't get it or decided to ignore it. Otherwise, the portrait might as well have been placed at the head of *Sir Thopas.* In Gaylord's opinion, the portrait is with *Melibee* because the makers wanted Chaucer's portrait to be associated with the more serious of the two tales in order to give a sense of importance to the manuscript and appeal to the patron who commissioned it ("Portrait" 138).[24] Again, the pictorial and verbal texts produce a tension and constitute a unique graphic production that differs profoundly from any non-illustrated version of the work. It is this atmosphere of tension that gives this manuscript its unique character.

We can learn a great deal about medieval culture from the *Canterbury Tales*, and even more from its Ellesmere manifestation. First, orality still plays a major role in medieval life, but alongside it is a growing concept of words as visible representations of ideas apart from their spoken form. Chaucer and the producers of the Ellesmere Manuscript have used these tensions between orality and literacy, between telling and writing, to make a statement about their complex relationship at the end of the fourteenth and beginning of the fifteenth centuries.

Second, we see that society has become complex and layered in ways that are both subtle and obvious. A comparison of Chaucer's portrayal of social types with the artists' portrayals not only gives us a glimpse of how people in various roles were conceived, but demonstrates that not everyone understood characters and tales the same way. We have two different mirrors to reflect the age, and each shows a slightly different picture. The situation becomes especially interesting when the mirror is turned toward Chaucer himself and we see how the poet's persona has been constructed by two people with different desires - the poet himself and the person who supervised the making of the manuscript.

The Ellesmere Chaucer is not atypical of manuscripts of its time, and yet it is much more than a typical manuscript. Its visual aspects appear at first to be fairly straightforward and obvious, but the more we study it the more its complexity is revealed, and the more we come to appreciate its uniqueness.

Notes

1 All references to the *Canterbury Tales* are from *The Riverside Chaucer*.

2 Manly and Rickert argue that Thomas Chaucer had the manuscript made, and that it later passed to the de Vere family. See also Ralph Hanna, "Introduction." 1-17; and Alfred David 307-26.

3 The word "schemata" (and its singular form "schema") refers to the practice common in certain types of art such as medieval art, children's drawings, and the art of some tribal cultures, in which the artist draws all objects of the same type according the same model. Consequently, in most medieval art, all faces drawn by the same artist will look like the same person except for details such as hair length and color.

4 One of the earliest manuscript portraits that seems to be mimetic, as Janet Backhouse observes, is that of John Duke of Bedford in the Bedford Hours (BL Additional MS 18850, f. 256b), made around 1423 ("Illuminated Manuscripts" 3). In general, however, manuscript illustrations are schematized in the traditional manner. It has been a commonly held opinion that the Ellesmere portrait of Chaucer is meant to resemble the poet, but see the discussion of the portrait on pages 20-22 for a differing view.

5 For example, the Franklin's horse shows an indented outline in the parchment with no paint in it, indicating that the form was traced with a stylus or other instrument from a pattern placed over the page.

6 Emmerson provides a chart wherein he compares the verbal and pictorial portraits and lists which characteristics appear in each (159-63).

7 See Jill Rickets, *Visualizing Boccaccio: Studies on Illustrations of the Decameron from Giotto to Pasolini* for examples.

8 Saenger seems to believe that silent reading would have been much more difficult if the words were not separated by some space.

9 Saenger points out that Augustine's *Confessions* was given chapter divisions, and Isidore also divided his *Etymologies* during this time (376).

[10] Another example of a manuscript where the figures are placed next to the lines they speak is the Douce *Piers Plowman* (Oxford Bodleian Library, MS Douce 104).

[11] All illustrations are from the Ellesmere Chaucer: San Marino, Huntington Library MS El 26 C9 and are used by permission of the Huntington Library, San Marino, California.

[12] I am referring to V.A. Kolve's idea of a cultural pool of images which he describes in *Chaucer and the Imagery of Narrative.*

[13] Ruth Mellinkoff's *Outcasts: Signs of Otherness in Northern European Art of the Middle Ages* gives extensive coverage of this topic.

[14] For example, the Lutrell Psalter (London, BL MS. Add. 42130 f. 53v.), the Fitzwarin Psalter (Paris, Bibliothèque Nationale MS lat. 765, f. 11r), the Ramsey Psalter (New York, Pierpont Morgan Library MS. 302 f.2v), the Holkham Bible (London, BL MS. Add.47682 f. 6v), The Hours of Elizabeth the Queen (London, BL MS. Add. 50001 f. 7r), and the M.R. James Memorial Psalter (London, BL MS. Add. 44949 f.3v), all from the 14th century.

[15] For example, the flagellation scenes from the 13th-century Chichester Psalter (Manchester, John Rylands Library MS. lat. 24 f. 151r) and the Fitzwarin Psalter (f.12r).

[16] Another example, the description of Dame Ragnell, shows attention to the same features:

> Her face was red, her nose snotid withalle,
> Her mouithe wide, her teethe yallowe overe alle,
> With blerid eyen gretter than a balle;
> Her mouithe was not to lake;
> Her teethe hing overe her lippes;
> Her cheekis wide as wemens hippes
> A lute she bare upon her back
> Her neck long and therto great;
> Her here cloterid on an hepe;
>
> In the sholders she was a yard brode;
> Hanging pappis to be an hors lode;
> And like a barelle she was made;
> And to reherse the foulness of that lady,
> Ther is no tung may telle securly.
> (*The Wedding of Sir Gawain and Dame Ragnell* ll. 231-244)

[17] Curry has shown that Chaucer was thoroughly familiar with these ideas.

[18] Hanna's opinion is that because the portrait comes at the head of the tale rather than at the prologue, the emphasis is on the tale rather than the teller ("Introduction" 14). However, the emphasis is inherently on the teller for the prologue. It is when the pilgrim leads the audience into the world of the narrative that the teller is likely to be forgotten.

[19] In the *Book of the Duchess*, for example, the narrator consistently fails to understand the import of the knight's words, "Thow nost what thow menest;/I have lost more than thou wenest" (1137-38); in the *House of Fame* as he walks in a field, an eagle swoops down and picks him up, though he tries to run away. He protests that he is not important enough to be stellified like the characters in *Metamorphoses*(529-591).

[20] Even if the pilgrims' horses may have been smaller than the horse in the photo, the difference in proportion is still marked.

[21] Ann Astell has argued convincingly in *Chaucer and the Universe of Learning* that the *Canterbury Tales* belongs to the didascalic genre which includes encyclopedic works such as Hugh of St. Victor's *Didascalicon,* Isidore of Seville's *Etymologies*, and Pliny's *Natural History.*

[22] At the beginning of the Canterbury pilgrimage, the host proposes "sentence and solaas" as criteria for judging the merit of the tales. The *Riverside Chaucer* glosses these terms as "significance" and "pleasure" respectively.

[23] See for example, W. W. Lawrence, "The Tale of Melibeus," *Essays and Studies in Honor of Carleton Brown,* New York, London: New York University Press, 1940, 100-110; Gardiner Stillwell, "The Political Meaning of Chaucer's *Tale of Melibee*," *Speculum* 19 (1944): 433-44; William Askins, "The *Tale of Melibee* and the Crisis at Westminster, November, 1387," *Studies in the Age of Chaucer*: Proceedings 2 (1986): 103-12; and Lynn Staley Johnson, "Inverse Counsel: Contexts for the *Melibee*," *Studies in Philology* 87.2 (Spring, 1990): 137-55. James Flynn shows how what appears to be contradictory advice in the use of quoted aphorisms is really a prioritizing of advice and correction: "The Art of Telling and the Prudence of Interpreting in The *Tale of Melibee* and Its Context," *Medieval Perspectives* 7 (1992): 53-63.

[24] Richard Emmerson argues that if the quires were distributed among the three illustrators to work on simultaneously, then Melibee received the portrait because it is close to the beginning of quire 20, and Artist 1 would still have been working on quire 19 (152). This scenario is quite possible, but I think the question of placement is more compelling than the convenience of an available quire.

Bibliography

Alexander, Jonathan J.G. "Art History, Literary History, and the Study of Medieval Illuminated Manuscripts." *Studies in Iconography* 18 (1997): 51-66.

Amodio, Mark C., ed. *Oral Poetics in Middle English Poetry*. The Albert Lord Bates Studies in Oral Tradition 13. New York and London: Garland, 1994.

Askins, William. "The *Tale of Melibee* and the Crisis at Westminster, November, 1387." *Studies in the Age of Chaucer*: Proceedings 2 (1986): 103-12.

Backhouse, Janet. "French Manuscript Illumination 1450-1530." *Renaissance Painting in Manuscripts: Treasures from the British Library*. Ed. Thomas Kren. New York: Hudson Hills, 1983.

--- "Illuminated Manuscripts and the Early Development of the Portrait Miniature." *Early Tudor England: Proceedings of the 1987 Harlaxton Symposium*. Ed. Daniel Williams. Woodbridge, Suffolk; Wolfeboro, N.H: Boydell, 1989. 1-18.

Benson, C. David. "Their Telling Difference: Chaucer the Pilgrim and His Two Contrasting Tales.*" The Chaucer Review* 18.1 (1983): 61-76.

Burrow, J. A. "'Sir Thopas': An Agony in Three Fits." *Review of English Studies* 22 (1971): 54-59.

Camille, Michael. *Image on the Edge: The Margins of Medieval Art*. Essays in Art and Culture. Cambridge: Harvard UP, 1992.

Chaucer, Geoffrey. *The Canterbury Tales: The New Ellesmere Monochromatic Facsimile (of Huntington Library MS EL 26 C9)*. Ed. Daniel Woodward and Martin Stevens. San Marino: Huntington Library, 1997.

--- *The Canterbury Tales: A Facsimile and Transcription of the Hengwrt Manuscript, with Variants from the Ellesmere Manuscript*. Ed. Paul G. Ruggiers. Norman: U of Oklahoma P, 1979.

--- *The Riverside Chaucer*. Ed. Larry D. Benson. 3rd ed. Boston: Houghton Mifflin, 1987.

Colette, Carolyn. "Heeding the Counsel of Prudence: A Context for the *Melibee*." *The Chaucer Review* 29.4 (1995): 416-33.

Curry, Walter Clyde. *Chaucer and the Medieval Sciences*. New York: Oxford UP, 1926.

David, Alfred. "The Ownership and Use of the Ellesmere Manuscript." Stevens
and Woodward 307-26.

Doyle, I. A. "The Copyist of the Ellesmere *Canterbury Tales*." Stevens and
Woodward 49-67.

---   and M. B. Parkes. "Paleographic Introduction." *The Canterbury Tales:
Geoffrey Chaucer: A Facsimile and Transcription of the Hengwrt
Manuscript*. Ed. Paul G. Ruggiers. Norman: U of Oklahoma, 1979. ix-
xlviii.

---   "The Production of Copies of the *Canterbury Tales* and the *Confessio
Amantis* in the Early Fifteenth Century." *Medieval Scribes, Manuscripts
and Libraries: Essays Presented to N.R. Ker*. Ed. M.B. Parkes and
Andrew Watson. London: Scolar, 1978. 163-205.

Emmerson, Richard K. "Text and Image in the Ellesmere Portraits of the Tale-
Tellers." Stevens and Woodward 143-70.

Flynn, James. "The Art of Telling and the Prudence of Interpreting: *The Tale of
Melibee* and Its Context." *Medieval Perspectives* 7 (1992): 53-63.

Gaylord, Alan T. "Chaucer's Dainty 'Dogerel': The 'Elvyssh' Prosody of *Sir
Thopas*." *Studies in the Age of Chaucer* 1 (1979): 83-103.

---   "Portrait of a Poet." Stevens and Woodward 121-42.

---   *Sentence* and *Solaas* in Fragment VII of the *Canterbury Tales*: Harry
Bailly as Horseback Editor." *PMLA* 82.2 (1967): 226-35.

Hanna, Ralph III. "(The) Editing (of) the Ellesmere Text." Stevens and Woodward
225-43.

---   "Introduction." *The Ellesmere Manuscript of Chaucer's* Canterbury Tales:
A Working Facsimile. London: D. S. Brewer, 1989. 1-17.

Illich, Ivan. *In the Vineyard of the Text: A Commentary to Hugh's Didascalicon*.
Chicago and London: U of Chicago P, 1993.

Johnson, Lynn Staley. "Inverse Counsel: Contexts for the *Melibee*." *Studies in
Philology* 87.2 (Spring, 1990): 137-55.

Kempton, Daniel. "Chaucer's *Tale of Melibee*: 'A Little Thyng in Prose.'" *Genre*
21 (Fall 1988): 263-78.

Kolve, V.A. *Chaucer and the Imagery of Narrative: The First Five Canterbury
Tales*. Stanford: Stanford UP, 1984.

Lawrence, W. W. "The Tale of Melibeus." *Essays and Studies in Honor of Carleton Brown*. New York and London: New York UP, 1940. 100-110.

Lerer, Seth. "'Now holde youre mouth' : The Romance of Orality in the Thopas-Melibee Section of the *Canterbury Tales*." Amodio 181-206.

Luria, Maxwell S. and Richard L. Hoffman, eds. *Middle English Lyrics*. New York and London: Norton, 1974.

Machan, Tim William. "Editing, Orality, and Late Middle English Texts." Alger Nicolaus Doane and Carol Braun Pasternack, eds. *Vox intexta: Orality and Textuality in the Middle Ages*. Madison: U of Wisconsin P, 1991. 229-45.

Manly, John M. and Edith Rickert. *The Text of the Canterbury Tales*. 8 vols. Chicago: U of Chicago P, 1940.

Mann, Jill. *Chaucer and Medieval Estates Satire: The Literature of Social Classes and the* General Prologue *to the* Canterbury Tales. Cambridge: Cambridge UP, 1973.

Mellinkoff, Ruth. *Outcasts: Signs of Otherness in Northern European Art of the Late Middle Ages*. 2 vols. California Studies in the History of Art. Berkeley, Los Angeles, Oxford: U of California P, 1993.

Middle English Verse Romances. Ed. Donald B. Sands. New York, Toronto, and London: Holt, Rinehart, Winston, 1966.

Ong, Walter. *Orality and Literacy: The Technologizing of the Word*. London and New York: Methuen, 1982

Parks, Ward. "Oral Tradition and the *Canterbury Tales*." Amodio 149-80.

Patterson, Annabel. " 'The Human Face Divine': Identity and the Portrait from Locke to Chaucer." *Crossing Boundaries: Issues of Cultural and Individual Identity in the Middle Ages and the Renaissance*. Ed. Sally McKee. Arizona Studies in the Middle Ages and the Renaissance 3. Turnhout, Belgium: Brepols, 1999. 155-86.

Patterson, Lee. "What Man Artow?: Authorial Self-definition in *The Tale of Sir Thopas* and *The Tale of Melibee*." *Studies in the Age of Chaucer* 11 (1989): 117-75.

Randall, Lilian M. C. *Images in the Margins of Gothic Manuscripts*. Berkeley and Los Angeles: U of California P, 1966.

Rickert, Margaret. "Illumination." Manly and Rickert 1:561-605.

Ricketts, Jill. *Visualizing Boccaccio*: *Studies on Illlustrations of the Decameron from Giotto to Pasoliti.* Cambridge Studies in New Art History and Criticism. New York: Cambridge UP, 1997.

Saenger, Paul. "Silent Reading: Its Impact on Late Medieval Script and Society." *Viator* 13 (1982): 366-414.

Scott, Kathleen. "An Hours and Psalter by Two Ellesmere Illuninators." Stevens and Woodward 87-119.

Secretum Secretorum: *Nine English Versions.* Ed. M.A. Manzalaoui. Early English Text Society 276. Oxford: Oxford UP, 1977.

Shultz, Herbert. *The Ellesmere Manuscript of Chaucer's Canterbury Tales.* San Marino: Huntington Library, 1966.

Silvia, Daniel S., Jr. "Glossses to the *Canterbury Tales* from St. Jerome's *Epistola adversus Jovinianum.*" *Studies in Philology* 62(1965): 28-39.

"Sir Degrevant." *Middle English Romances*. Ed. A. C. Gibbs. York Medieval Texts. Evanston: Northwestern UP, 1979. 136-158.

Stevens, Martin. "The Ellesmere Miniatures as Illustrations of Chaucer's *Canterbury Tales*." *Studies in Iconography* 7-8 (1981-82): 113-26.

---   "Introduction." Stevens and Woodward, 15-28.

---   and Daniel Woodward, eds. *The Ellesmere Chaucer: Essays in Interpretation*. San Marino, CA: Huntington Library, 1995.

Stillwell, Gardiner. "The Political Meaning of Chaucer's *Tale of Melibee*." *Speculum* 19 (1944): 433-44.

Tschann, Judith. "The Layout of Sir Thopas in the Ellesmere, Hengwrt, Cambridge Dd.4.24, and Cambridge Gg.4.27 Manuscripts." *The Chaucer Review* 20.1 (1985): 1-13.

Waterhouse, Ruth and Gwen Griffiths. "'Sweete Wordes' of Non-Sense: The Deconstruction of the Moral *Melibee*, Part I." *The Chaucer Review* 23.4 (1989): 338-61.

---   "Sweete Wordes' of Non-Sense; The Deconstruction of the Moral *Melibee*, Part II." *The Chaucer Review* 24.1 (1989-90): 53-63.

"The Wedding of Sir Gawain and Dame Ragnell." *Middle English Verse Romances*. Ed. Donald B. Sands. New York, Chicago, San Francisco, Toronto, London: Holt, Rinehart, & Winston, 1966. 323-347.

Chapter 2

Presenting the Text: Pictorial Tradition in Fifteenth-Century Manuscripts of the *Canterbury Tales*

Phillipa Hardman

The Pictorial Tradition

The manuscript tradition of Chaucer's *Canterbury Tales* is characterized by an embarrassing dearth of illustrations. Popular editions of the text have to resort to illustrations taken from manuscripts of other works to provide images for dust-jackets and paperback covers. The *Riverside Chaucer*, for example, carries a picture of the company of pilgrims taken from a sumptuously illustrated copy of Lydgate's *Siege of Thebes* (London, British Library MS Royal 18 D ii, fol.148), while the Oxford World's Classics translation of the *Canterbury Tales* represents a scene from the Knight's Tale with a miniature from an illuminated manuscript of Boccaccio's *Il Teseida* (Vienna, Österreichische Nationalbibliotek MS 2617, fol.53).[1] Although the Ellesmere MS preserves its complete programme of illustration and six other *Canterbury Tales* manuscripts contain one picture or more, none of them offers the kind of illustration of narrative incidents that picture researchers seem to require. V. A. Kolve's study of the imagery of narrative in the first five Canterbury Tales is profusely illustrated with images relating to narrative events in the tales, but they all derive perforce from pictorial sources unconnected to the manuscript tradition of the *Canterbury Tales*.[2]

There is nothing in the history of Chaucer's text to compare with the pictorial traditions of French or Italian vernacular classics such as we find in the *Roman de la rose* picture cycle or in illustrated manuscripts of the works of Dante. It is, however, instructive to note that the illustrative tradition of Dante's *Divina Commedia*, for example,

involves only a small proportion of the hundreds of surviving manuscripts, and varies from simple schemes where miniatures function as
indicators of the tripartite structure of the text, typically with a representation of Dante himself placed in an historiated initial at the opening of each *cantica*, to very elaborate copies produced as luxury volumes for wealthy aristocratic patrons, where frequent detailed illustrations accompany the textual narrative.[3] One reason for the paucity of
illustration in Chaucer manuscripts may therefore be a consequence of
the book-patronage habits of the English: for when aristocratic patrons
did purchase expensively produced vernacular texts they were still
likely to be in French, as they had been a century before,[4] and, as
Kathleen L. Scott notes, fifteenth-century English patrons on the whole
seem to have preferred their luxury illustrated books to be works
of devotion.[5]

Derek Pearsall points also to the contrast between Chaucer's apparent lack of concern to prepare his works for publication and the care
shown by a number of his contemporaries, including Gower, whose
personal organization of the presentation of his *Confessio Amantis*,
including a modest programme of illustration, was perhaps instrumen-
tal in ensuring the survival of the scheme in later manuscripts.[6]
However, it is important to take into account the probably fragmentary
and unfinished status of the *Canterbury Tales* at the time of Chaucer's
death; manuscripts of his completed masterpiece, *Troilus and Criseyde*,
give some evidence that Chaucer may not in fact have been quite so
unconcerned with the presentation of his text.[7] It is unfortunate that no
autograph copy of any of Chaucer's poems has survived; but a further
instructive Italian parallel is provided by copies of Boccaccio's works.
The autograph manuscript of *Il Teseida* shows the author's intentions
for the presentation of his text: a single-column layout with wide margins accommodating his *chiose*; interlineated glosses; rubricated sum-
maries within the text column; a system of large and small coloured initials to mark textual divisions and subdivisions; and spaces for a
planned programme of illustrations. Despite the clarity of this scheme,
however, no scribal copy of Boccaccio's poem reproduces the author's
presentation of the text. Most notably, only one contains a programme
of illustrations.[8] In the absence of authorial copies of Chaucer's texts,
therefore, it is as well to be cautious about deducing the author's concern for or intentions towards the presentation of his works on the evidence of the surviving manuscripts. As George Keiser argues, the contrasting treatment of manuscript glosses in modern editions of Gower's

Confessio Amantis (where they are included) and of the *Canterbury Tales* (where they are mostly omitted) has obscured 'the likelihood that Chaucer himself prepared the glosses'.[9] Maybe we should not exclude the possibility that Chaucer, like Gower, might also have planned to use illustrations as part of the presentation of his framed narratives.

The manuscript evidence of a pictorial tradition for the *Canterbury Tales* is not extensive, but it does provide examples of several distinct illustrative procedures. Three different formats are used: historiated initials (British Library MS Lansdowne 851, Bodleian Library MSS Rawlinson poet. 223 and Bodley 686, and the 'Devonshire' MS),[10] marginal illustrations (the Ellesmere MS), and illustrations within the text column (Cambridge University Library MS Gg.4.27 and the 'Oxford' MS).[11] Cutting across these differences in format, we find three distinct approaches to the relation between illustration and text: a pictured figure at the opening of the work, possibly representing in some way the author of the whole; pictured pilgrim-narrator figures placed in relation to individual tales; and pictured figures representing some aspect of the content of the adjacent tale. None of these groupings, either of format or of illustrative approach, reflects the textual affiliations between manuscripts as shown by Ralph Hanna in the critical apparatus to the *Canterbury Tales* in the *Riverside Chaucer*: evidently the pictorial tradition, such as it is, developed independently of the textual tradition.[12] Interestingly, examples of all three formats and all three illustrative approaches occur in illustrated manuscripts that are among the earliest copies of the text: the Ellesmere MS, dated by Kathleen Scott to the five years following Chaucer's death (1400-05);[13] BL MS Lansdowne 851 (c.1407-10);[14] and CUL MS Gg.4.27 (c.1420-25).[15] This diversity strengthens the impression of independent illustrative projects rather than a coherent tradition; although as Scott suggests, while there is no evidence that artists working on one of the manuscripts modelled their work directly on another, ideas may still have circulated, for 'it is likely that exceptional manuscripts like Ellesmere were talked about in the trade' (*LGM*, II, 145). Given the early occurrence of illustrations in the manuscript tradition of the *Canterbury Tales*, it seems all the more surprising that so few surviving copies present the text as illustrated.

Mutilated manuscript copies indicate possible sites of other lost illustrations, though it has to be admitted that the evidence is inconclusive in distinguishing between what may have been illustration and elaborate non-pictorial decoration: as Christopher de Hamel observes, 'manuscripts of Chaucer's *Canterbury Tales* were frequently illuminated but seldom illustrated' (p. 157). In several cases the first folio is missing, and while this is a common accidental result of wear and tear telling us nothing about the presence or absence of illustration, the appearance of the rest of the manuscript sometimes suggests that it probably had an initial page with exceptional decoration that may have been excised deliberately.[16] Other missing folios that contained the opening lines of individual tales provoke similar suspicions.[17] Occasionally, excised folios have left a ghostly presence in the survival of offsets on the margins of facing folios showing the outline and sometimes the colours of lost decorative features.[18] If any instances of such lost folios were indeed excised because they carried illustration, a calculation of the missing lines suggests it is likely to have been in the form of an historiated initial, as in the four manuscripts with extant illustrations in this format identified above. There is, however, a tantalizing glimpse of what could conceivably have been yet another approach to illustrating the *Canterbury Tales* in the best known of those manuscripts where folios that probably contained collectable decorative or pictorial images have been excised, CUL MS Gg.4.27.

The loss of illuminated folios from CUL MS Gg.4.27 is particularly keenly felt because the remaining illustrations and border decoration show what an exceptionally sumptuous manuscript it once was. But it was not a copy of the *Canterbury Tales* alone: as the editors of the facsimile edition indicate in their title, *The Poetical Works of Geoffrey Chaucer*, 'Gg.4.27 is the earliest surviving example of an attempt to collect Chaucer's poetry between two covers' (III, 64). The monumental character of this project may explain the unique provision of what appears from its vestigial remains to have been a full-page frontispiece to the *Canterbury Tales*. Henry Bradshaw, the eminent nineteenth-century bibliographer and Chaucer scholar who was Cambridge University Librarian from 1867 to 1886, conducted a reconstruction and collation of the manuscript and identified the five excised folios between the now defective end of *Troilus* and the mutilated opening of the *Canterbury Tales* as three folios from the second half of a regular twelve-leaf quire plus two singletons bound into the quire. His calculation of missing lines indicates that *Troilus* would have ended on the recto of the leaf before the singletons, and that the *Canterbury Tales* began on the verso of the second singleton. The remaining stub of the first singleton shows on the verso traces of decoration, described by Parkes and Beadle as 'the border or frame of a full-page illustration' and 'identifiable as an architectural motif' (III, 10, 59), and though it is of course impossible to recover the subject of the lost picture, it is in a position clearly appropriate for the function of frontispiece to the following text. On the stub of the second singleton, the remaining final letters 'e' of the General Prologue lines 2 and 8 in the inner margin indicate that the text must have been set to the right to accommodate a large and presumably ornamented initial. A possible explanation for the use of the two singletons here may therefore be that they were illuminated and/or illustrated by one or more artists working separately from those responsible for the rest of the decoration. There is a parallel case in Bodleian MS Fairfax 16, another collection of poems by Chaucer and others, where the elaborate frontispiece illustrating the first text, *The Complaint of Mars* combined with *The Complaint of Venus*, is on a single leaf added to the quire.[19]

When it was complete, then, CUL MS Gg.4.27 presented the *Canterbury Tales* as a major component in a monumental 'collected works' - a text given special prominence by blank pages separating it from the texts on either side, a full-page frontispiece, and a programme of illustration that consisted of twenty-two or twenty-three pictures of pilgrim-narrators (six survive) and seven paired images of Deadly Sins and Virtues (three remain) to illustrate the Parson's Tale. The 'Oxford' MS preserves a few relics of an at least partly similar programme, in that these fragments (totalling thirteen folios) of a manuscript copy of the *Tales* contain the openings of the Miller's, Cook's, and Man of Law's tales, each illustrated by a picture of the pilgrim-narrator. Kathleen Scott posits an informal iconographic 'tradition' connecting the pilgrim portraits back to the Ellesmere miniatures: 'Although the Cambridge sequence as it has survived shows no evidence of direct copying, certain themes seem to have been transmitted, whether by an intermediary copy, memory, or hearsay' (*LGM*, II, 145). The artists in the other four manuscripts, however, illustrating the text by one or more historiated initial/s, are working within a different aspect of the tradition, exploiting the illustrative opportunity offered by the system developed in Ellesmere and other manuscripts of presenting the text articulated by large illuminated capitals signalling each major structural or narrative division.[20]

Presenting the Text

In a fully developed system of presentation, the text of the *Canterbury Tales* would be divided and marked up for the reader with a whole range of identifying signs: large initials with attached marginal decoration signalling the first word of each prologue and tale, usually distinguishing the start of the tale with a larger initial and more extensive marginal decoration; *incipits* and *explicits*, often rubricated; blank space sometimes used in addition to create distance at textual divisions; running heads naming the teller or sometimes the subject of the tale. Within the units of text, further degrees of subdivision are appropriately indicated by correspondingly reduced signs: smaller decorated initials, paraphs, and so on. An excellent example of this developed system of *ordinatio* can be seen in Bodleian MS Arch. Selden B.14, a mid-fifteenth-century copy of the *Tales* with full apparatus of degrees of illumination and decoration, and interpretative rubrics, all designed to make the text easily accessible to the reader. This is the context within which the manuscript illustrations consisting of historiated initials must be understood.

Three manuscripts (MS Lansdowne 851, MS Bodley 686, and the 'Devonshire' MS) have a single illustration, in the illuminated initial letter at the beginning of the General Prologue, which forms part of an elaborately decorated introductory page. The open form of the capital letter - one U imposed on another instead of the W often adopted in manuscripts with an illuminated but not historiated initial in this position - allows a generous picture space. Full bar-frame borders surround the text area and lavish use of pigments and gold accentuate the element of display.[21] A major consideration in producing these introductory pages was the statement they make about the importance of the vernacular text thus presented (and, by analogy, of the owner of the manuscript). Despite the similarity in layout and function of all three pages, however, there is considerable variation in the styles of decoration and in the treatment of the pictured figure in the historiated initial.

MS Lansdowne 851 (color plate 17) is the earliest and in art-historical terms perhaps the most important of the three, for the full-length figure of a man depicted in its initial has been attributed to the hand of the celebrated illustrator Herman Scheerre.[22] The illuminated letter occupies a square space equivalent to ten lines of text, and the letter itself, painted in pink and blue on a gold ground, forms a frame through which the viewer looks into a spaciously designed interior scene. The depth of vision is created by the perspective drawing of a tiled floor extending from behind the frame to a wall-like background, and by the solidly placed feet of the figure standing in the middle of the floor. The man is shown in a three-quarter stance, facing towards the text, with a pale complexion, small, carefully drawn features, and a neatly trimmed beard. He is bare-headed, with cropped brown hair in early-fifteenth-century style, and wears a high-necked, ankle-length grey gown, loose-fitting and long-sleeved, with scarlet hose, and black shoes with strap fastening - the costume of a prosperous, civilian layman. He has a penner hung around his neck, indicating his clerkly profession, and holds with both hands a written text,[23] while his head and eyes are inclined to indicate reading. The quality of draughtsmanship and painting are high, as Kathleen L. Scott recognizes in attributing the work to Scheerre:

> The expressive face rendered in white, the costume, the green filigree background (typical of Scheerre at this period), and the floor lines coloured in receding shades of yellow to orange (as in Gough liturg. 6, f. 22v) support the attribution. (p. 111)

The stance and attire of the figure bear some resemblance to the far less elegant portrait of Chaucer that illustrates Hoccleve's *The Regement of Princes* in BL MS 17.D.vi (fol. 93v), dated some twenty or more years after MS Lansdowne 851. It is thus not surprising that scholars regularly identify Scheerre's pictured figure also as a representation of Chaucer.[24] Derek Pearsall is surely correct, however, to see it less as an attempt at individual portraiture than as a 'product of the long-established tradition of portraying the author in some stylized form in the initial miniature'; and he extends the same analysis to the 'miniatures of Chaucer as author' in MS Bodley 686 (color plates 18 and 19) and the 'Devonshire' MS (color plates 20 and 20a), although 'in the last two, Chaucer is pictured as beardless and youthful, and in the Devonshire, most unusually, as seated outdoors on a bank of flowers' (p. 291). None of the miniatures relates to the conventional author portrait as developed in representations of the four evangelists, figuring the act of composition as writing in a book; nor do they situate the first-person narrator within the narrative by showing him enacting some event. However, bearing in mind the function of these historiated initials within the system of decoration in presenting the text to the reader, it is interesting to consider what different signals the three variant 'Chaucer as author' pictures might convey.

In MS Bodley 686 the initial is less prominent than in MS Lansdowne 851, occupying the space of six lines of text, and seeming less the site from which the bar-frame borders spring than a decorative outgrowth into the text area from the border. Instead of the simple lines of the initial letter elegantly framing Scheerre's image, here the letter is constructed of heavily foliated lines entwined with the acanthus decoration of the border. The full-length figure is somewhat cramped within the space, his head and the toe of his left foot pushing against the upper and lower confines of the letter. As in the Scheerre miniature, the young man is shown in three-quarter stance on a terracotta tiled floor (in this case with black designs on the tiles) in front of a green background decorated with gold sprays. He has a well-drawn boyish face, clean-shaven, with brown typically cropped hair, and his eyes look towards the adjacent text. His blue calf-length gown, belted at the waist, is expensively and fashionably trimmed with fur at hem, cuffs, and neck; a red undergarment is visible at neck and cuffs, and he wears pink hose. With his raised left hand he seems to gesture towards the text, while holding in his right hand a scarlet hat with rolled brim and long floppy crown. Vying with the historiated initial for the reader's attention are trompe-l'oeil scrolls wound around the vertical bars of the border and inscribed with mottoes in gold letters. The left-hand scroll reads: ': / : pences d / : de mai : / : pences / de m / || Jhc / merci : / : ladi : / help :' and the right-hand scroll reads: 'in god is : / : al : mi truste / : in god : || As fortune / : faulit : As fort / : faulit :'[25] The decorative effect of the page is completed by a dense scattering in the margins of tiny green tendrils and gold dots in the French manner. All these details of costume and decorative style fit a date of 1430-40.

The initial page in the latest of the three manuscripts, the 'Devonshire' MS (1450-60), seems to conflate the characteristics of both the others. It has a very large, spaciously designed initial (twelve lines), and dense French-style marginal decoration, with space in the lower bar-frame (now filled with pink acanthus scrolls) that looks as if it might have been provided to accommodate optional inscriptions. The opulence of the page is enhanced by elaborate interlace patterns on a gold ground in the bar-frame border on three sides. The 'Chaucer as author' figure in the initial is indeed unusual. Not only is he sitting on a flowered turf bench; he is depicted turned away from the text, pointing in the opposite direction, with an expression of sadness. The outdoor setting is indicated by the grass and flowers covering the ground under the young man's feet, and by the stylized representation of the sky as blue clouds peeping from the upper left-hand corner of the framing initial and the sun from the right corner. The background, between the sky and the turf bench, is painted crimson, outlined in gold and decorated with gold filigree work. But on the right-hand side, the rays of the sun replace the filigree, extending down the crimson background and onto the turf bench beside the seated figure, while on the left, blue raindrops spatter the gold filigree and the turf bench, which is represented as a rectangular block covered with the same grass and flowers as the ground. Behind it, a grass-green area with flowers arranged in scroll patterns is perhaps intended to represent a rose hedge forming a little arbour around the bench. The posture of the seated young man is inconsistent: while his lower body is turned towards the right of the picture, his head and shoulders twist to the left, as his inclined head rests upon his raised right hand, and he points to the left with his other hand. He wears a tall brown hat under which his short fair hair is visible and his facial features are strongly marked, especially the arched eyebrows and large eyes, downcast to the left. A high-necked, tight-sleeved brown jerkin, laced at the throat, can be seen under his long scarlet houppelande, trimmed with fur at neck, cuffs, and hem, and belted at the waist with a blue and white girdle from which hangs a prominent drawstring purse. The unusual details of this illustration have led scholars to associate it with the *Legend of Good Women* or with Chaucer's 'Complaint to His Purse';[26] though it is not entirely obvious why such a pictorial reference would be appropriate at the opening lines of the *Canterbury Tales*.

Each of these three 'author' figures presents the text differently, according to the way its particular detail is read. In MS Lansdowne 851 the miniature dramatizes the act of reading a written text, and although the solitary figure might at first seem to be engaged in private reading, his standing position in a setting something like the 'paved parlour' where Criseyde and her companions hear 'a mayden reden hem the geste | Of the siege of Thebes' (*Troilus*, II. 81-84) suggests on the contrary a social performance directed to the present audience of the text. It thus conflates the voice of the author as narrator with the voice of the reading performer to create the voice of the text - a voice characterized through the figure and costume as urbane and prosperous. The illustration in MS Bodley 686 functions similarly, but more directly: the 'author' figure points towards the actual words of the text written on the page, representing the act of speaking with this traditional manual gesture and also indicating the words as being spoken. The voice of the text in this case is characterized as youthful and stylish, perhaps sharing the association of youth, fashion, springtime, and love that marks the Squire (General Prologue, 79-100), and is especially appropriate to the passage of text immediately adjacent to the illustration with its echoes of the spring settings of dream visions and *reverdie* poems, whose subject is commonly love.[27] The whole setting of the page contributes to this reading, for the mottoes inscribed on the scrolls are somewhat reminiscent of the 'posies' often engraved on love tokens such as rings.

In the 'Devonshire' MS, the characterization of the 'author' figure as a lover is taken further. His sorrowful expression, while surrounded by the signs of spring and life, marks him out as a stereotypical unhappy lover. The characterization is imaged in the double aspect of the sky: the sun shining on one side of the figure and rain falling on the other serve to typify the contrasts of joy and woe in love, and the woeful lover is shown inclining to the rainy side. The pointing gesture in this case does not indicate the text or any visible object, but probably represents the act of dictating a composition.[28] The purse hanging from his belt perhaps alludes to the trope of the purse or treasury of memory from which the material for composition is drawn.[29] The opening of the text mentions April showers and the sun, together with the flowers and birdsong suggestive of love visions, so that what the illustration seems to be offering is the figure of an author composing, in the persona of a lover, the text written down on the page (as if from dictation) by the scribe. Whether the artist simply took his cue from the first few lines of text (as may be the case with the conventional image in the initial of the *Purgatorio* of Dante guiding his metaphorical *navicella*),[30] or whether the illustration was designed to represent a known aspect of the work of the poet Chaucer, as described in the Man of Law's Prologue and in Chaucer's Retraction, we cannot know; but both come to much the same thing, as Chaucer was apparently re-working his reputation as a poet of love in constructing the persona of the author/narrator in the *Canterbury Tales*.

In a recent study of the way the author-figure is constructed in manuscripts of Gower's *Confessio Amantis*, Ardis Butterfield draws attention to the existence of four 'Gowers' in the poem: the historical author, the Gower named in the glosses, the Gower identified as Amans, and the more slippery Gower as narrator.[31] It is possible to discern a similar quartet in the *Canterbury Tales*: Chaucer the historical poet, the Chaucer cited in the Man of Law's Prologue, the 'Chaucer' identified in manuscript tradition as the pilgrim-narrator of *Sir Thopas* and *Melibee*, and Chaucer the narrator. In over a dozen *Confessio Amantis* manuscripts, a miniature representing Amans kneeling to Genius conventionally occurs at the beginning of the confession in Book I, long before the moment in the text when Amans is named as Gower and revealed as an old man; but interestingly, while Amans is most often shown as a fashionable young man, in at least one case he appears as a mature bearded figure (CUL MS Mm.2.21), and he is twice shown as an older man with a white beard (Bodleian MS Bodley 902; Cambridge, Pembroke College MS 307).[32] This uncertainty surrounding the identity of author/narrator/lover is exactly parallelled in the kind of variation seen in representing 'Chaucer' in *Canterbury Tales* manuscripts, in the three historiated initials described above and in the marginal portrait of the Ellesmere MS.

In the light of this variation, it is worth considering the case of MS Rawlinson poet. 223 (c.1450-60). This is a lavishly executed manuscript, copied by the same scribe who produced the 'Devonshire' MS (called the 'hooked g scribe' on account of his characteristic form of this letter).[33] Having lost its first folio, there is no evidence as to whether or not it had an historiated initial at the opening of the text, but it has what may be an 'author' illustration in the initial letter A that begins the tale of *Melibee* (fol. 183, color plate 21), though it has also been tentatively identified as a representation of Melibeus, the eponymous male character named in the first sentence of the tale.[34] The end of *Sir Thopas* is marked with the rubric 'Here endith the tale of Maister Chaucer', followed by an *incipit* for the next tale: 'And here ye shal fynde a moral tale of Melibe and Prudence'. The rubric does not make clear who tells this second tale, nor do the running heads, which give 'Chaucer' for *Sir Thopas* and 'Melibe / Prudence'.

The juxtaposition of *Sir Thopas* and *Melibee* is a site of some confusion in the *ordinatio* of many manuscripts. MS Arch. Selden B.14 has an almost perfect system of 2/3-line initials for prologues and 4/5-line initials for tales, with explanatory rubrics, and running heads signalling 'the [Pilgrim's] / prolog' or 'the / [Pilgrim]' throughout, except that prologue-style decoration is used both for the Host's words to Chaucer and for the opening of *Sir Thopas* (uniquely referred to in the rubrics without mention of the word 'tale', which is reserved for *Melibee*),[35] and tale-style decoration is used only for *Melibee*. The running heads also depart from the norm in giving the titles of the tales: 'Sir / Thopas', 'Mellibe / and Prudence', whereas 'Chauncers' [*sic*] is named repeatedly in the rubrics identifying *Melibee* as his tale. Bodleian MS Laud Misc. 600, where the running heads usually identify the teller, has 'Thopas' followed by 'Chaucer'. A third copy of the *Canterbury Tales* by the 'hooked g scribe', Cambridge, Trinity College MS R.3.3, has no running heads, but unusual rubrics for Chaucer's tales: 'A Prolog and a tale tolde by Maister Chaucer' (fol. 87); no separate rubric for *Sir Thopas* (which is severely abbreviated); 'Anothir tale in prose | tolde be master Chaucer | of Melibe and Prudence' (fol. 87v); 'Hiere endeth the tale of Melibe | And Prudence compiled by M | Chaucer' (fol. 98v). Oxford, New College MS D 314 produces an unattributed 'Ryme of Ser Topas' (fol. 208) and identifies *Melibee* simply as 'Chauceris tale' (fol. 211v). Other manuscripts name no teller for either tale in the rubrics.[36] The rubric to *Melibee* in BL MS Sloane 1686 uniquely addresses the reader/audience directly: 'Plesith you to here the Tale of Maister Chaucer' (fol. 247v) - an invitation that the Ellesmere MS illuminator renders in visual terms by placing his portrait of the poet Chaucer adjacent to the tale of *Melibee* rather than *Sir Thopas*. All these anomalies indicate considerable scribal anxiety about the attribution of the two tales and about the identity of 'Chaucer' (expanded to 'Geoffrey Chaucer' in some manuscript rubrics).[37]

A site of similar anxiety occurs in many manuscripts of the *Roman de la rose*, at the point where the narrator reveals that a second author, Jean Chopinel, took over the role of narrator from the first author, Guillaume de Lorris, many lines earlier. There is commonly an illustration at this point, showing an unnamed 'author' figure at a desk with a book, seemingly emphasizing the continuity of the authored text, irrespective of the personal identity of either named poet.[38] The figure in the historiated initial A in the Rawlinson MS, showing a man seated beside a lectern that supports an open book, very likely functions in a similar way. Like the three 'author' initials in the Lansdowne, Bodley, and 'Devonshire' MSS, and the miniature of the dictating author in BN MS n. acq. fr. 24541,[39] this shows the man in three-quarter view, facing the reader. He is pointing with his right hand towards the written text adjacent to the miniature, indicating the act of speaking (or possibly dictating) the text, while the presence of the book on the reading stand seems additionally to assert the authority of the written text. The 'voice of the text' is characterized in this illustration as authoritative and learned: the posture of the figure seems to be modelled on traditional representations of persons of authority such as kings and teachers, and the interior setting of the scene shows a study with boarded wooden vault, plastered wall, and tiled floor, furnished with a chair and reading desk, while through an arch to the right there is an opening to the starlit night sky with trees. The face is clean-shaven and has finely drawn strong features - a long nose and heavy-lidded eyes - and the costume indicates a man of substance: his large black hat lined with green has a gold cord around the crown, and his blue gown, open at the neck to reveal a laced doublet, is held together by a gold chain round the collar. It seems less likely that all these details are meant to portray directly either 'Maister Chaucer' or Melibeus (who notably neglects the teachings of books and authorities) than that they are working to support the authority of the text through a generic 'author' image.

'And hath so verray hys lyknesse | That spak the word'

In *The House of Fame* Chaucer expresses a traditional theory of the 'voice of the text' that may be helpful in discussing both the 'Chaucer' figures and the illustrations of pilgrim-narrators in *Canterbury Tales* manuscripts.[40] The Palace of the Goddess of Fame in a sense stands for the hazardous enterprise of publication, and the words sent out to seek fame speak both themselves and the author:

> Whan any speche ycomen ys
> Up to the paleys, anon-ryght
> Hyt wexeth lyk the same wight
> Which that the word in erthe spak,
> Be hyt clothed red or blak;
> And hath so verray hys lyknesse
> That spak the word, that thou wilt gesse
> That it the same body be,
> Man or woman, he or she.
>
> (1074-82)

Words 'clothed red or blak' remind us of the 'Twenty bookes, clad in blak or reed' that the Clerk would like at his bed's head (General Prologue, ll.293-94), and of the black ink and rubrication of the manuscript text: both 'embodiments' of the author's speech. In a multi-vocal text such as the *Canterbury Tales*, however, there is more than one 'voice of the text', and the elaborate system of *ordinatio* in many manuscripts is designed to differentiate the utterances of distinct voices. In illustrated manuscripts the difference is additionally realized in speaking representations of 'Chaucer' and the pilgrim-narrators.

Before considering the remnants of a possibly Ellesmere-derived set of pilgrim illustrations in CUL MS Gg.4.27 and the 'Oxford' MS, there is another miniature to be discussed in MS Rawlinson poet. 223 (color plate 22). This occurs at the beginning of the Prologue to the

Friar's Tale (fol. 142), in a ten-line initial T, and clearly represents the Friar. The design is simpler than in the *Melibee* initial, showing the Friar in a polygonal wooden pulpit placed on a grassy ground against a plain gold background. He wears a brown habit, with a large hood folded round his neck and ample folds hanging over the front of the pulpit, girded at the waist with a knotted cord that he fingers with his right hand, while raising his left in a preaching gesture. He is tonsured and clean-shaven with a youthful face, and there seems no attempt to illustrate in his expression the adjacent reference in the text to his 'louryng chiere', but his eyes are very conspicuously turned towards the words of the rubric: 'And here beginneth the Prolog of the Frere'. It is immediately obvious that this runs counter to the normal *ordinatio* of the manuscript, with illuminated initials at the beginnings of tales but penwork initials for prologues.

The running heads may hint why it was decided to place a miniature of the Friar here. The Friar's Tale is headed 'Frater de / Apparitore' and the juxtaposed Summoner's, 'Apparitor / De Fratre': the opportunities for confusion between the pilgrim-narrator Friar and the Friar-protagonist in the Summoner's Tale are obvious. The rubric introducing 'the Prolog of the Frere' does not differentiate conclusively between a prologue to the Friar's Tale and a prologue to a tale concerning the Friar, but the placing of the illustration of a Friar apparently in full spate indicates that the Friar owns the following tale as narrator. By comparison with the pilgrim-narrator illustrations in the Ellesmere MS, it might seem odd that the Rawlinson Friar is shown not on horseback as if on pilgrimage, but in his customary preaching posture in a pulpit. However, the intention may have been, as with the illustration to *Melibee*, to produce a generic rather than an individual representation of the 'voice of the text', signalling unmistakeably that what we hear in the following tale is the voice of a Friar.[41] Seen in the light of the Rawlinson MS illustrations, Lichfield Cathedral Library MS 29 has a very interesting pattern of excisions: it lacks, together with its first folio, the folios originally carrying the beginnings of the Friar's tale and Chaucer's tales of *Sir Thopas* and *Melibee*, suggesting that there might have been unusual decoration at similar junctures in this manuscript. Whether historiated or illuminated initials, they would, like the Rawlinson MS illustrations, have testified to a felt need to clarify the organization of the work at these points: local solutions to particular scribal problems, giving extra visual authority to the voice of the text.

The placing of the pilgrim-narrator illustrations in CUL MS Gg.4.27 and the 'Oxford' MS is an equally important consideration. Like the Ellesmere MS, both these manuscripts seem (as far as can be judged from the mutilated or fragmentary remains) to have received illustrations as a planned supplement to a system of *ordinatio* that presents the text to the reader as a coherent series of narrations in different voices, each prefaced by an introductory discourse or dialogue. The picture of each pilgrim-narrator is placed at the beginning of the tale that he or she narrates, and functions as a representation of the voice of the text, a visual equivalent of the typically worded rubric: 'Here beginneth the [Pilgrim] his tale'.[42] In the Cambridge MS the relation between rubric and illustration is particularly close: each of the six surviving pictures is placed immediately above or below the rubricated *incipit*, and in four cases the rubric is written as an interrupted line, broken by the pilgrim's head or his horse's legs. The 'Oxford' MS adopts a more formal arrangement, with each pilgrim illustration enclosed by a plain frame, but still maintains the close combination of rubric, picture, and tale; in the case of the Miller's Tale, where the page-turn interrupts the sequence, the scribe has made clear the continuity with a special rubric: 'Here endithe the myller his Prolog | And owir the leff begynnyth þe tale'.

Even in its mutilated state, it is obvious that the *ordinatio* of the Cambridge MS was never as consistently carried out as the execution in the Ellesmere MS. The Knight's Tale finishes two-thirds of the way down folio 174v, and the Prologue to the Miller's Tale begins with an illuminated initial and border at the top of the next recto; in the intervening space it appears that a picture was inserted, since roughly cut out, but with a border of pen-work scrolls still visible. It seems likely that this was an illustration of the Miller, whose tale begins on folio 176 with another illuminated initial and border, a rubric: 'here endith the prologe & here begynnyth the tale', but with no space at all for an illustration. Thus in at least one instance, the pilgrim-narrator was apparently pictured at the start of the framing link passage rather than the tale.

The sequence of illustration, text, rubric, and decoration at this point might suggest that the picture was opportunistically added to an already completed scheme of presentation; and the same supposition could be made in relation to the illustrations of the Reeve, the Cook, and the Wife of Bath, all of which appear at the foot of a page before the start of their tale on a fresh page with an illuminated initial and border (the Cook's has been excised). However, it is clear that illustration was intended from the outset for the tales later on of the Pardoner, the Monk, and the Manciple, for at the beginning of each of these tales a space of between a third and a half of the text area has been left at the top of the folio, partly outlined by the bar-frame border. The same variation can be seen in the three surviving illustrations to the Parson's Tale: Envy and Charity appear without any framing device at the foot of folio 416, while the appropriate section of text follows on the verso with large initial and border; Gluttony and Abstinence, however, and Lechery and Chastity are pictured later in spaces left either at the top of the folio or in the middle, above the text which begins with large initial and bar-frame border.[43] Was the design for this copy of the *Canterbury Tales* changing and developing as work proceeded? Did an opportunity for illustration provided by the habit of starting a new division of the text on a fresh page perhaps lead to a deliberate choice to include spaces for illustrations in the design of the pages? Kathleen Scott suggests that some of the oddities in the appearance of the pilgrim-narrators may be due to adaptation from a model with marginal illustrations:

> The idea of using a sequence of mounted Pilgrims instead of narrative scenes from their tales probably derives from the Ellesmere Chaucer or from a similar lost manuscript where they were placed in the margins. In the Cambridge book the ('marginal') Pilgrims had to be adapted to a space for a roughly half-page miniature. Indications of a transference between a marginal and a miniature format probably survive in the stretching of some figures and their mounts in order to fill the space . . . and in the lack of a background, which is not unusual for marginal figures but rare for figures rendered in pigments in a standard miniature space. (*LGM*, II, 144-45)

Putting all these observations together, one might hypothesize that an original intention to provide marginal illustrations (with no need to leave spaces) could have changed in the course of designing the book into a plan to provide specific sites in the text column for standard miniatures, and that the (probable) picture of the Miller was inserted in the only available space.

Previous commentary on the Cambridge illustrations has assessed what they have in common with the Ellesmere portraits, both in general (variation in types of horses and faces, interest in costume and in horse harnesses as status symbols) and in particular (the Wife of Bath's whip, the Man of Law's gourd, the lack of any attribute for the Reeve)

- enough at any rate to support the thesis that some kind of tradition connects them.[44] What I shall do in addition is to look at the Cambridge pictures in the context so far explored of 'voicing the text'. The first surviving miniature, depicting the Reeve (color plate 23), is the only one to show the characteristic speaking gesture of the raised hand: the figure holds the reins in his left hand and indicates with his right towards the start of the tale overleaf. He rides a dark bay horse with flowing mane and tail, quite unlike the dapple-grey 'stot' mentioned in the General Prologue and pictured in the Ellesmere MS (color plate 5), yet many details in the appearance of the Cambridge MS Reeve follow Chaucer's description very closely:

> The Reve was a sclendre colerik man.
> His berd was shave as ny as ever he kan;
> His heer was by his erys ful round yshorn;
> His top was dokked lyk a preest biforn. . . .
> A long surcote of pers [*dark blue*] upon he hade,
> And by his syde he baar a rusty blade. . . .
> Tukked he was as is a frere aboute.
> (587-90, 617-18, 621)

Although the Prologue to the Reeve's Tale, immediately preceding the picture in the manuscript, stresses the Reeve's white hair as a sign of his age, his hair is here painted a reddish brown; evidently, if the reader was expected to recognize specific features of the Reeve, it was a memory of the General Prologue that was to provide the repertoire of identifying details: his lean figure, cropped hair, clean-shaven chin, long blue gown tucked up at the waist to reveal his legs, and rusty-looking sword hanging at his left. The reason for this careful identification may well be the result of an anxiety about the voice of the text similar to that surrounding the Friar's Tale, as discussed above. In a number of manuscripts, the 'tit-for-tat' pairing of the Miller's and Reeve's Tales is signalled in the rubrics; for example, in BL MS Sloane 1686 they read: 'here begynneth the Mellers tale of the Reve' and 'Here endith the tale of the Reve that he tolde be the Meller' (fols 51, 69v); Bodleian MS Hatton donat.1 is more elaborate: 'next biginneþe the Millers tale of þe Carpenter of Oxenford' and 'next beginneth þe Carpenters tale of þe Miller of Trumpyngdoun' (fols 37, 45v). The Reeve's Tale is called the Carpenter's Tale in rubrics and running heads in several manuscripts, adding to the potential for confusion. The designer of the Cambridge illustrations, like the Rawlinson illustrator, was perhaps concerned to make clear whose voice should be heard in this tale, and chose to remind the reader of the portrait of the Reeve in the General Prologue.

The Cook of London (color plate 24), on the other hand, is depicted entirely independently of any descriptive detail in Chaucer's text. Instead of 'a povre man' (l. 4341) with 'a mormal' on his shin (Gen. Prol., l. 386), we see an apparently well-to-do figure wearing a lavender grey houppelande lined and trimmed with fur and an extravagantly large green hood, though his horse is a short-legged beast with its tail roughly knotted up, and a saddle and bridle far simpler than the Reeve's.[45] However, unlike the identifying objects in the Ellesmere portrait (meat-hook and food bowl), the items carried by the Cambridge Cook are frankly puzzling. In his right hand, resting on his shoulder, he holds what has been called a long whip, although the two knotted cords do not protrude from the end of the whip handle as normal but seem to be attached to the cord wrapped round it. It is twice as long as the Wife of Bath's whip, and its lower end is differently shaped: it looks more like the mouthpiece of a pipe, and there even seems to be a fipple visible. From under the Cook's right sleeve a green and white object projects backwards, partly resembling a sword (and more or less tentatively identified as such in previous descriptions), but with a red disc at its end. It seems as if some confusion or misunderstanding has occurred in the pictorial tradition, and the portraits of the Miller in the Ellesmere (color plate 1) and 'Oxford' MSS (figure 1) provide some interesting comparisons (though why the Cook and Miller should have been confused is not clear). The Ellesmere Miller plays a bagpipe whose drone, resting on his shoulder, looks very like the Cambridge Cook's 'whip'; the 'Oxford' Miller plays a fipple flute with his right hand, and has a short two-thonged whip in his left; the Ellesmere Miller also bears a sword and buckler that could perhaps explain the Cook's 'sword' and disc as a rearrangement of their constituent shapes. Nevertheless, whatever the history of the accessories in the design of the Cambridge Cook picture, the general impression created by the rider and his horse is ambivalent: a highly prosperous citizen astride a poor and ill-equipped mount, and this ambivalence might be thought a good visual referent for the voice of the Cook's Tale, with its urban identity and sober sympathy for the master (a victualler like the Cook),[46] but also its narrative commitment to the predictable fate of the downwardly mobile reveller.

Fig. 1 - The Miller

Although, as Kathleen Scott observes, most of the 'facial renderings are heavily modelled' (p. 145) in the Cambridge MS, the Wife of
Bath is an exception (color plate 25). Her face and neck are smoothly
painted and her small chin and simply drawn features give her a sweet,
youthful appearance. The focal point of the design is her enormous
head-dress, with its large quantity of pleated coverchiefs (probably of
the fine linen mentioned in the General Prologue), surmounted by an
extravagantly draped crimson hood.[47] A gored and dagged tippet of the
same colour with gold pendants completes the frame for her face. Her
green gown is visible at the breast and cuffs, but otherwise covered by
the voluminous dark blue travelling cloak that falls to below her feet.
With her left hand she holds up the reins that, like the trappings, are
scarlet and studded with what appear to be small gold bells, and in her
right hand she brandishes aloft a whip with three knotted thongs. In the
context of the Wife's Prologue, just concluded above the illustration, it
is tempting to see these prominent details as having metaphorical force:
the Wife has proclaimed herself the 'whippe' of tribulation in marriage
to her old husbands (III. 175), and has succeeded in obtaining 'the
bridel in myn hond' to signify her governance over her last husband

(III. 813). Altogether, the portrait expresses quite well the complex femininity of the voice of the Wife of Bath's Prologue and Tale in its combination of attractive, ostentatious, and domineering features.

In the case of the Pardoner (color plate 26), there is no doubt that the illustration draws upon the detail of his Prologue, for in his right hand the Pardoner displays one of his 'relics', a bone (l. 348). It is clearly a jaw-bone, whereas Chaucer mentions unidentified bones in a crystal reliquary and a shoulder-bone, but the illustration may be influenced by the pictorial topic of Samson with the jaw-bone of an ass. Apart from the bone, the only detail in the appearance of the pilgrim that could relate directly to Chaucer's text is the Pardoner's beardless chin: 'As smothe it was as it were late shave' (Gen. Prol., l. 690). He wears a crimson houppelande with large bag-sleeves, belted at the waist, and a scarlet hood. (The Ellesmere portrait also includes the beardless chin and red clothes.) The Pardoner's horse has notably better conformation than the three previous pilgrims' mounts and the most extensive trappings.[48] As an expression of the voice of the text in the Pardoner's Prologue and Tale, the illustration conveys a sense of prosperity and dignity that well suits the Pardoner's blatantly avowed intention to tell a moral tale, but solely for the purpose of winning himself more wealth and luxury goods.

The illustration heading the Monk's Tale (color plate 27) is perhaps the most interesting in terms of an attempt to embody the voice of the text. It shares with the Ellesmere portrait (color plate 28) a detail unrelated to Chaucer's description of the Monk - the broad-brimmed black hat - but whereas the Ellesmere MS also depicts the bridle bells and hunting dogs mentioned in the General Prologue, the designer of the Cambridge illustration seems instead to have noticed, in the Prologue to the Monk's Tale, the Host's reference to the Monk's cloak: 'Allas, why werestow so wyd a cope?' (VII. 1949). An all-enveloping brown cloak shrouds the Monk from head to ankle, the hood covering part of his face, shown in profile, while the black hat is tipped towards the reader, masking the Monk's brow and eyes from view. All that is visible of his face is a small triangle from the tip of the nose, to the chin, to the corner of the mouth. He wears black boots and the horse has a plain black bridle. Unlike all the other Cambridge illustrations, his shoulder is turned away from, instead of towards, the reader, so he appears to be turning his back, shunning the society of others. A comparison with Chaucer's description of the Man in Black in *The Book of the Duchess* (lines 445-447) suggests that the illustrator was perhaps intending to convey by the colouring and the bodily posture an impression of deep melancholy, a mood entirely in keeping with the unmixed tone of tragic lament voiced throughout the Monk's Tale.

The last surviving pilgrim-narrator illustration in the Cambridge MS depicts the Manciple (color plate 29), a character for whom Chaucer provides no descriptive detail. Comparing it with the Ellesmere portrait (color plate 15), it is striking how much the two have in common, although one is the reverse image of the other. As has been noted before, the 'gourde . . . of wyn' mentioned in the Prologue to the Manciple's Tale (IX. 82-83) is prominently displayed by both figures: the Ellesmere Manciple holds it aloft in his right hand while keeping the reins in his left, and the Cambridge figure holds the gourd down by his side with his right hand and lifts up the reins with his left. Both wear a full-bodied, high-necked light blue houppelande reaching almost to the ankle, held in neat pleats by a white or green and white belt at the waist, and both wear a soft cap of the same design, with the crown folded forwards, though the Cambridge cap is a more extreme example of the fashion. The set of the Cambridge Manciple's body looks as if it should be supporting a head in three-quarter view, like the Ellesmere figure; however, the face is shown in profile, the eye rolling upwards (though with nothing to look at) and the chin thrust forwards. One explanation could be that the head and body were modelled upon two different exemplars. The Manciple's horse is equally unusual: larger in relation both to the rider and to the picture space than any of the other mounts (and bearing less resemblance to a natural equine). But the gourd of wine, centrally placed in the illustration, is evidently the pivotal detail, drawing attention to the Manciple's prudent intervention in pacifying the Cook with wine before commencing his Tale of the Crow, a complementary parable on prudent speech.

It seems very likely that the designers of both the Ellesmere and Cambridge illustrations had access to a common tradition, for besides the features reflecting the verbal details of the General Prologue and link passages, which could independently have been selected from the text, there are a number of other similarities that look more than accidental. The Cambridge designer, however, seems (from the surviving sample) to have been less concerned to remind the reader of the individual pilgrim as described in the General Prologue, and more interested in the immediate context of the prologue to each tale to provide the visual details that will characterize the voice of the ensuing tale. By contrast, the designer of the three pilgrim-narrator illustrations in the fragments of the 'Oxford' MS, representing the Miller, the Cook (figure 2), and the Man of Law (figure 3), looks forward to the tradition established in the printed editions from Caxton onwards of identifying some of the pilgrims by attributes relating to their trades or professions, irrespective of the details given in Chaucer's text.

Fig. 2 - The Cook

Unlike the Ellesmere and Cambridge illustrations, the 'Oxford' miniatures are not painted in full colour but are tinted drawings, with plain backgrounds behind the figures and painted undulating ground beneath the horses' hooves, shading from very light green to dark olive on the horizon. The drawing is exceptionally accomplished, with a lively line, solid modelling, and convincing detail, but all economically achieved. All three pilgrims are shown riding towards the left, in three-quarter view, with round, clean-shaven faces, and good-humoured expressions. There is a clear hierarchy of status in the treatment of the horses: the Man of Law rides a noble-looking animal with elaborate trappings; the Cook of London has a good horse with a simple saddle but no stirrups, and a bridle but a knotted rope instead of reins; while the Miller is mounted on a mule with no saddle and a rope halter. No doubt the designer of the illustration knew the bestiary tradition that derives the word *mule* from the Latin *mola*, 'mill', because the mule turns the miller's grindstone, and indeed, the Miller is seated on two large sacks (presumably full of grain or flour) that his beast of burden is carrying. These sacks identifying the Miller reappear in the woodcut portrait used and reused from Caxton's to Thynne's editions, and so does the fipple flute that the 'Oxford' Miller plays in place of Chaucer's bagpipes. The costume is appropriate to the Miller's status and trade: a cap, a simple buttoned jerkin, stout boots, and a large apron fastened at his waist. He holds a whip - he is the only pilgrim pictured in any of the manuscripts with a whip except the Wife of Bath - ready to beat his proverbially stubborn mule.[49]

Fig. 3 - The Man of Law

The illustration of the Cook is dominated by the large meat cleaver that he holds aloft like a badge of his trade and, like the Ellesmere Cook, he wears a long apron tied around his waist that suits his calling. Apart from these attributes, though, the Cook's appearance seems less typical of his humble status than the Miller's: his hair is cropped and elaborately curled; his high-necked laced doublet, attached to his hose with points, has fashionable puffed sleeves (but folded back at the fore-arm as if to stop their getting soiled); his feet are shod in soft leather crakowes with extravagantly long points (far in excess of the six inches beyond the foot decreed the limit for non-gentry in the Sumptuary Laws of 1363). A marginal note 'Prentise' in the manuscript, in a hand described by Manly and Rickert as 'a small scribble' (I, 396), could suggest an alternative reading of this illustration, identifying the subject as Perkyn Revelour, the apprentice-victualler in the story, rather than the Cook, narrator of the tale.

However, the name 'Constance' noted by the illustration of the Man of Law can have no relevance to the picture as drawn; either it represents, as M. C. Seymour suggests, 'an original direction (never carried out) to insert pictures of hero and heroine (not the narrators) of their tales' (p. 253), or it is simply a marginal note indicating the story's subject matter as an additional finding device, such as is seen in the rubrics and running heads in several manuscripts. The 'Oxford' MS folio with the miniature of the Man of Law is in a poor state, but fortunately damage to the picture mostly affects the horse, not the rider, who is clad in a long, full gown and a hood with tippet and liripipe. He wears a coif, as in the Ellesmere illustration, and carries a scroll in his right hand as an attribute of his profession, both details that are replicated in the Caxton woodcut.

In BL MS Harley 1758, spaces of between seven and thirty-three lines have been left between the *explicit* rubrics of tales and the *incipit* rubrics of the following prologues, and it has often been assumed that at least the larger of these spaces were intended for pilgrim portraits. But in previous accounts of the spaces an important difference from the placing of the picture spaces in the Cambridge and 'Oxford' MSS has sometimes been overlooked.[50] Neither of those manuscripts places its illustrations at the start of the link passage or prologue rather than at the head of the tale (except the case of the Cambridge [Miller?] illustration, discussed above), nor does Caxton (with the perhaps understandable exception of the Wife of Bath). It seems more likely that these spaces in the Harley MS are simply part of the *ordinatio* of the manuscript, using the blank parchment to emphasize the separation between one pilgrim-narrator's tale and the next.[51] If illustration *was* part of the design in this manuscript, it would probably have been in the form of historiated initials beginning the tales on the folios that have since been excised (see note 16).

Picturing the Tale

If we accept the historiated initial at the beginning of *Melibee* in the Rawlinson MS as representing an 'author' figure, then the illustrations of Sins and Virtues in the Cambridge MS copy of the Parson's Tale have the distinction of being the only extant record of a medieval interest in providing illustrations for the subject matter of the tales (color plates 30-32). There was no shortage of other opportunities: rubrics and running heads often name characters and subjects in the tales that could have been illustrated as finding devices just as easily as the pilgrim-narrators that were selected. As has often been noted, however, manuscript programmes of illustration depend very much on the availability of pictorial models, and it is likely that the untypical decision to illustrate the Parson's Tale was prompted by the existence of an iconographic tradition picturing the Seven Deadly Sins.[52]

A glance at the three surviving illustrations suggests not only that the plan of including picture spaces seems to have developed in the course of executing the design for the manuscript, as outlined above, but that the disposition of the elements within the illustrations was also a matter of trial and error. Each picture juxtaposes two figures, one seated on a beast, representing a Sin, and the other standing, personifying a Virtue. In the first, the word 'Inuidia' is written in display script but in the same ink as the text to announce the subject of the following section (as 'Sequitur Gula' appears at the foot of folio 430v before the picture of Gluttony and Abstinence on folio 431). The word 'Charite' in red follows, and red has been used to highlight the initial letter of 'Inuidia' also. Below and to the left of each word, the appropriate allegorical figure has been painted, awkwardly placed on the page so that the beast's hindquarters fall in the margin and its tail disappears into the binding. There is a better arrangement in the two later designs, where the Virtue figure stands at the far right of the picture space, forming a kind of border, and the Sin figure is positioned in the centre of the rest of the space, while the English name, in red, appears to the left of each figure. The contrast seems to suggest that the first illustration was experimental, but the later two were planned and improved designs.[53]

All six figures draw on traditional iconographic representations of the abstract nouns they personify. The three Sins may be compared with the descriptions in Gower's *Miroir de l'homme*, where each of the (female) Seven Deadly Sins rides in procession on a beast and holds a bird on her hand, like a parody of a courtly hawking party. 'Dame

Envye' is mounted on a dog and holds a sparrowhawk; 'dame Gloutonie' rides a wolf and holds a kite; 'Leccherie' sits on a goat, holding a dove 'soutz sa constreinte' (ll. 865-936). The Cambridge illustrations show Envy and Gluttony as male, but all three Sins appear youthful and well-dressed. The illustrator has taken pains to make clear that the beast on which Envy rides is a dog by giving it a collar and lead and placing a large bone in its mouth. Envy carries no bird in the painting, but the visible red crayon under-drawing immediately above his raised right hand suggests that one was intended at exactly the point to which his eyes are directed.[54] Gluttony is seated on a bear, another beast traditionally associated with this vice (supposedly on account of its proverbial greed for honey), and holds a green and black bird, probably meant for a cormorant, described by Chaucer in *The Parliament of Fowls* as 'the hote cormeraunt of glotenye' (l. 362), to which he is feeding an eel. The details of this bird, if it is a cormorant, are carefully observed: its wings are spread in the typical drying posture, when the green sheen on its plumage is most visible, and it takes the eel (its staple diet) with its large, hooked yellow beak. Lechery, figured as a fashionable lady, is closest to Gower's description; she rides on a horned he-goat and carries on her finger a small bird identifiable by its accurately portrayed plumage and beak as a sparrow, in a traditional representation of wantonness or lust ('the sparwe, Venus sone', *PF*, l. 351; 'lecherous as a sparwe', *CT*, Gen. Prol., l. 626), while a chain and lock dangle from her wrist to signify the idea of constraint.

Unlike Gower's descriptions (or Spenser's two centuries later in *Faerie Queene*, Book I, canto 4), the Cambridge illustrations show no attempt to treat the physical features or clothes of the Sins in emblematic fashion, beyond a suggestion of obesity in the figure of Gluttony, with his prominent, low-slung belt, and a hint of luxurious excess in the enormous split sleeves and extravagant length of Lechery's elegant green gown. Although a figure wearing green clothes might signify promiscuity, as in the Chaucerian balade 'Against Women Unconstant' with its refrain 'In stede of blew, thus may ye were al grene', the choice of colour seems less symbolic (Lechery has an elaborate blue under-sleeve) than simply aesthetic: each double illustration varies the distribution of the same three pigments, green, blue, and crimson. The power of these representations of the Sins resides rather in the easily recognized formula of 'figure riding on beast with bird' and the traditional association of the selected beast and bird with each Sin. Similarly, the figures of the Virtues are distinguishable chiefly by the objects they carry: Charity's winged, flaming heart; the pitcher denoting Abstinence (or Temperance). These first two Virtues seem to be based on similar models: inclined head in three-quarter view, veiled and crowned, with red nimbus outlined in white dots, wearing a close-fitting plain gown and long cloak lined with white. Charity has in addition a triple coronet (perhaps a reference to Charity's position as chief of the three theological virtues) and carries a sceptre in her right hand, while Abstinence has a stylized flower in her left. The figure of Chastity, however, appears to come from a different kind of model. Her face is shown in profile, with uncovered, loose long hair, against an awkwardly placed red halo; she has a crimson, ermine-lined cloak, and her feet appear beneath her gown, placed firmly on a fearsomely toothed tawny and green beast with a very long tail, presumably a dragon, whose head she has pierced with the cross-spear held in her right hand. As Kathleen Scott suggests, there may well be influence from paintings of the popular virgin martyr, St Margaret, behind this image of Chastity (p. 145). However, although the representation of Chastity trampling the dragon reflects a well-known iconographic tradition that shows Virtues triumphing over Vices, the illustrator has not exploited this example; no attempt has been made to combine the Sin and the Virtue into a single design, beyond placing each Virtue to the right, facing towards her paired Sin.

Finally, the function of these three pairs of figures as illustrations of the text of the Parson's Tale remains to be considered. There is no direct translation from text to image: none of the iconographic details pictured here has been employed by Chaucer in constructing his representations of the Sins and their Remedies. In the first illustration even the names do not directly correspond, as the Latin 'Inuidia' serves to label the sin Chaucer discusses as Envye, and 'Charite' is used for the remedy that the Parson calls 'love'. It is noteworthy, however, that male personifications were chosen for Envy and Gluttony, and a female figure for Lechery. Both Envy and Gluttony are discussed in the Parson's Tale exclusively from the point of view of a male sinner, but not only is Lechery considered in relation to both men and women, the section also begins with examples from the Old Testament of the punishments decreed for different classes of women taken in adultery.[55] There may also be some correspondence between the painted and verbal portraits of Lechery, in that the fashionable gown in the miniature is perhaps an example of reprehensible 'queyntise of array' in women (*CT*, X. 932), though this is a conventional accusation. But indeed, convention is what connects the miniatures to the text as illustrations of the Parson's teaching: traditional associations between ideas and images that allow the images to function as memory sites for recollecting what is known. Charity's flaming heart thus signals succinctly the Parson's argument that active love of God and neighbour cures envy, and Abstinence's pitcher, signifying moderation or temperance, makes the same point as does the Parson in naming 'attemperaunce' and 'mesure' as 'felawes' of Abstinence (X. 834). Representing Chastity in the manner of a virgin martyr sums up the perfection of the virtue, just as the Parson does in the midst of his advice on living chastely in the married or widowed state by briefly praising the life of virginity: 'Thanne is she spouse to Jhesu Crist, and she is the lyf of angeles./ She is the preisynge of this world, and she is as thise martirs in egalitee' (X. 949).

Conclusion

Modern readers' appetite for illustrations that reflect their own closely detailed reading of the text of the *Canterbury Tales* has in the past led to some misinterpretations of the illustrations we do have, and of their function in relation to the text, as well as to regret that they are so few and so limited. However, very significant advances in understanding the use of imagery and images in Chaucer's text and in manuscript illustrations have been made in recent years. Richard K. Emmerson, for example, questions the widely held assumption that the Ellesmere portraits are predominantly 'realistic' and 'dramatic', stressing instead their function as 'visual titles' reinforcing the manuscript's *ordinatio*, representing 'the *tale-tellers* rather than . . . the General Prologue pilgrims on their way to Canterbury', and he draws attention to the artists' use of traditional details, 'relying on the reader's familiarity with a larger signifying context' (pp. 156-58, 146-47). These are the same kinds of approach that have informed my discussion of the illustrations in manuscripts other than the Ellesmere MS. Kathleen L. Scott, surveying the whole range of fifteenth-century English book illustration, stresses the positive choice that seems to have been made in so many cases to represent a 'static' figure rather than a narrative event ('Design', p. 47). This choice gives a clear indication of a different conception of illustration in books with narrative from our modern expectation that pictures should parallel or supplement the story in the text. Mary Carruthers, examining the role of the trained memory in medieval writing and reading, explains the use of pictures in texts primarily as memory sites.[56] V. A. Kolve, in his discussion of the *Canterbury Tales*, stresses the way Chaucer uses narrative imagery to evoke mental images, drawing on a traditional bank of culturally shared pictorial ideas.

Drawing on all this scholarship, therefore, I would argue that the provision of illustrations in manuscripts of the *Canterbury Tales* be understood in relation to what must have been the most commonly expected model of a reading of the tales: that is, of reading as a social experience in which one reader delivers the text to a group of listeners.[57] The pictures are seen by the reader, and they are intended primarily for him or her: they are tools, memorial stimuli, to help the reader to construct the appropriate voice of the text. (Of course, the same procedure would hold in the case of an individual reading alone to his/her inner ear.)[58] We may compare the very common occurrence of names of speakers in marginal annotations beside passages of dialogue in manuscript copies of many texts, including Chaucer's, sometimes giving it almost the appearance of a dramatic script. The words of the text are what convey narrative images to the listeners; the pictures convey to the reader the manner of delivery. I am not suggesting some kind of impersonation, the reader hamming a performance now of the peasant Miller, now of the domineering Wife of Bath, but rather a delivery of each tale in the appropriate rhetorical voice, the fitting register, with the right level of formality, and corresponding bodily expression, exactly as Chaucer describes the tale-telling technique of the 'strange knyght' in the Squire's Tale:

> He with a manly voys seide his message,
> After the forme used in his langage, ...
> And for his tale sholde seme the bettre,
> Accordant to his wordes was his cheere,
> As techeth art of speche hem that it leere.
> (V. 99-104)

The pictures in manuscripts of the *Canterbury Tales* thus make present the voice of the text not only to the reader's eye, but to the reader's and listeners' ears.

Notes

[1]   *The Riverside Chaucer*, ed. by Larry D. Benson and others, 3rd edn (Oxford: Oxford University Press, 1988). All quotations from Chaucer's works are taken from this edition. David Wright, *The Canterbury Tales: A Verse Translation* (Oxford: Oxford University Press, 1986).

[2]   V. A. Kolve, *Chaucer and the Imagery of Narrative: The First Five Canterbury Tales* (London: Arnold, 1984).

[3]   See Rachel Owen, 'Dante's Reception by 14th- and 15th-Century Illustrators of the *Commedia*', *Reading Medieval Studies*, 27 (2001), 163-225; Julia Schewski, 'Illuminated Manuscripts of the *Divine Comedy*: Botticelli and Dante Illustration in the 14th and 15th Centuries', in *Sandro Botticelli: The Drawings for Dante's 'Divine Comedy'*, ed. by Hein-Th. Schulze Altcappenberg (London: Royal Academy of Arts, 2000), pp. 312-17.

[4]   Derek Pearsall, 'The Ellesmere Chaucer and Contemporary English Literary Manuscripts', in *The Ellesmere Chaucer: Essays in Interpretation*, ed. by Martin Stevens and Daniel Woodward (San Marino, CA: Huntington Library; Tokyo: Yushodo, 1997), pp. 263-80 (p. 266); Christopher de Hamel, *A History of Illuminated Manuscripts* (London: Phaidon, 1994), pp. 157-59.

[5]   Kathleen L. Scott, 'Design, Decoration and Illustration', in *Book Production and Publishing in Britain 1375-1475*, ed. by Jeremy Griffiths and Derek Pearsall (Cambridge: Cambridge University Press, 1989), pp. 31-64 (pp. 46-47).

[6]   Pearsall, 'The Ellesmere Chaucer', pp. 268, 272.

[7]   Phillipa Hardman, 'Chaucer's Articulation of the Narrative in *Troilus*: The Manuscript Evidence', *Chaucer Review*, 30 (1995), 111-33.

[8]   Fifty-three medieval copies of *Il Teseida* are described in Edvige Agostinelli, 'A Catalogue of the Manuscripts of *Il Teseida*', *Studi sul Boccaccio*, 15 (1986), 1-83.

[9]   George R. Keiser, '*Ordinatio* in the Manuscripts of John Lydgate's *Lyf of Our Lady*: Its Value for the Reader, Its Challenge for the Modern Editor', in *Medieval Literature: Texts and Interpretation*, ed. by Tim William Machan (Binghamton, NY: Center for Medieval and Early Renaissance Studies, 1991), pp. 139-57 (p. 141).

[10] This manuscript is now in a private collection in Japan, Takamiya MS 24. I am very grateful to Professor Takamiya for generously providing me with digitized full-colour images of this manuscript.

[11] Fragments of this copy survive in two libraries, as Manchester, John Rylands Library MS English 63 and Philadelphia, Rosenbach Library MS 1084/2. Spaces

apparently left for an intended but unexecuted scheme in BL MS Harley 1758 seem to imply it too would have used the text column format, but see below.

12 The same scribe has been identified as copyist in both MS Rawlinson poet. 223 and MS Takamiya 24, but a different illustrative approach is used in each. The same kind of 'random' variation occurs in scribal copies of Boccaccio's works.

13 Kathleen L. Scott, 'An Hours and Psalter by Two Ellesmere Illuminators', in *The Ellesmere Chaucer: Essays in Interpretation*, pp. 87-119 (p. 106).

14 Kathleen L. Scott, *A Survey of Manuscripts Illuminated in the British Isles*, Volume 6: *Later Gothic Manuscripts 1390-1490*, 2 vols (London: Harvey Miller, 1996), II, 87. Henceforth *LGM*.

15 The dating of this manuscript is problematic. Scott states that the borders are in the style of c. 1400, while the illustrations cannot date from before 1420, and argues for a date post 1420, with borders executed by 'retrograde illuminators', possibly 'imitating borders in an exemplar of c. 1400' (*LGM*, II, 146). M. B. Parkes and Richard Beadle, in the introduction to *The Poetical Works of Geoffrey Chaucer: A Facsimile of Cambridge University Library MS Gg.4.27*, 3 vols (Cambridge: Brewer, 1980), date the copying of the text on palaeographical grounds to the first quarter of the fifteenth century, and note that localized, dated script analogues belong to the years before 1420. Their suggested date, based on all the evidence combined, is 'in the first quarter of the fifteenth century, and most probably in the second half of that quarter' (III, 6-7).

16 Examples of expensively produced manuscripts where folio 1 has perhaps been excised are: CUL MS Mm.2.5; Bodl. MS Rawlinson poet. 223; Lichfield Cathedral Library MS 29; BL MS Sloane 1685; Bodl. MS Laud misc. 600; Oxford, Corpus Christi College MS 198; MS Takamiya 32.

17 See, for example, BL MSS Harley 1758 and Sloane 1685; Lichfield Cathedral MS 29; Oxford CCC MS 198; MS Takamiya 32.

18 M.C. Seymour, *A Catalogue of Chaucer Manuscripts*, Volume 2: *The Canterbury Tales* (Aldershot: Scolar Press, 1997), laments the 'multiple losses' suffered by BL MS Egerton 2863 'due to the excision of illuminated leaves, of which offsets are faintly visible on opposite margins', and speculates that 'probably an initial vinet began the Prologue and demi-vinets began each prologue and tale, but all have been excised' (pp. 108, 110).

19 For discussion of the frontispiece in MS Fairfax 16, see *Bodleian Library MS Fairfax 16*, with an introduction by John Norton-Smith (London: Scolar Press, 1979), pp. xi-xiii. The celebrated frontispiece to *Troilus* in Cambridge, Corpus Christi College MS 61, while executed on a folio integral to the quire, may be the only miniature this illustrator was intended to contribute to the manuscript, as argued by Scott (*LGM*, II, 182).

[20] See A. I. Doyle and M. B. Parkes, 'The Production of Copies of the *Canterbury Tales* and the *Confessio Amantis* in the Early Fifteenth Century', in *Medieval Scribes, Manuscripts and Libraries: Essays Presented to N. R. Ker*, ed. by M. B. Parkes and Andrew G. Watson (London: Scolar Press, 1978), pp. 163-210; M. B. Parkes, 'The Influence of the Concepts of *Ordinatio* and *Compilatio* on the Development of the Book', in *Medieval Learning and Literature: Essays Presented to Richard William Hunt*, ed. by J. J. G. Alexander and M. T. Gibson (Oxford: Clarendon Press, 1976), pp. 115-41.

[21] The 'Devonshire' MS differs slightly, in that exaggeratedly elongated text ('han that aprille') takes the place of the bar-frame in the upper border.

[22] See Kathleen Scott, *LGM*, II, 111.

[23] In some other miniatures by Herman Scheerre, legible lettering forms part of the design; here the letters are not real.

[24] Margaret Rickert, 'Illumination', in John M. Manly and Edith Rickert, *The Text of the Canterbury Tales*, 8 vols (Chicago, IL: University of Chicago Press, 1940), I, 561-605, states: 'The picture is clearly intended for a portrait of Chaucer: he holds a book in both hands, presumably his *Canterbury Tales*' (p. 584); Scott calls it 'the full-length figure of Chaucer' (*LGM*, II, 111); M. C. Seymour, 'Chaucer's Portraits in Manuscript', in *A Catalogue of Chaucer Manuscripts*, Volume I: *Manuscripts Before the Canterbury Tales* (Aldershot: Scolar Press, 1995), pp. 157-62, comments: 'Though influenced by the "Hoccleve" tradition, as a portrait it is without authenticity' (p. 159); Derek Pearsall, 'The Chaucer Portraits', in *The Life of Geoffrey Chaucer: A Critical Biography* (Oxford: Blackwell, 1992), pp. 285-305, makes a similar point about all three images; 'The miniatures are of good quality, but the portraits are highly stylized, and have little if any connection with the tradition that is being described here as "authentic"' (p. 291).

[25] These mottoes have not been accurately read in previously published descriptions. Similar scrolls appear in the border of Chapel Hill, NC, Library of Professor Robert G. Heyneman, Brut Chronicle, folio 1; the only legible motto reads 'mercy ihc […] helpe'. Kathleen Scott suggests the mottoes may be those of the original owner or the illuminator (*LGM*, II, 225).

[26] Derek Pearsall sees the portrait 'presumably in allusion to Chaucer's representation of himself in the Prologue to *The Legend of Good Women*' ('The Chaucer Portraits', p. 291); Hilton Kelliher suggests the picture alludes to Chaucer as author of 'The Complaint to His Purse', in 'The Historiated Initial in the Devonshire Chaucer', *Notes and Queries*, 222 (1977), p. 197.

[27] The description of the Squire has been likened to manuscript illustrations of the month of May (Rosemund Tuve, 'Seasons and Months: Studies in a Tradition of Middle English Poetry' (Paris: Librairie Universitaire, 1933), p. 92). For the

association with dream visions, see Larry D. Benson, *The Riverside Chaucer*, 3rd edn (Boston, MA: Houghton Mifflin, 1987), p. 799.

[28] The gesture of pointing to indicate dictation can be seen, for example, in the copy of Gratian's *Decretals* illuminated by the Parisian artist Honoré, Tours, Bibliothèque Municipale MS 558, fol. 1, showing a king dictating the law to a scribe. Particularly interesting is the treatment of the same gesture in a copy of Gautier de Coincy's *Les Miracles Nostre Dame*, Paris, BN n. acq. fr. MS 24541, fol. 2, in which Gautier is shown seated, his head resting on his raised left hand, while he points with his right towards a scribe, indicating that he is dictating his work; beside him stands a desk supporting a book, a representation of the complete, authoritative work (see below for a similar scene in the Rawlinson MS).

[29] For the purse as memory trope, see Mary Carruthers, *The Book of Memory: A Study of Memory in Medieval Culture* (Cambridge: Cambridge University Press, 1990), pp. 34-35, 39, 251.

[30] *Navicella*: 'little boat'. George Keiser discussed manuscript evidence for scribes' not reading far in advance of their copying in 'Changing Verses in Mid-Stream: Lydgate's Intention and the Scribal Response', a paper given at the London Medieval Manuscripts Seminar, March 1995.

[31] Ardis Butterfield, 'Articulating the Author: Gower and the French Vernacular Codex', in *Medieval and Early Modern Miscellanies and Anthologies*, ed. by Phillipa Hardman, *Yearbook of English Studies*, 33 (2003), 80-96.

[32] See J. A. Burrow, 'The Portrayal of Amans in *Confessio Amantis*', in *Gower's 'Confessio Amantis': Responses and Reassessments*, ed. by A. J. Minnis (Cambridge: Brewer, 1983), pp. 5-24 (p. 12, n. 7).

[33] See A. S. G. Edwards and Derek Pearsall, 'The Manuscripts of the Major English Poetic Texts', in Griffiths and Pearsall, pp. 257-78 (pp. 265-66 and notes).

[34] Scott, *LGM*, II, 141; Seymour, II, 192; Otto Pächt and J. J. G. Alexander, *Illuminated Manuscripts in the Bodleian Library*, 3 vols (Oxford: Clarendon Press, 1966-73), III, 164. Margaret Rickert firmly identifies the figure as Melibeus (I, 587).

[35] 'Here Chauncers tellith of Sir Thopas' (fol. 167v); 'Here oure Ost letteth Chauncers his rymyng' (fol. 170v); 'Here bigineth Chauncers another tale off Mellibe and Prudence & Sophia. Chauncers tale' (fol. 171); 'Here endith Chauncers his tale of Mellibe and Prudence' (fol. 193v).

[36] See, for example, Philadelphia, Rosenbach Library MS 1084/1: 'Here endeth the tale of Sir thopas | And here bygynneth the tale of Mellybe and Prudence' (fol. 155).

[37] Princeton, Firestone Library MS 1009, fol. 180; Tokyo, Professor Takamiya MS 32, fol. 108; BL MSS Egerton 2864, fol.192v; Add. 5140, fol. 238; Lansdowne 851, fol. 206; Paris, BN, fonds anglais MS 39, fol. 72.

38 Ardis Butterfield ('Articulating the Author') observes that it is sometimes unclear whether the figure is an author, a scribe, or a reader. But any of these functions may represent the continuing 'voice of the text'.

39 See note 26 above.

40 See Mary Carruthers, *The Book of Memory*, p. 225, for discussion of this passage in relation to the medieval concepts of *parole* and *painture*.

41 Some other manuscripts adopt different strategies to cope with the potential for confusion. In MS Arch. Selden B.14, for instance, unusually descriptive rubrics are provided: 'Here endith the Frere his prolog And next folwith his tale to angre with the Sompnour' (fol. 100v); 'Here endith the Sompnour is Prolog And next folwith his tale to angre with the Frere' (fol. 106v).

42 For discussion of illustration and *ordinatio* in the Ellesmere MS, see Richard K. Emmerson, 'Text and Image in the Ellesmere Portraits of the Tale-Tellers, in *The Ellesmere Chaucer*, pp.143-70.

43 All nine illustrations in CUL MS Gg.4.27 are reproduced in colour and briefly described in the commentary by M. B. Parkes and Richard Beadle at the end of the facsimile edition of the manuscript; Kathleen L. Scott further discusses the stylistic and iconographic associations of the illustrations in *Later Gothic Manuscripts*, where the Cambridge MS is Catalogue No. 43. See also the discussion by Margaret Rickert (I, 596-604). Some slight inaccuracies occur in the printed descriptions: the Wife of Bath's whip has three (not two) lashes (Parkes and Beadle, III, 58); Chastity (not Charity) resembles paintings of St Margaret, and the placing of pilgrim portraits at the heads of tales is not an unsubtle variation by the designer of the Cambridge MS but normal practice (Scott, *LGM*, II, 145).

44 Scott, *LGM*, II, 145; Parkes and Beadle, III, 59-59. Margaret Rickert takes the opposite view (I, 593).

45 V. A. Kolve discusses this illustration in relation to the Cook's status as 'the skilled professional … hired by five London guildsmen', 'who would do his new patrons credit', and who is capable of 'wit and urbanity' in his exchange with the Host (*Chaucer and the Imagery of Narrative*, pp. 263-67).

46 V. A. Kolve identifies the voice as 'bourgeois' (p. 269).

47 The head-dress was apparently designed to be even larger: faint preliminary drawing is visible to the right of the Wife's hood and to the left of the horse's head.

48 The Cambridge illustrator shows a particular interest in the bridles, bits, and reins. The bit in the illustration of the Monk has been drawn, but not painted. Apart from the Cook's, all the bridles have double reins attached to an early version of a

pelham bit, a massive piece of metalwork that would give the rider extra leverage to control the horse. I am indebted to Nicholas Hardman for this information.

49 The Cambridge Cook's so-called 'whip' is discussed above. The Wife of Bath does not need her whip to urge on her horse, as the text, illustrated in the Ellesmere portrait, mentions the 'paire of spores sharpe' on her feet (Gen. Prol. l. 473); her feet in the Cambridge illustration are hidden by her cloak. Many of the pilgrims in both Ellesmere and Cambridge MSS are wearing prominent spurs.

50 Manly and Rickert, I, 201; Seymour, II, 120.

51 A good comparison is the *Troilus* manuscript, Cambridge, Corpus Christi College MS 61, where space has been left between the rubrics signalling the ends and beginnings of Proems and Books, distinct from the picture spaces elsewhere in the manuscript.

52 For the pictorial tradition of the Seven Deadly Sins, see Morton W. Bloomfield, *The Seven Deadly Sins* (East Lansing: Michigan State University Press, 1952); Siegfried Wenzel, 'The Seven Deadly Sins: Some Problems of Research' *Speculum*, 43 (1968), 1-22; Joanne S. Norman, 'Sources for the Grotesque in William Dunbar's "Dance of the Sevin Deidly Synnis"', *Scottish Studies*, 32 (1989), 55-75.

53 See Parkes and Beadle, III, 59, for the argument that the Sin and Virtue figures derive from different exemplars.

54 The artist seems to have had difficulty in representing swords worn by riders: the Reeve's is largely hidden, the Cook's(?) is scarcely recognizable, and Envy's large weapon hangs apparently in mid-air beside him.

55 Joanne Norman illustrates a late-fifteenth-century French series of the Deadly Sins mounted on beasts in which a female Lust rides a goat, while Envy and Gluttony are shown as male (fig. 2). The two sins given most extensive treatment in homiletic treatments generally are Avarice and Lechery, often dealt with as typically male and female sins respectively.

56 *The Book of Memory*, pp. 221-26.

57 For discussion of this topic, see Joyce Coleman, *Public Reading and the Reading Public in Late Medieval England and France* (Cambridge: Cambridge University Press, 1996).

58 An interesting contrast is provided by manuscript copies of works by Lydgate, who, as Kathleen Scott points out, 'received more extensive narrative illustration than any other author of the later period in England' ('Design', p. 46). Derek Pearsall suggests of Lydgate's major works, especially his *Troy Book* and *Fall of Princes*, that their 'chief reason for existence, it might unkindly be said, was to

provide the opportunity for ownership of large handsome books of English writing with pictures' ('The Ellesmere Chaucer and Contemporary Literary Manuscripts', p. 273). Both works are associated in the text with a royal dedicatee or patron, part of Lydgate's efforts 'to cultivate a reputation at court' (Carol M. Meale, 'Patrons, Buyers and Owners: Book Production and Social Status', in Griffiths and Pearsall, pp. 201-38 (p. 218)). A number of these luxury picture books were owned by the nobility and might conceivably have functioned in a context of courtly gift-giving, where elaborate illustration would enhance the value of the object. This is not the case with copies of the *Canterbury Tales*, where it seems more likely that purchasers would have valued illustration as an element of design for purposes of social reading.

Chapter 3

The Woodcut Illustrations in Early Printed Editions of Chaucer's *Canterbury Tales*

David R. Carlson

T wo related series of woodcuts remained in use for illustrating Chaucer's *Canterbury Tales* throughout the period of their black-letter publication. The first was cut for William Caxton's second edition of the *Tales*, published in 1483, and this series was reused, more and less intact, in Wynkyn de Worde's 1498 *Tales*, the 1532 edition of Chaucer's complete works, edited by William Thynne and printed by Thomas Godfray, and the 1542 reprint of the 1532 edition, produced by Richard Grafton. Individual woodcuts added to the Caxton series after its initial appearance recurred in the 'Printers' edition of c. 1550, the Stow edition of 1561, and the Speght editions of 1598 and 1602. The second series was cut for Richard Pynson's 1492 edition of the *Tales* and was reused in Pynson's 1526 edition of the same work, though for this second appearance of the series a number of the designs were copied on new blocks. In addition, the Pynson series reappeared in one of the two issues of the 1561 Stow edition, now as a combination of blocks from both 1492 and 1526. The last black-letter edition, a 1687 reprint of the 1602 Speght edition, did not illustrate the *Canterbury Tales* at all.[1]

In terms of invention and influence, the program of illustrations that Caxton first printed in 1483 is the only program of consequence. The Pynson woodcuts were copied from Caxton's; likewise, for positioning particular illustrations in relation to the texts, Pynson, de Worde, and the other printers who illustrated the *Tales* in the sixteenth century looked to Caxton's edition as their model. After Caxton, the use of woodcuts to illustrate the *Tales* is characterized by an increasing parsimony, accelerating a propensity already apparent in Caxton's

Fig. 1 - Manuscript illumination of The Cook

practice, and by the peculiar shrewd myopia that can characterize the doings of technically adept employees working to the directions of businessmen trying to better profit. Generally, later printers reduced the number of woodcut illustrations printed with the *Tales* and avoided the expense of designing and cutting new blocks. Typically innovating only when forced to do so by the loss or destruction of blocks, later printers used whatever blocks remained available to them with still less attention to the illustrations' appropriateness to particular pilgrims than even Caxton had used. The story of woodcut illustrations for the *Canterbury Tales* in the sixteenth century is the story of an initially effective marketing device falling into casual misuse and obsolescence.

The Caxton Series

In its first appearance in 1483, Caxton's series of illustrations was printed from twenty-three woodcut blocks, all of them new, apparently cut specifically for the edition, impressions from them occurring at forty-seven places in the book.[2] With the exception of an illustration showing the whole group of pilgrims seated together at table (20C),[3] all of the illustrations are equestrian portraits of single pilgrims; and without exception, all of the illustrations take the form of framed rectangles, printed within the single text-column of Caxton's page, in space that would otherwise have been occupied by type-set verses.

In their delineation of the pilgrims and format, the Caxton series woodcuts probably derive from a program of miniatures in a manuscript of which only a few leaves now survive, the "Oxford Fragments." Only three still extant manuscripts of the *Canterbury Tales* have or appear once to have had complete sets of pilgrim miniatures: the Ellesmere manuscript, in which a series of twenty-three miniatures remains intact; Cambridge, Cambridge University Library, Gg.4.27, of which remain after mutilation only the miniatures of the Reeve, the Cook, the Wife of Bath, the Pardoner, the Monk, and the Manciple; and the Oxford Fragments, now thirteen discontinuous leaves, two in the John Rylands Library, Manchester, and eleven in the Rosenbach Museum and Library, Philadelphia, containing among them three miniatures, of the Miller, the Cook, and the Man of Law. As far as can be determined, these three programs are artistically independent of one another; none appears to have copied any other.[4]

The three surviving Oxford Fragments miniatures share anomalous details with the corresponding Caxton series woodcuts, the similarities

Fig. 2 - Woodcut illustration of The Cook

arguing that, although the woodcuts are not close copies, they derive from this set of hand-painted illustrations, freely and possibly at some remove or other. The Cooks of the two series are not much alike (nor does either have much to do with Chaucer's Cook). The Oxford Fragments miniature gives the figure a big meat cleaver and a healthy head of curly hair, whereas the Caxton woodcut shows an undistinguished figure, without attribute, that could well have been meant to represent some other pilgrim (figs. 1 and 2). On the other hand, the Man of Law holds up a rolled parchment in the cognate illustrations of the Oxford Fragments and Caxton, and he has distinctive head-gear besides (figs. 3 and 4); and the Miller, who is seated on a distinctive flour-sack and plays a recorder of some sort or a tabor-pipe, rather than the bagpipe specified by Chaucer (figs. 5 and 6). In neither instance does the peculiar attribute - the rolled parchment in the one case and the recorder in the other - occur in any other extant illustration, nor is the attribute mentioned in Chaucer.

The similarities between the Oxford Fragment miniatures and Caxton's woodcuts extend also to matters of format and style. Unlike the Ellesmere miniatures, which appear in the outer margins of pages, the Oxford Fragments miniatures and the Caxton woodcuts occur

Fig. 3 - Manuscript illumination of The Man of Law

within the text area, across columns of writing; and unlike the miniatures in the Cambridge manuscript, which are similarly positioned on the page, the Oxford Fragments miniatures and the Caxton woodcuts are framed on four sides by straight lines, single in the printed edition and double in the Oxford Fragments. Finally, unlike the other manuscript miniatures, which are paintings, the Oxford Fragments miniatures are line drawings, within the outlines of which color has been applied. Consequently, the Oxford Fragments miniatures would have been amenable to copying for woodcut in a way that other kinds of illustrations would not have been.

I am unaware of any evidence indicating that the manuscript from which survive the Oxford Fragments did or did not pass through Caxton's hands,[5] and it must be possible that the model for Caxton's woodcuts was some no longer extant manuscript, related to the Oxford Fragments as exemplar or copy. In view of the similarities between the remaining Oxford Fragments miniatures and the cognate Caxton woodcuts, however, and in view of the rarity of programs of illustration in manuscripts of the *Canterbury Tales*, such as to militate against the possibility that there would have been yet another illustrated manuscript that Caxton could have used, it seems not unlikely that Caxton

Than Robys riche or fydyl or salterye
But al be that he was a phylosophre
Yet hadde he but lytyl golde in cofre
But al that he myghte of hys frendys lent
On bokys and on lernynge he it spent
And besely gan for the soulis praye
Of hem that yaf hym wherwyth to scolaye
Of study took he most cure and hede
Not a worde spak he more than nede
And that was sayd in fourme and reuerence
Short and quyk and ful of hygh sentence
Solwnynge moral vertu was hys speche
And gladly wolde he lerne and gladly teche

A Sergeaunte of lawe waar and wyse
Was there that ofte hadde be at the peruyse
That was also ful riche of excellence
Discrete he was and of grete reuerence

Fig. 4 - Page with woodcut illustration of The Man of Law

used the Oxford Fragments manuscript itself. Be that as it may, the unparalleled concurrence in anomalies of the manuscript miniatures and the woodcuts in two of the three cases for which evidence survives indicates relationship of some kind, if not immediate derivation.

The disparity between the number of blocks Caxton used to make illustrations for his *Canterbury Tales* - twenty-three - and the number of illustrations distributed throughout the edition - forty-seven - is to be accounted in large part by the fact that Caxton put woodcuts both at the heads of the descriptions of each of the pilgrims within the "General Prologue" and at the heads of each of the pilgrims' tales, usually using the same block for the same pilgrim in both places.[6] This doubling was costly, from a certain perspective: it gave space to illustrations which would otherwise have gone to letter-press, so inflating the edition's page-count and paper-consumption. On the other hand, the doubling also made using and appreciating the book easier, by guiding the book's users from pilgrim to tale, encouraging them to see connections between the prologue with its framing fiction and the individual tales within, the connections between tellers and tales.

This index-like function that the woodcuts fulfill was disturbed, however, by Caxton's occasional use of one block to represent more than one pilgrim, both within the "General Prologue" and among the tales proper. Caxton used a single woodcut for both the Shipman and the Canon's Yeoman (12C); another for both the Physician and the Parson (13C); and another for both the Manciple and the Franklin (17C). Most remarkably, he used a single woodcut for all three of the Merchant, the Franklin, and the Summoner (7C [fig. 7]).

Such dissonant re-use was possible because of the generic proper-ties of the designs of Caxton's woodcuts. Some part of the value of the pilgrim miniatures in the Ellesmere manuscript rests in their fidelity to Chaucer's writing. Each depicts details of appearance, furnishings, or attitude mentioned in the text, and each is peculiar to a single pilgrim.[7] Caxton's woodcuts, however, like Pynson's later series, lack the Ellesmere miniatures' qualities of individuation and specificity to the writing. Excepting egregious failures, and a few comparative success-es, the pilgrims of Caxton's woodcuts are more or less stock figures: male or female, religious or lay, but in most instances not further dif-ferentiated from one another.

Fig. 5 - Manuscript illumination of The Miller

Here tales al be they better or werse
Or ellis falsen some of my matere
And therfore who so lysteth not to here
Turne ouer the leef and chese another tale
For he shal fynde ynowe bothe grete and smale
Of hystoryal thynge that toucheth gentylnesse
And eke moralyte and holynesse
Blameth not me yf that ye chese amys
The Myllere is a cherle ye knowe wel thys
So is the Reue and eke other mo
And harlotrye they tolde bothe two
Aduyseth you and put me out of blame
And eke men shul not make ernest of game

¶ Here begynneth the myllers tale

Fig. 6 - Woodcut of The Miller

Fig. 7 - Woodcut illustration of The Merchant

Fig. 8 - Woodcut illustration ot The Clerk

One of the woodcuts of Caxton's series is strikingly inappropriate to the pilgrim it is used to represent: the woodcut of the Clerk, showing him equipped with an unscholarly bow and arrows (8C [fig. 8]). Nevertheless, the influence of Caxton's example was such that this unsuitable illustration, perhaps designed for a yeoman and misplaced in the text, continued in use for the Clerk among the heirs of Caxton's blocks and again in the copies made for the Pynson series. At the other extreme, a number of the Caxton illustrations delineate Chaucer's pilgrims with sufficient particularity for them to be identified without reference to their textual situation in the edition: the woodcuts used for the Knight (1C), the Squire (2C), the Yeoman (3C), the Man of Law (9C), the Wife of Bath (14C), the Miller (16C), and the Reeve (18C). These woodcuts are consequently found in Caxton's edition illustrating only the "General Prologue" descriptions and the tales of these pilgrims.

Even these, however, the most specific of the pilgrim cuts in the Caxton series, are not as specific as the corresponding Ellesmere miniatures. In fact, the better part of the illustrations in Caxton's series make little effort at being specific. From this perspective, the most characteristic woodcuts of Caxton's series are the four that occur as representations of more than one pilgrim in the 1483 edition. The recurrence of other Caxton series woodcuts in later editions as representations of different pilgrims, still without the illustrations seeming inappropriate, is another indication of the generic qualities of Caxton's designs: the 1483 edition's Plowman (15C) was later used for the Parson, for example; its Pardoner (19C) for the Franklin; a close copy of its representative Guildsman (cl0C) for the Pardoner; its Prioress (4C) for the Second Nun and its Second Nun (21C) for the Prioress.[8]

The nature of woodcut printing may have encouraged Caxton's use of such stock illustrations, by virtue of the economies that could accrue from the use of woodcuts in place of hand-painted illustrations. If the patron of an illustrated manuscript such as the Ellesmere Chaucer would have settled for stock pilgrims, as Caxton's customers had to do, much of the labor and cost of conceiving or designing such a hand-painted series might have been saved. Artists' pattern-books addressed such a wish to conserve conceptual labor in design.[9] Stock hand-painted miniatures, however, did not save the painter so much labor in the execution of the designs. Each miniature would still have to be painted individually, by hand, in any case. Use of woodcuts brought with it a greater incentive to repeat the same illustration for more than one pilgrim. The illustration would not have to be cut in wood more than once. The same block could simply be reused, conserving the woodcutter's labor in a way not possible for a painter of miniatures.[10]

By comparison with the cost of designing and executing a hand-painted series of illustrations, resulting in a single saleable manuscript book, Caxton's procedures represent a considerable economy, not so much in terms of the labor expended on designing such a series as in terms of the labor of executing and replicating it. Caxton's outlay in commissioning the series was considerable, however, compared to the costs his heirs incurred in reusing it. They cut few or no new blocks, being content in most instances to borrow blocks cut for some other use, to replace losses from the original series, and they availed themselves of Caxton's precedent for distributing the illustrations within the Tales.

On Caxton's dying in 1491, the blocks of his *Canterbury Tales* series came into the possession of Wynkyn de Worde, along with the rest of Caxton's shop, and de Worde reused the blocks when he reprinted the Tales in 1498.[11] Three blocks were lost in the interval, and two new blocks made first appearances illustrating the Tales in his edition. De Worde had to hand twenty-two blocks, in other words, one fewer than Caxton, and these he used less lavishly. De Worde illustrated his edition at only thirty-two places, compared with the Caxton edition's forty-seven, a reduction accomplished largely by a different treatment of the "General Prologue." Here, where Caxton's edition had illustrated each of the descriptions and the conclusion of the "Prologue" - in

twenty-three places - de Worde's "Prologue" used only seven woodcuts: four around its beginning and end, including one at the head of the
Caxton prologue to the *Tales*, which Caxton himself had not illustrated, and three heading the descriptions of the Parson, the Summoner,
and the Pardoner. In illustrating the tales, de Worde followed Caxton
more closely. With but five exceptions, the same woodcuts recur in the
same locations. The few changes de Worde made in no sense comprise
amelioration or correction of Caxton. De Worde simply replaced stock
figures with other stock figures, apparently at random or in ways dictated by loss of the original blocks.[12]

By 1532, thirteen blocks remaining from Caxton's series had come
into the possession of the London printer Thomas Godfray, who used
them for illustrating the *Canterbury Tales* portion of an edition of
Chaucer's complete works prepared by William Thynne. The book is
not illustrated elsewhere. With two new blocks - another new Knight
(27Cx), and a figure used for the Squire (28Cx), which Hodnett
describes as showing rather a king, wearing a crown on the side of his
head, carrying a scepter - Godfray had fewer blocks at his disposal,
only fifteen, and he used them still less lavishly, to make only twenty
illustrations.[13] The edition illustrates the "General Prologue" not at all,
and the tales themselves not altogether thoroughly. No illustration
occurs with either of the tales told by Chaucer, nor with those of the
Monk and the Nun's Priest, which follow Chaucer's tales immediately
in the edition's order, occupying signatures Q-V.[14] Except for these
four omissions and seven substitutions, all apparently resulting from a
need to make up for blocks lost from the series in the thirty-four years
since its last use, the 1532 edition's program of illustrations replicates
that of the cognate portions of de Worde's 1498 edition. With one possible exception, the edition's innovations again have the character of
improvisations rather than efforts to ameliorate or rationalize
the program.[15]

Other evidence besides reduction of the program also suggests that
Godfray was concerned to use as little paper as possible in manufac-
turing his inevitably still sizeable edition. The 1532 complete works is
printed in two columns; used in combination with a smaller-bodied
type, the layout enabled Godfray to print as many as ninety-six lines of
verse per page. Woodcut illustrations confounded this economy. As
originally sized, they occupied both columns of a folio page, reducing
the number of lines per page by nearly half. As few as fifty lines are
printed on the illustrated pages. To reduce the amount of space given
over to them, Godfray   reduced the number of illustrations

considerably; also, the borders were removed from all the blocks remaining from the Caxton series, making them smaller. In addition, four of the thirteen remaining blocks were substantially trimmed down, two of them being made small enough thereby to fit in a single column (fig. 9), and the two new blocks were both narrow, one of them narrow enough to be printed in a single column space.[16]

In 1542, nearly sixty years after their first appearance, blocks from Caxton's original series were used for the last time in an edition of the *Canterbury Tales*, in a reprint of the 1532 Thynne edition, printed by Richard Grafton for William Bonham and John Reynes, who would have had to come to terms with Godfray to obtain the remaining wood-cut blocks, if not also use of the texts. All thirteen of the blocks from the original 1483 series that had appeared in the 1532 edition reappear in 1542, though the two illustrations that had been new in 1532 do not. They were replaced by a single new woodcut (29Cx), used only to replace them: tall and narrow like the 1532 Knight (27Cx), it shows a knight and a squire and occurs at the heads of the tales of both the Knight and the Squire.[17] An inconsequential, inexplicable substitution, of one generic illustration for the others used previously at the same point, occurs at the head of the "Franklin's Tale," and the edition's incorporation of the apocryphal "Plowman's Tale" among the *Canterbury Tales*[18] prompted its only other innovation. Otherwise, this last appearance of impressions from Caxton's original blocks replicates the illustrative program of the 1532 edition.

No edition subsequent to that of 1542 offered a *Canterbury Tales* illustrated with blocks from the original Caxton series; none of them was much illustrated at all.[19] The Printers edition of c. 1550 had at the head of its "Squire's Tale" a close copy (c28Cx) of the Squire woodcut unique to the 1532 edition, and yet another new Knight (30Cx) at the head of the "Knight's Tale"; otherwise, its *Tales* are plain. In all issues of the 1561 Stow edition, both those with an illustrated "General Prologue" and those without, and in both the first and second Speght editions, of 1598 and 1602 respectively, this Knight of the Printers edition recurs at the head of the "Knight's Tale"; otherwise, their *Tales* too are plain.

The Pynson Series

Pynson copied Caxton. The woodcuts making up his 1492 series were executed with greater sophistication, perhaps, and by their banners, longer and more skilful curves, and relative wealth of detailed

For though this sōpner wode were as an hare
To tel his harlotrye I wol not spare
For we ben out of his correction
They haue of vs no iurdiction
Ne neuer shullen/terme of al her lyues.
¶Peter so ben women of the stewes.
(Qd this Sompner) yput out of our cure.
   Peace with mischaūce/& with misauenture
Sayd our hoste/and let him tell his tale
Nowe telleth forthe/& let the Sompner gale
Ne spareth not/myn owne maister dere.
¶This fals thefe/this Sōpner (qd the frere)
Had alway baudes redy to his honde
As any hauke to lure/in Englonde
That telleth him al the secre that they knewe
For her aquayntāce was not come of newe
They weren his aprouers pryuely
He toke him selfe a great profyte therby
His maister knewe not alwaye what he wan
Without maundement/a lewde man
He coude sōmon/on payne of chriftes curse
And they were glad to fyllen his purse
And made him great feestes at the nale
And right as Iudas had purses smale
And was a thefe: right suche a thefe was he
His maister had but halfe his deutie
He was (if I shal yeuen him his laude)
A thefe/a sompner/and eke a baude.
   He had eke wenches of his retinue
That whether sir Roberde/or sir Hue
Or Iohan/or Rafe/or who so that it were
That lay by hem/they tolde it in his eere
Thus were the wenches and he of one assent
And he wolde fetche a fayned maundement
And sōmon hem to the chapitre bothe two
And pylle the man/and let the wenche go
Than wolde he say/frende I shal for thy sake
Do stryken the out of our letters blake
The dare no more as in this case trauayle
I am thy frende/there I may the auayle
Certayne he knewe of brybies mo
Than possible is to tell in yeres two
For in this worlde nys dogge for the bowe
That can an hurte dere from an hole knowe
Bet than the Sompner knewe a slye lechour
Or auouter/or els any paramour
For that was the fruite of al his rente
                         Ther

Hylom there was dwellyng in my coūtre
W An archedeken/a man of hye degre
   That boldly dyd execution
In punisshyng of fornycation
Of witchcrafte/and eke of baudrie
Of defamacion/and aduoutrie
Of churche reues/and of testamentes
Of contractes/and lacke of sacramentes
Of vsure/and of symonye also
But certes lechours dyd he moche wo
They shulden synge/if they weren hente
And smale tythers they were foule ishente
If any person wolde vpon hem playne
There might asterte hem no pecunyal payne
For smale tythes / and small offrynge
He made the people pitously to synge
For er the bisshop caught hem with his hoke
They were in the archedekens booke
And than had he (thorough his iurdiction)
Power to done on hem correction
He had a Sompner redy to his honde
A slyer boye was there none in Englonde
For subtelly he had his espiayle
That taught him where he might auayle.
   He couthe spare of lechours one or two
To techen him to foure and twenty mo

Fig. 9 - Page with woodcut illustration of The Friar

work, suggest a knowledge of contemporary continental woodcutting on his artist's part that Caxton's artist did not possess or would not use (fig. 10). Nevertheless, all of Pynson's woodcuts derive from Caxton's, as adaptations or free copies; and for placing impressions of his copies in his first edition of the *Tales* in 1492, Pynson likewise simply followed what Caxton had done.[20] He illustrated his edition in precisely the same forty-seven places Caxton had illustrated in 1483. A number of mismatches occur, half of them due to carelessness, apparently, and half to Pynson's failure to obtain a complete set of copies. He had copies of only twenty-one of Caxton's twenty-three designs. Nevertheless, Pynson was in most instances able to set his derivatives at those points in his text where the Caxton's originals had been, no doubt using a copy of the Caxton edition as a guide. The result was that, in terms of its program of illustrations, Pynson's first edition mostly reprints Caxton's, substituting new derivative woodcuts for the old.[21]

Issued in 1526, Pynson's second edition of the *Canterbury Tales* is less extensively illustrated than his first, in only twenty-six places. Pynson achieved this economy by the means used by Wynkyn de Worde in 1498: to an even greater degree than de Worde, Pynson reduced the received program for the "General Prologue," offering only two illustrations, one near the beginning and another near the end. For locating illustrations among the tales proper, however, Pynson followed the precedent of his 1492 edition closely, with but two deviations.[22]

Fig. 10 - Woodcut illustration of The Franklin

Pynson resorted to use of a large number of new blocks in 1526, in a way that suggests - though the inference turns out to be in part mistaken - an unusually high rate of attrition for the 1492 blocks. Although the blocks had neither been reused nor changed hands, eleven of the twenty-one blocks of 1492 do not reappear in 1526 (1P, 2P, 5P, 7P, l0P, 13P, 15P, 16P, 18P, 19P, 22P). Pynson moved shop in 1500, from Westminster to London. By way of contrast, however, only ten of the twenty-three blocks of Caxton's original series disappeared from use between 1483 and 1532, an interval longer by fifteen years, during which the Caxton series also moved from Westminster to London with de Worde, again in 1500, was printed from three times, and changed hands three times. Pynson made up for the loss of these eleven by using eight new blocks. One is an original, independent design (26Px).[23] The rest are close copies - so close as to be practically indistinguishable - from blocks used previously. Five of the close copies are from illustrations that Pynson had used in his own 1492 edition which do not recur in 1526 (c2P, c5P, c7P [fig. 11; cf. fig.10], cl3P, cl6P), while the other two are from illustrations that Caxton had used in 1483 (c10C [fig. 12] and c17C). Of one of these Caxton illustrations (10C [fig. 13]), Pynson had already had made in 1492 a free adaptation (l0P [fig. 14]), but this free adaptation was not reused in 1526, and the other of these Caxton illustrations (17C) is one of the two that Pynson omitted to have copied in 1492.

Fig. 11 - Woodcut illustration of Thopas

Fig. 12 - Woodcut illustration of The Pardoner

Pynson must have had access to a copy of the 1483 Caxton edition as he was preparing to print his 1526 edition, inasmuch as he had new illustrations copied from it. The Caxton edition may also have served Pynson as a model for distributing his now substantially recut series throughout his new edition; the evidence is equivocal.[24] In any case, for matching illustrations with locations, Pynson's 1526 edition followed no model so closely as his previous edition had followed Caxton's, though the innovations appear inconsiderate.[25]

The 1561 Stow edition of Chaucer's works emulates the 1550 Printers edition in its illustration of the tales proper: that is to say, the tales themselves in the 1561 edition are not illustrated, except that at the head of the "Knight's Tale" a woodcut first used in the same spot in the Printers edition (30Cx) turns up again. Extant copies of the 1561 edition, however, exhibit different issues of the "General Prologue." Some copies offer an unillustrated "General Prologue," congruent in page design with the rest of the edition, along with other preliminaries occupying a single six-leaf signature (collating A^6) at the beginning of the book. Others offer a "General Prologue" illustrated with woodcuts from the Pynson series occupying, again with other preliminary matter, three signatures, one of four leaves, one of six, and one of four (collating ♣^{4}✠^{6}A^4). Apart from these different "General Prologue" issues, the text and illustration of the rest of the edition is, as far as is known, made up of a single printing.

A N haberdaſſher ther was and a carpenter
A webbe a dyer and a tappyſer
And they were clothed alle in o lyuere
Of a solempne and grete fraternyte
Ful freſſh and newe her geer pyked was
Here knyuys chapyd were not wyth bras
But al wyth ſiluer wrought ful clene and wel
Here gyrdelis and hyr powchys euerydel
Wel ſemed ece of hem a fayr burgeys
To ſitten in the yeld halle at the deys
Euerych for the wyſdom that he can
Was happely forto be an aldyrman
For catryll hadde they ynow and rent
And here wyuys wold it wel aſſent
And ellis certayn they were to blame
Hyt is ful fayr to be callyd madame
And go to the Uygyllis al before

G iij

Fig. 13 - Woodcut illustration of A Guildsman

Fig. 14 - Woodcut illustration of A Guildsman

The most plausible explanation seems to me to be that James Kingston and John Wight, the printer and the publisher of the edition, came into possession of the woodcuts belatedly, after most of the press work for the edition had been done, including the work of printing some though not all copies of a preliminary signature without illustrations. After obtaining the blocks, they ran up a new issue of the beginning of the book, incorporating a "General Prologue" illustrated with woodcuts from the Pynson series, longer by several pages but still comprising a discrete set of signatures capable of being substituted for the previously printed single quire. Combining copies of the first unillustrated preliminaries with copies of the sheets of the rest of the edition until the supply of the unillustrated prelims was exhausted, then substituting illustrated prelims for them, they manufactured the two versions of their edition, without wasting printing that had been done. In all documented cases, the unillustrated "General Prologue" occurs with a title-page showing the Chaucer arms, dated 1560 at the top of the shield, even though the colophon dates the edition 1561 (fig. 15). A different title-page, dated 1561, is found in copies incorporating the illustrated "General Prologue" (fig. 16).[26]

The 1561 illustrated "General Prologue" uses a mixture of blocks: old ones first used in 1492, others cut for the 1526 edition, and a

❡The woozkes of Geffrey Chau-cer, newly pzinted, with diuers ad-

dicions, whiche were neuer in pzinte befoze: with the siege and
destruccion of the wozthy citee of Thebes, compiled
by Jhon Lidgate, Monke of Berie.
As in the table moze plainly
dooeth appere.

Vertue florisheth in Chaucer still,
Though death of hym, hath wrought his will.

Fig. 15 - Title page from Chaucer's Canterbury Tales

single block new in 1561. The mixture of new and old, however, is not as it had been in 1526. In the thirty-six years since the Pynson series was last used, three more blocks of 1492 vintage, all of which had appeared in the 1526 edition, were lost (14P, 20P, 23P); also lost was the single block that had made its first appearance in 1526 (26Px). To the fourteen remaining blocks used in 1526, the edition of 1561 added a single new one (31Px) and, oddly, six blocks that had not been used since 1492 (1P, 13P, 15P, 18P, 19P, 22P). Most remarkable is the appearance in this 1561 edition of impressions from both a 1526 close copy of a 1492 block (cl3P [fig. 17]) and the original 1492 block itself (13P [fig. 18]). On this evidence of their reappearance in 1561, six of the eleven 1492 blocks that, because they did not occur in the 1526 edition, seemed to have disappeared, were not in fact lost. At least some of them were simply not used, though they remained capable of use later, and at least one of the 1526 close copies was made from a block that survived to 1561. For Pynson's failure to use surviving blocks in 1526, and for his having a close copy made of at least one still surviving block, reasons do not occur to me.

The 1561 edition enjoyed a certain independence from the 1526 edition in its access to blocks from the original 1492 Pynson series. It also appears to have disposed illustrations from these blocks independently of the example of Pynson's editions, and to have followed Caxton's example instead. It deviates from precedent only four times, all of them cases in which lost blocks and wanting copies necessitated substitutions. The substitutions were made economically, without recourse to new blocks, and more or less circumspectly: stock figures were replaced with stock figures.[27] The only sensible difference between Caxton's illustration of the "General Prologue" and that of the 1561 edition is that the 1561 edition equivocates less often - less often than any other extensively illustrated edition, in fact: only once does it represent two pilgrims by a single illustration.[28]

N. F. Blake has argued that the woodcuts of Caxton's 1483 *Canterbury Tales* were part of an effort on Caxton's part to create a new market for a work he had published only a few years before, in 1477.[29] It is conceivable that demand for printed copies of the *Tales* found a readier market than Caxton had anticipated and that his second edition was born of exhaustion of supplies of the first and an ambition to exploit demand. Were such the case, however, a simple reprint, less

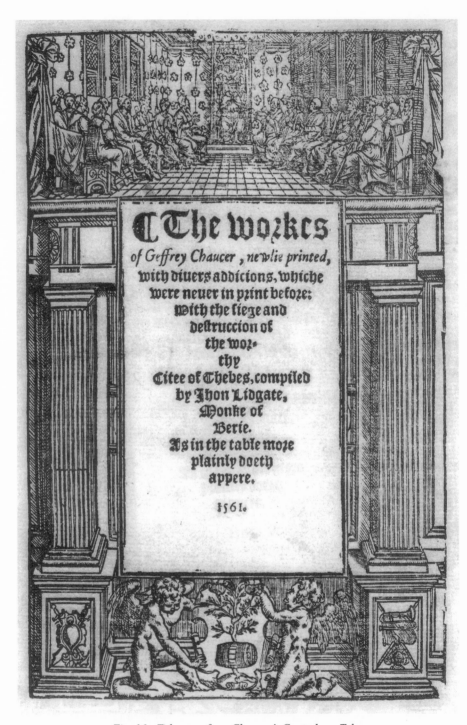

Fig. 16 - Title page from Chaucer's Canterbury Tales

Fig. 17 - Woodcut illustration of The Physician

costly to produce, would have served. That his second edition of the *Tales* is anything but a simple reprint suggests that Caxton was not only taking advantage of market demand. In view of the features of his second edition - the improvements of the text that Caxton advertises in his preface, as well as the addition of woodcut illustrations - it seems more likely that Caxton was seeking to open a new market for the book, as well as to encourage second-time buying, by means of a two-fold appeal, innovative for Caxton though it was to become standard among Chaucer's sixteenth-century publishers: the appeal of the new and the improved.[30] The appeal entailed, on the one hand, a promise of more and, on the other, a promise of betterment of something now stipulatively obsolete. To those who had not been induced to buy his first edition, Caxton offered his second edition's something new, the woodcuts. To those who had bought the first edition, as well as to those who had not, Caxton offered not only this attractive something more, but also his promise of textual improvement: the preface to the second edition attempts to insinuate into the perceptions of consumers a dis-satisfaction with the first edition, by depreciating its text and promis-ing to have rectified it.[31]

The character of Richard Pynson's first edition of the *Tales* sug-gests a perception on his part that the appeals of Caxton's second edi-tion were the proper ones and that, by its particular array of appeals,

Fig. 18 - Woodcut illustration of The Physician

it had succeeded in creating exploitable demand. Pynson had no patron. Venturing his new edition of the *Tales* must have proceeded from Pynson's belief that there was business to be done. It may be that, by 1492, supplies of Caxton's second edition were exhausted, while demand persisted. More likely, it was the lapse of Caxton's business, after his death in the autumn of 1491 and before de Worde's resumption of it about mid-year 1492, that made Pynson's opportunity. That Pynson's edition is effectively a simple reprint of Caxton's second edition - identical to it in all but the physical materials from which it was produced - suggests that, rather than seeking to compete against Caxton's edition, an enterprise that would have called for improving Caxton's work or innovating, Pynson was seeking only to make up for a want of Caxton's edition.[32] In any event, that Pynson went to the expense of having Caxton's woodcut blocks replicated indicates his belief that Caxton had done well to use illustrations in the first place. Only if Pynson believed that illustration had contributed to the success of Caxton's enterprise could he have justified the cost of his own series of woodcut blocks.

Investment in such series of woodcuts as these was of two kinds: an investment of manual effort, in drawing, cutting, emplacing, and printing the blocks, and an investment of conceptual effort beforehand, in conceiving the illustrations and their disposition, in relation to one another and to a body of writing, as a series of illustrations for a book. Already in 1483, there are signs of a tendency to skimp on both kinds of expenditure in producing illustrations for the *Canterbury Tales*. Use of a program of manuscript illustrations as a model, presumably for the woodcuts' disposition as well as their design, would have obviated for Caxton the need for some conceptual effort, which he or those whom he hired seem disinclined to have expended in any case. Moreover, stock illustrations, however harmful their use may have been to the possibility of realizing illustrative ideals, saved manual effort.

The tendency accelerated from this point. From Pynson's point of view, apparently, Caxton seemed to have invested already all the conceptual work that was called for, and so Pynson put in only as much material and manual effort as was necessary to replicate Caxton's product. Caxton and Pynson having invested what they did to produce the two series of illustrations in 1483 and 1492, their heirs as publishers of the *Canterbury Tales* - de Worde in 1498, Pynson himself again in 1526, Godfray in 1532, Grafton in 1542, the Printers c. 1550, and Kingston and Wight in 1561 - were content to use what was to hand, adding a new block or two and haphazardly rearranging illustrations as required by the inevitable destruction of original blocks, but never again investing, either conceptually or manually, even to the (limited) extent that Caxton or Pynson had. Their reluctance to spend is understandable. Caxton's and Pynson's books remained accessible, as repositories of models for individual illustrations and arrangement; and, more importantly, perhaps, many of the original blocks of the two series remained capable of use for a long time, for nearly seventy years in the case of some of Pynson's 1492 blocks.

There is, in addition, evidence to suggest that the market for printed editions of Chaucer's work matured in the interval between Caxton's first *Canterbury Tales* of 1477 and the Stow edition of 1561, in such a way as to justify the sixteenth-century printers' reluctance to reinvest in woodcut illustrations. In issuing as many editions of Chaucer's writings as they did, England's early printers were availing themselves of such reputation as had already accrued to Chaucer's name - which from their perspective would have had the value of a brand name - out of the first century or so of Chaucer "criticism and allusion" and of trade in manuscript copies of his writings. At the same time, by the same printed editions, they were also in turn contributing to the further aggrandizement of Chaucer's exploitable reputation. The printers' work as promoters of Chaucer, calculatedly or not, no doubt contributed to the emergence of a sizable, relatively sophisticated audience for Chaucer's writings by the middle of the sixteenth century.[33]

Repackagings of the works subsequent to the Thynne edition of 1532 and its reprints of 1542 and c. 1550 appealed to this potential market still by versions of Caxton's two-fold appeal, of the new and of the improved. The innovations offered were different, however: no longer woodcut illustrations, but more writings, previously unpublished; more by way of introduction and explanatory annotation; and eventually, in the 1598 Speght edition, the first also to offer a life of the poet and a glossary, in place of woodcut illustrations for the *Tales* or elsewhere, an engraved frontispiece portrait of the author, soon to be followed by the better known, kindred portraits of Shakespeare, Milton, Pope, and others.[34] To the extent that woodcut illustrations for the *Canterbury Tales* originated as a marketing tool, neglect of them, finally to the point of their disappearance, bespeaks the obsolescence of their appeal to Chaucer's printers' markets over the course of the sixteenth century.

Notes

This paper is a revision of "Woodcut Illustrations of the *Canterbury Tales*, 1483-1602," *The Library*, 6th ser., 19 (1997), 25-67, chiefly by way of incorporating references to materials published since 1995, when the earlier version was finished, most significantly Ruth Samson Luborsky's work on the *Canterbury Tales* illustrations, making it possible to understand the wider, later sixteenth-century circulation of a number of the illustrations; that research is now published in Luborsky and Elizabeth Morley Ingram, *A Guide to English Illustrated Books 1536-1603,* 2 vols. (Tempe, Arizona, USA: MRTS, 1998), henceforth cited as "Luborsky." Thanks are due, again to the staffs of the institutions where I studied copies of the various editions - the Huntington Library, the British Library, and the Folger Shakespeare Library - and to Michael Johnson, for help with data construction, W. W. Barker, and Fred Unwalla; and now also to Martin Davies and Martha Driver.

[1]   The editions are listed, with *STC* references, in the headnote to the "Catalogue of Woodcuts" appended below; I use the dates given for them in the revised *STC*, although in some cases the dates cannot now be determined with precision.

[2]   The particulars of the programs of illustrations in the several editions are given in the "Synopsis of Editions" appended below. For the techniques of production and use, an especially valuable and well illustrated survey is Martha Wescott Driver, "Illustration in Early English Books: Methods and Problems," *Books at Brown* 33

(1986), 1-57; see now also Driver, "The Illustrated De Worde: An Overview," *Studies in Iconography* 17 (1996), 349-403, and Lotte Hellinga, "Printing," in *Cambridge History of the Book in Britain 1400-1557* (Cambridge: Cambridge University Press, 1999), esp. pp. 97-106. On the Caxton edition, see also Beverly Boyd, "William Caxton," in *Editing Chaucer: The Great Tradition*, ed. Paul G. Ruggiers (Norman, Oklahoma, USA: Pilgrim Books, 1984), pp. 20-27, with remarks about the woodcuts on p. 27, and *Chaucer and the Medieval Book* (San Marino, California, USA: Huntington Library, 1973), pp. 125-130; and George D. Painter, *William Caxton* (London: Chatto & Windus, 1976), pp. 130-135. Painter, *William Caxton*, p. 132, identifies the woodcutter who made the illustrations for Caxton's second edition of the *Game of Chess* as responsible for the *Canterbury Tales* series as well. The *Canterbury Tales* series is also discussed in Arthur M. Hind, *An Introduction to a History of Woodcut* (1935; rpt. New York: Dover, 1963), II, 710, and in Edward Hodnett, *English Woodcuts 1480-1535* (1935; rpt. with additions London: Bibliographical Society, 1973), p. 3, where de Worde's and Godfray's reuse of the blocks and Pynson's copying of them are also mentioned; see now also Betsy Bowden, "Visual Portraits of the Canterbury Pilgrims, 1484 (?) to 1809," in *The Ellesmere Chaucer: Essays in Interpretation*, ed. Martin Stevens and Daniel Woodward (San Marino, California, USA: Huntington Library, 1995), pp. 171-204.

3   These parenthetical references within the body of the paper are to the items listed in the "Catalogue of Woodcuts" below.

4   On the three manuscript illustration schemes, see Margaret Rickert, "Illumination," in John M. Manly and Edith Rickert, *The Text of the Canterbury Tales* (Chicago: University of Chicago Press, 1940), I, 590-593, who remarks on the stylistic similarities between the Oxford Fragments miniatures and "early woodcuts" (p. 593); also, Boyd, *Chaucer and the Medieval Book*, pp. 38-41. A. S. G. Edwards, "ISTC, the Literary Historian, and the Editor," in *Bibliography and the Study of 15th Century Civilisation*, ed. Lotte Hellinga and John Goldfinch (London: British Library, 1987), pp. 232-233, expresses skepticism about the hypothesis that the Caxton woodcuts derive from an illustrated manuscript of the *Tales*, "given both the apparently attenuated tradition of manuscript illustration for the poem and the presence of some curious anomalies in the cuts themselves;" cf. now Hellinga, "Printing," in *Cambridge History of the Book in Britain 1400-1557*, p. 103. The Ellesmere miniatures have been often reproduced and discussed, e.g., in James Thorpe, *Chaucer's Canterbury Tales: The Ellesmere Manuscript*, 2nd ed. (San Marino, California, USA: Huntington Library, 1978). The Gg miniatures are reproduced in M.B. Parkes and Richard Beadle, *Poetical Works, Geoffrey Chaucer: A Facsimile of Cambridge University Library MS Gg.4.27* (Cambridge: Brewer, 1979-1980), with discussion, III, 58-60. The Miller portrait of the Oxford Fragments is reproduced with Guthrie Vine, "The Miller's Tale: A Study of an Unrecorded Fragment of a Manuscript in the John Rylands Library in Relation to the First Printed Text," *Bulletin of the John Rylands Library* 17 (1933), following 346; the Cook portrait is reproduced as a frontispiece to the Rosenbach Company catalogue *An Exhibition of Fifteenth Century Manuscripts and Books in Honor of*

the Six Hundredth Anniversary of the Birth of Geoffrey Chaucer (1340-1400) (New York: Rosenbach Company, 1940), with some discussion, p. 8; and the Man of Law portrait has not to my knowledge been reproduced before.

5   There is nothing to suggest that the textual improvements that characterize Caxton's second edition came from the Oxford Fragments manuscript. Textually, the Oxford Fragments are related more closely to Caxton's first edition than to his second; see Vine, "The Miller's Tale," esp. pp. 336-340. Nor am I aware of physical evidence in the Oxford Fragments that would suggest that they had passed through Caxton's or some other printer's shop, like the offsets of type discovered in the Malory manuscript (see Hellinga, *Caxton in Focus* [London: British Library, 1982], pp. 90-92) or the compositorial markings that occur in some of the manuscripts used for setting up the 1532 edition of Chaucer, for example (see James E. Blodgett, "Some Printer's Copy for William Thynne's 1532 Edition of Chaucer," *The Library*, 6th ser., 1 [1979], 97-113).

6   The exceptions can be found by comparing the pertinent columns of Tables 1 and 2 below.

7   The most thorough discussion is that by Martin Stevens, "The Ellesmere Miniatures as Illustrations of Chaucer's *Canterbury Tales*," *Studies in Iconography* 7-8 (1981-1982), 113-134. See now also Richard K. Emmerson, "Text and Image in the Ellesmere Portraits of the Tale-Tellers," in *The Ellesmere Chaucer*, pp. 143-170; and, on the manuscript, Ralph Hanna III and A. S. G. Edwards, "Rotheley, the De Vere Circle, and the Ellesmere Chaucer," *Huntington Library Quarterly* 58 (1995), 11-35.

8   These repeats can be located by reference to the "Catalogue of Woodcuts" below. Other woodcuts in the 1483 series are likewise generic in design - imparticular, poorly individuated - but were not apparently used later for different pilgrims: 5C always occurs for the Monk; 6C, always for the Friar; 11C, always for the Cook; 22C, always as a Chaucer portrait; and 23C always as the Nun's Priest.

9   On the uses of pattern-books for conserving artists' labours, see Lesley Lawton, "The Illustration of Late Medieval Secular Texts, with Special Reference to Lydgate's 'Troy Book'," in *Manuscripts and Readers in Fifteenth-Century England*, ed. Derek Pearsall (Cambridge: Brewer, 1983), pp. 45-47. The more extraordinary expedient of pasting pieces of printed decoration in books in place of manual decoration - discussed most recently by Mary C. Erler, "Pasted-In Embellishments in English Manuscripts and Printed Books c. 1480-1533," *The Library*, 6th ser., 14 (1992), 185-206 - was also a means of conserving artists' labours.

10 The conservative reuse of generic woodcut illustrations and the bibliographic problems it can cause are discussed in Ruth Samson Luborsky, "Connections and Disconnections between Images and Texts: The Case of Secular Tudor Book Illustration," *Word & Image* 3 (1987), 74-85, and "Woodcuts in Tudor Books: Clarifying Their Documentation," *Papers of the Bibliographical Society of America* 86 (1992), esp. 77-81.

[11] Painter, *William Caxton*, pp. 182-190, esp. 189. De Worde's reuse of Caxton's *Canterbury Tales* woodcuts is noted in Hind, *Introduction*, II, 728, and Hodnett, *English Woodcuts*, p. 3; and cf. Driver, "Illustration in Early English Books," pp. 6-9, and "The Illustrated De Worde," pp. 351-354 and 363-369, showing a broader range of evidence.

[12] De Worde transposed Caxton's Second Nun (21C) and Prioress (4C), using the one's illustration at the head of the other's tale and vice versa, and he used Caxton's Plowman (15C) - an illustration that would otherwise have been wasted on de Worde, since the Plowman (not yet a tale-teller) was not one of the three pilgrims whose descriptions he illustrated in his "General Prologue" - at *ParsT*. De Worde also put illustrations at the beginning (22C) and end (20C) of the "Retractions," without precedent, and he omitted to illustrate *Th*. Elsewhere, he only replaced stock figures with other stock figures, seemingly at random (i.e., at *MerT*) or in ways dictated by the loss of blocks (i.e., at Kn, *KnT*); cf. the "Synopsis of Editions" appended below. Similarly casual reuse of a received program of woodcut illustrations, by de Worde and other, later printers, is documented in Josephine Waters Bennett, "The Woodcut Illustrations in the English Editions of *Mandeville's Travels*," *Papers of the Bibliographical Society of America* 47 (1953), 59-69, esp. 64-67. In response to evidence of textual derivation, it has been opined that the copy of Caxton's 1483 edition from which de Worde would have typeset his 1498 edition was defective, wanting pages that contained some or all of *PrT*, *Th*, *Mel*, and *MnkT*, where de Worde appears to have relied on a textually independent manuscript; see Thomas J. Garbáty, "Wynkyn de Worde's 'Sir Thopas' and Other Tales," *Studies in Bibliography* 31 (1978), 66-67. While de Worde's program of illustrations too deviates from Caxton's in this same section (see Table 2 below), the differences are not such as to confirm that de Worde had to do without Caxton's example here.

[13] The 1532 edition is not illustrated except in its *Canterbury Tales* section, and the later editions of the complete works of Chaucer discussed herein are the same: not illustrated with woodcuts except in the *Canterbury Tales*. On the 1532 edition, see esp. Blodgett, "William Thynne," in *Editing Chaucer*, ed. Ruggiers, pp. 35-52. For later reuses of the second of Godfray's new blocks, 28Cx, see Luborsky, *A Guide to English Illustrated Books 1536-1603*, II, 82, in reference to 6451/10 and 6452.

[14] The hypothetical missing section of the copy of the 1483 edition that de Worde may have been using in 1498 (see above, n. 12) would have encompassed some of these same tales that went unillustrated in the 1532 edition. The omissions meant that the woodcut that had served as an author-portrait (22C) - de Worde, evidently understanding Caxton's woodcut as such, had placed it at the beginning of the "General Prologue" and at the head of the "Retractions," as well as at the appropriate point within the *Tales* proper, as had Caxton - passed out of use altogether, and it was not replaced in the 1532 edition by any alternative image of the poet.

15 The possible melioration is the 1532 edition's innovation in representing the Canon's Yeoman: it again uses Caxton's inappropriate Clerk (8C) at *ClT*, as had de Worde as well, but it also uses this yeoman-like image at *CYT*, where Caxton and de Worde had used something else, which remained available in 1532 (12C). For this and the edition's other substitutions and omissions, see the "Synopsis of Editions" below. In some cases, it might seem that the 1532 edition returned to Caxton's 1483 edition as its model, instead of the 1498 edition, but the evidence is equivocal. The 1483 and 1498 editions are too like one another, and the 1532 edition's innovations are too characterless, to licence conclusions. For example, in placing at *PrT* the block de Worde had used at *SNT* (4C), the 1532 edition reverts to Caxton's practice. However, whereas both Caxton and de Worde had had two representations of female religious (4C and 21C), one for the Prioress and one for the Second Nun, in 1532 there appears to have remained only one such representation (4C), and the 1532 edition uses it indifferently for both the Prioress and the Second Nun. Evidently, the 1532 usage in this instance was determined by the availability of blocks rather than by the Caxtonian model. The 1532 edition also uses the same block as had Caxton at *MerT* (7C), where de Worde had used one of his new blocks (24Cx), evidently lost to the 1532 edition; and in place of the block that both Caxton and de Worde had used at *FranT* (17C), a block also evidently lost to the 1532 edition, it substituted the block that Caxton, though not de Worde, had used to illustrate the description of the Franklin in his original illustrated "General Prologue" (7C). However, the block replacing the two evidently lost ones (24Cx and 17C) is the same in both instances (7C); and the fact that the 1532 edition uses the block again at *ManT*, again in place of one of these lost blocks (17C), though without the precedent of either Caxton's or de Worde's practice, suggests rather that the 1532 edition was using the block, where convenient, as a stock replacement for lost representations of stock secular male pilgrims. The block in question is the one used most variously in the editions of 1483, 1498, and 1532, even without counting the 1532 edition's idiosyncratic uses of it.

16 The blocks trimmed down for the 1532 edition were 6C, 7C, 12C, and 18C. 6C was used in a single column; though it was not, 18C was trimmed small enough that it could have been printed in one column. Only one of the two new blocks (28Cx) was printed in a single column.

17 On the 1542 edition, see H. S. Bennett, *English Books and Readers 1475-1557,* 2nd ed. (Cambridge: Cambridge University Press, 1969), pp. 146-147 and 236, and the remarks of Derek Pearsall, "Thomas Speght," in *Editing Chaucer*, ed. Ruggiers, p. 71. Luborsky, *A Guide to English Illustrated Books 1536-1603,* II, 44, in reference to 5069/1, describes the new woodcut, 29Cx, as a copy of Hodnett 1122, which was widely copied and variously used in the sixteenth century.

18 The 1542 edition used a block (19C), which had been since 1483 and remained in 1542 in use at *PardT*, at *FranT* as well, where 1532 had had another block (7C) - one that recurs elsewhere in 1542 - and the 1483 and 1498 editions had had something else again (17C), which had not survived. At the head of the "Plowman's

Tale," the edition used the block that had been since 1483 and remained in 1542 in use as a portrait of the Miller (16C). On the publication history of the "Plowman's Tale," see now Joseph A. Dane, "Bibliographical History versus Bibliographical Evidence: The Plowman's Tale and Early Chaucer Editions," *Bulletin of the John Rylands Library* 78 (1996), 47-61.

19 On the Printers edition, see Bennett, *English Books and Readers 1475-1557,* pp. 146-147 and 236, and Pearsall, "Thomas Speght," p. 71. On the Stow edition of 1561 (also discussed below), see Anne Hudson, "John Stow," in *Editing Chaucer,* ed. Ruggiers, pp.53-70. And on the Speght editions of 1598 and 1602, see Pearsall, "Thomas Speght," pp.71-92.

20 Hind, *Introduction*, II, 732, notes the derivation of Pynson's woodcuts from Caxton's, finding Pynson's "even more crudely designed and cut;" see also Hodnett, *English Woodcuts*, pp. 32-33, where the illustration of both Pynson's editions is discussed. Julie A. Smith, "Woodcut Presentation Scenes in Books Printed by Caxton, de Worde, Pynson," *Gutenberg-Jahrbuch 1986* (Mainz: Gutenberg-Gesellschaft, 1986), pp. 326 and 331-332, mentions other instances in which Pynson copied Caxtonian woodcuts. The continental influences are put in context in A. S. G. Edwards, "Continental Influences on London Printing and Reading in the Fifteenth and Early Sixteenth Centuries," in *London and Europe in the Later Middle Ages*, ed. Julia Boffey and Pamela King (London: Centre for Medieval and Renaissance Studies, Queen Mary and Westfield College, University of London, 1995), esp. pp. 234-236.

21 Pynson lacked copies of one of Caxton's stock secular male figures (17C, used in 1483 at Man, *FranT*, and *ManT*) and of one of Caxton's female religious (21C, used in 1483 at *SNT*). Because neither of these Caxtonian illustrations is distinctive, it is possible that they were simply overlooked when Pynson ordered copies made. In any case, where impressions from these two blocks had occured in Caxton's edition, Pynson substituted other, more or less suitable stock figures (2P at Man, 7P at *FranT*, 4P at *SNT*, and 19P at *ManT*). For the rest, Pynson's other substitutions - four further instances in which he failed to place his derivatives in the same locations in the text where had occurred the corresponding Caxtonian originals, using 18P in place of 7C at Mer, 13P in place of 9C at ML, 15P in place of 11C at Ck, and 7P in place of 12C at Sh - appear to have been carelessly made, occurring despite the fact that, elsewhere in his edition, Pynson used properly (i.e., in accord with the model established by Caxton's use of the originals from which Pynson's woodcuts derive) his derivatives of each of the woodcuts for which he substituted: 7P at Fran, Sum, *MerT*, and *SumT*; 9P at *MLT*; 11P at *CkT*; and 12P at *CYT* and *ShT*.

22 At *MerT* and *WBT*. Pynson's other Chaucerian publications of the same date - perhaps to be regarded, with the 1526 *Canterbury Tales* edition, as the part-issued components of a complete Chaucer - were also illustrated with woodcuts, though less extensively than the *Canterbury Tales*, and with predominantly borrowed woodcuts, designed for use with other texts: Pynson's *Troilus* (= *STC* 5096) had

five woodcuts (in order, Hodnett nos. 1933, 1628, 1629, 1625, and 1630), as did also his collection of various minor poems of Chaucer and Chaucerian apocrypha, including the *House of Fame* and the *Parliament of Fowls* (= *STC* 5088, with Hodnett nos. 1500, 1502, 1944, 1326, and 1494, in order). See Hodnett, *English Woodcuts,* pp. 45-46.

[23] Later reuses of this new woodcut, 26Px, are listed in Luborsky, *A Guide to English Illustrated Books 1536-1603,* at 14282/1 and 1989/1.

[24] Four of the close copies from 1492 blocks (c2P, c5P, cl3P, cl6P) occur in the 1526 edition strictly in place of the 1492 originals from which they were copied, but these 1492 originals had all occurred in place of the Caxtonian originals from which they derive more freely. On the other hand, although the woodcut occurs also in the 1526 edition anomalously, not in accord with any model, at *SumT*, in place of a lost block from the 1492 series (7P), the 1526 edition's other uses of its second close copy directly from a Caxton block (c17C) suggest a dependence on Caxton's edition for placement. The block is used in 1526 at *FranT* and *ManT* where the Caxtonian original had occurred, but where the 1492 edition had had to use a pair of unrelated woodcuts (7P and 19P), since at that time Pynson had nothing derivative from this illustration of Caxton's.

[25] An exception may occur at *CYT*, where the 1526 edition uses fittingly, as if thoughtfully, a woodcut that had appeared in 1492 only to represent the Yeoman in the "General Prologue" (3P). At the same spot, Pynson's first edition and Caxton's had had something less suitable (12P and 12C respectively). This innovation may have been motivated as much by a desire to make use of an available block as by concern for illustrative propriety, however. The Yeoman of Pynson's series derives from a woodcut Caxton had used only for his Yeoman in the "General Prologue" (3C), and this woodcut of Caxton's had not been reused by de Worde in 1498. Had Pynson not devised some such use as he did for his 1492 Yeoman, the block would have been wasted on him in 1526, because he did not illustrate his "General Prologue," just as the Caxtonian original appears to have been wasted on de Worde in 1498.

[26] The revised *STC*, at nos. 5076 and 5076.3, describes two anomalous copies, having the "1560" armorial titlepage but also a "General Prologue" with woodcuts. The woodcuts in the "General Prologue" and other differences between the two issues of the 1561 edition are discussed in Hudson, "John Stow," pp. 57-58.

[27] In instances where Caxton's and Pynson's practices accord, the 1561 edition follows (Kn, Sq, Yeo, Pr, Mk, Fr, Cl, Phy, Pars, Pl, Mil, Rv, Pard); in instances where Caxton's and Pynson's practices diverge, the 1561 edition follows Caxton's example (Mer, ML, Gu, Ck, Sh, Man), except in the four instances in which, always for want of an appropriate block, it follows neither (Fran, WB, Sum, Conc); in no instance, however, does the 1561 edition emulate Pynson's practice against that of Caxton. See Table 1 below.

[28] Where the Caxton series had had illustrations of three women, used strictly for the Prioress (4C), the Wife of Bath (14C), and the Second Nun (21C), the Pynson series had never had more than two, both appearing in both of Pynson's editions: a derivative from Caxton's Wife of Bath (14P) used exclusively for her, and a derivative from Caxton's Prioress (4P) used indifferently for both of the female religious pilgrims. By 1561, there remain only one of Pynson's women, the Prioress (4P), and the 1561 edition used it for both the Prioress and the Wife of Bath. The edition's only alternative would have been to use a male figure, however; interestingly, this alternative would appear to have seemed less conceivable than use of an incongruously religious figure for the Wife.

[29] N.F. Blake, "Caxton Reprints," *Humanities Association Review* 26 (1975), esp. 173-177, and "William Caxton: The Man and his Work," *Journal of the Printing Historical Society* 11(1976), esp. 71-75.

[30] Painter, *William Caxton*, p. 134, in discussing Caxton's reasons for issuing the second edition, strikes a characteristically judicious balance: "Caxton's motives in this painstaking but patchy textual revision were no doubt mixed. He was glad, as always, to be on amicable terms with 'a gentleman', liked to feel he was doing his favorite poet a good turn, took a professional pride in the editorial tradition, rare among printers, which he had acquired from Colard Mansion and his fellows, and saw the story made a good selling point." See also Blake, "Caxton and Chaucer," Leeds Studies in English, N.S. 1 (1967), 19-20, and Boyd, *Chaucer and the Medieval Book*, pp. 126-127. On "Caxton's marketing acumen" (p. 460) in general, see Russell Rutter, "William Caxton and Literary Patronage," *Studies in Philology* 84 (1987), 440-470; and now also esp. William Kuskin, "Reading Caxton: Transformations in Capital, Authority, Print, and Persona in the Late Fifteenth Century," *New Medieval Literatures* 3 (2000), 149-183. On the importance of woodcuts for marketing, see A. S. G. Edwards and Carol M. Meale, "The Marketing of Printed Books in Late Medieval England," *The Library*, 6th ser., 15 (1993), 112.

[31] On the textual rectification of Caxton's second edition, see Boyd, "William Caxton," pp. 24-27, or Blake, "Caxton and Chaucer," pp. 20-25.

[32] Painter, *William Caxton*, pp. 189-190. In his edition's prologue (sigs. A1r-A1v), which he signed "by Richard Pynson" even though the better part of it is a verbatim reprint of Caxton's prologue, Pynson emphasized the propinquity of his work to that of "my worshipful master William Caxton," asserting that he had printed his edition "by a copy of the seid master Caxton."

[33] Cf. A. S. G. Edwards, "Chaucer from Manuscript to Print: The Social Text and the Critical Text," *Mosaic* 28/4 (1995), 1-12; also, on the early growth of the Chaucer industry generally, Seth Lerer, *Chaucer and his Readers: Imagining the Author in Late-Medieval England* (Princeton: Princeton University Press, 1993).

34 On this engraved frontispiece portrait of Chaucer, see Hind, *Engraving in England in the Sixteenth & Seventeenth Centuries,* Pt. I (Cambridge, 1952), 286-289; and now Driver, "Mapping Chaucer: John Speed and the Later Portraits," *Chaucer Review* 36 (2002), 228-249. On the development of the frontispiece author portrait, see David Piper, "The Development of the British Literary Portrait up to Samuel Johnson," *Proceedings of the British Academy* 54 (1968), 56-57.

Catalogue of Woodcuts
Used to Illustrate the *Canterbury Tales*
1483-1602

The distinctive individual designs are listed in a numerical sequence running from 1 to 31; Caxton's originary realizations of the designs are designated "C" and Pynson's secondary realizations of them, derived as comparatively free adaptations from Caxton's, are designated "P;" close copies are indicated by a "c" preceding the other designations; and extensions of the original series - i.e., new designs added after 1483 and 1492 - are designated "Cx," if they extend the Caxton series, or "Px," if they extend the Pynson series. For example: "1C" designates Caxton's woodcut illustration of the Knight, the first illustration to appear in the first illustrated edition; "1P" designates the illustration Pynson used that derives from 1C; "cl0C" designates a close copy of Caxton's realization of the tenth design, while "10P" designates Pynson's free adaptation of the same; "24Cx" indicates that the twenty-fourth design used to illustrate the *Canterbury Tales* occurs as an extension of Caxton's original series of illustrations, occurring in a later edition; and so on.

For each item in the catalogue is supplied the number assigned the item in Edward Hodnett, *English Woodcuts 1475-1535,* in which descriptions of the woodcuts are to be found, and now also, where pertinent, cross-references to Ruth Samson Luborsky, *A Guide to English Illustrated Books 1536-1603.* Occasionally, I add a few words by way of supplement to Hodnett's descriptions, and in cases where the woodcut is not catalogued by Hodnett I supply descriptions. The information about borders (where the border is other than a simple single rule) and about dimensions (in millimetres, height before width) is based on my own observations, though for the most part these have served only to confirm Hodnett's.

Also provided is a list of each occurence of the item, arranged chronologically according to edition (designated 1483 = Caxton's second edition, *STC* 5083; 1492 = Pynson's first edition, *STC* 5084; 1498 = de Worde's edition, *STC* 5085; 1526 = Pynson's second edition, *STC* = 5086; 1532 = the Thynne edition, *STC* 5068; 1542 = the Grafton reprint of Thynne, *STC* 5069-5070; 1550 = the Printers reprint of Thynne, *STC* 5071-5074; 1561 = the Stow edition, *STC* 5075-5076.3; 1598 = the first Speght edition, *STC* 5077-5079; and 1602 = the second Speght edition, *STC* 5080-5081), and within the individual editions from first page to last, including indication of the occurence's location in the edition (e.g., "sig. A3v") and its location in relation to the edition's text of the *Canterbury Tales*, always immediately preceding the line number mentioned here, by means of the following series of abbreviations (line-number references are to *The Riverside Chaucer*, 3rd ed., gen. ed. Larry D. Benson [Boston, 1987]):

CaxPro = the head of Caxton's preface to his 1483 edition, often reprinted preceeding the *Tales*. Within the "General Prologue," with the exceptions of In = I. 1 and Conc = I.747, before the first line of the descriptions of the individual pilgrims: Kn = I.43; Sq = I.79; Yeo = I.101; Pr = I.118; Mk = I.165; Fr = I.208; Mer = I.270; Cl = I.285; ML = I.309; Fran = I.331; Gu = I.361; Ck = I.379; Sh = I.388; Phy =I.411; WB =I.445; Pars =I.477; Pl =I.529; Mil = I.545; Man = I.567; Rv = I.587; Sum = I.623; Pard =I.669. Within the "Tales" proper, before the first line of the individual tales and prologues: *KnT* = I.859; *MilT* = I.3187; *RvT* = I.3921; *CkT* = I.4365; *MLT* = II.134; *MerT* = IV.1245; *SqT* = V.9; *FranT* = V.729; *WBP* = III.1; *WBT* = III.857; *FrT* = III.1301; *SumT* = III.1709; *ClT* = IV.57; *SNT* = VIII. 120; *CYT* = VIII.720; *PhyT* = VI.1; *PardT* = VI.463; *ShT* = VII.1; *PrT* = VII.488; *Th* = VII.712; *Mel* = VII.967; *MkT* = VII.1991; *NPT* = VII.2821; *ManT* = IX.105; *ParsT* = X.75; *PlT* = "The Plowman's Tale," line 1; and *Ret* = X.1081.

The order of the "Tales" in the tables (as likewise in this list of abbreviations) is that of the Caxton edition of 1483; later editions deviate from this order in some particulars. The synopsis and the tables of locations appended below use these same abbreviations.

1C = Hodnett 214. 100 x 122.
        1483: sig. A3v (Kn); sig. C5v (*KnT*)

1P = Hodnett 1640. 86 x 115.
        1492: sig. A2v (Kn); sig. C4v (*KnT*)
        1561: sig. [cross]2r (Kn) [= Luborsky 5075/1]

2C = Hodnett 215. 101 x 122.
        1483: sig. A4v (Sq); sig. N8v (*SqT*)
        1498: sig. M2r (*SqT*)

2P = Hodnett 1641. 5mm border. 85 x 114.5.
        1492: sig. A3v (Sq); sig. B7r (Man); sig. O8v (*SqT*)

c2P = Hodnett 1642. Somewhat irregular 5mm border. 86 x 121.
        1526: sig. A1r (titlepage); sig. G3r (*SqT*)
        Double thin border. 86 x 120.
        1561: sig. [cross]2v (Sq) [= Luborsky 5075/2]

3C = Hodnett 216. 101 x 121.
        1483: sig. A5r (Yeo)

3P = Hodnett 1643. 6mm border. 85 x 114.5.
        1492: sig. A4r (Yeo)
        1526: sig. M6r (*CYT*)
        Double thin border.
        1561: sig. [cross]3r (Yeo) [= Luborsky 5075/3]

4C = Hodnett 217. 101 x 119.
        1483: sig. A5v (Pr); sig. 2H6v (*PrT*)
        1498: sig. N6v (*SNT*)
        Border removed. 89 x 119.
        1532: sig. N6r (*SNT*); sig. Q4v (*PrT*)
        1542: sig. M6v (*SNT*) [= Luborsky 5069/11]; sig. P4v (*PrT*)

4P = Hodnett 1645. 2mm border. 85 x 114.
        1492: sig. A4v (Pr); sig. 2E3r (*SNT*); sig. 2K7v (*PrT*)
        1526: sig. M2v (*SNT*); sig. 06v (*PrT*)
        1561: sig. [cross]3r (Pr) [= Luborsky 5075/4]; sig. A1r (WB)

5C = Hodnett 218. 92 x 127.
        1483: sig. A6v (Mk); sig. 3C6r (*MkT*)
        1498: sig. T2v (*MkT*)

5P = Hodnett 1646. 5mm border. 86 x 114.
        1492: sig. A5v (Mk); sig. 2C2v (*MkT*)

c5P = Hodnett 1647. 6mm border. 85 x 121.
        1526: sig. R2v (*MkT*)
        Double thin border. 85 x 119.
        1561: sig. [cross]3v (Mk) [= Luborsky 5075/5]

6C (fig. 9) = Hodnett 219. 93 x 126.
        1483: sig. A7v (Fr); sig. S8v (*FrT*)
        1498: sig. H4r (*FrT*)
        90 x 83.
        1532: sig. K5r (*FrT*)
        1542: sig. K1r (*FrT*) [= Luborsky 5069/8]

6P = Hodnett 1648. 5mm border. 85 x 114.
        1492: sig. A6v (Fr); sig. V6r (*FrT*)
        1526: sig. I6v (*FrT*)
        Double thin border.
        1561: sig. [cross]4r (Fr) [= Luborsky 5075/6]

7C (fig. 7) = Hodnett 220. 95 x 127.
        1483: sig. A8v (Mer); sig. B2r (Fran); sig. Clv (Sum); sig. L8r
                MerT); sig.T6v (*SumT*)
        1498: sig. B3v (Sum); sig. I1r (*SumT*)
                Border removed. 90 x 120.
        1532: sig. H3r (*MerT*); sig. L1r (*SumT*); sig. M6v (*FranT*); sig. V3v
                (*ManT*)
        1542: sig. G6v (*MerT*) [= Luborsky 5069/6]; sig. K3r (*SumT*); sig.
                T2v (*ManT*)

7P (fig. 10) = Hodnett 1653. 5mm border, crossed top and right by white zigzags, and bottom and left by white diagonals. 86 x 115.
        1492: sig. B1r (Fran); sig. B3r (Sh); sig. B8r (Sum); sig. M6r
                (*MerT*); sig.Q4r (*FranT*); sig. 2A4v (*SumT*)

c7P (fig. 11) = Hodnett 1654. 6mm border. 86 x 119.
        1526: sig. P2r (*Th*); sig. P4r (*Mel*)
        Double thin border.
        1561: sig. [cross]4v (Mer) [= Luborsky 5075/7]

8C (fig. 8) = Hodnett 221. 94 x 125.
        1483: sig. B1r (Cl); sig. 2A2r (*ClT*)
        1498: sig. I5r (*ClT*)
        Border removed. 85 x 125.
        1532: sig. L5r (*ClT*); sig. O3v (*CYT*)
        1542: sig. K6v (*ClT*) [= Luborsky 5069/9]; sig. N4r (*CYT*)

8P = Hodnett 1650. 5mm border. 85 x 115.
        1492: sig. A8r (Cl); sig. 2B7r (*ClT*)
        1526: sig. K6v (*ClT*)
        3mm border. 82 x 112.
        1561: sig. A1r (Cl) [= Luborsky 5075/14]

9C (fig. 4) = Hodnett 222. 95 x 126.
        1483: sig. B1v (ML); sig. I7v (*MLT*)
        1498: sig. F1v (MLT)
        Border incompletely removed, still evident at top and bottom.
        1532: sig. F4r (*MLT*)
        1542: sig. F2r (*MLT*) [= Luborsky 5069/5]

9P = Hodnett 1663. 4mm border. 85 x 114.
        1492: sig. K5r (*MLT*)
        1526: sig. E2v (*MLT*)
        1561: sig. [cross]5r (ML) [= Luborsky 5075/8]

10C (fig. 13) = Hodnett 223. 92 x 126.
        1483: sig. B3r (Gu)

10P (fig. 14) = Hodnett 1655. 4mm border. 85 x 115.
        1492: sig. B2r (Gu)

c10C (fig. 12) = Hodnett 1656 (describing it as "a reversed copy of no. 1655 [sc. 10P] with a spear instead of a whip" although it is significantly closer to 10C = Hodnett 223). 7mm border. 85 x 124.
        1526: sig. N7v (*PardT*)
        Double thin border.
        1561: sig. [cross]5r (Gu) [= Luborsky 5075/10]

11C (fig. 2) = Hodnett 224. 95 x 125.
        1483: sig. B3v (Ck); sig. I5r (*CkT*)
        1498: sig. E5v (*CkT*)
        Border removed. 91 x 125.
        1532: sig. F3r (*CkT*)
        1542: sig. F1r (*CkT*) [= Luborsky 5069/4]

11P = Hodnett 1667. 4.5mm border. 85 x 114.
    1492: sig. K2v (*CkT*)
    1526: sig. D5r (*RvT*)
    1561: sig. [cross]6r (Ck) [= Luborsky 5075/11]

12C = Hodnett 225. 92 x 125.
    1483: sig. B4r (Sh); sig. 2D7v (*CYT*); sig. 2G7v (*ShT*)
    1498: sig. 04v (*CYT*); sig. Q3v (*ShT*)
    Border removed. 92 x 121.
    1532: sig. Qlv (*ShT*)
    1542: sig. Plv (*ShT*) [= Luborsky 5069/13]

12P = Hodnett 1664. 4mm border. 85 x 115.
    1492: sig. 2F4v (*CYT*); sig. 2I7v (*ShT*)
    1526: sig. Elv (*CkT*); sig. 03v (*ShT*)
    1561: sig. [cross]6r (Sh) [= Luborsky 5075/12]

13C = Hodnett 226. 95 x 125.
    1483: sig. B4v (Phy); sig. B6r (Pars); sig. 2F2r (*PhyT*); sig. 3G2v (*ParsT*)
    1498: sig. B2v (Pars); sig. P3r (*PhyT*)
    Border removed. 90 x 125.
    1532: sig. P2r (*PhyT*)
    1542: sig. 02r (*PhyT*) [= Luborsky 5069/12]

13P (fig. 18) = Hodnett 1651. State 1: 5mm border; state 2: double border. 85.5 x 115.
    1492: (state 1) sig. A8v (ML); (state 2) sig. B3v (Phy); sig. B5r (Pars);
    sig. 2G8r (*PhyT*); sig. 3Glr (*ParsT*)
    1561: (state 2) sig. Alv (Pars) [= Luborsky 5075/15]

cl3P (fig. 17) = Hodnett 1652. 7mm border. 85 x 120.
    1526: sig. N5r (*PhyT*); sig. Tlv (*ParsT*)
    Double border.
    1561: sig. [cross]6v (Phy) [= Luborsky 5075/13]

14C = Hodnett 227. 91x 126.
    1483: sig. B5v (WB); sig. Q6v (*WBP*)
    1498: sig. G2v (*WBP*)
    Border removed.
    1532: sig. I3v (*WBP*)
    1542: sig. H6v (*WBP*) [= Luborsky 5069/7]

14P = Hodnett 1658. 5mm border. 85 x 115.
    1492: sig. B4r (WB); sig. S2r (*WBP*)
    1mm border. 81 x 91.
    1526: sig. H5v (*WBP*); sig. I4r (*WBT*)

15C = Hodnett 228. 92 x 126.
    1483: sig. B7r (Pl)
    1498: sig. X6v (*ParsT*)
    Border removed. 87 x 126.
    1532: sig. V5v (*ParsT*)
    1542: sig. T4v (*ParsT*) [= Luborsky 5069/14]

15P = Hodnett 1657. Uneven 4 - 5mm border. 86 x 114.
    1492: sig. B2v (Ck); sig. B6r (P1)
    1561: sig. A2r (P1) [= Luborsky 5075/16]

16C (fig. 6) = Hodnett 229. 92 x 125.
    1483: sig. B7v (Mil); sig. G4v (*MilT*)
    1498: sig. D7r (*MilT*)
    Border removed. 85 x 125.
    1532: sig. E2r (*MilT*)
    1542: sig. D6v (*MilT*) [= Luborsky 5069/2]; sig. Y5v (*PlT*)

16P = Hodnett 1659. 6mm border. 85 x 115.
    1492: sig. B6v (Mil); sig. G8r (*MilT*)

c16P = Hodnett 1660. 6mm border top and bottom; 8mm border left and right. 85 x 120.
    1526: sig. D1r (*MilT*)
    Double border top and bottom; triple border left and right. 83 x 120.
    1561: sig. A2r (Mil) [= Luborsky 5075/17]

17C = Hodnett 230. 92 x 127.
    1483: sig. B8r (Man); sig. P2v (*FranT*); sig. [3]F5v (*ManT*)
    1498: sig. M6r (*FranT*); sig. X4r (*ManT*)

c17C = Hodnett 1668. Somewhat irregular 5mm border. 86 x 120.
    1526: sig. H1r (*FranT*); sig. K3r (*SumT*); sig. S5v (*ManT*)
    Double border left and right.
    1561: sig. A2v (Man) [= Luborsky 5075/18]

18C = Hodnett 231. 95 x 127.
    1483: sig. B8v (Rv); sig. H6v (*RvT*)
    1498: sig. E3v (*RvT*)
    Border removed. 90 x 97.
    1532: sig. E6r (*RvT*)
    1542: sig. E4v (*RvT*) [= Luborsky 5069/3]

18P = Hodnett 1649. 2mm border, crossed with white diagonals. 83 x 112.
    1492: sig. A7v (Mer); sig. B7v (Rv); sig. I3v (*RvT*)
    1561: sig. A3r (Rv) [= Luborsky 5075/19]

19C = Hodnett 232. 95 x 127.
    1483: sig. C2v (Pard); sig. 2F8v (*PardT*)
    1498: sig. B4r (Pard); sig. P6r (*PardT*)
    Border removed. 87 x 123.
    1532: sig. P4v (*PardT*)
    1542: sig. M1v (*FranT*) [= Luborsky 5069/10]; sig. O4v (*PardT*)

19P = Hodnett 1661. 5mm border, crossed with white diagonals. 85 x 115.
    1492: sig. C1r (Pard); sig. 2H7v (*PardT*); sig. 3F3r (*ManT*)
    1561: sig. A3v (Pard) [= Luborsky 5075/21]

20C = Hodnett 233. 102 x 121.
      1483: sig. C4r (Conc)
      1498: sig. A3v (Kn); sig. Clr (Conc); sig. [ ]4r (Ret)

20P = Hodnett 1662.4mm border. 85 x 115.
      1492: sig. C2v (Conc)
      1526: sig. A6r (Conc)

21C = Hodnett 234. 97 x 128
      1483: sig. 2C6r (*SNT*)
      1498: sig. Q6v (*PrT*)

22C = Hodnett 235. 95 x 126.
      1483: sig. 2I2v (*Th*); sig. 3A1r (*Mel*)
      1498: sig. A3r (In); sig. R4v (*Mel*); sig. [ ]3r (*Ret*)

22P = Hodnett 1665. 5mm border. 85 x 115.
      1492: sig. 2L3r (*Th*); sig. 3Alr (*Mel*)
      3 mm border.
      1561: sig. [cross]5r (Fran) [= Luborsky 5075/9]

23C = Hodnett 236. 94 x 127.
      1483: sig. 3E3r (*NPT*)
      1498: sig. V4v (*NPT*)

23P = Hodnett 1666. 5mm border, crossed with white diagonals. 85 x 115.
      1492: sig. [3]D7v (*NPT*)
      1526: sig. Slv (*NPT*)

24Cx = Hodnett 19. 102 x 123.
      1498: sig. A2r (CaxPro); sig. Llr (*MerT*)

25Cx = Hodnett 18. 103 x 122.
      1498: sig. C2r (*KnT*)

26Px = Hodnett 1943 [cf. Luborsky 14282/1 and 1989/1]. Double border joined at left corners. 110 x 80.
      1526: sig. A2r (Kn); sig. B1r (*KnT*)

27Cx = Hodnett 2067. Double border joined at corners. 135 x 95.
      1532: sig. Clr (*KnT*)

28Cx = Hodnett 2066 [cf. Luborsky 6451/10 and 6452]. Somewhat uneven 2mm border. 98 x 73.
      1532: sig. G5r (*SqT*)

c28Cx. Close copy of 28Cx, with, i.a., the addition of a banner at the top and upper left. 1mm border. 98 x 72.
      1550: sig. E6v (*SqT*) [= Luborsky 5071/2]

29Cx. A copy of Hodnett 1122: in the foreground, a knight, shown in profile, armored but wearing a fabric hat with plumes, holding a drawn sword upright in his right hand, riding right. His horse is fully armored, with a plumed chaffron; its left foreleg is raised. In the background at upper left, another mounted man, not armored, carrying a lance which rests on his right shoulder, in his right hand, riding right. His horse is not fully visible. Eight plants. Uneven 1mm border. 115 x 88.

      1542: sig. C1r (*KnT*) [= Luborsky 5069/1]; sig. G2v (*SqT*)

3OCx. Knight, armoured cap-à-pied, plumed helmet with visor open, carrying a blank shield in his right hand and a lance in his left, riding left. Both his horse's forefeet are raised. In the background, a castle wall with crenelations. Numerous plants; one rock. 2mm border. 92 x 92.

      1550: sig. B1r (*KnT*) [= Luborsky 5071/1]
      Border removed left and right. 92 x 86.
      1561: sig. B1r (*KnT*) [= Luborsky 5076/1]
      Border removed top.
      1598: sig. B1r (*KnT*) [= Luborsky 5077/2 and 5078/2]
      1602: sig. B1r (*KnT*) [= Luborsky 5080/2 and 5081/2]

31Px. Man, shown in profile and with his back turned, backwards hunter's cap, beads around shoulders, spear point and haft showing above his left shoulder, evidently held in his left hand, which is not visible, riding right. The horse is turned round to face the rider; both its forelegs are raised. Triple border top, right, and left; double border bottom. 85 x 115.

      1561: sig. A3r (Sum) [= Luborsky 5071/2]

Synopsis of Editions
Using Woodcuts to Illustrate the *Canterbury Tales*, 1483-1602

What follows is an attempt to describe, compendiously, the illustrative programs in the several black-letter editions of the *Tales*. Using the same systems of reference and abbreviations as the "Catalogue of Woodcuts," the descriptions tell how many (and which) blocks were used for illustrating the edition; how many illustrations were printed from these blocks (and where the illustrations are located in relation to the texts); how many times blocks were repeated within the edition, from greatest to least frequency (with lists of the blocks so repeated; e.g., "3x: 2 (20C, 22C)" = two woodcuts were repeated three times each, the two being catalogue numbers 20C and 22C); and how often (and where) the illustrative program deviates from its model, by adding, omitting, or substituting illustrations.

1483 Caxton (= *STC* 5083)

    blocks used: 23
        new: 23 (1C-23C)

    places illustrated: 47
        GP: 23 (Kn, Sq, Yeo, Pr, Mk, Fr, Mer, Cl, ML, Fran, Gu, Ck, Sh, Phy, WB, Pars, Pl,

Mil, Man, Rv, Sum, Pard, Conc)
Tales: 24 (*KnT, MilT, RvT, CkT, MLT, MerT, SqT, FranT, WBP, FrT, SumT, ClT,
          SNT, CYT, PhyT, PardT, ShT, PrT, Th, Mel, MkT, NPT, ManT, ParsT*)

repeats:
5x: 1 (7C)
4x: 1 (13C)
3x: 2 (12C, 17C)
2x: 13 (1C, 2C, 4C, 5C, 6C, 8C, 9C, 11C, 14C, 16C, 18C, 19C, 22C)
1x: 6 (3C, 10C, 15C, 20C, 21C, 23C)

1492 Pynson (= *STC* 5084)

blocks used: 21
new: 21 (1P- 16P, 18P-20P, 22P-23P)

places illustrated: 47
GP: 23 (Kn, Sq, Yeo, Pr, Mk, Fr, Mer, Cl, ML, Fran, Gu, Ck, Sh, Phy, WB, Pars, P1,
          Mil, Man, Rv, Sum, Pard, Conc)
Tales: 24 (*KnT, MilT, RvT, CkT, MLT, MerT, SqT, FranT, WBP, FrT, SumT, ClT,
          SNT, CYT, PhyT, PardT, ShT, PrT, Th, Mel, MkT, NPT, ManT, ParsT*)

repeats:
6x: 1 (7P)
5x: 1 (13P)
3x: 4 (2P, 4P, 18P, 19P)
2x: 9 (1P, 5P, 6P, 8P, 12P, 14P, 15P, 16P, 22P)
1x. 6 (3P, 9P, 10p, 11P, 20P, 23P)

innovations:
substitutions: 8 (Mer, ML, Ck, Sh, Man, *FranT, SNT, ManT*)

1498 De Worde (= *STC* 5085)

blocks used: 22
inherited (from 1483): 20 (2C, 4C, 5C, 6C, 7C, 8C, 9C, 11C, 12C, 13C, 14C, 15C,
          16C, 17C, 18C, 19C, 20C, 21C, 22C, 23C);
and lost (since 1483): 3 (1C, 3C, 10C)
new: 2 (24Cx, 25Cx)

places illustrated: 32
GP: 7 (CaxPro, In, Kn, Pars, Sum, Pard, Conc)
Tales: 25 (*KnT, MilT, RvT, CkT, MLT, MerT, SqT, FranT, WBP, FrT, SumT, ClT,
          SNT,.CYT, PhyT, PardT, ShT, PrT, Mel, MkT, NPT, ManT, ParsT, Ret*
          [bis])

repeats:
3x: 2 (20C, 22C)
2x: 6 (7C, 12C, 13C, 17C, 19C, 24Cx)
1x: 14 (2C, 4C, 5C, 6C, 8C, 9C, 11C, 14C, 15C, 16C, 18C, 21C, 23C, 25Cx)

innovations:
additions: 4 (CaxPro, In, *Ret* [bis])
omissions: 19 (Sq, Yeo, Pr, Mk, Fr, Mer, Cl, ML, Fran, Gu, Ck, Sh, Phy, WB, Pl,
                Mil, Man, Rv, *Th*)
substitutions: 6 (Kn, *KnT, MerT, SNT, PrT, ParsT*)

1526 Pynson (= *STC* 5086)

blocks used: 18
    inherited (from 1492): 10 (3P, 4P, 6P, 8P, 9P, 11P, 12P, 14P, 20P, 23P);
    and lost (since 1492): 11 (1P, 2P, 5P, 7P, l0P, 13P, 15P, 16P, 18P, 19P, 22P)
    new: 8 (c2P, c5P, c7P, cl0C, cl3P, cl6P, cl7C, 26Px)

places illustrated: 26
    GP: 2 (Kn, Conc)
    Tales: 24 (*KnT, MilT, RvT, CkT, MLT, SqT, FranT, WBP, WBT, FrT, SumT, ClT,
                SNT, CYT, PhyT, PardT, ShT, PrT, Th, Mel, MkT, NPT, ManT, ParsT*)

repeats:
    3x: 1 (cl7C)
    2x: 6 (4P, c7P, 12P, cl3P, 14P, 26Px)
    lx: 11 (c2P, 3P, c5P, 6P, 8P, 9P, cl0C, 11P, cl6P, 20P, 23P)

innovations:
additions: 1 (*WBT*)
omissions: 22 (Sq, Yeo, Pr, Mk, Fr, Mer, Cl, ML, Fran, Gu, Ck, Sh, Phy, WB, Pars, P1,
                Mil, Man, Rv, Sum, Pard, *MerT*)
substitutions: 16 (Kn, *KnT, MilT, RvT, CkT, SqT, FranT, SumT, CYT, PhyT, PardT, Th,
                Mel, MkT, ManT, ParsT*)

1532 Complete Works, ed. Wm. Thynne (= *STC* 5068)

blocks used: 15
    inherited (from 1483): 13 (4C, 6C, 7C, 8C, 9C, 11C, 12C, 13C, 14C, 15C, 16C, 18C,
                            19C);
    lost (since 1483): 7 (2C, 5C, 17C, 20C, 21C, 22C, 23C)
    and (since 1498): 2 (24Cx, 25Cx)
    new: 2 (27Cx, 28Cx)

places illustrated: 20
    GP: 0
    Tales: 20 (*KnT, MilT, RvT, CkT, MLT, MerT, SqT, FranT, WBP, FrT, SumT, ClT,
                SNT, CYT, PhyT, PardT, ShT, PrT, ManT, ParsT*)

repeats:
    4x: 1 (7C)
    2x: 2 (4C, 8C)
    lx: 12 (6C, 9C, 11C, 12C, 13C, 14C, 15C, 16C, 18C, 19C, 27Cx, 28Cx)

innovations:
omissions: 11 (CaxPro, In, Kn, Pars, Sum, Pard, Conc, *Mel, MkT, NPT, Ret*)
substitutions: 7 (*KnT, MerT, SqT, FranT, CYT, PrT, ManT*)

1542 Grafton (=*STC* 5069-5070)

>   blocks used: 14
>   inherited (from 1483): 13 (4C, 6C, 7C, 8C, 9C, 11C, 12C, 13C, 14C, 15C, 16C, 18C,
>   19C);
>   and lost (since 1532): 2 (27Cx, 28Cx)
>   new: 1 (29Cx)
>
>   places illustrated: 21
>   *GP*: 0
>   *Tales*: 21 (*KnT, MilT, RvT, CkT, MLT, MerT, SqT, FranT, WBP, FrT, SumT, ClT,
>   SNT, CYT, PhyT, PardT, ShT, PrT, ManT, ParsT, PlT*)
>
>   repeats:
>   3x: 1 (7C)
>   2x: 5 (4C, 8C, 16C, 19C, 29Cx)
>   lx: 8 (6C, 9C, 11C, 12C, 13C, 14C, 15C, 18C)
>
>   innovations:
>   additions: 1 (*PlT*)
>   substitutions: 3 (*KnT, SqT, FranT*)

1550 Printers (= *STC* 5071-5074)

>   blocks used: 2
>   inherited: 0;
>   and lost (since 1483): 13 (4C, 6C, 7C, 8C, 9C, 11C, 12C, 13C, 14C, 15C, 16C, 18C,
>   19C)
>   and (since 1542): 1 (29Cx)
>   new: 2 (c28Cx, 30Cx)
>
>   places illustrated: 2
>   *GP*: 0
>   *Tales*: 2 (*KnT, SqT*)
>
>   repeats:
>   lx: 2 (c28Cx, 30Cx)
>
>   innovations:
>   omissions: 19 (*MilT, RvT, CkT, MLT, MerT, FranT, WBP, FrT, SumT, ClT, SNT, CYT,
>   PhyT, PardT, ShT, PrT, ManT, ParsT, PlT*)
>   substitutions: 2 (*KnT, SqT*)

1561 Stow (= *STC* 5075-5076.3)

>   blocks used: 22
>   inherited (from 1550): 1 (3OCx);
>   (from 1526): 14 (c2P, 3P, 4P, c5P, 6P, c7P, 8P, 9P, cl0C, 11P, 12P, cl3P, cl6P, cl7C);
>   reappearing (not used since 1492): 6 (1P, 18P, 13P, 15P, 19P, 22P);
>   and lost (since 1526): 4 (14P, 20P, 23P, 26Px)
>   new: 1 (31Px)

places illustrated: 23
 GP: 22 (Kn, Sq, Yeo, Pr, Mk, Fr, Mer, Cl, ML, Fran, Gu, Ck, Sh, Phy, WB, Pars, P1,
    Mil, Man, Rv, Sum, Pard)
 Tales:1 (KnT)

repeats:
 2x: 1 (4P)
 1x: 21 (1P, c2P, 3P, c5P, 6P, c7P, 8P, 9P, cl0C, 11P, 12P, 13P, cl3P, 15P, cl6P, cl7C, 18P,
    19P, 22P, 30Cx, 3lPx)

innovations:
omissions: 1 (Conc)
substitutions: 13 (Sq, Mk, Mer, ML, Fran, Gu, Ck, Sh, Phy, WB, Mil, Man, Sum)

1598 Speght first ed. (= STC 5077-5079) and 1602 Speght second ed. (= STC 5080-5081)

blocks used: 1
 inherited (from 1550): 1 (30Cx);
 and lost: 0
 new: 0

places illustrated: 1
 GP: 0
 Tales: 1 (KnT)

repeats:
 lx: 1 (30Cx)

innovations: 0

TABLE 1

Woodcuts and locations of Woodcuts

in the Illustrated Versions of the ``General Prologue``

	1483	1492	1498	1526	1561
CaxPro			24Cx		
In			22Cx		
Kn	1C	1P	20C	26Px	1P
Sq	2C	2P			c2P
Yeo	3C	3P			3P
Pr	4C	4P			4P
Mk	5C	5P			c5P
Fr	6C	6P			6P
Mer	7C	18P			c7P.
Cl	8C	8P			8P
ML	9C	13P			9P
Fran	7C	7P			22P
Gu	10C	10P			c10C
Ck	11C	15P			11P
Sh	12C	7P			12P
Phy	13C	13P			c13P
WB	14C	14P			4P
Pars	13C	13P	13C		13P
Pl	15C	15P			15P
Mil	16C	16P			c16P
Man	17C	2P			c17C
Rv	18C	18P			18P
Sum	7C	7P	7C		31Px
Pard	19C	19P	19C		19P
Conc	20C	20P	20C	20P	

Table 1

TABLE 2

Woodcuts and Locations of Woodcuts

in the Canterbury Tales

	1483	1492	1498	1526	1532	1542	1550	1561	1598	1602
KnT	1C	1P	25Cx	26Px	27Cx	29Cx	30Cx	30Cx	30Cx	30Cx
MilT	16C	16P	16C	c16P	16C	16C				
RvT	18C	18P	18C	11P	18C	18C				
CkT	11C	11P	11C	12P	11C	11C				
MLT	9C	9P	9C	9P	9C	9C				
MerT	7C	7P	24Cx		7C	7C				
SqT	2C	2P	2C	c2P	28Cx	29Cx	c28Cx			
FranT	17C	7P	17C	c17C	7C	19C				
WBP	14C	14P	14C	14P	14C	14C				
WBT				14P						
FrT	6C	6P	6C	6P	6C	6C				
SumT	7C	7P	7C	c17C	7C	7C				
ClT	8C	8P	8C	8P	8C	8C				
SNT	21C	4P	4C	4P	4C	4C				
CYT	12C	12P	12C	3P	8C	8C				
PhyT	13C	13P	13C	c13P	13C	13C				
PardT	19C	19P	19C	c10C	19C	19C				
ShT	12C	12P	12C	12P	12C	12C				
PrT	4C	4P	21C	4P	4C	4C				
Th	22C	22P		c7P						
Mel	22C	22P	22C	c7P						
MkT	5C	5P	5C	c5P						
NPT	23C	23P	23C	23P						
ManT	17C	19P	17C	c17C	7C	7C				
ParsT	13C	13P	15C	c13P	15C	15C				
PlT						16C				
Ret			22C 20C							

Table 2

Chapter 4

Tales Told and Tellers of Tales: Illustrations of the Canterbury Tales in the Course of the Eighteenth Century

Betsy Bowden

(Note: All figures referred to in text appear at end of this chapter's Appendix)

Part I

The Battle of Ancients vs. Moderns, in Britain waged on fronts ranging from Grub Street to the universities, pitted Greek and Latin canonical texts against literature composed in English by Milton, Shakespeare, and more. Intellectual tumult fanned eighteenth-century sparks that flared into "medievalism," i.e., the nation's recovery and re-creation of its own vernacular past, as distinguished from Greco-Roman classical culture taught in schools and shared with the rest of Europe. *Paradise Lost* had raised hopes for an English national epic to rival the *Aeneid*, *Iliad*, and *Odyssey*—hopes that led variously to the wit of Alexander Pope, the stupifying fecundity of Sir Richard Blackmore, the ballad collecting of Bishop Thomas Percy, and the Ossianic fabrications of James Macpherson.[1]

Much in Macpherson's style, it turned out, had come straight from Shakespeare. For his compatriots Shakespeare's superiority over the three extant Roman playwrights (Plautus, Terence, and Seneca) made his case ironclad compared to quests for an indigenous Virgil. During the eighteenth century, burgeoning attention to Shakespeare led not only to multiple editions and stagings but also to newly appropriate subjects for imaginative visual art. History and Greco-Roman mythology and the Bible did not, after all, exhaust the potential for picturable events. Shakespearean scenes and characters proliferated at exhibitions at the Royal Academy (founded in 1768), the Society of Artists, and other venues, as well as in book illustrations and published series of engravings such as John Boydell's Shakespeare Gallery (begun 1789, dispersed at auction, 1805).

Peeking from behind that Elizabethan-era stage presence, nudging fellow players, winking at the audience, mouthing dialect hard to understand but assuredly English, stood Chaucer. He who had never been lost was welcomed heartily into the eighteenth century. Each generation therein would, as usual, reconfigure Chaucer to reflect its own concerns and its own self-image.

Compared to Shakespeare's writings, those by Chaucer seldom served as basis for artwork in high-profile exhibits or publications. In the course of the century numerous modernizers, however, were acquainting the public with Chaucer's bawdiest tales, and one scholar (Thomas Tyrwhitt, to be discussed) was establishing and annotating his Middle English text.[2] Meanwhile, book illustrators did supply two publications of Chaucer's collected works with, respectively, portraits of the pilgrims and scenes from the tales told en route to Canterbury. The scenes appear in frontispieces designed by Thomas Stothard for the pocket-sized series of Bell's British Poets (1782-1783). The only complete set of pilgrim portraits that was published during the eighteenth century, probably drawn as well as engraved by several hands, remains uncredited. Each pilgrim on horseback occupies an oval medallion at his or her tale opening in the 1721 folio that was sponsored by entrepreneurs at Oxford and was blamed upon John Urry, who died well aware of his lack of qualifications for editing Middle English.[3] In hopes of encouraging future research, I will be proposing the name of an artist potentially linkable to the Urry edition's portrait series of lively, meaningfully differentiated, Canterbury-bound horses and the pilgrims that they bear.

Besides those two widely accessible sets of book illustrations, examples from which will be discussed here, and besides a few paintings and separate engravings to be listed, eighteenth-century visual Chauceriana includes two substantial but rarely seen items. The bulk of this article will present them for the sake of future scholarly consideration: a nine-piece set of scenes from *Canterbury Tales*, drawn by John H. Mortimer and engraved for a deluxe edition that never came to fruition; and a twenty-four-piece set of pilgrim portraits, drawn by James Jefferys and never prepared for reproduction.

As a final category awaiting analytic attention, several eighteenth-century artists depicted groups of pilgrims gathered at the Tabard or riding toward Canterbury. Mortimer's series includes a departure scene. Two anthologies illustrated by Stothard contain three travelling parties (e.g., figure 34). A pilgrim group by Edward

Francesco Burney (Fanny's cousin) opens volume one of the 1794-1795 Poets of Great Britain series compiled by Robert Anderson. Earliest by half a century is the Urry-edition titlepiece, engraved though not drawn by George Vertue, wherein miniatures of the medallion portraits of a dozen pilgrims ride out from the Tabard innyard. Each of the six group scenes gives a major role to the Wife of Bath, who stars thereafter also in the rival conceptions by Stothard (1807) and William Blake (1809).[4] To conclude this article, with gratitude to Robert N. Essick and G. E. Bentley, Jr. for the suggestion, and with apologies to Blake, I will explicate an early book illustration by Stothard that bridges the gap between the Urry-edition "Departure to Canterbury" and the two artists' paintings.

The present article's survey will select eighteenth-century pictures that have not already been reproduced and discussed in my publications since 1980. (See appendix to this chapter.) During these two decades, materials available for analysis have increased. Most hearteningly, because art historians had stated that Jefferys' pilgrim portraits were lost, I was thrilled to discover his original drawings at the Houghton Library, one year too late, however, for inclusion in my book that reproduces ten eighteenth-century items of visual art related to the Prioress, Pardoner, and Merchant. Jefferys' depiction of the Prioress, for instance, provides a thought-provoking counterweight to the twentieth-century critics who regard as sinfully sensual her "mouth ful smal, and therto softe and reed."[5] Jefferys pictures instead a stern, dignified nun with lips pursed, apparently to stave off observers' potential disapproval of her pet dogs (figure 27).

As a second criterion of selection for this survey, the Wife of Bath does not appear because my research in progress will result in a book on visual and verbal interpretations of herself and her narratives throughout "the long eighteenth century." Accordingly, try as she might to yoo-hoo from the wings, everybody's favorite pilgrim will have to wait for center stage.

For the book-buying public, the Wife of Bath's Tale and other Chaucerian works were first modernized-i.e., paraphrased into Modern English-by John Dryden in *Fables Ancient and Modern*, just before his death in 1700. In 1714 Alexander Pope modernized the Wife's Prologue on the model of his first-ever publication, the Merchant's Tale, modernized in 1709. With such precedent, more writers proceeded to modernize other Canterbury tales, mostly the fabliaux.[6]

Among many eighteenth-century reprintings of the Dryden and Pope modernizations, some with illustrations, this article will address only one item. Diana Beauclerk-Horace Walpole's cherished "Lady Di "-illustrated a folio edition of Dryden's *Fables* (1797) using two distinctive styles that might be termed adult vs. juvenile, or neoclassical vs. proto-Victorian (figures 3-7). Herein I give Beauclerk exceptional status in order to wonder to what extent her two styles might epitomize two Augustan-era attitudes toward the Father of English Literature, who lived during the childhood of the English language. Might sentimentality or caricature or rebelliousness or some other intention predominate in, for example, Beauclerk's rendering of Palamon and Arcite as bare-naked toddlers sporting Cupid-like wings, baby-bonnet helmets, and toy swords?

Other than illustrations to the tales modernized by Dryden and Pope, visual art accompanies the work of only two other eighteenth-century modernizers: one of the Squire's Tale, the other of the Clerk's. As rendered in 1794 by John Penn (grandson of the founder of Pennsylvania), the Squire's Tale was reprinted with his collected *Poems* (1801) featuring two designs by Robert Smirke, a prolific illustrator of Shakespeare. Both were engraved on March 1, 1801. One Squire's Tale scene features the knight brandishing his mirror toward galleries crowded with courtiers. The brass steed behaves as would any flesh-and-blood one, whirling in fear at the unfamiliar situation. In Smirke's other scene, with palm trees and castle looming behind, Canace and three of her women gaze up at the perching falcon.

An excerpt from the other modernization to be illustrated, the Clerk's Tale done by George Ogle in 1739, was reprinted in *Angelica's Ladies Library, or, Parents and Guardians Present* (1794). Within an oval medallion, humbly dressed Griselda curtsies with gratitude to nattily dressed Walter. The scene perforce occurs early in the tale, for *Angelica's Ladies Library* bids farewell to the couple just after the wedding, in bliss prior to the onset of Walter's testing behavior. The anthology's illustrations, including this one engraved on February 20, 1794, were done by Angelica Kauffman, famed as one of few female members of the Royal Academy.[7]

Although the engraving specifies "Painted by Angelica Kauffman," she contributed no paintings on Chaucerian subjects to the well-documented annual exhibitions at the Royal Academy. In 1785, however, her colleague John Francis Rigaud exhibited one with the same title as Kauffman's plate, *Gualtherus and Griselda* (#136 on that year's exhibition list), plus a painting set later in the tale, *Griselda Returning to Her Father* (#130 on the list). I hope that researchers will pursue the fortunes of the Chaucerian paintings by Rigaud and Kauffman, as well as three that Richard Westall exhibited at the Royal Academy in 1785 (*January and May*, #583, and *The Wife of Bath's Tale*, #598) and 1788 (*Chaucer's Wife of Bath's Tale*, #123). Also, for a painting not exhibited there but datable "before 1812," Henry Fuseli envisioned the moment at which *The Knight Finds the Hag Transformed into a Beautiful Young Wife*. "On the evidence of this picture," remarks Richard D. Altick, "the magical transformation fell short of complete success."[8]

By the time of the cluster of Chaucer paintings at Royal Academy exhibitions, 1785-1788, Thomas Tyrwhitt's 1775 edition was making the Middle English text more accessible than it had previously been. However, the choices of topic by Kauffman, Rigaud, Westall, and Fuseli imply that their audiences would more likely be familiar with the modernizations by Ogle, Pope, and Dryden of the tales of the Clerk, Merchant, and Wife of Bath. In addition to reprints elsewhere, these works appeared with other modernizations and Ogle's tale links in his uncompleted but widely distributed *Canterbury Tales of Chaucer, Modernis'd by Several Hands* (1741).

It is certainly Dryden's *Palamon and Arcite* and another modernization from Ogle's 1741 collection, rather than Tyrwhitt's Middle English text, that underlie a publication venture involving Royal Academicians in the 1780s. The Poets' Gallery of Thomas Macklin would have melded verbal and visual art toward a history of English literature. Subscribers were to receive, at regular intervals, engraved artwork accompanied by relevant passages from major British writers. One hundred paintings and subsequent engravings were planned. The twenty-four completed plates included *Constantia* by John Francis Rigaud, with a passage from the Man of Law's Tale modernized by Henry Brooke, and two designs by William Hamilton for the Knight's Tale, *Palamon and Arcite* and *The Death of Arcite*, accompanied by Dryden's modernization.[9] For pragmatic reasons, I must exclude from this survey not only the exhibited paintings but also Macklin's abandoned enterprise.

Part II

Having established into what realms this lengthy article will not be expanded, at a knyght than wol I first bigynne. The tale told first on the road to Canterbury, thanks to aventure or sort or cas there at the Wateryng of Seint Thomas, appealed to eighteenth-century tendencies toward the somber and heroic-which coexisted, of course, with eighteenth-century tendencies toward the spirit of the fabliaux that follow. This long, serious narrative poem is told by the pilgrim regarded as the embodiment of England's glorious medieval past.[10] As literature, the Knight's Tale approaches Greco-Roman epic. Analogously, as subject for artwork it evokes the genre most exalted by eighteenth-century authorities, that of history painting. It is the only tale illustrated by both John H. Mortimer and Thomas Stothard, well demonstrating their divergent interests and styles, and illustrated also by the intriguing Lady Di, displaying her divergent or indeed oppositional styles.

Of the two males Mortimer was a visionary artist, Stothard a hard-working artisan. The former was best known "as a painter of historical and romantic bandit subjects" and "for the freedom and extravagance of his life."[11] Mortimer's innovative techniques continued to influence the British art world long after his short lifetime. He died of profligacy and excess at age thirty-eight, just after a special grant from King George III declared him worthy of Royal Academician status despite his not having followed proper procedures.

Stothard, like his friends William Blake and John Flaxman, was inspired by a Royal Academy retrospective in the year of Mortimer's death, 1779. Having begun a course of study there two years earlier, Stothard duly proceeded to establish himself in London artistic circles and to earn election to the Royal Academy in 1794. By the time of his death in 1834, just short of his eightieth birthday, he had created so many book designs that one might more easily list the major British authors whose works Stothard did not illustrate than those he did.[12] By his own estimate he created about 5,000 designs including, but by no means limited to, book illustrations. Today the Balmanno collection at the British Museum has about 2,200 engravings after Stothard, the Boddington collection at the Huntington Library about 2,500, a twelve-volume collection at the Royal Academy many others, and so on. Moreover, this husband and father supported his double-digit offspring by fashioning delicate silverwork, by executing vast murals and decorated staircases and cabinets and ceilings, by producing piecework in various media such as china, by painting anything that anybody requested in oil or water-color, and by both teaching and serving as chief librarian at the Royal Academy. Stothard did not, however, do engraving.

Influential in a less dramatic way than was Mortimer, Stothard kept on giving the public what it wanted to see. As tastes shifted, someone so omnipresent deserves credit not just for following but rather for helping to create public expectation and appreciation for the softened, romanticized style and subjects that were to prevail during the Victorian era.

Marked differences in style and subject surely appear between Mortimer's epic/heroic conception of the Knight's Tale (figure 1) and Stothard's love-story scene (figure 2). Charles Grignion's engraving of Stothard's design serves as frontispiece to volume two of the British Poets series compiled by entrepreneur John Bell. For twenty-five of Bell's 109 volumes, Mortimer had done frontispieces illustrating such poets as Milton, Spenser, and Swift. Stothard did twenty-eight plates illustrating eighteen minor poets, as well as the fourteen frontispieces for Chaucer's genuine and spurious works. For his texts, John Bell reprinted from the 1721 Urry edition everything except the *Canterbury Tales*, for which he used (unattributed) the well-wrought text that Thomas Tyrwhitt, Chaucer's first philologically responsible editor, had published in 1775 and had genially neglected to copyright.[13]

The tale order of Tyrwhitt's edition provides evidence of a thwarted publication goal for Mortimer's folio-sized series of scenes from *Canterbury Tales*. With two exceptions, the engraving of each Mortimer design supplies a volume and page number (figures 8-12). The page sequence discloses a plan for a sumptuous Chaucer edition in accord with Tyrwhitt's tale ordering, which differs from that of all print editions prior to 1775 and also from the order of Ogle's collected modernizations (1741).

Prior to publication of the 1775 edition, Mortimer could have discussed Chaucerian matters in person with Tyrwhitt. The scholar was active in London intellectual circles, being elected a fellow of the Royal Society in 1771 and a trustee of the British Museum in 1784. Mortimer was famed as a stunningly fast worker, though. Even starting after 1775, he could easily have conceptualized and executed the nine Chaucer scenes presented in 1778 "To S[r.] JOS[A] REYNOLDS President of the Royal Academy" as part of "*Mortimer's Works. A Collection of Fifty Historical Designs* by J. H. Mortimer, and chiefly etched by that admired artist, in his most spirited manner." Engraved by artists other than Mortimer, the scenes from *Canterbury Tales* were published independently in 1787. Engravings then were bound into some but not all copies of the second edition of Tyrwhitt's *Tales*, printed a dozen years after the editor's death in 1786. Next, the Chaucerian scenes were published in 1816 along with the rest of the fifty designs that had qualified Mortimer for the Royal Academy in November 1778, three months before his death.[14]

Thus Mortimer's designs for the Tales were first prepared for public sale in 1787, coincident in time with the several Chaucer paintings exhibited at the Royal Academy (1785, 1788) and with those engraved for Macklin's Poets' Gallery (begun in 1788). The date of Tyrwhitt's death also coincides. It seems probable that, for about a decade, several Royal Academy associates were collaborating with Tyrwhitt toward a lavishly illustrated Chaucer edition that was to differ from the 1721 Urry edition by having a reliable text, and by showing scenes from the tales rather than equestrian portraits of the tellers.

Evidence of the enterprise's magnitude survives as volume and page numbers on the Mortimer engravings. Quite a large typeface would have conveyed the Middle English text. For example, the Miller's Tale would have occupied about twenty-five folio pages, at perhaps thirty lines per page. (Pagination is approximate because a given scene may have been intended for positioning at the point of action portrayed, rather than at a tale's opening.) No doubt each page would have contained more than Chaucer's text *per se*: decorative borders, marginal glosses and indicators, footnotes, perhaps the same text in black-letter typeface, perhaps even a modernization of each tale - although no modernizations then available would have aligned with the Middle English even passage for passage, much less line for line.

Extant page numbering begins at volume two. What was intended for volume one? Presumption of a pending first volume increases the likelihood of input from Tyrwhitt himself. Following his annotated *Canterbury Tales* in 1775, Tyrwhitt in 1778 published a glossary of obsolete words found not only in the *Tales* but also elsewhere in Chaucer's writings-specifically, though, only in "what [Tyrwhitt] conceive[d] to be *the genuine* works of Chaucer" as distinguished from those "falsely ascribed to him, or improperly intermixed with his."[15] Sifting and winnowing the spurious, Tyrwhitt remained engrossed in primary Chaucer scholarship until his death at age fity-six. Probably volume one of the deluxe edition was being held in reserve for whichever dream visions and other poems Tyrwhitt deemed genuine, which he either had started to edit or, as he succumbed to lifelong ill health, was still hoping someday to edit.

For the projected edition's volume two, Mortimer's *Departure of the Canterbury Pilgrimes* could have served as frontispiece; it has no page number (see appendix). Mortimer's series proceeds straight through the first fragment of *Canterbury Tales*, beginning with the Knight's Tale at volume two, page 63 (not visible on figure 1 as cropped). Next follow the tales of the Miller at volume two, page 168; Reeve at volume two, page 193; and Cook at volume two, page 212 (figures 8-10). At this point Tyrwhitt's edition places the tales of the Man of Law and Wife of Bath, both substantial in length, neither one illustrated by Mortimer but both (as noted above) featured during the mid-1780s in paintings by Royal Academy associates John Francis Rigaud and Richard Westall.

Mortimer's designs for the projected edition re-start part way into its third volume: the Friar's Tale at volume three, page 71/72; Summoner's Tale at volume three, page 93; and Merchant's Tale at volume three, page 191 (figures 11-12, appendix). Into the hundred-page interval between Summoner and Merchant, Tyrwhitt's tale order positions the Clerk's Tale. Might the two Clerk's Tale paintings exhibited by Rigaud in 1785, or the painting by Kauffman not engraved until 1794, have initially been associated with this luxury edition? In 1785 at the Royal Academy also, however, Westall exhibited a Merchant's Tale painting with the same title as both Pope's well-known modernization and Mortimer's page-designated scene: *January and May*. Likewise, of William Hamilton's two Knight's Tale scenes for Macklin's Poets' Gallery, one shares its title *Palamon and Arcite* with both Dryden's modernization and Mortimer's page-designated plate. If the unrealized edition did involve individual Canterbury tales illustrated by associates of the Royal Academy, the tale assignments must have allowed for flexibility, overlap, or perhaps indeed competition.

In Mortimer's series the remaining item lacks volume and page number. It illustrates the Pardoner's Tale, which Tyrwhitt's edition situates three tales past that of the Merchant (see appendix). The Pardoner's Tale was not modernized until 1792, by Yorkshire clergyman William Lipscomb. In London, therefore, Mortimer was reading the Middle English text. He understood it well enough to propose an allegorical interpretation for the tale's still mysterious Old Man: Mortimer's four-person scene is entitled *Three Gamblers and Time*.

Mortimer's contemporaries remark not only upon his wildness of spirit-eating wineglasses while drunk, alienating potential patrons, and the like-but also upon his diligence: "Before he attempted any work of importance, he always devoted some time to the perusal of that author which would give him the most information."[16] His unaided reading and sophisticated interpretation of a Middle English text would therefore be conceivable, given Mortimer's multifaceted genius that some observers then or indeed now might well label madness. It seems more probable, though, that Mortimer and other London artists would have consulted with Tyrwhitt himself, the world's only Chaucer scholar.

Overall, evidence points toward a respectable but overambitious enterprise under the aegis of the Royal Academy. The attempt collapsed around the time of Tyrwhitt's death in 1786. Some or all of the contributing artists, including Mortimer posthumously, were at least able to show their work elsewhere. In 1880 F. J. Furnivall urged future scholars to investigate this magnificent scheme to honor (and perchance to profit from) Chaucer. As of 2003, I second that emotion.

Part III

For this projected edition Mortimer was envisioning Chaucer's original four-part Knight's Tale, rather than Dryden's three-part modernization illustrated by Hamilton (for Macklin's Poets' Gallery) and by Beauclerk (discussed below). From Chaucer's tale Mortimer chose a scene midway through Part Two: Palamon and Arcite battling in the grove. (See figure 1.) Mortimer's goals were artistic, not interpretive, in portraying violent human action using lines and angles that run parallel to immobile background objects. Nonetheless, the visual effect resembles twentieth-century textual interpretation of the Knight's Tale, as articulated most influentially by Charles Muscatine: "This subsurface insistence on disorder is the poem's crowning complexity....The impressive, patterned edifice of the noble life, its dignity and richness, its regard for law and decorum, are all bulwarks against the ever-threatening forces of chaos" (189-190).

In Mortimer's conception the chaos appears as negative natural forces within human psyches, as they strive to kill one another, and also as non-human nature, in that the background trees both large and small lean forty-five degrees from the vertical. Trees die slow natural deaths, however, unlike warring cousins. The tilting trees set up a different sort of contrast to the background object that, as would a growing tree, points skyward: a tower constructed by Athenians, perhaps the very tower in which Palamon and Arcite were imprisoned. That one cultural construct, aligned in Mortimer's composition with the two fighters' backbones, signifies the cultural customs and regulations that soon will serve to divert the savage nature of their anger toward a grand ritualistic tournament.

Besides the background tower, the tale's pending reimposition of cultural controls appears at the exact center of the picture's foreground. On the buckler, the crossed bands form an angle parallel to the trees and to the swordsmen's legs and arms, implying disorder. At the buckler's midpoint, however, an ornament that resembles dramatic masks of comedy/tragedy instead displays a stern, straight-lipped facial expression of authoritative disapproval. The disembodied face implies the imminent arrival of Theseus' party, and the consequent cessation of uncontrolled War set into motion by disorderly Love.

Mortimer thus gives visual form to the text's unresolvable ambiguity, as anlyzed by Muscatine and others. To make the rival lovers indistinguishable from one another, Chaucer-the-author substantially changed Boccaccio's *Teseida*, which is a tragedy because the hero Arcita dies and leaves Emilia for second-best Palemone. Instead, the Knight's Tale can be categorized as neither a tragedy nor a comedy with happy ending, because neither Arcite nor Palamon deserves Emelye more. Without knowing that Chaucer changed the *Teseida*, Mortimer used that centered, straight-mouthed mask to convey the idea that the Knight's Tale is neither tragic nor comic.

Other pictorial details also showcase the impossibility of choosing the worthier hero and/or the more deserving husband. In Mortimer's design Arcita [sic] and Palamon, whichever is which, sport different faces and different body types. Neither one, however, looks markedly nobler or stronger or more handsome or better proportioned than the other. The left-hand fighter is short-waisted, with a beard and a larger nose than has his clean-shaven, long-waisted cousin. Making glaring eye contact, the cousins are leaping into mirror-image stances such that both men's hair and garments billow. A brawny chest, with right arm raised to chop, does symmetrical battle against a brawny back with right arm lowered to stab. They wear equivalent, approximately authentic Athenian garb that exposes musculature for their entire upper bodies, arms, and lower legs.

The conventions of narrative art, for Mortimer and other artists to be discussed, call for each illustration to depict an exact moment from the text. Herein, which is it? On the ground below the swordfighters lie broken spears and a helmet cast aside, evidence that the duel has lasted for some time. It may be that Mortimer found comic relief at a particular line in the midst of tragic grandeur, but that he refrained from literally picturing Chaucer's line 1660, " Up to the ancle foghte they in hir blood."

In contrast to the broken war gear strewn underfoot in Mortimer's folio-sized conception, an upright helmet and an intact spear hover above Stothard's tiny medallion frontispiece for the Bell edition. (See figure 2.) The scene is specified by quotation of Chaucer's lines 1053-1054. It captures the moment at which the glum prisoner, presumably Palamon, who will claim first sighting, first turns his eyes toward Emelye. In Stothard's design, therefore, precariously balanced weaponry crowns the very moment at which Love for an oblivious female is about to spark War between the two captured cousins. The medallion's frame thus helps to convey the tale's complexity. In other of Stothard's Bell-edition frontispieces, framing devices likewise enrich the scene portrayed. As an example besides the two pictures discussed below, for the "Departure to Canterbury" a valid religious pilgrimage goal is signified by scallop shells that decorate the frame atop a scene of male pilgrims ogling the Wife of Bath (figures 13-14, appendix).

Besides the loose weapons in both artists' conceptions of the Knight's Tale, the background of Stothard's picture corresponds to that in Mortimer's. Both use curving trees and underbrush to evoke the wilderness of nature against which human culture tries to erect mental and social structures regulating Love and War. Stothard makes the Athenian tower more prominent than does Mortimer, probably for the pragmatic reason that everything significant has to be visible within a two-and-a-half-inch circle.

Resembling Mortimer also, indeed resembling any artist influenced by Greco-Roman classical standards, Stothard reveals the maximum musculature allowable in an increasingly restrictive society that sought to repress what Blake calls the Human Form Divine.[17] Emelye's seamless, tight-fitting upper garment clings to biceps and forearms appropriate to her Amazonian heritage. Likewise it lightly covers her breasts, including a nipple more noticeable in the enlargement than on the Bell-edition page. Emelye's large hand fearlessly grasps a rose's thorny stem. Her hair "a yerde long, I gesse," as specified in the Knight's Tale, is flowing free rather than "broyded in a tresse" (I:1049-1050).

These pictorial hints of female strength and freedom, alongside the imprisoned and marginalized male head, give to Stothard's Emelye the central role denied her by the male characters in a tale wherein her only speech is a futile prayer to Diana. Chaucer's text itself, of course, creates the tension whereby Stothard and many other readers would like to give Emelye more of a voice.

Lady Diana Beauclerk, artiste and woman-about-town, shared her own name with the "chaste goddesse of the wodes grene" to whom Emelye prays for a husbandless lifespan (I:2297). For one of the three folio-sized illustrations to Dryden's three-part *Palamon and Arcite*, Beauclerk chose dramatic action that focusses upon her namesake's two altars, one still flaming and the other billowing black smoke. (See figure 3.) She shows the exact moment of Diana's divine signal, which Dryden bowdlerized such that the "blody dropes" (I:2340) spurting from a phallic firebrand, for example, become dripping "Sweat of Sanguin Hue." In the modernization Emily turns her eyes from the ill omen, then rends the sky "with loud Shrieks and Clamours" until Diana appears.[18] Beauclerk's white-clad Emily, startled but not yet clamouring, is reaching for a female attendant's support at the last moment in her lifetime that she can still believe that rituals and prayers to Diana might bring results. Exactly embodying the literary text at hand, Beauclerk's Emily wears the unbound hair and oak-leaf crown described by Dryden. Well exemplifying eighteenth-century strictures on the education of female artists, who were excluded from "life drawing" of nude or near-nude models, Emily and her attendants pose before neoclassical columns and walls while wearing loose draperies that reveal musculature for no more than their arms, necks, and upper chests. Three children are permitted knee-length gowns, though; the youngest even uncovers some thigh. The discrepancy implies Beauclerk's exasperation toward the hypocrisy, verging on pedophilia, of an artistic establishment that stifled aesthetic appreciation for human bodies excepting those enveloped in baby fat.

In another Beauclerk design, the rivals for Emily's reluctant hand wear neoclassical warriors' attire that, in addition to arm and neck areas, exposes allowable male calf muscles. (See figure 4.) Although the background trees appear unkempt, civilization looms nearby. This grove near Athens is much frequented by lovers and others who dismount to complain or relax, and who then go their way, for someone has installed there a mounting block. Arcite's horse watches the action, anticipating a longer rest break now that the mounting block is occupied by some human other than its rider.

Again Beauclerk, following the conventions of eighteenth-century narrative artwork, pinpoints a precise moment in the literary text being illustrated. At Dryden's line 141 the unarmed figure has just declared, "I am *Palamon* thy mortal Foe," while the other has not yet "His Sword unsheath'd." As a counterpart to Emily's last moment of potential spinsterhood, therefore, Beauclerk depicts the separated cousins' first moment of mutual recognition and mutual wrath. Anon Arcite will resheathe, and will promise to return with a second set of weapons.

Come the actual fight, though, my goodness gracious, laddies, what a cute little bum and what a cute little belly. (See figure 5.) The chubby cherubs Palamon and Arcite draw swordlets above the title to Dryden's Book Two, while a disembodied head implies authorities' disapproval (as does the shield ornament in Mortimer's conception). To what extent is Beauclerk rebelling against an artistic climate wherein Greco-Roman-inspired naked adult flesh was increasingly disallowed? Is she idiosyncratic? Or part of a Zeitgeist whereby England's medieval past was being regarded, sentimentally or sarcastically or seriously, as the childhood of the nation? Is her bipolar response specific to Dryden's medieval and classical *Fables*? Or applicable to other literature as well? Might Beauclerk simply be indulging a fondness for caricature, aside from any large issues of nudity in visual art or interpretation in literary history? Because this article deals with illustrations to Chaucer's text itself, holding at bay the complications aroused by its paraphrased modernizations, herein I merely hope to encourage research by reproducing this and two more of Beauclerk's marginal decorations to the poem *Palamon and Arcite*.

At the end of Dryden's Book One, a pre-pubescent Emily arranges her garland. (See figure 6.) In the misty distance stands an adult male observer atop a tower, not imprisoned in it, supporting a flag that signals martial interests, not marital ones. From that distance, moreover, he could scarce distinguish the rosebush from the back of the little girl's beflowered head. Might Beauclerk be suggesting that the male world ought to mind its own business?

Above the title to Dryden's Book Three, as a final example, Emily and Palamon mourn the death of Arcite. (See figure 7.) His laurel wreath lies fallen; his spear serves as bedpost. Only the one mourner's drapery and the other's bare chest show these children to be respectively female and male. With grief so unisex and everybody underage, perhaps Beauclerk's marginal Emily will be allowed to retain her maidenhood for a little while longer after all.

Part IV

Two decades before Beauclerk's tribute to Emily's unwed state, John Mortimer's many friends hoped that his marriage on February 11, 1775 would help to calm him down; but he died just three years and fifty-one weeks later. It was probably around the time of his leaving bachelorhood behind that Mortimer talked with Tyrwhitt about creating nine scenes for *Canterbury Tales*, including the Knight's Tale discussed above and including three reproduced and analyzed elsewhere (figure 1, appendix).

Like those four, Mortimer's five designs to be next considered seem action photographs snapped during five stage plays (figures 8-12). I will suggest that Mortimer was adapting not only the recent genre of artwork illustrating British plays and other British literature but also a satiric genre wherein pictures themselves create a serial narrative caricaturing society, best known from William Hogarth (1697-1764). In a series like "Rake's Progress" or "Marriage à la Mode," Mortimer perhaps found inspiration not only for his own "Progress of Vice" but also for illustrating Chaucer's given tale order as a "Progress of" something not so allegorically succinct. From his opening scene of the pilgrims' mounting up in the Tabard innyard and flirting outrageously, Squire with Prioress as well as Friar with Wife, Mortimer's series moves to the pre-Christian world of the Knight's Tale, which disallows celibacy whether sacred or secular (figure 1, appendix). Subsequent to the five fabliaux designs to be discussed next, Mortimer illustrated a fabliau even more disrespectful toward marriage as an institution. Therein, as May climbs onto January's back to reach her ready lover in the pear tree, her foot reveals a devilish cloven hoof (see appendix). Next, in face of the variety still awaiting illustration in Tyrwhitt's tale order, such as the Franklin's Tale that offers closure to the "marriage group" discussed by twentieth-century commentators, Mortimer leapt on ahead to the Pardoner's Tale (see appendix). In his final scene chosen, Time brings certain death to young rowdies regardless of any such cultural controls as marriage or a religion of forgiveness.

Whether or not Mortimer intended linear narrative by his choice of scenes from each tale, the five interrelated fabliaux (figures 8-12) gave him the opportunity to portray disorderly events that encroach upon the everyday lives of ordinary people at home, within bourgeois households like his own just beginning, in place of the bandits and

romance heroes and historical juggernauts that had inspired his artwork so far. In terms of the "roadside drama" of Chaucer's frame
story, furthermore, these five designs illustrate the tales for which
interpilgrim conflict is most definitively rechanneled toward story-
telling: the Friar's insulting account of a summoner cursed to hell; the
infuriated Summoner's response in which a greedy friar gets the hot
air that he deserves; the disclaiming Miller's story of three amorous
men each getting his just deserts; the infuriated Reeve's response dis-
gracing millers; and the unfinished Cook's Tale aimed at requiting the
Host's banter.[19]

In each of Mortimer's illustrations to the five interlinked fabliaux,
as was usual in the genre of narrative artwork based foremost upon
Shakespeare, the characters' facial expressions and bodily gestures
capture a moment frozen in time, i.e., a single line or couplet of
Chaucer's text. Three of the five dramatic moments feature, as predominant emotion, the one that Chaucer's fictional storytellers are projecting and that amateur actors find easiest to perform: anger. Likewise
Mortimer chose an angry encounter from many potential scenes within the first Canterbury tale, itself calmly told (figure 1).

Unlike the Knight's Tale, though, the fabliaux could offer Mortimer
but minimal opportunity to depict rippling musculature in epic/heroic
poses. For these five tales, he displays artistic virtuosity instead at a
range of male body types, clad in a variety of more-or-less medieval
garments probably deduced from stage drama. The protagonists'
diverse physiques interact either inside or in front of precisely detailed
lower- and middle-class homes, framed by women and household
goods and horses' rear ends. Chaos and disorder loom, we will see, not
only close to the epic/heroic Athens of the Knight's Tale but also close
by or inside the coziest of typical British homes. It is as if Mortimer
were trying to figure out, in excruciating visual detail, how any shape
of a man can possibly costume and mask himself to pretend to fit into
ordinary, everyday home life.

For the Miller's Tale Mortimer depicts lines 3474-3475: "This carpenter. . . hente hym [Nicholas] by the sholdres myghtily." (See figure
8.) Just two lines earlier, bulky Robyn hove in the door; just one line
later, the old man will start shaking hende Nicholas, upon whom sunlight pours as if it were divine revelation. The latter's doublet, hose,
and other attire look more appropriate to an Elizabethan-era stage than
to an Oxford study, and Cambridge students wear collegiate robes in
Mortimer's conception of the Reeve's Tale (figure 9). Therefore, the

intentionally anachronistic clothing emphasizes Nicholas' thespian skill at gazing "upward into the eir" (I:3473). He might well double as Hamlet seeing the ghost.

Each of the three figures' musculature bulges within tightfitting garments, Robyn's so snug that only a hole lets his elbow bend. He and Nicholas are both long-waisted in physique, Robyn hunch-backed besides. Two styles of curly dark hair signal the young men's respective attitudes, short and servile vs. flowing and visionary. In contrast to them John is short-waisted, bearded, behatted, and elderly but (being a carpenter) far from frail. His face tilts sideways and downward, counterpart to Nicholas' face tilting upward at the same sideways angle. Robyn's profile aligns with the musical instrument so carelessly tossed atop books, about to slide off the ledge along with the dangling document.

Within Nicholas' room, disarray appears also as strewn papers and books, dishevelled bedcurtains, remnants of the broken-down door (angled like the student's lower legs), and on the stool a hat with feather that links it visually to the precariously balanced inkwell. On the lit-up windowsill, however, in sharp contrast to clutter elsewhere, a perfect right triangle is formed by a rod (possibly but not obviously music-related) and a vase containing "herbes swoote" (I:3205). The room's corner timbers form right triangles less decisively than do the rod and window frame, for the walls are otherwise constructed of randomly scattered blocks and blotches.

The picture's lighting and composition draw an observer's eye in the direction of Nicholas' gaze, thereby toward that right triangle formed by a sweet-smelling room decoration and an indeterminate rod, both standing tall at the sunlit window. Nicholas' disorderly lifestyle and his dramaturgical skill will let him use that window to escape, as it were, from the confines and expectations of a married couple's home. Thus Mortimer's visual details echo Chaucer's patterns of poetic imagery, which accumulate meaning in the course of the Miller's Tale to culminate in pitch darkness where rods, both metaphorical and literal, are wielded in the course of not-so-sweet-smelling action athwart a windowsill.

Elsewhere in the *Tales*, on a windowsill near Trompington leans a disproportionately small twenty-year-old daughter. (See figure 9.) From the bedroom Malyne is watching the action of Reeve's Tale lines 4024-4025: "Aleyn, welcome," says her dad Symkyn, gladhanding the good-looking college guys, "by my lyf! / And John also, how now, what do ye heer?" Mortimer puts the two students into collegiate robes, wearing the kind of caps later called "tam-o-shanters" (after Robert Burns's poem, according to the *Oxford English Dictionary*) but long associated with Scotland and the north of England, the birthplace of John and Aleyn.

In profile and at three-quarters facial angle, respectively, the students smile and attempt to make eye contact with the would-be grain thief, who avoids meeting their eyes. Their two shapes of pointed nose are differentiated from his "camus" one (I:3934, pug). Mortimer need not have perused Tyrwhitt's glossary-in-progress for basic meanings of "camus" and other obsolete words, such as Symkyn's visible "panade" or the "thwitel" hidden in his hose (1:3929-3934, two kinds of dagger). Most were defined in the earliest glossary, in Thomas Speght's 1598 edition, and reprinted thereafter.[20]

Mortimer's re-creation of Chaucer's descriptive text falters only for the "typet bounden aboute his [Symkyn's] heed," shown more like a turban (I:3953). Its jaunty feather visually connects the conversational interlude below to the gigantic dead bird nailed to the wall above, alongside a framed half-Malyne whose full size would not much surpass that of the bird. As comparison, in Mortimer's Summoner's Tale scene the woman appears small because distant (figure 12). Here Mortimer's juxtaposition of tiny daughter and immense bird, both displayed on the same visual plane, conveys the implication from Chaucer's text that Malyne's tender feelings matter to the visitors not much more than do those of the tender goose that she will help to roast for their dining pleasure.

The tender feelings of the packhorse are, of course, central to the plot. Fluttering eyelashes signal the urges that will impel Bayard not to the nearest grainbin, upon release, but rather with a "wehee" in pursuit of wild mares (I:4066). Pricking his ears and tossing his forelock, he paws the ground in eager anticipation.

Bayard appears knock-kneed while pawing, thereby resembling several Urry-edition horses as well as the Knight's horse in Mortimer's departure scene (figures 29-32, appendix). Like many artists fully proficient at landscapes, still life, and the human body, Mortimer tends to evade the ultimate equine challenge. The bone structure of horses, their thin-skinned musculature, their complex movements, their disinclination to pose: such characteristics make them notoriously difficult to portray. Most difficult of all, as will be noted in reference to the Urry-edition pilgrims, is the fitting of a rider's leg to a horse's convex body shape. Even the phenomenal Mortimer may have experienced humility upon seeing the work of a colleague at the Society of Artists, George Stubbs. Born a currier's son in 1724, Stubbs researched equine anatomy and specialized his artwork such that by 1756 he could charge a hundred guineas to paint a horse's portrait.[21]

Upon the beast of burden rendered to the best of Mortimer's ability, light falls such that exactly half of the grainsack in the foreground is illuminated, with that sunlit part tied in half. In effect the lighting marks off grainsack divisions that reflect relationships among the three men: a smaller matched pair of grain guardians wear dark garments as contrast to the temporarily successful beguiler, in light-colored sunlit clothing, whom they then will beguile regarding not only their college's grain but also his daughter and wife. Although the light-colored attire signals the miller's verbal skill at pretended innocence, he will be left with neither the dark nor the light half of the grainsack that he covets.

The protagonists stand on a bridge over the millstream. The archway beneath them mirrors mechanistic forms elsewhere, notably the discarded millstone behind Symkyn and the functional gears indoors. Less directly, the arch shares its shape with the grainsack and with the rounded edges of plaster smeared onto irregular wooden walls. Like the lighting, these partly unifying effects of composition contribute toward the visual sense that Symkyn, despite bourgeois social pretensions, is ultimately unable to keep even his own millhouse in order.

Mortimer's father owned a mill at Eastbourne, according to the *DNB*, and sometimes served as collector of customs. In this Reeve's Tale design, thus, the irregularities appear in a backdrop that Mortimer would have associated with his own boyhood, while the human interactions cast a cloak of superficial cultural pleasantries over feelings of mutual distrust and ill intentions. From a tale with no shortage of action-driven scenes, that is, Mortimer chose a moment in which powerful emotions remain repressed and conflict latent. There is no reason to suppose that Mortimer's rural childhood was anything but happy, in a well-off two-parent household. At some point after an artistically inclined uncle sponsored his apprenticeship to a master painter in London, however, the young Mortimer began exhibiting erratic behavior inextricable from artistic brilliance.

In contrast to his design for the Reeve's Tale, and as a possible reflection of the course of Mortimer's own life, his design for the Cook's Tale shows potential disorder not repressed but instead ejected decisively from a neatly kept urban household. (See figure 10.) Of the fragment's fifty-seven lines, Mortimer illustrates line 4412, in which the apprentice's master "bad hym go, with sorwe and with meschance." By entitling his picture *The Coke and Perkin*, Mortimer has shifted the tale's situation toward autobiography. In Middle English the master of the rotten-apple apprentice is not a cook but a "vitaillier," spelled differently at Mortimer's time (I:4366, *Oxford English Dictionary* s.v. victualler). As the keeper of an eating-house or inn like the Tabard, the character in Chaucer's tale figures into the pilgrim Cook's reciprocal bantering with Harry Bailly.

Mortimer directs attention instead to the interpersonal conflict within the narrative, that of responsible maturity vs. unbridled youth. The two figures' gestures and facial expressions approach caricatured allegory: full-faced adult Anger shouting "Get outta here and good riddance," and near-profile adolescent Anger snarling, "Getcher blankety-blank hands offa me" while defiantly tossing the "lokkes blake, ykembd ful fetisly" specified by Chaucer (I:4369).

The short, tubby authority figure wears a chef's hat and a simple short gown; at his belt dangle chopping knives. The ex-apprentice has yet to give back his set of chopping knives and his apron, which protects far fancier clothing than his master's: ornamented shoes and hosiery, elegant waistcoat, shirt with multi-buttoned cuffs, feathered cap. A slight sense of guilt about the boy's mouth, a slight sense of uncertainty in his downcast eyes-nothing else prevents Perkyn from whirling to smother the man with his own apron and stab him with his own knives and thus earn punishment well beyond those after-revel occasions at Newgate gaol. Instead the lad leaves a well-constructed home, with bread cooling on the windowsill, for the shop that fronts his friend's wife's swyving business.

Compared to Mortimer's design for the Reeve's Tale, which shows the off-center doorway of a multi-use building depicted at an angle, here the action is squarely centered in front of the entryway to a solid middle-class domicile complete with boot-scraper, lintel ornaments, and decorative foliage. Among Mortimer's fabliaux scenes, only this one hints at a positive outlook for a male householder and his domain. It is anger and anger alone, though, anger aimed at destroying youthful impetuous spirits, that may perhaps serve to shield domestic life from ever-looming chaos.

For the two tales bitterly spewed at one another by the pilgrim Friar and Summoner, Mortimer's two designs incorporate variations on the emotion of anger so central to his conception of the Cook's Tale (figures 10-12). In the Friar's Tale, the old woman's righteous anger sets off the action depicted of line 1639, " And with that word this foule feend hym hente." The exact line illustrated for the Summoner's Tale is less apparent. At first glance, the three facial expressions and the friar's gestures might seem applicable to either of two situations: either his delivery of a long-winded sermon on the deadly sin of Ire, or else his angry reaction to Thomas' gift of (as it were) wind. Before considering that choice, let us look to the assuredly hell-bent summoner in the Friar's Tale.

As compositional strategy for his Friar's Tale design, Mortimer uses the same device as in his portrayal of the anger of Palamon and Arcite. (See figure 11, cf. figure 1.) In each design, the motionless trunk and limbs of a leaning tree establish parallel lines that heighten contrast to the violently active human trunks and limbs in the foreground. In the background of each picture rises a tower, here that of the local church, each implying a cultural construct above and beyond the foreground's display of disorderly human nature.

For the Friar's Tale, old Mabely is aligned with the base of the tree that shades her humble home. Rooted there "upon hir knees," she has already repeated her curse with an offer of repentance (III: 1625-1629). The central figure, having rejected that repentance, has just heard from the devil his due (III:1630-1638). The summoner makes terrorized eye contact with Mabely's slit eyes glaring in profile. Clutching the pan included in her curse, he is jerked backward so abruptly that his hat-feathered, but resembling in shape a king's crown-is sliding forward.

At the same moment the seizer, aligned with tree limbs and rooftop, is lurching forward so abruptly that his hat-black, though lacking the fringe specified at line 1383-is sliding backward to reveal devilish horns. Thus Mortimer reveals to observers what the pictured summoner sees instead in Mabely's eyes: that he is inextricably in league with the devil himself. The two male figures, though met by chance, wear correspondingly lavish garments with matching neck ruffs and sleeve scallops. Their faces, shown in three-quarters profile from opposite angles, mirror one another in beard and nose shape. The fiend has shorter hair and no mustache, though. Perhaps future researchers will seek and find his prototype among eighteenth-century visual representations of the hero...excuse me, the villain of *Paradise Lost*.

The fiend differs also from his soul brother in that he bears bow and arrows, as specified at line 1381, rather than the sword so inappropriate to a representative of the church. Mabely's pan could have had another size or shape. By making the hell-bound pan look like a buckler, Mortimer emphasizes the sword at the summoner's side.

Sunlight plays upon the churchman's last chance for heaven, just refused, and his consequent last moment on earth, Also illuminated are the little house and the two horses, such that the lighting implies earthly values that will endure after line 1640, "Body and soule he with the devel wente." Now, horses do not follow bad riders to hell; indeed, lines 1537-1570 of this tale speak against any equine's dispatch there even for its own inadequacies. Mortimer could have depicted the same dramatic moment with horses nowhere in sight. Their prominent position indicates that, although Mabely has lost that one pan, she will retain her tidy cottage and her household goods, and will furthermore become rightful owner of quite a magnificent team.

At far left, bony haunches reveal that the overdressed summoner has cruelly been underfeeding his mount. However, an enterprising widow can sell one pricey piece of harness, such as the devil's scalloped breastplate, in order to buy sufficient fodder and then set herself up in some lucrative business. Both equine partners will cooperate. Despite startling activity on its back, the fiend's horse pricks calm ears and peers straight toward Mabely with a sympathetic expression. The summoner's loosed horse, starved though he be, turns away not to graze but to gaze toward spiritual nourishment: the church tower. In Mortimer's interpretation of this Canterbury tale, an angry but unvictimized woman kneels in the process of her vindication both sacred and secular. She belongs right there in her own home, alone.

In Mortimer's design for the Summoner's Tale, the woman instead just worries and keeps to the background. (See figure 12.) Nor is there any sign of the animal whose world the friar violates, in that most quintessentially Chaucerian of details, "And fro the bench he droof awey the cat" (III:1775). Doubtless it has reclaimed its rightful spot just beyond the left margin of the picture, for by this point in the tale Friar John no longer occupies the bench. After arising to embrace the wife at line 1802, perhaps he sat back down on the bed to deliver his tedious sermon. If so, because Thomas' mouth is open, this scene would represent the homeowner's interjection either at lines 1948-1953, in tandem with the friar's response, "O Thomas, dostow so?" or else at lines 2094-2098, with the response, "Yif me thanne of thy gold."

However, according to the conventions of British narrative artwork in general and of Mortimer's Chaucer drawings in particular, it is likelier that this scene illustrates a precise moment of heightened drama. That moment occurs just past line 2149, "Amydde his hand he leet the frere a fart." With both hands upraised, having just jerked one out from under the covers, the friar is poised to "up stirte as dooth a wood leoun" (III:2152). The lightcolored bedclothes draw an observer's eye toward Thomas' open mouth. It emits a belch, as visible counterpart to what is unfit for artwork unless by the likes of Hieronymus Bosch and the illuminators of just a few medieval manuscripts.

Thematic connections between the tales of Miller and Summoner-i.e., intestinal gas as major plot element-led Mortimer to envision scenes set in two bedchambers with meaningful similarities and differences. Compared to the house of John the carpenter (figure 8), Thomas' domain displays evidence of wealth and an orderly lifestyle. Although both stage settings (as it were) feature exposed beams, panels cover Thomas' ceiling and much of the walls. His flooring consists of inlaid blocks, not rough boards like John's, and a proper bedcurtain drapes symmetrically. On the mantelpiece, in contrast to Nicholas' overflowing shelf, the couple's household goods stand in neat array. To the right of the fireplace is propped a musical instrument, which must see far less action than the one flung aside by Nicholas.

In front of the centered fireplace frets the wife, apparently sprouting out of the friar's neck. She does seem oddly placed and too small, like Malyne at the mill (figure 9). However, her size is proportionate to the fireplace and to objects on its mantelpiece, albeit not to the huge feathered hat hung far above human reach. It therefore seems probable that Mortimer distorted the perspective somewhat, having intended to make the wife and the wall seem further away, and the bedroom thus notably larger than Nicolas' cozy chamber. It appears larger also than the entire cottage controlled by a justly angry woman in its companion piece (figure 11). Inside such a spacious and wealthy home, though, a woman like Thomas' wife has no control over her husband's anger or his bodily emissions or his finances or religion or impending death. The ultimate in upper-middle-class cultural values, therefore, keep chaos at bay no more effectively than does the idealized, fully fictional worldview of the epic/heroic Knight's Tale.

Mortimer's lightning-fast working practices were such that he might well have drawn the six pictures discussed here one right after the other, in the same order that they appear in the projected multi-volume Chaucer edition. The three scenes not discussed here also could fit into a nine-item progression involving exuberance and domesticity and anger and death. The series opens with unrepressed sexuality among pilgrims both sacred and secular, and moves on past the Summoner's Tale to the pear-tree scene of the Merchant's Tale, followed by Time sending three riotours up the crooked way to their violent end (see appendix). Regardless of order of execution, and regardless of the artist's intentions toward linear progression, the nine designs do inter-relate as a thematically unified set in which Mortimer-the-newly-wed (or perhaps Mortimer-the-betrothed, or Mortimer-the-urged-to-wed-by-well-meaning-friends) was giving visual shape to his worries about doing what was normally done by Londoners in their thirties, in his case with a Miss Jane Hurrell toward whom he ought to feel what the Athenian cousins felt for Emelye. In the sequence of tales told en route to Canterbury, Mortimer found an outlet for his suspicions that the institution of marriage might not have such a soothing effect after all upon what might nowadays be termed his brain-chemical imbalance.

Imbalanced or no, madman or genius, Mortimer raised the stakes on existing traditions of narrative artwork. He was using visual-art techniques both obvious and subtle, both established and innovative, to transform his own imagined performance of the Middle English text into a series of implied audiovisual stagings, each one stopframed at a moment in time. Contemporary artists were doing the same for the more accessible language of Shakespeare and other post-medieval writers. Nobody prior to Mortimer, though, took on Chaucer.

It is tempting to wonder whether Mortimer's sketches for other Canterbury tales may someday surface, thanks to art historians' ongo-ing documentation efforts-sketches that he did not have time to finish before preparing for presentation of his Royal Academy portfolio, and then dying. If so, evidence may turn up intermingled in drawers or files with never-reproduced work by the many younger artists who began their careers by imitating Mortimer's unconventional style, such as William Blake, John Flaxman, Henry Fuseli, James Jefferys (figures 15-28), and Thomas Stothard (figures 2, 13, 14).

Part V

Initially inspired by Mortimer, Stothard developed his own style in accord with public expectations and with the need to support his grow-ing family. Like his Knight's Tale scene discussed, two of Stothard's other plates for specific Canterbury tales in Bell's British Poets exem-plify his scrupulous carrying out of the task assigned to him by a pay-ing publisher. As frontispiece to volume five Stothard illustrated the Second Nun's Tale, for which no modernization yet existed. (See fig-ure 13.) He chose it instead of three other tales that were likewise available only in Middle English. For volume five also, however, he decided against the Nun's Priest's Tale, well-known from Dryden's modernization, which Stothard would illustrate two decades later.[22]

As an art student in his mid-twenties, with no special language training, Stothard conscientiously read and envisioned for himself Tyrwhitt's Middle English text of the Second Nun's Tale and other works. If my reconstruction is valid concerning Tyrwhitt's participation in a grandiose Royal Academy project, perhaps he would have spoken with a lowly student there, Stothard, who confided an interest in Chaucer. However, the scholar could not have known that said student's conceptions were intended to illustrate Tyrwhitt's own pirated text. In a letter regarding the Bell series, he expresses surprise at its use of his edition and disdain toward its purchasers: "Having given them a picture at the beginning of each volume, he [Bell] seems to have thought (and perhaps with reason) that they would be perfectly unconcerned about everything else."[23]

More likely, therefore, Stothard unaided read through the five tales for volume five. He found a dramatic moment, suitable for the medallion's shape and size, in lines 222-223 of the Second Nun's Tale. One might quibble with details. If the open book is the one with is "wordes all with gold ywriten," it ought to be three miles away (VIII:210, 173); and the angel ought to bear a second lily-rose crown to reward Valerian at line 224. Perhaps a crown will blossom from the angel's clenched left hand, though, and maybe the book is just a book. For this very small round space, Stothard has successfully delineated a three-person indoor scene with sacred connotations and with easy-to-interpret emotions: the dark-clad man's amazement, the barefooted woman's humble devotion, and the white-robed angel's air of authority, reinforced by a second angel's head topping the frame of the medallion.

Both in composition and in sacred vs. secular subject matter, the Second Nun's Tale design invites comparison with the frontispiece to Bell's volume four. (See figure 14.) For the latter Stothard chose, from eight tales therein, the only bawdy one. The Shipman's Tale happens also to be the sole one of the eight that was modernized, albeit not widely distributed, prior to William Lipscomb's 1795 collection. Because Chaucer's bawdiest tales were those most often modernized, the coincidence does not change the likelihood that Stothard read in Middle English all eight tales for Bell's volume four.[24]

There Stothard quotes lines 156-157 of the Shipman's Tale beneath a scene that, both visually and ethically, counterbalances the frontispiece to Bell's volume five. Set outdoors not indoors, emanating sinfulness not saintliness, betokening a wife's reward for adultery not chastity, Stothard's design positions on the left a dark-clad male expressing an overt emotion: lechery. The monk's dangling cross points toward his large bare foot, poking suggestively out from his robe. The merchant's wife reciprocates by revealing just the tip of her shoe. While moving her left leg and elbow coyly away, she thrusts her right side toward Daun John. She makes haughty eye contact beneath an elaborate hairdo, counterpart to his hypocritical tonsure, and beneath a peaked hat-this shape being both associated with witches and, in the course of eighteenth-century fashion, sometimes worn by stylish ladies.[25]

At the right of the picture, placed parallel to the hovering angel and open book of the frontispiece to Bell's volume five, is the "mayde child" who may or may not be overhearing the adults at play in Chaucer's text (VII:95). Stothard has her heedlessly chase a butterfly and ignore the sexual transaction between mother and monk-ignore it, that is, within the medallion itself. To indicate this tale's complexity, on the frame overhead Stothard reproduces the face, with assymetrically billowing hair, of that same little girl. At the analogous position above the Second Nun's Tale medallion, the adult male angel head gazes outward from the page (figure 13). In contrast, this girl fixes her eyes downward in order to keep watch over worldly activities below. The maid-child's apparent innocence sees all, knows all, and (much like Chaucer's text itself) forces us observers to make our own decisions about right and wrong.

Besides the three plates reproduced and discussed here, Stothard did eleven more Chaucer frontispieces for Bell's British Poets. In volume eight, for example, a youthful Pandarus peeks at Troilus and Criseyde lolling in bed.[26] For every design, the artist seems conscientiously to have read the assigned Middle English. Beyond Chaucer, and beyond Bell's British Poets, Stothard also envisioned scenes and characters from hundreds of other works of literature. By the early nineteenth century, Stothard's book illustrations dominated readers' visualizations of the creative output of nearly every British author in print. Only for Shakespeare did Stothard have numerous artistic rivals. His designs were known to all readers of English literature, appreciated by some, and taken for granted by the rest.

Part VI

In contrast, another artist from the generation of Blake and Stothard remained little-known even to his contemporaries because he died in his early thirties, at an even younger age than had his role model Mortimer. In 1771, James Jefferys first exhibited his artwork with Mortimer's colleagues at the Society of Artists. According to the art historians who rediscovered him in 1976, "the early drawings of Jefferys are sufficiently close in style to Mortimer for confusion."[27] In 1772 Jefferys entered the Royal Academy Schools and began absorbing other artistic influences, such that his Canterbury pilgrims tend toward caricature much more than does anything from Mortimer's hand.

In 1774 Jefferys won major prizes from both the Society of Artists and the Royal Academy, plus the first "travelling scholarship" awarded by the Society of Dilettanti. With the stipend he led a productive albeit rowdy life in Rome, returning to England at the approximate time of Mortimer's death, 1778-1779. While executing his Chaucerian portrait gallery, probably on assignment, Jefferys resided at the rural home of a well-off friend of his well respected father. He completed the task on September 12, 1781. Publication must have been intended, had he not died in 1784, for an engraving of the Friar accompanies Jefferys' original drawings now at the Houghton Library (figure 15). Engraved reproductions of his Host and Pardoner may await discovery elsewhere, on the evidence of an 1848 estate-auction catalogue.[28]

Examination of thirteen of these drawings, plus the engraving of the Friar, will demonstrate the young artist's combining and surpassing of techniques and genres taught to him (figures 15-28). The most highly regarded genre at his time, history painting, was a relatively recent development based on the tradition of picturing quasi-historical events from the Bible and Greco-Roman legend. More recent yet was the depiction of scenes from plays, narrative poems, and even novels. Its genesis lay in Restoration-era portraits of costumed actors and actresses posed in roles that won them fame, the earliest example being Alexander Pope's mentor Thomas Betterton portrayed as Bajazet in Christopher Marlowe's *Tamburlaine*.[29] A third genre, portrait painting, was long-established and lucrative for trained artists. Although most subjects posed in their own home settings, some requested costumes and backgrounds. Such a staged portrait would convey implicit narrative by showing three sisters as three Muses, for example, or a rural landowner as war hero, or a daughter as Ophelia or Desdemona or perhaps Una in Spenser's *Faerie Queene* (the last done by both George Stubbs and Joshua Reynolds, for example).

Jefferys' innovation was to create artwork that, although based upon a literary text, is not illustrating events in that text. Any reader may well notice that Chaucer's verbal portraits of the pilgrims, in the General Prologue, are reminiscent of visual portraiture. Jefferys noticed the similarity, then acted upon his perception. Adapting elements from all three narrative-related genres, he decided to have each Chaucerian character pose for a portrait session during his or her everyday life at home in the late fourteenth century, prior to or separate from the pilgrimage, or in some cases pose during solitary pursuit of private interests upon arrival at Canterbury.

Even more strikingly than the snapshot-like narrative artwork by Mortimer and others, Jefferys' full-length pilgrim portraits prefigure photography. Characterization, conveyed by body language and eye direction, is such that some of the subjects delight in having their images preserved for posterity. Some feel suspicious, others puzzled, as to the artist's motives. Several pilgrims, with more important business on their minds, hope that he will finish soon; and several do not even notice the artist's presence or ours. Representing the extremes are two pilgrims juxtaposed midway through the General Prologue. Jefferys' oblivious Parson glides past the picture space intent on heavenly matters (figure 26), whereas the Wife of Bath basks in her element. Striking a pose that flatters her best features while diverting attention from, for example, those pesky double chins, she radiates oft-practiced charm during this "photo op" so long denied her. She will have to forgive my shifting the limelight to dwell briefly upon each of fourteen pictures that present twenty of her travelling companions, five of their horses, and two well-fed small hounds. For each of the pictures (figures 15-28) my comments here remain preliminary. My primary motivation is to reproduce for other researchers' perusal all the remainder of this lately unearthed evidence, excepting only Alisoun.

I have shown elsewhere that Jefferys did antiquarian research in books as well as in and around his patron's estate near Beccles, Suffolk, his own hometown of Maidstone, Kent, and other locations including Canterbury.[30] Even Jefferys' deteriorating health need not have precluded a visit there to sketch the cathedral and other buildings for later use as backdrops. Elsewhere than Canterbury, he could continue to research and accurately reproduce fourteenth-century interiors, furniture, household goods, riding gear, and clothing (with special attention to footwear). Besides establishing an authentic material context, Jefferys also shows each pilgrim in the process of doing something appropriate to that sort of fourteenth-century person as described in the General Prologue and as projected by the tales and tale links. Like his contemporary Stothard, that is, Jefferys on his own was capable of reading and visualizing the contents of a text in Middle English.

To portray the Friar, who flirts with the Wife of Bath and fights with the Summoner in tale links, Jefferys largely concentrates upon the General Prologue's account of "a wantowne and a merye...ful solempne man." (See figure 15, I:208-209.) The artist gives him the expensive cloak specified, the wrestler's white neck, the musical interests, and-taking noteworthy precedence over a crucifix-the typet...ful of knyves...for to yeven faire wyves" (I:233-234).

In accord with conventions of British narrative artwork, but based instead upon the General Prologue's descriptive passage, this picture pinpoints one specific moment in the text. At lines 266-267, now "that he hadde songe" and has set aside his instrument, the Friar's eyes are twinkling. The twinkle's lecherous nature is manifested by the finger hooked in clerical belt and by the intensity and direction of his gaze. If today's fair wife should happen to be just outside the picture space, bending over an oven, her haunches would be at the level of his stare. The Friar's jutting feet, bare of sandal straps, also exude sexuality.

Jefferys seats the Friar on solid wooden furniture, of a style that can survive four centuries, in light from a window through thick stone walls. Unlike Mortimer, Jefferys had no interest in visual details of ordinary people's ephemeral homes. Regardless of class rank, all Canterbury pilgrims pose before the kind of massive stone architecture built before or during the late fourteenth century and still standing in Jefferys' milieu.

The Manciple, at the corner of a carved but windowless stone wall, sits beside a different wooden table on the same sort of bench as the Friar. (See figure 16, I:567-586.) His clothing distinguishes him from the cleric, whom he resembles in age and in body type--husky but not obese-and resembles also, with intentional artistic variations, in leg and arm positions, face and nose shape, beard, and balding hairline. The Manciple bears keys at his side, not a disrespected cross at his chest as does the Friar; and he has put aside some sort of counting device rather than a musical instrument. Most notable is the nature and direction of the Manciple's gaze. Making tentative eye contact with the observer of the picture, he hopes that readers of Chaucer's text will refrain from revealing his financial skulduggery so far kept secret from those know-it-all law students whom he serves.

The Cook shares beard length, age, and body type with the Friar and Manciple both. (See figure 17, I:379-387). In practical terms Jefferys would have asked the same servant or good-natured neighbor to pose more than once. 'Twere to consider too curiously, that is, to suppose the visual overlap significant on some such grounds as that the drunken Cook is berated then forgiven by the Manciple, and the Friar also drinks. The artist does intend to vary characterization using the same model, however, particularly by means of facial expressions and other aspects more subtle and compelling than just costume changes. Thus the Cook's eyes, half-closed with exhaustion and blankly staring off into space, provide a definitive contrast to the Friar's eyes, also half-closed but peering at something specific that is hidden from our view (figure 15).

The Cook poses before another stone corner and window, using yet a third sturdy table. By providing him with pillow and stool for the diseased leg, Jefferys shows more sympathy concerning the mormal than do twentieth-century critics. Despite his handicap, the Cook must keep working at the only trade that he knows. Perhaps future researchers will discover whether actual cooks, two and/or six centuries ago, maintained long shapely fingernails like his, and if so why (cf. figure 10). Among the foods listed in the General Prologue portrait of the Cook, Jefferys chose the pie and the ready-to-boil chicken.

Years of yummy chicken pies have metamorphosed into the grossly obese abdomens and limbs of the Cook's five employers. (See figure 18, I:361-378.) The Five Citizens "clothed alle in o lyveree" offered an artistic opportunity for a sketchbook-like series of poses and facial angles, using a model other than the one for Friar/Manciple/Cook. In so doing Jefferys was rising to the challenge of Chaucer's text, which denies the Five Citizens the individualized attention given to every other pilgrim excepting the Prioress' retinue. From left to right in the picture Jefferys presents a view of the model's profile, characterized as a guildsman who does not notice the artist at work; then the full-face view, just noticing the artist and wondering what's going on, then the three-quarters-right view, pleased at the attention and starting to assume a portrait stance; then the three-quarters-left view, irritated that #3 is distracted from their very important conversation; then another three-quarters-right-facing Citizen, who differs from

#3 in that he has already turned his body and adjusted his gaze with immortalizing portraiture in mind. Even though the faces of #3 and #5 are shown at much the same angle, that is, #3 is making eye contact with the artist/observer, #5 strikes an heroic pose in which he affects the gaze of a thinker of profound thoughts. Beneath identical noses and above identical beards, dissimilar sets of smiling lips reinforce the contrasting attitudes. Whereas #3 smiles toward the artist/observer, expressing glad surprise, #5 is directing his smile inward in proud contemplation of his own great deeds now so justly commemorated.

Without and with spurs, respectively, #3 and #5 wear the extravagant riding boots that Jefferys knew were authentic to the fourteenth century. Two generations earlier, already, the "long piked Shoes, so long as to be tied up by Strings or small Chains to their Knees" were assigned to Chaucer's sociohistorical context by George Vertue, the engraver of two Urry-edition illustrations and an enthusiastic member of the Society of Antiquaries.[31]

Having elsewhere documented Jefferys' intentions for antiquarian authenticity,[32] I will but add that an entire monograph could address costume below the knees for this portrait series. The pilgrims ready to ride, in particular, model footwear ranging from the Merchant's costly but practical "bootes clasped faire and fetisly" (I:273, figure 22), through fitted lower-leg protectors quite like what are now called "half-chaps," through inexpensive cloth wrappings resembling the "puttees" of soldiers' uniforms in the 1914-1918 Great War.

Like the Five Citizens' knee-high boots, their sunhats and codpieces and close-fitting trousers equip them for long-distance travel in optimum comfort. Reachable without dismounting are all of the girdles, pouches, and knives specified in the General Prologue, and more. Citizen #3 clasps a riding crop, for example, which the artist has positioned so as to reinforce vertical lines of the stone alcove behind the group. One of the horizontal lines that shaped Jefferys' composition remains visible, in this as in other pictures.

The same model who posed as five guildsmen, now hatless and longer-bearded, sits facing three-quarters-left to become the Franklin. (See figure 19, I:331-360.) His arm position, eye direction, and slight smile make him most resemble, among the Five Citizens, the one furthest right. Minute differences in facial expression shift visual characterization away from a pretentious bourgeois striking an heroic pose toward a satiated one mulling future food, not past glory. Above body so bloated that it barely fits between the arms of a massive chair, the

Franklin's contemplative gaze appears somewhat more outer-directed than is that of Citizen #5. "Seint Julian am I in my contree," he seems to ponder. "Might I therefore have responsibilities?" Should hungry peasants drift into his thoughts, though, he would nudge them aside for the sake of neighbors to invite over as excuse for yet another feast. From the Franklin's girdle hang, as specified in the General Prologue, both "anlaas" and "gipser" (I:357, dagger, purse).

Standing up and wearing much plainer clothing, to characterize Harry Bailly, the same hefty model tilts his head backward and makes eye contact forward. (See figure 20, I:751-756 and passim.) The "large man...with eyen stepe" doffs his hat and nods toward us observers as an invitation to enter the doorway and once inside, of course, to pay for what we eat. The word "stepe," obsolete but not yet in glossaries, occurs for the Host's eyes and the Monk's eyes (I:201, 753, *Oxford English Dictionary* s.v. steep). In both portraits, Jefferys interprets it as meaning a firm gaze straight at the artist/observer (see appendix). The Host's accoutrements indicate that, besides the General Prologue, the artist has taken into account at least the prologue to the Monk's Tale, "I am perilous with knyf in honde," and the epilogue to the Pardoner's Tale, "Unbokele anon thy purs" (VII:1919, VI:945).

Having observed Harry Bailly and other pilgrims still at home, puttering about their everyday lives, we now fast-forward past the journey to find ourselves at Canterbury, making eye contact with the Man of Law. (See figure 21, I:309-330.) In addition to him, the Shipman and the Clerk pose before cityscapes that Jefferys most likely sketched in Canterbury (see appendix). The foregrounded stone wall usefully hides most of the horse, especially the problematic position of its rider's leg. Horses accompany twelve pilgrims in Jefferys' portrait gallery, among whom only the Man of Law is mounted. Because Jefferys served an apprenticeship to engraver William Woollett, one of whose steady clients was George Stubbs, perhaps he learned humility in equine matters even more directly than did his early exemplar Mortimer.

The Man of Law, reluctantly accommodating, has scheduled precious time to pose for the artist before proceeding to important affairs upon his long-anticipated arrival in town. Like Chaucer, Jefferys lets us observers decide for ourselves to what extent one condemns or appreciates a man who "semed bisier than he was" (I:322). The confident gaze makes him a presence to be reckoned with, one way or the other. Of all Jefferys' pilgrims he is the best-looking by far, i.e., the one whose unseen body likeliest resembles Greco-Roman male statuary. To clothe such a healthy physique, Jefferys takes care to provide the "array" specified: "a medlee cote / Girt with a ceint of silk, with barres smale," the last detail interpreted plausibly as stripes (I:328-329).

It came as more of an artistic challenge to give to another busy pilgrim a respectable appearance, for line 271 of the General Prologue specifies that the Merchant wears "mottelee." (See figure 22, I:270-284.) It and the Man of Law's "medlee" share an etymology such that both words, at Chaucer's time, meant cloth woven of mixed colors (I:271, 328). In the eighteenth century, "medley" remained a neutral textile term. Two centuries earlier, though, the melancholic Jaques had begun ranting onstage of his encounter with "a fool i' th' forest / A motley fool." Due to Shakespeare's innovative usage, "motley" quite abruptly became limited to the garish garb of a professional fool.[33] Unaware of the change in meaning, Jefferys was nonetheless able to adapt the textual image toward a Merchant who wishes to impress potential customers. He therefore wears not only expensive boots and a "Flaundryssh bever hat" (I:272) but also an outfit that shows his staid English customers the height of fashion in some exotic foreign land, well beyond Flanders, where he has travelled on successful business. While resident in Rome, Jefferys might have seen wealthy Italian merchants don just such attire during Carnavale and other public displays of grandeur.

The Merchant's mount, with forelegs very like tree trunks and hindlegs carefully hidden, helps to showcase its master's solvency. The luxurious equine equipment includes authentically medieval bardings and a bejewelled breastplate, even fancier than what Mortimer gave to the devil's steed (figure 12). While the horse makes wary eye contact with the artist/observer, the Merchant keeps his own eyes fixed on its ears. He will intervene instantly whenever those mood barometers signal imminent restlessness that would make the artist's task last even longer.

Restless himself, Jefferys' Merchant may pass the time pondering implications of the long beard thrust upon him by early printers. Beginning with Speght's second edition (1602) the Merchant again wears the "forked berd" of most manuscripts. It therefore seems probable that the artist was working from a 1598 Speght edition. Older sixteenth-century printings with long-bearded Merchants include no glossaries or readers' aids whatsoever, whereas Jefferys knows obsolete clothing terms and other information readily available in Speght's apparatus beginning in 1598.

What analogous details might future researchers someday reveal about this innovative but overlooked artist's sources, working conditions, and creative process? "Don't ask me," says the Yeoman. "I'm just here to water the horses." (See figure 23, I:101-117.) Warily, unfamiliar with portraiture and not sure that he likes the idea, the Yeoman makes respectful but somewhat impatient eye contact with the artist/observer. He has led this horse to water and he wants it to drink whether thirsty or not, in preparation for travel, whereas its ear and eye direction show it instead distracted by the artist's presence. While worrying about one of his assigned tasks, the Yeoman stands before the same entryway that appears in the portraits of his employers, the Squire and Knight (see appendix). Future scholars may discover more about Jefferys' artistic practices by identifying this detailed doorway, perhaps still standing in Canterbury or near the artist's known dwellings.

Like the Yeoman's counterpart in the Urry edition (figure 33), this one cuts almost a comic figure simply by managing to carry all of the weaponry demanded by the General Prologue. Although an experienced rider, he will find it difficult to keep his one-handed grip on the reins while bearing the mighty bow, the sheaf of arrows, the arm guard, the sword, the buckler, the horn, and the well-harnessed dagger. For travel in daytime, he wears a sunhat and has flung back the specified hood, held in place by the "Cristopher on his brest" (I:115).

The same model, having flung back another specified hood and flexing even brawnier arms, climbs stone steps to emerge as the Miller. (See figure 24, I:545-566.) Jefferys has adapted the model's features to accord with the General Prologue, such that the Miller appears broader, thicker, and more short-shouldered than the Yeoman. Above a larger mouth and wider nostrils, though, the hairy wart belongs to him alone. These two lower-class characters' contrasting spurs and shoes and legwear, in particular their two styles of practical "half-chaps," well exemplify the need for further research into Jefferys' (knowledge of) fourteenth-century costume.

In accord with Chaucer's text the none-too-honest Miller appears shifty-eyed, his pupils peering sideways. Jefferys makes visual also the metaphorical "thombe of gold" (I:563). The Physician likewise wears a thumb ring signifying love of gold (see appendix). The Miller is welcomed along on the pilgrimage, however, not for the sake of ethical niceties but rather for his defensive capabilities. Although the General Prologue names only the larger weapons, Jefferys gives him also a dagger, as carried by other pilgrims, and at his belt a purse. The Miller decisively positions his stash of valuables where he and only he can reach it on horseback, with his dagger ready at hand to protect it.

Just by illustrating what the General Prologue states, that the Miller and Yeoman and many others bear multiple weapons, Jefferys' drawings emphasize the aspect of fourteenth-century social history whereby parties of pilgrims to Canterbury and elsewhere rode in mortal danger of ambush. Bagpipes are associated with pilgrimages elsewhere than in Chaucer's work. Perhaps the distinctive sound served to announce alert travellers on the defensive, such that robbers would think twice before pouncing. Jefferys implies such a connection, at any rate, by having the Miller sling together all three implements with which he will ride foremost of the company: sword, buckler, bagpipes.

The Urry-edition "Departure to Canterbury" shows a different reason for the Miller's riding out in front (see appendix). In the 1721 picture his placid mount makes the best lead horse, i.e., the one least likely to spook at the invisible horse-eating monsters that line the route of a high-strung horse like the Squire's, second in line and already rearing. Jefferys, reading the same Middle English passage as did the Urry-edition artist, has interpreted the Miller's lead position in terms of human brawn rather than equine calm. The two visual conceptions provide a succinct example of ways in which readers across six centuries have been able to find whatever they seek in Chaucer's chameleon-like text.

Slimmed down but still posing on steps, the same model as for Yeoman and Miller becomes the lower-class pilgrim who is juxtaposed and contrasted to the Miller in the General Prologue: the hard-working Plowman. (See figure 25, I:529-541.) He steps up into a building that must be a church, indicated by the archway behind and the carved doorposts with hooks for short-term hitching. Thus Jefferys shows the Plowman in the process of enacting line 539, "His tithes payde he." He wears hat and boots and other clothing practical for horseback travel, including the "tabard" specified (I:541). This term exemplifies ones obsolete by Jefferys' time, but mentioned by antiquarians and defined in the glossary of the 1598 Speght edition.

It is acceptable to bring into church a dagger but not a sword. Carrying the empty sheath, the Plowman hopes that God will protect from thieves both his sword and his horse left outside. Not even noticing the artist's presence, the mare's master has just looped the reins and now shifts his gaze beyond the hook, toward those same heavenly matters that so fully occupy his brother (figure 26).

Having lived in Rome, Jefferys needed no glossary to supply the Parson with an appropriate robe, sandals, walking staff, and rosary. (See figure 26, I:477-528.) A thin, elderly Parson, with sagging features and balding head, may represent Jefferys' awareness of the cleric aged "Sixty Years" who "made almost a Sin of Abstinence" in Dryden's "Character of a Good Parson; Imitated from Chaucer, And Inlarg'd."[34] Also, or instead, circumstances may have presented an elderly man as model. As the globe-trotting artist-in-residence in a rural community, Jefferys might well have invited the local parson to pose for the portrait series in progress. Perhaps he asked the same of a local lawyer in the prime of life (figure 21). Whatever the cause, Jefferys portrays Chaucer's age-indeterminate Parson as a much older brother of the Plowman. Totally unaware of the artist's presence, or of anything else save his sacred duties to the next impoverished parishioner on his daily rounds, the Parson passes a window that differs in style from those behind Friar and Cook.

That Jefferys sketched backgrounds during a visit to Canterbury, with its plentitude of windows and doorways datable to Chaucer's time, is further demonstrated by his portrait of the Prioress. (See figure 27, I:118-164.) In the background, the high windows resemble those on a cathedral shown more fully behind the Man of Law and the Clerk (figure 21, appendix). Thus the Prioress is entering a building located right beside the cathedral's sacred space. She does so while concealing one dog in her sleeve and shooing the other ahead of her up the steps, toward a private room where she could have kept them hidden for the duration of her stay...had this voyeuristic artist not stepped from the shadows to record for all posterity so small a sin.

The Prioress' downcast eyes watch one of her "smale houndes" (I:146). The direction of her gaze also expresses the blend of guilt and irritation on account of which she is avoiding eye contact with the intrusive artist/observer. Her small red mouth, as mentioned earlier, seems to Jefferys not sensual but instead pursed in anticipation of our disapproval. Consideration of her headpiece provides another counterbalance to the sort of interpretive issues created by the now-discredited construct "courtly love."[35] Whereas early-twentieth-century commentators tended to see as sinfully vain the Prioress' attention to "semyly" pinching of her wimple, Jefferys with equal plausibility sees stern propriety. There is one and only one correct way to pinch a wimple, and woe betide any lesser nun who deviates.

The Second Nun, with neck unseemly exposed, indeed appears intimidated as she lurks behind the Prioress. She is very pretty. In decisive contrast Jefferys portrays the Prioress as ugly, with facial frown lines and bags beneath her eyes. In addition to the specified rosary beads and brooch with crowned A, she carries a knife that betokens her devotion to table manners. Forks being not yet invented, that is, Jefferys envisions her carrying neat morsels to her well-blotted lips with a delicate knifepoint. Although potentially defensive, her dagger does not signify an offensive weapon useful for beheading the Nun's Priest. His glazed eyes, however, and his position sandwiched between two animal faces, do imply the Prioress' disregard for any member of her entourage who might be embarrassed by her sneaking the dogs upstairs.

From Jefferys' captive moment recording the Prioress' arrival at Canterbury, replete with General Prologue details, we turn in closing to a pilgrim whose portrait incorporates relatively few details of his appearance and no background setting at all. (See figure 28, I:669-714.) The beardless, blond, stringy-haired Pardoner, partly based on Chaucer's text, may be visually compared to others among Jefferys' pilgrims. Except that his small mouth expresses smugness not discomfiture, the Pardoner's deepset eyes and prominent nose make his face resemble that of the Prioress. Jefferys might well have used the same adolescent model for mannish woman and womanish man. As another comparison, in facial angle and in corporal attitude he resembles the Citizen furthest right in the group portrait, except that the Pardoner strikes a pose as if contemplating holy deeds rather than military ones (figure 18).

Among all twenty-four pictures, it is only behind the Pardoner and his singing partner the Summoner that Jefferys puts no background, save blank wall and floor line (see appendix). The implication is that such scoundrels continue to operate outside of the historical context of fourteenth-century England. While in Italy, Jefferys would have seen in person what he probably regarded as corrupt counterparts of the Pardoner and Summoner, openly representing the Roman Catholic church. To execute this portrait, Jefferys perhaps reworked sketches done in Rome of church officials and souvenir peddlers. While providing his subject with richly embroidered ecclesiastical robes, for that or another reason, Jefferys has neglected several General Prologue details. Here the Pardoner carries no "walet...in his lappe" or anything else in which to store pardons (I:686). In lieu of the many relics listed by Chaucer, he holds a vial of holy water (apparently) and a fistful of medallions. Also, his elaborate headgear must originate elsewhere than Chaucer's twice-specified "cappe" (I:683-685).

Those turban-like folds that deck the Pardoner's scraggly hair allow for visual display of two definitions of Chaucer's word "vernycle," both found early in Speght's unpaginated section "Corrections of some faults, and Annotations vpon some places" (I:685, *Oxford English Dictionary* s.v. vernicle). Unbeknownst to Jefferys, only one meaning was accurate. Speght misdefines the term as a "brooch or figure wherein was set the instruments wherewith Christ was crucified," which Jefferys renders as the Pardoner's cloak clasp. Speght continues, correctly now, "and withall a napkin, wherein was the print of his face."

When I first discovered these drawings, I supposed that Jefferys had chosen only the inaccurate meaning and had moved that single vernicle from head to chest. Now I am not so sure. The longer I stare, the more I think that I see the disapproving face of Jesus Christ himself— left eye, nose, downturned mouth—gazing out from the peak of the Pardoner's atextual headdress.

I hope that future scholars will bring expertise from other fields, such as art history and eighteenth-century studies, to reinforce or to call into question my initial interpretations of the signifying vernicle and other complexities in this unprecedented portrait gallery by yet another imaginative artist who died too young. Jefferys' death was caused by consumption and at last a cold, though, not by a lifestyle like Mortimer's bursting with genius or madness or profligacy.

Part VII

Two generations prior to Jefferys' time, there briefly lived an under-documented artist who exhibited a stunning range of profligacy and excess. He died at age 45, one year before Mortimer was born, and was famous for drawing horses. I hope that future scholars will uncover evidence for and against my proposal that John Vanderbank (1694-1739) might have had some connection with the pilgrim portraits in the 1721 Urry edition (e.g., figures 29-33). Indirect data may lurk in the notebooks of the influential engraver George Vertue, ten years his senior, who complained of Vanderbank's "high living" in maintaining multiple coach teams "in town and country," but who also called him "of all men born in this nation superior in skill" and who engraved some of his designs including the first two (only) among Vanderbank's seventy plates for a sumptuous *Don Quixote* (1738).[36]

In 1711 Vanderbank and Vertue were among the founding members of England's first art academy, at Lincoln's Inn Fields. By 1720 Vanderbank was attempting to run his own art academy in St. Martin's Lane. Despite enthusiastic pupils including William Hogarth, and despite a legacy in 1717 from his wealthy artisan father, from 1724 until his death Vanderbank meandered in and out of debtors' prison. While in a situation somewhat like parole, however, he "purchased a fine Horse as a Model for his Pencil" and thereby did extensive illustrations for a treatise on equitation and a collection of novels (both 1729).[37] As Vanderbank kept on spending far more than he earned and inherited, at his death his landlord claimed his possessions for unpaid rent.

During the same few years that young Vanderbank was annoying his colleagues at England's only art academy, entrepreneurs in Oxford were thrown off schedule by John Urry's sudden death in 1714/15. Re-assignment of editorial duties languished until late 1717. Origin of the illustrations is unknown, beyond an advertisement in 1715 mentioning "30 Copper Plates by the best Gravers."[38] Among them the only "Graver" identifiable, Vertue, reproduced from someone else's drawings the first two illustrations only: as frontispiece a head-and-shoulders portrait of Chaucer, and as titlepiece to page one the first "Departure to Canterbury" scene ever done (see appendix). Throughout a long career, Vertue is credited with drawing only one among the many hundreds of designs that he engraved.[39]

During the half-decade following Urry's death, I propose, the tolerant Vertue's high-living associate Vanderbank might have been looking to take on students without an obligation to the institution at Lincoln's Inn Fields. As the devil-may-care owner of several coach teams, he would revel in journeys back and forth between London and Oxford. There, where potential students abounded, illustrations were needed for a series of horseback riders.

In Oxford Urry had acquired for temporary consultation what is now Cambridge manuscript Gg.4.27, the direct source for several Urry-edition pilgrim portraits. Regardless of Vanderbank's involvement, there is no need to posit that the illuminated manuscript itself must have been transported not only from Cambridge to Oxford but also on to London, where most of England's visual-art community resided, in order to have its illuminations copied. More likely, an established artist would sometimes visit the university town to supervise the series and perhaps to contribute designs himself.

Accordingly, I will discuss five of the Urry-edition portraits with reference to a plausible situation whereby novice artists were learning how to draw horses in various positions and attitudes. (See figures 29-33.) As examples I have chosen designs that appear to be done by different hands. The five range in origin from the Cook, which is directly based on Cambridge ms. Gg.4.27 with no evidence of attention to Chaucer's text, through the Yeoman, which certainly illustrates lines 101-117 of the General Prologue.

For practicing artists, these five medallions first and foremost demonstrate equine bodies and faces from five representative angles. The artistic challenge resembles that taken on by Jefferys in individualizing five identically-clad fat men (figure 18). A horse in complete profile, represented by the Cook's mount, is far and away the easiest to draw. The Yeoman rides a horse with body in profile but face partly turned. The horses beneath the Franklin and Man of Law are both turning their forequarters, as well as their faces, part way toward the artist/observer. The Physician's mount shows its face full forward, its body almost so.

In the five poses, all ten hindlegs appear well-proportioned. Harder-to-draw forelegs look severely knock-kneed on three of the mounts, and problematic even for the profiled Cook and Yeoman. Furthermore, the five riders' legs each ought to bend not only front to back at the knee but also outward, around each horse's convex body. No legs quite do so. Moreover, the human legs all look too short excepting the Physician's, which are too long, even though all stirrups appear correctly placed in relation to equine underbellies. The Urry edition, in brief, showcases frustrations inherent in trying to draw horses.

Although drawing styles differ, it would be premature to begin assigning specific medallions to specific anonymous artists. The original drawings may have resembled each other more than do the engravings, in that some degree of difference could result from participation by more than two of England's "best Gravers" (i.e., more than one besides Vertue). Apparent stylistic distinctions might stem also from different horse breeds used as models. For example, the Franklin's well-bred horse has proportionately longer legs and neck, and a more delicate muzzle, than does the Yeoman's cob (figures 31, 33).

The Yeoman and his horse appear appropriate for and responsive to one another, in an effect that I have analyzed elsewhere for Urry-edition pilgrims other than the five discussed here.[40] The Monk prances on one of the prettiest from his stablefull of steeds, for example, while the Miller's draft horse plods benignly. This present article shifts away from "equitation as interpretation" in order to address more broadly what it was that early-eighteenth-century book illustrators, sellers, and purchasers expected to accomplish. Apt understanding of a late-fourteenth-century text lay somewhere well outside of the big picture.

At the turn of the eighteenth century, the producers of a folio volume elaborately illustrated with equestrian portraits were trying to associate Chaucer, and England's medieval past, with the twin peaks of Greco-Roman classical art and British restored royalty. One precedent for the Urry-edition portrait series goes back to Greco-Roman equestrian sculptures in honor of emperors and other alleged heroes, which Englishmen more likely knew from expensive engraved reproductions than from travel. After the Restoration, also, a more immediate precedent flourished. Many lavishly illustrated treatises on equitation saw publication for an intended readership with plenty of money to spend on frivolous books (because only practice can improve riding skill). Particularly prestigious was one that William Cavendish, Duke of Newcastle, published in exile: *La méthode et invention nouvelle de dresser les chevaux* (orig. Antwerp, 1658, with multiple translations and reworkings).[41] Cavendish was the much-honored governor and riding master to the prince who returned to England in 1660 as King Charles II.

The sensible British book-buying public, however, remained unconvinced of any need for a royal imperial Chaucer. They kept on reading their reliable black-letter Speght editions until the appearance of Tyrwhitt and then cheap pirated reprints. The 1721 edition, despite roman typeface, languished unsold until the college of Christ Church began to require that incoming students buy copies.[42] Thus Urry editions, owned but seldom opened, remain intact and abundant three centuries later.

Besides the upper classes brandishing horsemanship for artbook connoisseurs, more obvious prototypes for the Urry-edition series were the equestrian pilgrims in sixteenth-century Chaucer editions. The Oxford preparers of the Urry edition had access to such woodcut illustrations, known to postdate the author, as well as to the one and only illustrated manuscript from approximately Chaucer's time. (What is now the Ellesmere was privately owned and not publicized.) From Cambridge ms. Gg.4.27 one of the Urry-edition artists, notably unskilled, exactly copied attributes of the Manciple (color plate 29) and his high-strung horse. The Wife of Bath (color plate 25) and the Reeve (color plate 23) are copied from it not quite so slavishly, and with greater artistic expertise (see appendix).

The portrait of the Cook is analogous to those of the Wife and Reeve in its relationship to its model in Cambridge ms. Gg.4.27. (See figure 29, I:379-387.) Neither the manuscript Cook (color plate 24) nor his Urry-edition counterpart resembles either Chaucer's described pilgrim or a generic cook. Neither appears even to belong to the lower classes, except insofar as each rides a horse that sometimes works in harness (as indicated by tails-docked in the eighteenth century, tied up in the fifteenth). Instead, the manuscript's margin and the engraved medallion both portray bearded men wearing high-piled turbans, robes with fur collars, and soft (i.e., expensive) leather boots. The two richly clad Cooks assume near-identical postures, each resting a two-lash crop on his right shoulder. No details at all, certainly no mormal, come from the General Prologue.

The Urry-edition Physician may have been copied from one of the pictures now cut from the margin of Cambridge ms. Gg.4.27. (See figure 30, I:411-444.) His headgear resembles that worn by the Wife of Bath therein, and the males' turbans. Any other evidence is merely negative. The Physician seems awkwardly drawn, with minimal attention to the General Prologue. His face and body both look chubby, in contradiction to "his diete mesurable...of no superfluitee," and none of his accoutrements relate to medical interests (I:435-436). Wealth in general—i.e., love of gold-could be seen as the over-the-knee (i.e., soft and expensive) riding boots and his stallion's lush mane and tail. A decorative ribbon behind its ears may be replacing some item of fifteenth-century tack that the eighteenth-century artist did not recognize.

Of course we will never know anything about the Physician or other excised Gg.4.27 portraits, unless clippings surface at the back of a neglected cabinet somewhere in Oxford. It is surely possible also that, soon after 1721, the manuscript was returned to Cambridge with the same number of pictures clipped from its margins as when it arrived. In the latter case, the random appearance of the Urry-edition Physician lacks discernible cause.

In contrast to the Physican, the Urry-edition pilgrims to be discussed next were more likely created independently than copied from originals now missing from the manuscript (figures 31-33). Cambridge ms. Gg.4.27 came to Oxford with "Figures of some of the Pilgrims on horseback illuminated...and he [Urry] doubts not but this Book originally had them all."[43] Among illuminations already missing when the manuscript arrived were probably the Man of Law and his friend the Franklin, and almost certainly the Yeoman. All three, but most fully the Yeoman, appear conceptualized in direct reference to the General Prologue.

It is useful to examine together the Man of Law and the Franklin who, according to the General Prologue, rides "in his compaignye." (See figures 31-32, I:309-360.) Two of the Urry-edition artists (or possibly one artist rendered by two engravers) did the medallions as mirror images in which differentiation between the two humans depends upon details from the General Prologue.

Presuming multiple artists, they portray the riding companions as two men of similar age and dignity whose faces appear in three-quarters profile, angled in opposite directions. The Man of Law and the Franklin both ride long-legged, long-necked, anatomically correct stallions with medium-length manes and docked tails. The equine faces both appear in three-quarters profile but aimed toward opposite directions. In mirror image the horses display the same leg combination, with diagonals lifted equally, and both bodies are angled to expose their entire chests. Shadows show that each is moving toward the sun. (Compare the Cook illuminated from behind and the Physician from the front, figures 29-30.) Both horses wear fancy breastplates and beribboned cruppers, fashionably varied.

Because of compositional and equine similarities in the two pictures, the differences between the two riders themselves form a marked contrast. Background scenery signals the two men's occupations, respectively practiced in town (Man of Law) and country (Franklin). Other distinguishing features come straight from the General Prologue. The Man of Law wears a robe "girt with a ceint of silk, with barres smale" and the occupational hood of a lawyer (I:329). For the Franklin the General Prologue specifies the white beard and, hanging at his girdle, the "gipser" and oversized "anlaas" (I:357).

So that the two comrades both appear middle-aged, the artist has a bareheaded Franklin reveal that only his beard has prematurely turned white. After experiencing Jefferys' Franklin (figure 19) we must remind ourselves that the General Prologue praises culinary hospitality, but does not state outright that "Epicurus owene sone" was obese (I:336). In the Urry edition, visual manifestation of that textual hint takes second place to the artistic goal of two middle-aged, middle-class riding companions in mirror image but differentiated from one another via Chaucer's descriptions.

If the two pictures do come from two artists, and if John Vanderbank might be one, he more likely did the Man of Law. So far I have examined Vanderbank's illustrations only to *Don Quixote*. There the horse shown full-body at this angle is Rocinante, who is supposed to look silly. However, on the Man of Law's horse the squared-off muzzle and the deepset, expressive eyes make it resemble Vanderbank's Rocinante more than it does the bland-faced horse bearing the Urry-edition Franklin. The Franklin's horse shows no emotion. Therefore the rider, free of concern for his vehicle's behavior, can make eye contact with the artist/observer. In contrast, the Man of Law must keep his attentive eyes on the ears because his horse is glaring angrily at something just beyond the frame of the medallion.

Looking in isolation at the Man of Law's horse, one might hesitate to claim outright that its open mouth and frowning eyelid give it a cartoon-like expression of that emotion so basic to horses as well as to humans: anger. The artistic intention is clarified in reference to the thick-muzzled and possibly Vanderbankian horse ridden by the Yeoman, which expresses another emotion common to both species but expressed less selfconsciously by equines: fear. (See figure 33, I:101-117; cf. figure 32.) Both equine faces are shown at three-quarters profile, with mouths equally open. Compared to the Man of Law's horse, the Yeoman's is jerking its head upward rather than staring forward at something. It pricks its ears toward the perceived danger, rather than plastering them back in anger. The Yeoman's startled horse opens eyes wider than does the angry horse, also, and distends its nostrils in fear.

During this commonplace situation the human participant, being a rational animal, must exude courage in order to calm the horse. Thus the Urry-edition Yeoman, looking past the ears toward whatever has frightened his mount, just looks apprehensive and mildly exasperated. "Isn't my job hard enough," he seems to think, "without my having to deal one-handed with yet another invisible horse-eating monster, all the while bearing the mighty bow, the sheaf of arrows, the sword, buckler, horn, and on my other side the dagger all loaded upon me by Chaucer-the-author?"

The positioning of the hindquarters of the Yeoman's horse, compared to those calmly striding forward beneath the Man of Law and Franklin, exemplifies artistic techniques for portraying a skittish horse in the act of whirling counterclockwise. Its right hindleg is extended, its left hindleg poised to stomp. In addition, its tail swishes downward, as a standard equine reaction resembling the tail between legs of a frightened dog. However, it is not canine or feline but equine emotions of anger and fear and pride and love that humans must learn how to master-or, in Blake's worldview, learn how to emulate-in order to make progress along the nonrational road to Canterbury.[44]

Part VIII

In Stothard's 1807 painting, set on the road to Canterbury, the Yeoman's horse is whirling in the same direction as is its Urry-edition counterpart-whirling not in terror, but instead in doing its duty to protect the rest of the equine crowd from the contagious panic of the Squire's horse (see appendix). Stothard, as Royal Academy librarian, had opportunity to examine the Urry edition datable to his tenure. Besides the Yeoman he could observe, for example, the Urry-edition Squire's horse rearing and turning counterclockwise, not in fear but rather in a carefully signalled dressage movement (see appendix). It is more than possible that Stothard gleaned ideas for his own artwork from the Urry edition.

It is not at all possible that Stothard gleaned artistic ideas from Blake. However, it is not our duty to confront Blake with mere chronological discrepancy. Blake believed what he believed, and rechanneled his anger and other emotions to create what he created.

Prior to his 1809 painting, Blake was familiar with the "Departure to Canterbury" engraved by Vertue for the Urry edition, from which he copied two pilgrims and the frontispiece Chaucer portrait for William Hayley's library at Felpham (see appendix). At the Royal Academy library, Stothard had equal access to the same seminal illustration. At the far left of the 1721 titlepiece, pilgrims emerge from the archway of the Tabard innyard. Mostly in single file, the riders turn to their left (the observer's right) and head out toward Canterbury. Village houses line the route.

Stothard adapted the Urry-edition scene in order to create his own "Departure to Canterbury" published in 1794, an entire decade before Robert Cromek proposed a full-scale painting on the subject to him or, as Blake would vehemently claim, to Blake. (See figure 34.) In the tiny titlepiece for an English-literature anthology, Stothard has followed the conventions of eighteenth-century narrative artwork by capturing one dramatic moment in the text being illustrated. The Host appears nowhere in the Urry-edition illustrations. Stothard decided to portray him at the point of turning to address pilgrims behind him, apparently in the act of calling for a tale to be told.

One might quibble with details, the same as noted for a Bell-edition frontispiece (figure 13). If the moment shown were at lines 823-824 of the General Prologue-" oure Hoost...gadrede us togidre alle in a flok"—it would take place in the innyard prior to riding out. If it were at line 827-"there oure Hoost bigan his hors areste"-it would occur at the Wateryng of Seint Thomas, which cannot be located so close to the inn or they would have watered the horses before mounting. An equestrian Host calling for a tale makes visual sense, however, and is retained by Stothard for his 1807 painting. There Harry Bailly continues to ride second in line, as in the 1794 engraving, but he loses his centrality in the overall composition of the picture.

In Blake's mind, of course, Blake independently invented the centered Host turning backward to call for a tale. His fury against the money-mad art world, now represented by his former friend Stothard, ignited his explosive denial of any influence outside of his own creative genius.

Elsewhere in Stothard's 1794 conception, the bagpipe-playing Miller leads off (figure 34). He rides bareback with only a lead rope to steer, the same as in the Urry-edition precedent (see appendix) and in Stothard's later painting, but not Blake's. Behind the Host ride pilgrims who display a range of differing facial angles, an effect expanded in the paintings by both Blake and Stothard. In the book illustration two of the figures are identifiable as the Clerk and Chaucer. The same two pilgrims are juxtaposed near the midpoint of Stothard's painting and at almost the rear, save only the Reeve, of Blake's procession.

The Wife of Bath, who has squirmed into this article despite my firm decision to the contrary, holds a key position toward the rear of the 1794 procession, as she does in both later paintings. In the book illustration, which elaborates Stothard's Bell-edition "Departure to Canterbury" (see appendix), the Friar and a secular pilgrim stare at the back of Alisoun's head. For his painting Stothard, expanding his Bell-edition idea even further, surrounds "the Bath pilgrim...the gay wife" with a dozen menfolk both sacred and secular, entranced from every direction.[45] It is Blake who replicates (that is, in his worldview, independently invents) the framing of her head by two males staring from behind, the same as in Stothard's 1794 conception. My work in progress will address several other Alisounian features abandoned for

Stothard's painting but replicated (i.e., invented) by Blake. For example, in 1794 she rides sidesaddle to the off side.

In his painting Blake has "varied the heads and forms of his personages. . . the Horses he has also varied to accord to their Riders." He wisely chose to portray in simple profile all of the fully visible horses, and most of the back-row heads. His artistic intentions did not extend to an attempt to rival the equine angles and attitudes even in Stothard's book illustration, much less those executed with even more variety and skill in the painting, which was seen in progress and praised by George Stubbs himself just before his death in 1806.[46]

As background to his own painting Blake replicates (i.e., invents) the procession's emergence from the Tabard archway and its subsequent direction of travel, elements found in both the Urry edition and the 1794 illustration. Fuming, Blake also preserves elements of both pictures' village structures, which Stothard had eliminated in favor of painting the "Dulwich Hills, which was not the way to Canterbury; but, perhaps the painter thought he would give them a ride round about, because they were a burlesque set of scare-crows, not worth any man's respect or care."[47]

Turning our backs now on the eighteenth century, as if on the Tabard Inn, we look to the next two articles in this collection to address artistic motivation and execution in the rival paintings by Stothard and Blake. Like others who have come before and after them, on the long and winding road to Canterbury, both artists left significant evidence of the mental exercise regimens that enabled them to rechannel their respective brain-chemical imbalances into functional lifetime balancing acts between hard work and creativity.

Notes

[1] Pope composed such works as *The Rape of the Lock* (orig. 1712) and *The Dunciad* (1728) in the wake of parodies of the *Aeneid* by Paul Scarron (1648-52) and Charles Cotton (1664-1665). Blackmore wrote serious epic-length poems on Arthurian, philosophical, and theological topics. Percy published hundreds of ballads, regarded as proto-epics, as *Reliques of Ancient English Poetry* (1765). Macpherson attributed to "Ossian," supposedly a third-century bard, his own compositions beginning with *Fragments of Ancient Poetry. Collected in the Highlands of Scotland, and Translated from the Galic or Erse Language* (1760).

[2] For modernizations besides those available in the collected works of Alexander Pope and John Dryden, see Bowden, *Eighteenth-Century Modernizations*. On Tyrwhitt see B. A. Windeatt's chapter in Ruggiers 117-143.

3   On the Urry edition see Alderson and Henderson 69-140, excerpted in Ruggiers 93-115.
On its illustrations see Bowden items so listed in the appendix, esp. *Chaucer Aloud* 309-310
n. 25. Lam and Smith discuss the frontispiece portrait of Chaucer, not the pilgrims. Also see
Miskimin, taking into account flaws documented by Bentley.

For alphabetically arranged book illustrators see Hammelmann; for artists more generally
see *DNB* Graves (both items), Waterhouse, and Whitley. Much information comes ultimately
from thirty-nine notebooks kept by George Vertue between 1713 and 1756, which were purchased from his widow and excerpted by Horace Walpole in his *Anecdotes of Painting in
England* (1762-71), then published between 1930 and 1955 for the Walpole Society as vols.
18, 20, 24, 26, 29 (index), and 30, termed vols. 1-6 in standard citations. In this article I
quote Vertue from secondary sources.

For an account of the century's artistic interest in Shakespeare and, to a lesser extent,
other English authors, see Altick 1-55 and passim. For context also see Hutchison 1-64,
Lipking 109-207 and passim, and Solkin. In preparing this article I benefitted from an exhibition at the Philadelphia Museum of Art, "The Plot Thickens: Narrative in British
Printmaking, 1700-1900, " organized by Andrea W. Frederickson, May-June 2002.

4   See appendix for the locations of reproductions and discussions of five of the group
scenes (besides this article's fig. 34) in Bowden publications. Of the remaining two, Burney's
seems never to have been reproduced. Stothard's frontispiece to volume one of Bell's British
Poets is reproduced in Miskimin 45.

5   I:153, i.e., line 153 of the General Prologue, which is part of fragment one of *Canterbury
Tales*, in Chaucer 23-36. References in my text are to fragment and line numbers of thi edition.

6   Dryden 4:1703-1717 and passim, Pope 14-78, Bowden, *Eighteenth-Century Modernizations*.

7   For Smirke see *DNB* and Hammelmann 68. For Penn and reprint information see *DNB*
and Bowden, *Eighteenth-Century Modernizations* 244-49. For Kauffman see *DNB*,
Hammelmann 57, and Roworth (the last including references to four biographies between
1810 and 1972). For Ogle and reprint information see Bowden, *Eighteenth-Century
Modernizations* 80-118. The inaccurate *DNB* article on Ogle has been replaced (by B.
Bowden) for the *Oxford Dictionary of National Biography*, forthcoming.

8   Altick 341, providing a reproduction of Fuseli's painting. For alphabetically arranged
exhibition records see Graves, *Royal Academy*.

9   On the Poets' Gallery see Boase 148-155. For a preliminary list of reprints of the works
by Ogle, Dryden, and Pope, see Bowden, *Chaucer Aloud* 285-300.

10   See Bowden, " Visual Portraits " 177-181.

11   Qtd. respectively from Hammelmann 62 and *DNB*; also see Nicolson (an exhibition
catalogue).

12   This point is made by Altick 39. On Stothard primarily see Bennett, also see Coxhead,
DNB, and Hammelmann 68-71.

13   On Bell see Morison. On Tyrwhitt see B. A. Windeatt's chapter in Ruggiers 117-143.
Tyrwhitt is preceded by a responsible scholar Thomas Morell, who completed only the
General Prologue and Knight's Tale. He published his annotated text in 1737, along with

Dryden's modernization of the latter work and Pope's of the former, which Pope published under the name of Thomas Betterton. (See Bowden, *Eighteenth-Century Modernizations* 3-9.) 1 have recently become the astonished owner of Horace Walpole's personal copy of Morell's second edition (1740). It has no annotations and little evidence of use.

[14] Four of Mortimer's original drawings accompany the engravings of his Chaucer scenes in the copy of *Mortimer's Works* owned by the Victoria and Albert Museum. For other locating information see Bowden, *Chaucer Aloud* 311 n. 29, and captions to the scenes reproduced in this article. T. Palser published the 1816 collection; J. R. Smith published the separate engravings on February 12, 1787.

[15] Tyrwhitt 5. i (his emphasis), qtd. from Ruggiers 141.

[16] Anon. in *Monthly Magazine* (1796): 25, qtd. from Nicolson 11.

[17] Blake 32; also 13, 395, and elsewhere, but best known from "The Divine Image" in *Songs of Innocence* (1789).

[18] Dryden 4:1507, for Book 3, lines 260 (rendering Chaucer's I:2340) and 262. For qtns. below (Book 2, lines 140-42) see Dryden 4:1487. On Beauclerk see *DNB* and Hammelmann 14. The third of her folio-sized designs shows Theseus' party meeting the grieving widows.

[19] See Lindahl on these and other frame-story interactions.

[20] On glossaries see Kerling.

[21] On Stubbs see *DNB* and Taylor.

[22] On Stothard's illustrations to an 1806 edition of Dryden's *Fables*, see Coxhead 201-202 and Bennett 77. For William Lipscomb's 1795 modernization of the Second Nun's Tale, see Bowden, *Eighteenth-Century Modernizations* 233-236.

[23] Tyrwhitt in *Gentleman's Magazine* 53 (June 1783): 461-462, qtd. from Spurgeon 1:474.

[24] See Bowden, *Eighteenth-Century Modernizations* for details. The Shipman's Tale was modernized by John Markland in 1721, Henry Travers in 1731, and Andrew Jackson in 1750. The last was never reprinted, the first two reprinted once apiece (but not in Ogle's unfinished 1741 collection, due to tale order). In comparison, by 1785 Samuel Cobb's 1712 Miller's Tale modernization had appeared in at least ten miscellanies as well as in Ogle's collection.

[25] On the style of hat, also worn by the Wife of Bath in the Urry-edition illustrations, see Cunnington and Cunnington 163-164.

[26] Reproduced in Miskimin 49.

[27] Clifford and Legouix 152. On Jefferys also see Butlin. The *DNB* misdates Jefferys' birth and may contain other errors.

[28] For details see Clifford and Legouix 157, item 16.

29 Altick 1-2. For example, 282 portraits are extant of actor David Garrick (1717-1779), far more than of any eighteenth-century monarch.

30 Bowden, "Canterbury Pilgrims and Their Horses" and "Visual Portraits" 188-192.

31 Vertue in *Philosoiphical Transactions* 44.484 (1747): 575, qtd. from Spurgeon 1.394. On Vertue see *DNB* Hammelmann 88-89, Lam and Smith, and Evans 55 and passim.

32 See n. 30 above.

33 Shakespeare 414, for *As You Like It* 2.7.12-13; *Oxford English Dictiomary* s.v. medley, motley.

34 Dryden 4:1736, for lines 8 and 11.

35 For an account of the demise of "courtly love" with full bibliography, see Bowden, "Introduction to the Second Edition."

36 Vertue 6:170. See n. 3 above re Vertue's notebooks, here qtd. from Hammelmann 79, in the course of an extensive account of Vanderbank's life noting errors in the *DNB*.

37 Introduction (perhaps by Josephus Sympson) to *Twenty Five Actions of the Manage Horse* (London, 1729), qtd. from Hammelmann 80.

38 Anon. in *Daily Courant*, 27 January 1715, qtd, from Bond 336, On the Urry edition see Alderson and Henderson 69-140, excerpted in Ruggiers 93-115.

39 Hammelmann 88-89. Miskimin 30, in crediting Vertue with the Urry-edition medallions, does not distinguish between drawing and engraving.

40 See Bowden, " Visual Portraits " 181-187, and throughout "Artistic and Interpretive Context," "Canterbury Pilgrims and Their Horses," and *Chaucer Aloud*.

41 On Cavendish and counterparts see the bibliographical footnote to Bowden, "Before the Houyhnhnms." Herein, the Works Cited section gives but one example of an alternative title.

42 For more on distribution see Spurgeon 1.cxix-cxxi.

43 For references and discussion see Bowden, "Visual Portraits" 181-187, noting the error "Departure from [rather than "to"] Canterbury."

44 For development of this thesis see Bowden, "Transportation to Canterbury."

45 Carey 68-69. Concerning his commentary on Stothard's painting see Bowden, "Visual Portraits" 193-197, and throughout *Chaucer Aloud* and "Transportation to Canterbury."

46 Blake 533. On Stubbs' visit see Bowden, "Transportation to Canterbury" 79.

47 Blake 540. This and the previous qtn. come from the *Descriptive Catalogue* to his 1809 exhibition. I would like to thank the Research Council of Rutgers University for funding those nineteen of the illustrations to this article that were obtained before the mid-1990s,

when criteria shifted such that I would have had to apply and be rejected for at least one outside grant from some corporation or agency interested in eighteenth-century visual Chauceriana. I thank the U. S. Internal Revenue Service and my accountant, Philip Hughes, for the tax-deductibility of the other fifteen illustrations.

Works Cited

Alderson, William L., and Arnold C. Henderson. *Chaucer and Augustan Scholarship.* Berkeley: U of California P, 1970.

Altick, Richard D. *Paintings from Books: Art and Literature in Britain,1760-1900.* Columbus: Ohio State UP, 1985.

Bennett, Shelley M. *Thomas Stothard: The Mechanisms of Art Patronage in England circa 1800.* Columbia: U of Missouri P, 1988.

Bentley, G. E., Jr. "Comment upon the Illustrated EighteenthCentury Chaucer." *Modern Philology* 78 (1980-1981): 398.

Blake, William. *The Complete Poetry and Prose of William Blake.* Ed. David V. Erdman. Rev. ed. Berkeley: U of California P, 1982.

Boase, T. S. R. "Macklin and Bowyer." *Journal of the Warburg and Courtauld Institutes* 26 (1963): 148-177.

Bond, Richmond P. "Some Eighteenth-Century Chaucer Allusions." *Studies in Philology* 25 (1928): 316-339.

Bowden, Betsy. "The Artistic and Interpretive Context of Blake's 'Canterbury Pilgrims'." *Blake: An Illustrated Quarterly* 13 (1979-1980): 164-190.

--- "Before the Houyhnhnms: Rational Horses in the Late Seventeenth Century." *Notes and Queries* 237 (1992): 38-40.

--- "Canterbury Pilgrims and Their Horses in the Eighteenth Century: Two Artists' Interpretations." *Harvard Library Bulletin* ns 3 (1992-93): 18-34.

--- *Chaucer Aloud: The Varieties of Textual Interpretation.* Philadelphia: U of Pennsylvania P, 1987.

--- ed. *Eighteenth-Century Modernizations from The Canterbury Tales.* Rochester: Brewer, 1991.

--- "Introduction to the Second Edition." *The Comedy of Eros: Medieval French Guides to the Art of Love.* Tr. Norman R. Shapiro. 2nd ed. Urbana: U of Illinois P, 1997. ix-xviii.

--- "Transportation to Canterbury: The Rival Envisionings by Stothard and Blake." *Studies in Medievalism* 11 (2001): 73-111.

---   "Visual Portraits of the Canterbury Pilgrims, 1484(?)-1809." *The Ellesmere Chaucer: Essays in Interpretation*. Ed. Martin Stevens and Daniel Woodward. San Marino: Huntington Library; Tokyo: Yushodo, 1997. 171-204.

Butlin, Martin. "The Rediscovery of an Artist: James Jefferys 1751-1784." *Blake: An Illustrated Quarterly* 10 (1976-77): 123-124.

Carey, William P. *A Critical Description of the Procession of Chaucer's Pilgrims to Canterbury. Painted by Thomas Stothard, Esq., R.A.* 2nd ed. London: Glindon, 1818.

Cavendish, William, Duke of Newcastle. *La méthode et invention nouvelle de dresser les chevaux*. 1658. Trans. [anon.] as *A General System of Horsemanship*. 2 vols. London: Brindley, 1743.

Chaucer, Geoffrey. *The Riverside Chaucer*. Ed. Larry D. Benson. 3rd ed. Boston: Houghton, 1987.

Clifford, Timothy, and Susan Legouix. "James Jefferys, Historical Draughtsman (1751-84)." *Burlington Magazine* 118 (1976): 148-157.

Coxhead, A. C. *Thomas Stothard, R.A.: An Illustrated Monograph*. London: Bullen, 1906.

Cunnington, C. Willett, and Phillis Cunnington. *Handbook of English Costume in the Eighteenth Century*. Boston: Plays, 1972.

[*DNB*=]Dictionary *of National Biography*. Ed. Leslie Stephen and Sidney Lee. 22 vols. 1885-1901. London: Oxford UP, 1937-1938.

Dryden, John. *The Poems of John Dryden*. Ed. James Kinsley. 4 vols. Oxford: Clarendon, 1958.

Evans, Joan. *A History of the Society of Antiquaries*. Oxford: Oxford UP, for Society of Antiquaries, 1956.

Furnivall, Frederick J. "Mortimer's Illustrations to Chaucer's 'Canterbury Tales'." *Notes and Queries* 6th ser. 2 (1880): 325-326.

Graves, Algernon. *The Royal Academy of Arts: A Complete Dictionary of Contributors and Their Work from Its Foundation in 1769 to 1904*.1905. 4 vols. Wakefield, Yorks.: S. R.; Bath: Kingsmead, 1970.

---   *The Society of Artists of Great Britain, 1760-1791: The Free Society of Artists,1761-1783*. 1907. Bath: Kingsmead, 1969.

Hammelmann, Hanns. *Book Illustrators in Eighteenth-Century England*. Ed. and compl. T. S. R. Boase. New Haven: Yale UP, for Paul Mellon Centre, 1975.

Hutchison, Sidney C. *The History of the Royal Academy, 1768-1986*. 2nd ed. London: Royce, 1986.

Kerling, Johan. *Chaucer in Early English Dictionaries: The Old-Word Tradition in English Lexicography down to 1721 and Speght's Chaucer Glossaries.*The Hague: Nijhoff, for Leiden UP, 1979.

Lam, George L., and Warren H. Smith. "George Vertue's Contributions to Chaucerian Iconography." *Modern Language Quarterly* 5 (1944): 303-322.

Lindahl, Carl. *Earnest Games: Folkloric Patterns in the Canterbury Tales*. Bloomington: Indiana UP, 1987.

Lipking, Lawrence. *The Ordering of the Arts in Eighteenth-Century England*. Princeton: Princeton UP, 1970.

Miskimin, Alice. "The Illustrated Eighteenth-Century Chaucer." *Modern Philology* 77 (1979-1980): 26-55.

Morison, Stanley. *John Bell, 1745-1831: Bookseller, Printer, Publisher, Typefounder, Journalist, &c.* 1930. introd. Nicolas Barker. New York: Garland, 1981.

Muscatine, Charles. *Chaucer and the French Tradition.*1957. Berkeley: U of California P, 1969.

Nicolson, Benedict. *John Hamilton Mortimer, ARA, 1740-1779: Paintings, Drawings, and Prints*. London: Mellon, 1968.

Oxford English Dictionary, 2 vols. Oxford: Oxford UP, 1971.

Pope, Alexander. *The Rape of the Lock and Other Poems*. Ed. Geoffrey Tillotson. 3rd ed. London: Methuen; New Haven: Yale UP, 1962. Vol. 2 of *The Twickenham Edition of the Poems of Alexander Pope*. Ed. John Butt. 11 vols. in 12. 1939-1969.

Roworth, Wendy Wassyng. "Biography, Criticism, Art History: Angelica Kauffman in Context." *Eighteenth-Century Women and the Arts*. Ed. Frederick M. Keener and Susan E. Lorsch. Westport: Greenwood, 1988. 209-223.

Ruggiers, Paul G., ed. *Editing Chaucer: The Great Tradition*. Norman: U of Oklahoma P, 1984.

Shakespeare, William. *The Riverside Shakespeare*. Ed. G. Blakemore Evans. 2nd ed. Boston: Houghton, 1997.

Solkin, David H., ed. *Art on the Line: The Royal Academy Exhibitions at Somerset House, 1780-1835*. New Haven: Yale UP, for Paul Mellon Centre and Courtauld Institute, 2001.

Spurgeon, Caroline F. E. *Five Hundred Years of Chaucer Criticism and Allusion, 1357-1900*. 1908-1917. 3 vols. in 6 parts. New York: Russell, 1960.

Taylor, Basil. *Stubbs*. London: Phaidon, 1971.

Tyrwhitt, Thomas, ed. *The Canterbury Tales of Chaucer*. 5 vols. 1775-1778. New York: AMS, 1972.

Vertue, George. *Note Books*. 6 vols. numbered 18, 20, 24, 26, 29, and 30. Oxford: University Press, for Walpole Society, 1930-1955.

Waterhouse, Ellis. *The Dictionary of British 18th Century Painters in Oils and Crayons*. Woodbridge, Suffolk: Antique Collectors' Club, 1981.

Whitley, William Thomas. *Artists and Their Friends in England, 1700-1799*. 1928. 2 vols. New York: Blom, 1968.

Appendix

Analysis of visual art requires, of course, seeing it. Of the eighteenth-century artwork mentioned in this article, only the two paintings by Stothard and Blake have been reproduced at all frequently. Two of the other sources, although seldom reproduced, can be found in numerous libraries: the 1721 Urry edition of Chaucer's *Works* and the 1782-83 edition of Bell's British Poets. This appendix serves as a locating guide to reproductions from and discussions about these relatively accessible sources, citing my previous publications. (I have never before discussed the work of Diana Beauclerk, available in many libraries.)

In addition, this appendix both supplies citations and also reprints the pictures themselves for the two least accessible sources: the Mortimer series reproduced in 1816 but never widely distributed, and the Jefferys series never reproduced. Reprinted below, again by courtesy of the Houghton Library, Harvard University, are the three Mortimer scenes (figures 35-37) and the nine Jefferys pilgrims (figures 38-46) that I have discussed elsewhere. Each Mortimer engraving measures 15.5 cm.x. 21 cm., each Jefferys drawing 27.5 cm. x 36 cm.

In the citations, the following abbreviations refer to publications by Betsy Bowden:

BIQ = "The Artistic and Interpretive Context of Blake's 'Canterbury Pilgrims'." *Blake: An Illustrated Quarterly* 13 (1979-80): 164-190.
CA = *Chaucer Aloud: The Varieties of Textual Interpretation*. Philadelphia: U of Pennsylvania P, 1987.
HLB = "Canterbury Pilgrims and Their Horses in the Eighteenth Century: Two Artists' Interpretations." *Harvard Library Bulletin* ns 3 (1992-93): 18-34.
EC = " Visual Portraits of the Canterbury Pilgrims, 1484(?)- 1809." The Ellesmere Chaucer: Essays in Interpretation. Ed. Martin Stevens and Daniel Woodward. San Marino: Huntington Library; Tokyo: Yushodo, 1997. 171-204.
SM = "Transportation to Canterbury: The Rival Envisionings by Stothard and Blake." *Studies in Medievalism* 11 (2001): 731

> For the painting by William Blake (1809, engraved 1810) see BIQ, CA, EC, and SM.
> For the painting by Thomas Stothard (1807) see EC and SM (also discussed but not reproduced in CA).
> For the departure scene by Thomas Stothard in volume 14 of Bell's British Poets (engraved 1783) see BIQ, CA, and EC.
> For the anonymous illustrations to the *Works* of Chaucer, ed. John Urry (engraved before 1721) see as follows. The pilgrims are listed in the General Prologue order, not in the Urry-edition order of their tales. Departure scene: BIQ and CA. Chaucer: BIQ and HLB. Knight: HLB. Squire: HLB

and SM. Prioress: CA. Monk: HLB. Merchant: CA. Clerk: EC. Shipman: HLB. Parson: HLB. Miller: EC. Manciple: EC. Reeve:HLB. Summoner: EC. Pardoner: CA.

For the drawings by John H. Mortimer (before 1779, engraved 1787), see as follows (with reproductions below). *Departure of the Canterbury Pilgrimes* (fig. 35): BIQ, CA, and EC. *January and May* (fig. 36): CA. *Three Gamblers and Time* (fig. 37): CA.

For the drawings by James Jefferys (1781) see as follows, listed in General Prologue order (with reproductions below).

Chaucer (fig. 38): HLB.

Knight (fig. 39): HLB.

Squire (fig. 40): HLB.

Monk (fig. 41): HLB.

Clerk (fig. 42): EC.

Shipman (fig. 43): HLB.

Physican (fig. 44): EC.

Reeve (fig. 45): HLB.

Summoner (fig. 46): EC.

Fig. 1 - Palamon and Arcita

Fig. 2 - Scene from the Knight's Tale

Fig. 3 - Scene from the Knight's Tale

Fig. 4 - Scene from the Knight's Tale

Fig. 5 - Decoration for the Knight's Tale

Fig. 6 - Decoration for the Knight's Tale

Fig. 7 - Decoration for the Knight's Tale

Fig. 8 - Nicholas, the Carpenter, and Robin

MILLER of TROMPINGTON and TWO SCHOLARS. *Reeve's Tale* *Chaucer*
London Published Feb 1st 1787 by I.R. Smith, No 31 King Street Covent Garden

Fig. 9 - Miller of Trompington and Two Scholars

THE COKE and PERKIN. *Cokes Tale* *Chaucer*
London Published Feb 1st 1787 by I.R. Smith, No 31 King Street Covent Garden

Fig. 10 - The Coke and Perkin

THE SOMPNOUR DEVIL and OLD WOMAN. *Freere's Tale* *Chaucer*
London Published Feb 1st 1787 by I.R. Smith, No 31 King Street Covent Garden

Fig. 11 - The Sompnour, Devil, and Old Woman

THE FRERE and THOMAS. *Sompnour's Tale* *Chaucer*
London Published Feb 1st 1787 by I.R. Smith, No 31 King Street Covent Garden

Fig. 12 - The Frere and Thomas

Fig. 13 - Scene from the Second Nun's Tale

Fig. 14 - Scene from the Shipman's Tale

Fig. 15 - The Friar

Fig. 16 - The Manciple

Fig. 17 - The Cook

Fig. 18 - The Five Citizens

Fig. 19 - The Franklin

Fig. 20 - The Host

Fig. 21 - The Man of Law

Fig. 22 - The Merchant

Fig. 23 - The Yeoman

Fig. 24 - The Miller

Fig. 25 - The Plowman

Fig. 26 - The Parson

Fig. 27 - The Prioress

Fig. 28 - The Pardoner

Fig. 29 - The Cook

Fig. 30 - The Physician

Fig. 31 - The Franklin

Fig. 32 - The Man of Law

Fig. 33 - The Yeoman

Fig. 34 - Scene of departure to Canterbury

Drawn by Mortimer.   Engraved by Hogg.

EPARTURE of the CANTERBURY PILGRIMES. *Prologue.* Canterbury Tale.
Cha.

London Published Feby 2th 1727 by I R Smith N31 King Street Covent Garden.

Fig. 35 - Mortimer, Departure of the Canterbury Pilgrims

JANUARY and MAY *Merchantes Tale* *Chaucer*
London Publish'd Feb.^{ry}2 1727 by J.R. Smith N.31 King Street Covent Garden

Fig. 36 - Mortimer, January and May

Drawn by Mortimer.   Engraved by Blogg.

THREE GAMBLERS and TIME.   Chaucer.

London, Published Feb.y 2.th 1787 by Tho. Smith No 31 King Street Covent Garden

Fig. 37 - Mortimer, Three Gamblers and Time

Fig. 38 - Jefferys, Chaucer

Fig. 39 - Jefferys, Knight

Fig. 40 - Jefferys, Squire

Fig. 41 - Jefferys, Monk

Fig. 42 - Jefferys, Clerk

Fig. 43 - Jefferys, Shipman

Fig. 44 - Jefferys, Physician

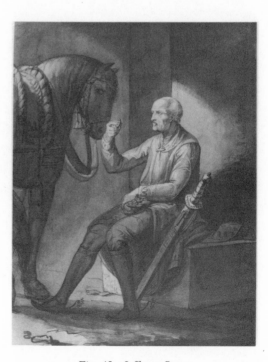

Fig. 45 - Jefferys, Reeve

Fig. 46 - Jefferys, Summoner

Chapter 5

From Canterbury to Jerusalem:
Interpreting Blake's *Canterbury Pilgrims*

Warren Stevenson

B lake's drawing of Chaucer's *The Canterbury Pilgrims*, begun in
1806, completed as a tempera painting in time for his ill-fated
exhibition of May, 1809,[1] and subsequently engraved, was one
of a series of dramatic pictures on literary themes that included the earlier series for Robert Blair's poem *The Grave*, Edward Young's *Night
Thoughts*, and the Milton and Bunyan series; culminated in the great
Illustrations to the Book of Job; and extended to the unfinished illustrations to Dante's *Commedia*. As Northrop Frye observed, in these
works Blake undertook "to illustrate other poets' vision so that their
readers may more easily understand their archetypal significance."[2]
There followed in the 1960s a brief commentary by S. Foster Damon
and a more substantial study by Karl Kiralis of what has since become
one of Blake's better known literary illustrations.[3] Kiralis invited further studies of *The Canterbury Pilgrims* in the hope that they might
throw more light on the symbolism of Blake's roughly contemporaneous Major Prophecies and receive reciprocal illumination therefrom.[4]
The following essay takes up Kiralis' invitation.

Any sound discussion of *The Canterbury Pilgrims* must take as its
point of departure Blake's *Descriptive Catalogue*, which he prepared
for the 1809 exhibition, and which includes not only, as Charles Lamb
observed, "a most spirited criticism of Chaucer,"[5] but also a commentary on the picture itself, without which we should be only imperfectly
aware of the subtleties of Blake's aim and method. In this catalogue
Blake declares,

> The characters of Chaucer's Pilgrims are the characters which compose
> all ages and nations: as one age falls, another rises, different to mortal sight,

Fig. 1 - Engraving of Blake's Canterbury Pilgrims

but to immortals only the same; for we see the same characters repeated again and again, in animals, vegetables, minerals, and in men; nothing new occurs in identical existence; Accident ever varies, Substance can never change nor decay.

Of Chaucer's characters as described in his Canterbury Tales, some of the names or titles are altered by time, but the characters themselves for ever remain unaltered, and consequently they are the physiognomies or lineaments of universal human life, beyond which Nature never steps....

As Newton numbered the stars, and as Linneus numbered the plants, so Chaucer numbered the classes of men.[6]

Of his own role as artist, Blake goes on to explain that he has "consequently varied the head and forms of his personages into all Nature's varieties; the Horses he has also varied to accord to their Riders; the costume is correct according to the authentic monuments" (K 567). This statement might be taken to imply a documentary or quasi-realistic approach to Blake's subject, limiting his more characteristic archetypal method. However, as we shall see, Blake does not hesitate to depart from Chaucer's text and even "the authentic monuments" when it suits his purpose to do so; and his remarks should be taken in

CANTERBURY PILGRIMS

conjunction with another passage that occurs later in *A Descriptive Catalogue*: "Thus the reader will observe, that Chaucer makes every one of his characters perfect in his kind; every one is an Antique Statue; the image of a class, and not of an imperfect individual" (K 570-571). These statements suggest a sculpturesque influence upon Blake's work reminding one of his earlier association with John Flaxman and his study of the Gothic cathedrals. In his theory of art Blake–like the medieval artisans who decorated those same cathedrals–is for clear and determinate outline and minute particularity in the delineation of character. He is against "generalization," which is another name for the vague or abstract: "A History Painter Paints the Hero, & not Man in General, but most minutely in Particular."[7] Accordingly, Blake recommends to the viewer's attention "every Lineament of Head, Hand & Foot, every particular of dress or Costume, where every Horse is appropriate to his Rider, & the Scene or Landscape with its Villages, Cottages, Churches, & Inn in Southwark is minutely labour'd...even to the Stuffs & Embroidery of the Garments, the hair upon the Horses, the Leaves upon the Trees, & the Stones & Gravel upon the road."[8]

In Blake's depiction of the Canterbury pilgrims it is morning (color plate 33 and figure 1). The first beams of the sun and the south wind (note the direction that the smoke is blowing from the chimneys in the distance) are pushing back the dark clouds which slant away towards the north. Thirty pilgrims are emerging from the Gothic portal of the Tabard Inn, led by the Squire and the Knight, and comprehending, in Dryden's fine phrase, "God's plenty."[9] They are being watched by some standing figures, and the sun is about to rise behind the Pilgrims, most of whom are facing west. Although their nominal journey takes them southeast to Canterbury, their symbolic journey is westward, in accord with what Blake elsewhere calls "the current of/Creation."[10] Thus Blake establishes an antithesis between the Pilgrims *as* pilgrims, and the Pilgrims as exemplars of the Divine Humanity—an antithesis which, it will be argued, is basic to his symbolic and archetypal method of portraying each of the individual figures as well as the universal types they represent.

Visible against the sky are the black silhouettes of four flying birds–probably ravens of dawn.[11] Five white, dove-like birds are also awake to greet the dawn; two of these are hovering in flight, and the other three are perched on the scalloped eaves of the Tabard. Perhaps they symbolize the five senses of man through which he may perceive eternity, as Blake wrote symbolically in the opening lines of *Europe: A Prophecy*.[12] Two of the perched doves appear to be billing and cooing, and one of the flying doves appears to be hovering over the planet Venus, also known as Lucifer and the morning star, visible through the clouds over the Gothic church in the distance. This image probably refers to Chaucer as the morning star of English poetry.[13] These nine birds, perhaps meant to recall the nine "Nights" of Blake's *The Four Zoas*, may also represent the joys of generation and poetry proceeding alike from a heavenly source whence our apprehension of human mortality and immortality also emanates.

Of the Pilgrims themselves, as Damon writes, "The upper classes lead the way, the lower classes follow, and democratic Harry Baily unites them."[14] A good example of Blake's skillful efforts to reconcile reasonable fidelity to Chaucer's text with faithfulness to his own vision may be seen in his portrayal of the Knight's group, of which he writes:

> The Knight is a true Hero, a good, great, and wise man; his whole length portrait on horseback, as written by Chaucer, cannot be surpassed. He has spent his life in the field; has ever been a conqueror, and is that species of

> character which in every age stands as the guardian of man against the oppressor. His son is like him with the germ of perhaps greater perfection still, as he blends literature and the arts with his warlike studies. (K 567-68)

In Chaucer's "General Prologue" the Knight comes first; in Blake's picture the Knight, whose "whole length portrait on horseback" is admirably rendered, is slightly preceded by his son, the Squire, whose handsome face framed with blond hair and cap with gay red plumes can perhaps best be described as Apollonian. The Squire's free-and-easy attitude is forward-looking, in contrast to the Knight's retrospective glance and gesture directing the viewer's eyes to the middle of the picture. Also, the Squire's gaily caparisoned mount is frisking and has a noticeably livelier expression than the Knight's war-horse, which has appropriately glaring eyes like the mastiff that trots between them.

A curious aspect of what may at first appear to be Blake's wholly favorable portrayal of the Knight, who has just returned from the Crusades, is that it sorts oddly with his view of war as "energy Enslaved," with his strong critique of warfare throughout the major Prophecies, and with his identification of "Religion hid in war" as the work of Rahab and Satan.[15] Four of Blake's other pictures from his exhibition of 1809 deal with the theme of warfare: *The Spiritual Form of Pitt Guiding Behemoth*, *The Spiritual Form of Nelson Guiding Leviathan*, *The Bard*, and *The Ancient Britons* (now lost). To these may be added a fifth, *The Whore of Babylon* (1809), at the bottom of which tiny figures are engaged in fighting. Thus, it is no exaggeration to say that Blake was preoccupied with the theme of warfare at this time, when Nelson and Pitt were dead, but the Napoleonic Wars were still raging.[16] And yet, how neatly he sidesteps the issue in his remarks about the Knight's military prowess and noble character. To see that the matter is far from being settled by Blake's referring to him as "a guardian of man against the oppressor"–the oppressor in this instance presumably being the Moors–one need only recall the lines, "Nought can deform the Human Race/Like to the Armour's iron brace" from *Auguries of Innocence* (ll. 99-100). And Blake's Knight, unlike Chaucer's, is portrayed wearing armor.[17] It is instructive to note that when Blake came to do his *Job* engravings some fifteen years later, he repeated the visual effect of the "good" Knight's scaled armor in the portrayal of Satan, whose upper breast, neck, shoulders, loins, and thighs are likewise covered in scales.[18] One may conclude that Blake calls the Knight "good" because Blake is distinguishing "between

States & Individuals of those States" (*The Four Zoas*, viii:380). To perceive the Knight as "good" requires a vision of forgiveness on the part of the beholder which it is the aim of Blake's art to evoke. It is also worth noting that in the overall placement of the figures the Knight, second from the beginning of the procession, counterbalances Chaucer himself, second from the end, reminding one that in Blake's myth the "war of swords" is the antithesis of "intellectual War" (*The Four Zoas*, ix:854).

As for the Knight's connection with organized religion, Blake portrays on his breast a small cross, thus introducing a visual motif that is repeated twice in the portrayal of the Prioress, who follows the Knight and in whose direction his extended right hand points, and three times in the portrayal of the Pardoner, who comes next among the full-length figures, and whose gloved right hand holding a gem-studded cross is extended towards both the Prioress and the Knight. Also, there hang from the Knight's armor-plated shoulders two red draperies—an almost feminine touch reminding the viewer of the biblical curtains of the tabernacle and Blake's veil symbolism,[19] about which more presently.

Paralleling Blake's ambivalent portrayal of the Knight there seems at first glance to be a discrepancy between the remarks concerning the Prioress in *A Descriptive Catalogue* and his handling of the themes of chastity and sexual restraint symbolized by Tirzah ("teaser"), daughter of Rahab, in the Prophecies. The opening tone of the former is deceptively suave:

> This Lady is described...as of the first rank, rich and honoured. She has certain peculiarities and little delicate affectations, not unbecoming in her, being accompanied by what is truly grand and really polite; her person and face Chaucer has described with minuteness; it is very elegant, and was the beauty of our ancestors, till after Elizabeth's time, when voluptuousness and folly began to be accounted beautiful. (K 568)

But Blake's portrayal of the Prioress, even more so than that of the Knight, is charged with mordant irony. Damon unhesitatingly (and rightly) glosses her as "Tirzah, the Prude."[20] His supporting evidence is drawn from Blake's myth, particularly a passage in the first chapter of *Jerusalem* (5:40-45) where Rahab and Tirzah, representing the superficially opposed states of licentiousness and prudery, divide the daughters of Albion between them, and from the following comment further on in *A Descriptive Catalogue*: "The characters of Women Chaucer has divided into two classes, the Lady Prioress and the Wife of Bath. Are not these leaders of the ages of men? The lady prioress, in some ages, predominates; and in some the wife of Bath, in whose character Chaucer has been equally minute and exact, because she is also a scourge and a blight" (K 572). Such scathing remarks notwithstanding, there is no use in our asking whether Blake praises or damns these characters. His praise or condemnation is directed at the class or state with which an individual has identified himself. Blake portrays his characters in all their human complexity, with a shrewd insight and humor comparable to, though subtly different from, that of Chaucer himself. It is not Blake's purpose to judge, but to delineate character.[21]

For Tirzah's beauty there is the precedent of the *Song of Solomon* (6:4), as well as Chaucer's own description of the Prioress. As to the inner symbolism of Blake's portrait of this figure, the net-like covering of her horse's body reminds one of his use of the net as a symbol of the snares of sex (see "The Golden Net"–in the tempera the Prioress' net is golden–and "How Sweet I roam'd"), and also the Net of Religion, which in the Major Prophecies is identified with the veil of Vala.[22] This veil motif is replicated in the diaphanous blouse or top that simultaneously covers and reveals the Prioress' shoulders and breasts, although not, curiously enough, her arms, which are covered by a dark material resembling that which she wears on her lower body. While this horizontal bifurcation of dress may reflect some monastic prohibition being honored more in the breach than the observance, it also signifies that the Prioress is sending mixed signals. One's overall impression of artificially retarded innocence is reinforced by her two long braids, cross-eyed look,[23] and somewhat stern, prudish expression.

The Prioress' greyhounds, faithfully reproduced from Chaucer's text, remind one of chaste Diana's hounds. Her scarlet saddle contrasting with her black clothing links her symbolically with the Knight, who is also portrayed in these colors, and with the Wife of Bath. Beneath the cross suspended from the chain on the Knight's chest is a tiny wrought figure of a knight on horseback inside what looks like a crescent moon, symbol of Diana, while above the cross hanging from the Prioress's rosary is a brooch inscribed, according to Chaucer, with the Ovidian motto, "Amor vincit omnia"(I:162).[24] The red, curtain-like draperies hanging from the Knight's shoulder armor symbolize his subjection to the "female will" of Vala as manifested in the religious institutions of Chaucer's day and dramatically embodied in the demure, slightly frowning Prioress, in whose direction the sad-faced Knight-at-arms is turning with chivalric deference.[25]   One is reminded of the passage in *Jerusalem* where one of the warriors exclaims, "I must rush again to War, for the Virgin has frown'd and refused" (68:63).

Contrasted with the Prioress is her attendant Nun, usually known as "the Second Nun," whose expression is more soulful and humane, and whose visible stigmatum on the back of her raised right hand may be compared with Blake's favorable reference to St. Teresa of Avilon in *Jerusalem*, 75:50.[26] The Second Nun looks considerably less covered up in the engraving than in the tempera, notwithstanding the down-to-earth practicality of her shawl protecting her head and shoulders, and her gorget guarding her throat from the early morning April air. In the engraving, beneath her dark shawl she, like the Prioress, is wearing a not unbecoming diaphanous blouse or top, perhaps out of diplomatic solidarity with her quixotically, if not strategically, risqué Mother Superior, who would have been the arbiter of fashion in their monastic community. All this in no way detracts from, but rather enhances, what Blake antithetically portrays as the Second Nun's fundamentally religious character.

In view of the persuasive arguments of Kiralis and Reisner, to be discussed below, that the face of the Plowman is based on Blake's own, and those of the Pardoner and Summoner derive from the physiognomies of Pitt and Fox respectively, one might ask whether this contemporaneity includes any of the other Pilgrims. When I first asked myself this question, the face that came as it were unbidden to mind was that of the Second Nun, who, unlike the Wife of Bath and the Prioress, is looking directly at the viewer, and whose genuine modesty and simple faith (sans benefit of crucifix) are evident once the stigmatum on the back of her raised right hand is recognized. Her face resembles that of Catherine Blake, who, according to Mona Wilson, had "a face full of beauty and character, with large dark eyes."[27] The Second Nun's dark eyes seem more accentuated in the painting than in the engraving, but her beauty and character, including what Northrop Frye describes as Catherine Blake's "unexpectedly strong face, with a twist of the mouth full of tough and resilient humor," are there in both.[28] In addition to exhibiting her sensibleness in wearing a shawl on an early April morning, the Second Nun is not sporting any jewelry. Further, her curly hair is arranged around her head in a becoming manner that once more reminds one of Blake's drawings of his wife, who wore her hair cut short, and whose beauty he compared in one of his letters to "a flame of many colours of precious jewels."[29]

In the engraving Blake goes a step further in drawing the viewer's attention to this unobtrusive but important character, who evidently represents a commendable balance between the Wife of Bath's licentiousness and the Prioress' teasing prudery and so is more characteristic of Jerusalem. Blake makes this point by showing (more clearly in the engraving than in the tempera) that portion of the Second Nun's bodice visible just below her dark cutaway shawl as being of a contrasting light-colored, translucent material similar to the Prioress' top. Moreover, Blake has moved the Second Nun's barely covered right forearm up into a position of greater prominence than it had in the tempera, and has made the scar or wound on her right hand more evident. The Second Nun's ample right breast (the only one visible), with what looks like a partially obscured nipple, is now if anything more prominent than that of the Prioress, both women wearing two-tone gowns anticipating the high-waisted dresses that were coming into fashion during the Regency. In the crook of the Second Nun's arm one can see quite clearly in the engraving, less so in the tempera, the dark, reinforced high waist of the lower portion of her dress serving as additional support for her breasts, thus imitating the Prioress. Blake thereby suggests that the Second Nun, like Catherine Blake, has a good character and figure, but is neither prude nor exhibitionist.

I shall pass over Blake's portrayal of the Friar and the Monk, since his own discriminating commentary on these two characters "of a mixed kind" should place their massive, sculpturesque portraits in adequate perspective and shall proceed to the Pardoner and the Summoner.[30] The Pardoner, whose full figure is turned away from the viewer toward "his freend and his compeer" (I:670), the Summoner, dominates this part of the picture. Blake refers to the Pardoner as "the Age's Knave," and to the Summoner as "also a Devil of the first magnitude," adding that "the uses to Society are perhaps equal of the Devil and of the Angel" (K 570), a remark that once more indicates Blake's antithetical method.

The jewel-encrusted cross held in the Pardoner's gloved right hand, replicated by the large red crosses on his back and wallet, highlights both his office and his flagitious hypocrisy. Frye points out that Blake associates triple-ness with the Anti-Christ, and Damon observes that for Blake the cross is "an instrument of execution, of the Vengeance for Sin, and therefore should not symbolize the true religion of forgiveness."[31] The Pardoner's long, lank hair and effeminate clothing, if not his earring (visible in the engraving), aptly hint at the nature of his relationship with the Summoner, who regards him with a sensual leer. The Pardoner's horse looks as though it is trying to get the bit between its teeth, and is enabled to do so because the Pardoner alone among the Pilgrims has relinquished his grip on the reins.

In a thoughtful article entitled "Effigies of Power: Pitt and Fox as Canterbury Pilgrims," E. M. Reisner presents the case for Pitt as Pardoner and his Parliamentary antagonist Fox as Summoner on the level of political satire, citing Blake's roughly contemporaneous Pitt and Nelson frescoes by way of analogy.[32] While Reisner observes that "the briefest comparison of Blake's Pardoner and Summoner with Gillray's (or Sayers's or Rowlandson's) standard representations of sharp-nosed Pitt and swarthy-jowled Fox demonstrates striking like-ness" (488), she also recognizes that Blake's purpose was larger than mere political satire: "The Pardoner and Summoner...[also] represent the principles in which Pitt and Fox participate....In Blake's day these two classes [of men] had taken over the leadership, but where in his own society could he see Harry Baily?" (502). The point of Reisner's shrewd rhetorical thrust, one supposes, is that Harry Baily, whom Blake describes as "equally free with the Lord and the Peasant" (K 569), tran-scends politics, something which a current critical fashion that Blake would have regarded with contempt has declared impossible.

Dominating the center of the picture, Harry Baily's firm figure with outspread arms assumes the position sometimes known as "the living cross," which, in contrast to the "dead cross" of the crucifix, symbol-izes forgiveness.[33] The living cross also contrasts with the Pardoner's swastika-like contortions. Certainly, what Blake elsewhere refers to as the Divine Vision is central to his purpose here. However, since a sim-ilar posture is assumed by Satan while afflicting Job in the *Job* series,[34] as well as by Pitt in *The Spiritual Form of Pitt Guiding Behemoth*, Harry Baily's outstretched arms may also represent a marriage of heav-en and hell, of Innocence and Experience, which enables him to com-mand the other Pilgrims. As Blake remarks, the Host "holds the cen-ter of the cavalcade, is a first rate character, and his jokes are no tri-fles;...though uttered with audacity, and equally free with Lord and Peasant, they are always substantially and weightily expressive of knowledge and experience" (K 569). Harry Baily, with both arms mag-nanimously extended in opposite directions, holds his horse's reins in his left hand and a whip in his right; both are held loosely, giving one the impression of an easy assumption of authority. This image accords well with his central position in the design. The impression of down-to-earth practicality is reinforced by the thick belt around the Host's waist and the dagger at his side. He has also had the foresight to bring along a bedroll or extra blanket. The feather in his cap repeats a motif introduced in the Apollonian portrayal of the Squire, replicated by the swirl of the tip of the reins held gesticulatingly over his horse's head. His ruddy countenance, jovial expression, and elegant ruff give him an irresistible charm.

According to Blake, the principal character in the next group of figures–those who follow the Host–is the Good Parson, whose full-length portrait balances that of the Pardoner. Blake calls the Parson "an Apostle, a real Messenger of Heaven, sent in every age for its light and its warmth," and adds, "He serves all, and is served by none; he is, according to Christ's definition, the greatest of his age" (K 570). The Parson's white-bearded, black-cassocked figure mounted on a small, gentle-looking horse attains a calm dignity that is subtly emphasized by the arrangement of the figure. His is the only one of the seven full-length figures which presents a perfect profile, and the stark, black-and-white coloration contrasts markedly with that of the other figures in the tempera. This rather severe effect is reinforced by the complete absence of adornment on his person and mount. Though he wears no spurs, his horse's tail has been docked with perhaps unwitting cruelty, granted the rudimentary awareness of animal rights in the fourteenth century.[35] He somewhat resembles the eponymous protagonist of "The Voice of the Ancient Bard" as portrayed in the illustration to that poem in *Songs of Innocence and of Experience*, and also, inevitably, Urizen; for as priest he is a pillar of the religious establishment. True, the Parson is a good pillar, but only insofar as one exercises the vision of forgiveness that distinguishes his true character or individuality from his institutional trappings. Once more, Blake's double vision or keen sense of paradox is evident.

Of the seven figures who appear between Harry Baily and the parson, six–the Sergeant of Law, the Plowman (whom Kiralis sees as Blake's low-keyed, self-portrait, neglecting to mention his broad-brimmed hat),[36] the Doctor of Physic, the Franklin, and two "Citizens of London" or Guildsmen[37]–are facing Harry Baily, and their horses are likewise looking at him, leading the viewer's gaze back towards the center of the design. The Franklin's plumed hat, like that of Harry Baily and the Squire, accords with the sanguine temperament and out-going, hospitable nature Chaucer assigns the Franklin in the General Prologue (I:331-360). Blake calls him "the Bacchus" of the group and observes that he contrasts with the dour Physician, whose exterior adornment belies his grave expression. Still, Blake insists that the Physician is "perfect, learned, completely Master and Doctor in his art," in keeping with Blake's dictum that "Chaucer makes every one of his characters perfect in his kind; every one is an Antique statue, the image of a class, and not of an imperfect individual" (K 570-571). The seventh figure of this group, who is looking over his shoulder at the others and wears a beaver hat, is not the Merchant, whom Chaucer describes thus attired, but the Shipman. Blake appears to have playfully transposed a detail of the Merchant's dress to the Shipman, whose shipboard thefts of wine Chaucer mentions, and whose uneasy posture and scowling expression highlight other details of Chaucer's portrayal.[38]

The fork-bearded Merchant appears between the Parson and the Wife of Bath. The Merchant looks at the Wife with an expression of doleful admiration. The Miller, playing his bagpipes, is looking over the Wife's right shoulder, and thus helps to provide an appropriate dramatic setting for this most flamboyant of Pilgrims, whose full-length portrait complements that of her counterpart, the Prioress, as Rahab complements her daughter Tirzah in Blake's myth. Each is seen as an aspect of Natural Religion masking the female will, or as respectively sexual licence and repression.

That Blake's Wife of Bath is portrayed as being in the state of Rahab, his mythic name for the Whore of Babylon, there can be little doubt, even though many of the details of her portrayal are taken straight from Chaucer's text, while others are elaborations of biblical passages. Thus, she appears with hose of scarlet red, a voluminous foot-mantle or riding rug over her large hips and thighs, sitting on the wrong side of a gaily bedecked horse, and holding a glass of wine that, on the literal level (like the Cook's tankard of foaming ale and the tavern boy and girl in the foreground) ties in with the departure-from-the-tavern setting, whereas on the symbolic level it is reminiscent of the golden cup of the Great Whore of *Revelation*.[39] In the tempera, the Wife's right hand holding the wine glass blocks out our view of the right eye of the Oxford scholar's horse—no doubt a horse of instruction. In the engraving Blake eliminated this detail, perhaps as being too didactic. Three strands of pearls circle the Wife's neck; the tripleness again recalls the Anti-Christ. From one of these strands hangs a heart-shaped locket and from another a small cross, which connects her with institutionalized religion, as does the fact that she appears beneath a hollow-looking Gothic church with seven or ten steeples, depending on whether or not one counts the three small steeples at the base of the large one on the right. These steeples ironically correspond to the seven heads and ten horns of the biblical beast that "was, and is not, and yet is."[40] What looks like a red horn surrounded by six smaller horns projecting from the Wife's elaborate headdress repeats this motif, which is carried on in the ten-pointed ruff around her neck. In her left hand is just visible (added in the engraving) the handle of a riding crop also resembling a scroll or hidden message.[41] Between the Wife's shapely ankles one of her "spores sharpe"(I:473) is visible, replicating the visual motif of Lucifer, the morning star, also called Venus, which appears between the two tallest steeples of the distant church.

The Wife's brazen expression, like her posture and shamelessly exposed breasts (somewhat muted in the engraving), contrasts with that of the demure Prioress, and her unlovely features are, as Blake observes, faithful to Chaucer's description. However, he chooses to ignore Chaucer's statement that she is "ywympled wel" (I:470), particularly if "wimpled" here means veiled, and instead endows her with a fantastic cobra-like hood, ingeniously improving on Chaucer's martial description of her large hat.[42] Blake's interpretation of the Wife's portrayal as involving her in the state of Rahab requires as much revelation as possible, and this apocalyptic context helps to explain both the serpent-like folds and design of her foot-mantle, a motif also evident in her horse's bridle, and the fact that the visible portion of the Miller's bagpipes just over her right shoulder resembles a trumpet. The basic principle at work here and, as Northrop Frye first convincingly showed, throughout Blake's Prophecies, is that the consolidation of error is a necessary prelude to the greater apprehension of truth.[43] Hence the deliberate ambiguity of the Wife's placement beneath the Gothic church;[44] the "star" called both Venus and Lucifer; and the four flying raven-like birds with their low-keyed apocalyptic irony, as well as the two dove-like birds hovering over both the star and the Wife, perhaps symbolizing the Holy Spirit which alone makes Mystery manifest.

An interesting aspect of the Wife's portrayal is that the arrangement of her figure, with knees apart and heels close together, closely resembles that of Amoret in Blake's analogous painting *Spenser's Faerie Queene*. But Amoret occupies the center of her cavalcade (which is also heading in the opposite direction), as does Harry Baily here, both figures having extended arms. As Damon observes of the later painting, Blake did not endorse Sir Guyon's prudery;[45] and it is instructive to note that Una is riding in the same position, with an open Bible in her lap. Once more, Blake's sense of ironic ambivalence enables him to give primacy to aesthetic rather than didactic considerations. This ambivalence, or suspension of judgment, expresses itself positively in what I have called Blake's "vision of forgiveness," which distinguishes, for example, the Wife of Bath's true individuality of character as expressed in the telling of her tale from the state with which she has allowed herself to become identified.

Chaucer himself is the last of the full-length figures on horseback, and the adjective that immediately springs to mind upon beholding his portrayal is "Christ-like." The modest, slightly bowed figure is richly appareled but without undue ostentation, and his black steed appears to be in fine fettle.[46] In his depiction of Chaucer, Blake draws on elements associated with other Pilgrims. Thus, Chaucer's embroidered clothing recalls the "General Prologue's" description of the Squire. The bearded face resembles the Knight's, as well as Jesus' in Blake's illustration *Christ and the Woman Taken in Adultery*. The rosary in his right hand recapitulates an aspect of the Prioress; his rolled up blanket is like Harry Baily's. His downcast eyes and composed attitude are reminiscent of the Parson. Even the Pardoner's demonic duplicity finds its appropriate analogue in what may be termed Chaucer's "angelic duplicity," since the latter's devout demeanor is at variance with the robust humor of *The Canterbury Tales*. Blake calls Chaucer "the great poetical observer of men" (K 569), whose "more comprehensive soul," to borrow a phrase from William Wordsworth's description of the prototypical poet, contains aspects of the various characters he so adeptly portrays.[47] Blake illustrates this quality by combining in the visual representation aspects of the characters Chaucer so adeptly portrays.

Last of all in the procession rides the choleric Reeve, whose sinister expression, taken in conjunction with Chaucer's description of him,[48] reminds one not merely of the plague, but also of the figure of Death riding on a pale horse in *Revelation*. The Reeve appears under the womb-like, tomb-like portal of the Tabard Inn from which the other Pilgrims have just emerged and to which, symbolically as well as literally, they must return. Chaucer and the Clerk of Oxford also ride beneath this portal, but whereas their figures are framed by solid arches, that of the Reeve is framed by a hollow one.[49]

Standing beside the portal at the far left is a group of people watching the procession, comprising an old man, a woman holding an active naked infant, a boy, and two girls, one of whom is holding a doll. This pleasant scene, taken together with the doves billing and cooing atop the roof of the Tabard, reinforces the idea that the picture as a whole illustrates an aspect of the Divine Vision seen as a procession from the State of Innocence in Blake's Beulah (Hebrew for "married"), through Generation or Experience, represented by the pilgrimage itself, to the supernal reality of Blake's fourfold Eden symbolized by the imminent sunrise and perhaps by the four adult figures who appear with a child in the distance at the far right, reminiscent of Blake's Four Zoas watching over life's journey in which they also participate as members of the Divine Humanity.

One may conclude that by virtue of Blake's antithetical methods of juxtaposition and contrast, his magisterial illustration *The Canterbury Pilgrims* invites the viewer to consider the classes of men in the light of eternity, and to participate in the human and divine vision of forgiveness by distinguishing "States from individuals in those States," so that the journey of the Pilgrims may be seen as metaphoric of that continuous dynamic progression which in his myth becomes Jerusalem, "a City, yet a Woman."   For as Blake wrote, "Every age is a Canterbury Pilgrimage."[50]

Notes

[1]   The unscrupulous publisher Robert Hartley Cromek, who had earlier cheated Blake out of the full reward for his set of commissioned designs to Blair's *The Grave* by breaking the contract and giving the work of engraving them to Luigi Schiavonetti, probably swindled Blake a second time, as Blake averred, after a visit to his studio by giving the idea for his work-in-progress *The Canterbury Pilgrims* to artist-engraver Thomas Stothard, whose florid style was more popular than Blake's Gothic one. See Mona Wilson, *The Life of William Blake* (London: Nonesuch Press, 1927), pp. 187-200, and G. E. Bentley, Jr., "'They Take Great Liberty's': Blake Reconfigured by Cromek and Modern Critics–The Argument from Silence," *Studies in Romanticism* 30 (1991): 657-684. For a dissenting view on the Blake-Cromek controversy see, for example, Aileen Ward, "Canterbury Revisited: The Blake-Cromek Controversy," *Blake: An Illustrated Quarterly* 22 (1988-89):80-92 and Dennis M. Read, "The Rival *Canterbury Pilgrims* of Blake and Cromek: Herculean Figures in the Carpet, *Modern Philology* 86 (1988):171-190. According to Read, "The idea to paint an illustration of the Canterbury pilgrims and make an engraving of the painting originated with Cromek, not Blake" (171).

[2]   *Fearful Symmetry: A Study of William Blake* (Princeton, NJ: Princeton University Press, 1947), 415. Hereafter "Frye."

[3] S.v. "Chaucer" in S. Foster Damon, *A Blake Dictionary: The Ideas and Symbols of William Blake* (Providence, RI: Brown University Press, 1965; revised ed., Hanover, NH: Published for Brown University Press by the University Press of New England, 1988)–hereafter "Damon;" Karl Kiralis, "William Blake as an Intellectual and Spiritual Guide to Chaucer's *Canterbury Pilgrims*," *Blake Studies* 1 (1969): 139-197–hereafter "Kiralis."

[4] Blake had recently finished *The Four Zoas* (1795-1804), was completing *Milton* (1804-1808), and beginning *Jerusalem* (1808-1820) at the time he was working on *The Canterbury Pilgrims*.

[5] To Bernard Barton, 18 May 1824, in *The Letters of Charles Lamb*, ed. E. V. Lucas, 3 vols. (London: J. M. Dent & Methuen, 1935), 2:425.

[6] *The Complete Writings of William Blake*, ed. Geoffrey Keynes (London: Oxford University Press, 1966; rpt, 1991, paperback), 567; hereafter "K" followed by page number.

[7] Blake's "Annotations to Sir Joshua Reynolds's Discourses" (London, 1798), K 465.

[8] "Draft for Prospectus of the Engraving of Chaucer's Canterbury Pilgrims," K 588.

[9] Preface to *Fables Ancient and Modern*, in *Of Dramatic Poesy and Other Critical Essays*, ed. George Watson, 2 vols. (London: Dent, 1962), 2:284.

[10] *Jerusalem* 77, K 717. See also Edward J. Rose, "Visionary Forms Dramatic: Grammatical and Iconographical Movement in Blake's Verse and Design," *Criticism* 7:2 (Spring 1966): 111- 125.

[11] Cf. the phrase "Raven of dawn" in *The Marriage of Heaven and Hell*, K 160, and see the entry under "Raven" in Damon. Cf. Also *Jerusalem* 66:70, K 703.

[12] "Five windows light the cavern'd man: thro' one he breathes the air;
"Thro' one hears music of the spheres; thro' one the eternal vine
"Flourishes, that he may receive the grapes; thro' one can look
"And see small portions of the eternal world that ever groweth;
"Thro' one himself pass out what time he please; but he will not,
"For stolen joys are sweet & bread eaten in secret pleasant." (*Europe*, ll.1-6, K 237)

[13] See Kiralis, 149, following S. Foster Damon, *William Blake: His Philosophy and Symbols* (New York: P. Smith, 1947), 218.

[14] Damon, 79.

[15] *The Four Zoas*, ix:152; *Jerusalem*, 75:20.

CP 1

CP 2

CP 3

CP 4

CP 5

CP 6

PLATE PAGE 1

CP 7

CP 8

CP 9

CP 10

CP 11

CP 12

PLATE PAGE 2

CP 13

CP 14

CP 15

CP 16

CP 17

CP 18

PLATE PAGE 3

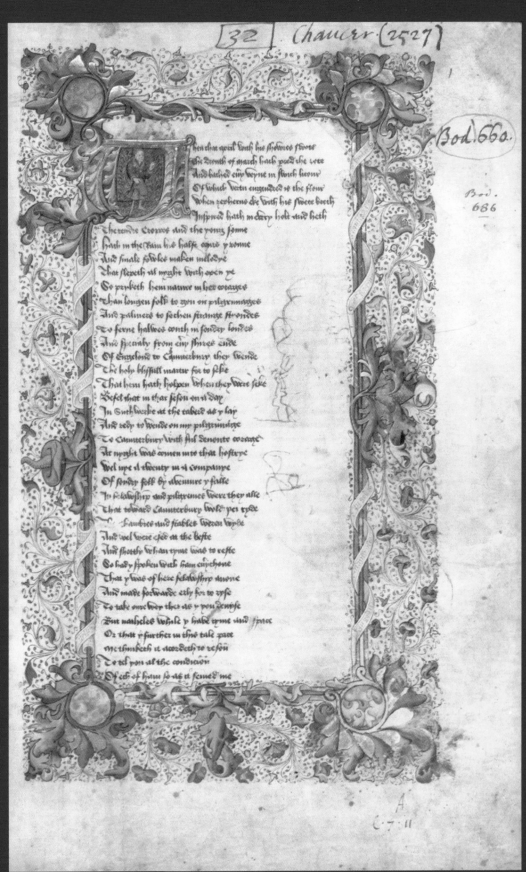

CP 20A

CP 20

PLATE PAGE 5

CP 21

CP 22

CP 23

CP 24

CP 25

CP 26

PLATE PAGE 6

CP 27

CP 28

CP 29

CP 30

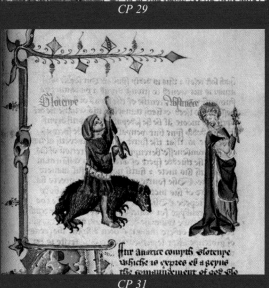

CP 31

CP 32

PLATE PAGE 7

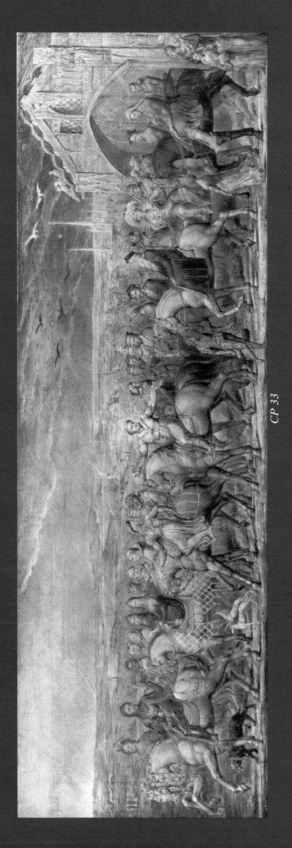

CP 33

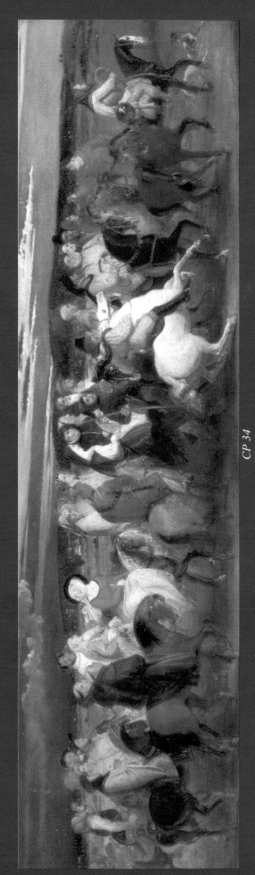

CP 34

PLATE PAGE 8

CP 36

CP 35

CP 37

CP 38

CP 39

CP 42

PLATE PAGE 11

CP 40

CP 41

PLATE PAGE 12

[16] Cf. Anthony Blunt, *The Art of William Blake* (New York: Columbia University Press, 1959), 97-103; William Gaunt, *Arrows of Desire* (London: Museum Press, 1956), 111-112; and David Erdman, *Prophet Against Empire: A Poet's Interpretation of His Own Times* (Princeton, NJ: Princeton University Press, 1954), passim.

[17] To be more precise, both mail and plate armor, a combination that was not uncommon in Chaucer's day, though the wearing of armor on a pilgrimage to Canterbury would have been, like some of the Wife of Bath's more outré accoutrements, inappropriate for the occasion. Blake, who was willing to sacrifice verisimilitude for dramatic and symbolic effect, opts for a narrowly literal interpretation of lines 75-78 of the "General Prologue" as suiting his purpose, with the result that one cannot see the besmottered "gypon" for the probably hypothetical "habergeon."

[18] See *Blake's Job*, Pl. VI and commentary. For other examples of Blake's early use of scaly figures see *Europe*, Pl. IX (Huntington), where the nude figure representing War is entirely covered with scales, *Goliath Cursing David* (c. 1805), and *Satan Comes to the Gates of Hell* (1807).

[19] See Frye, 381 and passim.

[20] Damon, p. 79. Cf. his entries under "Tirzah" and Rahab."

[21] Cf. "On Homer's Poetry," in which Blake states,
> Aristotle says Characters are either Good or Bad; now Goodness or Badness has nothing to do with Character: an Apple tree, a Pear tree, a Horse, a Lion are Characters, but a Good Apple tree or a Bad is an Apple tree still; a Horse is not more a Lion for being a Bad Horse: that is its Character: its Goodness or Badness is another consideration. (K 778)

[22] See Kiralis, 154-155 et passim. For Vala's net see *The Book of Urizen* 25:22; *Jerusalem* 42:81, et passim.

[23] I am indebted to Michael Thompson for this acute observation and for lending me his photolithograph of the engraving reproduced in this volume.

[24] All quotations from *The Canterbury Tales* are from *The Riverside Chaucer*, 3rd ed., ed. Larry D. Benson (Boston: Houghton Mifflin, 1987).

[25] See the entries under "female will" in the index to Frye.

[26] Corroborated by Samuel Palmer. See Mona Wilson, *The Life of William Blake*, p. 293.

[27] *The Life of William Blake*, p. 15. Wilson relied on contemporary accounts and Blake's drawings of his wife.

[28] Introduction to *Selected Poetry and Prose of William Blake*, ed. Northrop Frye (New York: Modern Library, 1953), xviii.

[29] Wilson, p. 15, quoting from a letter from Blake to William Hayley, in *The Writings of William Blake* (London: Nonesuch Press, 1925), 2: 185.

[30] Blake writes that Chaucer depicts the Monk
> as a man of the first rank in society, noble, rich, and expensively attended; he is a leader of the age, with certain humorous accompaniments in his character, that do not degrade, but render him an object of dignified mirth, but also other accompaniments not so respectable.

Of the Friar Blake writes,
> The Friar is a character also of a mixed kind...but in his office he is said to be a "full solemn man": eloquent, amorous, witty, and satyrical; young, handsome, and rich; he is a complete rogue, with constitutional gaiety enough to make him a master of all the pleasures of the world. (K 568)

[31] Frye, 300; Damon, s. v. "Cross."

[32] *Eighteenth-Century Studies* 12 (1979):481-503. For possible cartoon figures of Pitt, Fox, Burke, et al., in *Europe* (1794), see David V. Erdman, *The Illuminated Blake* (Garden City, NY: Anchor Press/Doubleday, 1974), 159-171.

[33] See *Blake's Job: William Blake's Illustrations of the Book of Job, with an Introduction and Commentary by S. Foster Damon* (Providence, RI: Brown University Press, 1966), Pls. XIII, XVIII, XX, and commentary. See also the discussion of the Summoner and the Pardoner below.

[34] See *Blake's Job*, Pl. VI.

[35] Since the horse probably has been hired, the Parson should perhaps not be held responsible for the state of his horse's tail. In the "General Prologue" Chaucer implies that the Parson does not own a horse, since he visits "The ferreste in his parisshe, muche and lite,/Upon his feet, and in his hand a staf" (I:494-495).

[36] Kiralis, 147-148. For Blake's broad-brimmed hat, see Mona Wilson's *Life of William Blake*, 150, and the pencil drawing by John Linnell that serves as that book's frontispiece.

[37] A third Citizen or Guildsman, clothed like the other two, appears between the Prioress and the Monk.

[38] The Shipman thus appears to have stolen the Merchant's hat, retaining his character of pirate even on land.

[39] See *Revelation* 17:1-6 and Blake's *The Whore of Babylon* (British Library). For the Wife's sitting "on the wrong side [of her horse] for a lady", see Kiralis, p. 148.

40 *Revelation* 13:1, 17:8.

41 For details of the riding crop (but not the "hidden message") see Kiralis, 148.
Cf. the tiny scroll-like book held between Albion's hands while he embraces
Jerusalem's lumbar loins in Pl. 99 of Copy C of *Jerusalem*, reproduced and com-
mented on in my *Romanticism and the Androgynous Sublime* (Madison, NJ:
Fairleigh Dickinson University Press,1996), 46-47. Both illustrations seem to refer
to the "improvement of sensual enjoyment" that Blake had predicted in *The
Marriage of Heaven and Hell* (14, K 154) would precede the apocalypse. Here the
conflation of whip and scroll may be meant to suggest sadomasochistic sexual play.

42 "and on her heed an hat/As brood as is a bokeler or a targe" (I:470-471).
    While Blake's Wife's headdress is fantastic, it is not without historical founda-
tion. "The simple coifs, gorgets, wimples, and veils of early medieval women gave
way (in the 14th cent.) to reticulated headdresses with jeweled gold cauls and
crespins, and later to conical hennins and large decorative butterfly and horn-shaped
headdresses with starched veils" (*The Columbia Encyclopedia*, s.v "hat").

43 *Fearful Symmetry* 61, 188, 357, et passim.

44 "Gothic is Living Form," from Blake's "On Virgil," K 778.

45 Damon, 384.

46 Beside Lavater's aphorism, "All finery is a sign of littleness," Blake wrote, "Not
always" (K 71).

47 Preface to *Lyrical Ballads*, 2nd ed. (London, 1800); reprinted with introduction
and notes by R. L. Brett and A. R. Jones (London: Methuen, 1968), 255.

48 "They were adrad of hym as of the deeth" (I:605).

49 This detail is more obvious in the engraving. Cf. the hollow steeple above the
Wife of Bath, first observed by Kiralis, p. 149.

50 *Jerusalem* 32:22, K 521; *The Four Zoas* ix:222; *A Descriptive Catalogue*, K 570.

Chapter 6

Thomas Stothard's *The Pilgrimage to Canterbury* (1806): A Study in Promotion and Popular Taste

Dennis M. Read

T homas Stothard's painting of *The Pilgrimage to Canterbury* (1806) and the subsequent engraving of it were a resoundingly popular sensation throughout the first half of the nineteenth century. Thousands viewed the painting in London and the provinces, and more than seven hundred subscribed to the engraving. The venture, while riddled with personal misfortune, broken promises, and a feud that remains unresolved to the present day, nevertheless can be called one of the most commercially successful enterprises of its kind. While the success of the design can be attributed to some extent to contemporary popular taste and to Stothard's artistic reputation, it probably has more to do with the orchestrations of publicity, endorsements, and huckstering by its proprietor, Robert Hartley Cromek, a tireless promoter of various literary and artistic schemes.

Part I

Thomas Stothard (1755-1834) was an artist who willingly undertook virtually any commission, ranging from shop-cards to the interior decoration of townhouses to designs for goldsmiths. He was best known for his book illustrations, which numbered in the thousands and covered literary works ranging from the classics to sentimental novels. Elected to the Royal Academy in 1794, he made comparatively few paintings during his long career. His artistic style shows versatility, but it most often expresses a gentle sentimentality. Contemporary commentators often used "charm" and "grace" in describing it.

Stothard had maintained a professional association with Cromek (1770-1812) for a decade before Cromek engaged him to paint *The Canterbury Pilgrims*. Cromek's first profession was engraving, and from the mid-1790s on, Stothard often chose Cromek to engrave his book and magazine illustrations. The largest commission of Cromek's chalcographic career was sixteen designs by Stothard illustrating *The Works of Salomon Gessner*, published by Cadell and Davies in 1802.

Engraving, however, was for Cromek too filled with drudgery. John Pye, who knew Cromek as early as 1801, when Pye was beginning his own engraving career, wrote that though Cromek "was nominally an Engraver; . . . his tastes and sympathies lay in another direction."[1] By late 1806 he had extricated himself from engraving and was attempting to make his mark as an impresario of art. He had already designated himself the proprietor of a lavish edition of *The Grave* by Robert Blair, with designs by William Blake engraved by Louis Schiavonetti. In promoting the edition, Cromek had secured endorsements from Henry Fuseli and eleven other members of the Royal Academy (including Stothard) and had traveled to Birmingham, Liverpool, and Yorkshire in search of subscribers. The volume was published in 1808 by Cadell & Davies.

After their marriage on October 24, 1806, Cromek and his bride, Elizabeth, moved into a house at 64 Newman Street in London, just down the street from Stothard's residence since 1794, 28 Newman Street. Benjamin West, President of the Royal Academy, had resided at 14 Newman Street since 1775. About forty other painters, sculptors, engravers, and others practicing the arts lived along its two-block length; it was popularly called "Artists' Street." Many years later John Scholey recalled in a letter to Thomas Cromek, "Your Father appeared to be on very Friendly terms with the Artists, many of whom then resided in Newman St & the neighborhood."[2]

If Stothard's biographer, Anna Eliza Bray, is correct in reporting a visit by George Stubbs while Stothard was finishing the painting,[3] Cromek settled his arrangement with Stothard in June 1806, before he left London to be married in Wakefield. Stubbs died July 10, 1806. Stothard made a number of sketches in preparation for his oil painting. According to Bray, he traveled to the outskirts of London to sketch the Surrey Hills "on the spot, from the Old Kent Road, near Peckham" in order to make the geography of the pilgrims' starting place as correct as possible.[4] Fidelity to medieval dress was another major consideration. According to Bray, "The painter, assisted by his son, Charles, collected from manuscripts of the time of Chaucer, preserved in the British Museum, also from monumental effigies, &c., his authority for the armour of the knight and all the other dresses; not the slightest accompaniment was neglected."[5] The "Biographical Sketch of Robert Hartley Cromek" in the 1813 *Grave* asserts that Cromek "made the most diligent researches into all records, whether written or pictorial, which characterized the age of Chaucer, and brought the result of them to Mr. Stothard" (xlix). Whatever Cromek's contribution, Stothard's son undoubtedly was the more valuable researcher. The researches uncovered, among other things, a likeness of Chaucer. In the Prospectus for the *Canterbury Pilgrims* engraving appended to the 1808 *Grave*, Cromek states, "The Portrait of Chaucer is painted from that in the British Museum, done by Thomas Occleve, who lived in his time, and was his scholar." Betsy Bowden suggests that Cromek is referring to Hoccleve's *Regement of Princes* (Harleian MS 4866), which contains "a picture of Chaucer in the margin (not actually painted by Hoccleve, of course)."[6]

The painting, Bray writes, "was executed in a comparatively short space of time."[7] If Stothard began the painting in the spring of 1806, that would mean that it required perhaps two months. The time would have been even shorter, but, according to Stothard, Cromek promised to raise his purchase price for the painting from sixty to one hundred pounds if Stothard "would give one month's additional attention to the picture, over and above what was first agreed."[8]

In February 1807 Cromek published the pamphlet *Proposal for a Print after Stothard's Canterbury Pilgrims*. In it Cromek asserts that Stothard's painting contains a verisimilitude achieved through

> . . . fidelity from the best authorities; from the British Museum, & other Public Depositories of rare manuscripts; from Monumental Remains; from the authority of Chaucer himself; & from ancient illuminated manuscripts, painted in his time, which serve to corroborate the Poet's testimony. . . . Gentlemen of the first taste in the Antiquarian Society, & particularly those who are celebrated for their knowledge of the ancient costume of this country, have been consulted: the Picture has derived considerable advantage from the liberal manner in which several of them came forward, & offered their libraries to Mr. Stothard's examination.[9]

In this pamphlet Cromek invokes the authenticity of medieval sources and the authority of members of the Antiquarian Society to promote the proposed *Canterbury Pilgrims* engraving. The Society of Antiquaries, with origins reaching to 1586, was a venerable organization with a venerable membership. The painting, Cromek asserts, is historical, an important distinction. History painting occupied the highest artistic status, while paintings of vernacular subjects were regarded as, at best, amusing local color. The grounding in medieval documentation and antiquarian authority is necessary to counter the impression that the depictions of the pilgrims border on caricatures similar to those in a Rowlandson satire. Stothard had recently completed a number of paintings for Robert Bowyer's Historic Gallery (1790-1806), and Cromek may well have been attempting a quick association of the *Canterbury Pilgrims* painting with them.

A month later, Stothard had completed the painting and Cromek was ready to exhibit it in his home. On March 5, 1807, Cromek ran a small advertisement on the first page of *The Times* of London:

> PROCESSION OF CHAUCER'S PILGRIMS to CANTERBURY.—
> The Nobility and Gentry are respectfully informed that a CABINET PICTURE,[10] painted from this most interesting and classical subject, by THOMAS STOTHARD, Esq. R. A. is now on view at 64, Newman-street. Tickets of admission may be had of Mr. Stothard, 23, Newman-street, or of Mr. Cromek, at the place of Exhibition.—It is particularly requested that no money be given to the servant.

Part II

The long and narrow painting showing the twenty-nine mounted pilgrims was much in accord with popular taste (color plate 34). It diminishes distinctions of class and emphasizes the simple pleasures of drink, song, and companionship, pursuits uniting the pilgrims as they begin their springtime journey. Stothard follows Chaucer's descriptions of the individual pilgrims, but augments the depictions with his own details. A good example is the Yeoman, who, Chaucer writes, "was clad in cote and hood of greene" (l. 103).[11] Stothard's Yeoman indeed wears a hooded forest green garment. He also holds his bow and displays his silver medal of St. Christopher on his chest, two other details included in Chaucer's description. But Stothard substitutes what looks like a leather pouch for the dagger Chaucer mentions.

Near the center of the painting is the Wife of Bath riding sidesaddle. Stothard allocates her more open space than any other pilgrim. All the others before and after her are bunched together in tight groups. Clearly she is on display. But Stothard does not depict her as bold-faced and brazen. Rather, she is younger and more willowy than Chaucer's Wife of Bath, with a soft face and lilting eyes. Her headdress is imposing, but it could not possibly weigh the ten pounds in Chaucer's description.

Chaucer himself is depicted as a thin, dispassionate observer garbed entirely in white, including a conical hat. His wry demeanor contrasts with the prevalent jollity of the other pilgrims. The many members of religious orders wear dark vestments suitable to their callings, but their demeanor is generally other than pious. Stothard shows the tonsured Monk and Friar riding just behind the Wife of Bath as gladsome and well-fed, like Tweedle-Dum and Tweedle-Dee. On the Wife of Bath's other side ride the corpulent, red-faced Summoner, his head wreathed in a garland, and the effeminate Pardoner, with long, flaxen hair, a pale blue gown, and a red cap adorned with a vernicle.

Stothard extensively revises the order of Chaucer's pilgrims as listed in the *General Prologue*, though he retains the bagpipe-playing Miller at the front of the procession and the drunken Reeve at its rear.[12] The other pilgrims are arrayed in no discernible pattern. Stothard has disregarded Chaucer's generally hierarchical arrangement of the pilgrims out of either a democratic impulse or, more likely, compositional considerations. In order to make the young Squire more prominent in the painting, for instance, Stothard positions him behind eight others. There, just to the left of the center of the painting, his rearing white charger commands greater attention.

Stothard's painting is a panorama of Chaucer's figures on horseback presented in a winning and winsome manner. Against the rich blue sky and the green, gently rolling hills of Surrey, the pilgrims show themselves in colorful diversity. Viewers can study each pilgrim individually, down to the sheen of their buckles and the gleam in their eyes. And they can admire the entire group as they move in undulant waves toward Canterbury. In his depiction of Chaucer's figures, Stothard concentrates on their personalities, expressing their moods through careful delineation of their smiling or, in some cases, stern faces. He may have costumed them in authentic medieval garb, but he has presented them as a group very much in tune with its nineteenth-century audience.

In his four-page Prospectus for the engraving appended to *The Grave*, published in July 1808, Cromek describes Stothard's picture in detail:

> It is the particular merit of this Piece, that the Story is immediately brought home to the Spectator. He becomes instantly one of the group, and sees them move before him, marked by their distinctive habits, characters, and

sensations, in the same manner as Chaucer has drawn them. The idea of the Poet is impressed at the first view,–a humour unforced, agreeable, and comic; *a pleasurable Tour, sanctified by the name of Pilgrimage*. The covert ridicule on these eccentric excursions, which Chaucer intended, is very happily preserved in his Face; the quiet indifference of one of the Monks, the hypocrisy of another, and the real piety of a third, are with equal excellency pourtrayed. The gay levity of the *Wife of Bath*, and the countenance of the *old Ploughman*, worn down with age and labour, are finely rendered. The Miller is an admirable character; and his Horse is as much in character as himself. *The Fop of Chaucer's Age* is exhibited as making a display of his riding; and *the Sea Captain* bestrides his Nag with the usual awkwardness of the Sailor. The pale and studious countenance of the Oxford Scholar; the stateliness of the Lady-Abbess; the facetiousness and homely humour of the Host, as contrasted with the Serjeant at Law and the Doctor of Physic;–all these peculiarities of character are very finely and delicately expressed. The costume of each Person is correct with an antiquarian exactness; and the whole Group is so well distributed, that each character is sufficiently seen, and in his due place.

The phrasing in Cromek's description is very similar to that of Dryden's in his *Preface* to his *Fables Ancient and Modern*, first published in 1700. In fact, Cromek included a passage from it in the five-page advertisement appended to his *Reliques of Burns*, published in early December 1808:

> We see all the Pilgrims, their humours, their features, and their very dress, as distinctly as if we had supped with them at the Tabard, in Southwark. . . . He must have been a man of most wonderful comprehensive nature, because, as it has been truly observed of him, he has taken into the compass of his Canterbury Tales, the various manners and humours of the whole English nation, in his age. All his Pilgrims are severally distinguished from each other, not only in their inclinations, but in their very physiognomies and persons. The matter and manner of their Tales, and their telling, are so suited to their different educations, humours, and callings, that each of them would be improper in any other mouth. Even the grave and serious characters are distinguished by their several sorts of gravity: their discourses are such as belong to their age, their calling, and their breeding; such as are becoming of them, and them only. The Re[e]ve, the Miller, and the Cook, are several men, and distinguished from each other, as much as the mincing Lady Prioress, and the broad-speaking Wife of Bath.[13]

Betsy Bowden has noted that Stothard's rendering of the pilgrims' horses had advanced significantly over the "forms very like dirigibles" he had depicted in his earlier *Pilgrimage to Canterbury* for Bell's *Poets of Great Britain*.[14] The famous painter of horses, George Stubbs, came to view the painting while Stothard was still working on it. Bray records Stubbs exclaiming, "Mr. Stothard, it has been said, that I understand horses pretty well; but I am astonished at yours. You have well studied those creatures, and transferred them to canvas with a life and animation, which until this moment, I thought impossible."[15] There could be no greater praise.

Bowden, in another essay, has examined the equestrian styles of the most prominent pilgrims in Stothard's painting.[16] She notes that Stothard is more intent on compositional arrangement and variety than on horsemanship, agreeing with Walter Scott, for instance, that the Squire is in great danger of tumbling over the head of his rearing white steed in the next instant. Most of the horses, however, are so sedate and tolerant of their riders—"babysitter horses"—that the other pilgrims are in little danger of losing their mounts.

Part III

Interest in Stothard's painting was immediate, and Cromek's home was visited daily by crowds of viewers willing to pay the admission charge of one shilling. Several weeks after the painting had been put on exhibition, it was reported that on March 20 the Royal Academician John Hoppner "had . . . the honour of presenting Stothard's 'Canterbury Pilgrims' to H.R.[H.] the Prince of Wales at Carlton House." Hoppner (1758-1810), a member of the Royal Academy since 1795, was portrait-painter to the Prince of Wales. A dashing and handsome man and extremely successful portraitist, he furnished entrée to royalty and the aristocracy. The account continues:

> The style in which the picture is painted reminds the connoisseur of the works of Holbein, Albert Durer and the pictures of that period. His Royal Highness, with a discrimination that proved his acquaintance with works of art, immediately made the same observation. . . . His approbation was confirmed by his graciously permitting Mr. Cromek to dedicate the print to him.[17]

The imprimatur of the Prince of Wales certainly lent more stature to the proposed engraving. The comparison of the painting with those of two preeminent portraitists, Hans Holbein (1497/8-1543) and Albrecht Dürer (1471-1528), is so high-flown as to be gratuitous.

In a second advertisement of the *Canterbury Pilgrims* painting published in the April 8 and 9 *Times*, Cromek announced that William Bromley (1769-1842) would engrave the design. He was busily selling subscriptions to the print; a small inducement to subscribers was viewing Stothard's painting for free. The real money to be made from this venture lay in the sale of its prints. The date on the earliest surviving receipt is March 27, 1807:

> RECEIVED [March 27 *written in*] 1807, of [Mr Major Burenger *written in*] the Sum of [1*l*.11*s*.6*d*. *crossed out;* 3.3.0 *written in*] being One-half of the Subscription to a [Proof *written in*] Print, from a Picture by Thomas Stothard, Esq. R. A. representing THE PROCESSION OF CHAUCER'S PILGRIMS TO CANTERBURY, which will be delivered early in the Year of 1810. /s/ R. H. Cromek[18]

Artists and connoisseurs alike made note of the remarkable success of Stothard's painting. In his letter of April 2, 1807 to the poet and newspaper editor James Montgomery of Sheffield, the engraver James Hopwood reported:

> Mr Cromek . . . has lately had a Picture painted from Chaucer's Pilgrims going to Canterbury, by Mr Stothard; which is considered amongst the greatest productions of the age. He (Mr Cromek) has for nearly two Months been exhibiting it at his House in Newman Street, and the people are still coming by hundreds in [a] day to see it[.][19]

Cromek repeated Hopwood's news in a letter he wrote to Montgomery two weeks later, on April 17, adding, "You must know that I give myself great Credit for thinking of such a glorious Subject—it is true that it was sufficiently obvious—but, it is equally true that what is obvious is [not *del.*] often overlooked."[20]

When the annual exhibition of the Royal Academy commenced in May 1807, Cromek arranged to have Stothard's painting moved to a location practically across the street from Somerset House in order to have it near the crowds of exhibition-goers. He advertised the new location in the April 27 *Times*:

> EXHIBITION—STOTHARD's popular PICTURE of the PROCESSION of CHAUCER's PILGRIMS to CANTERBURY, will be on view, during the Exhibition at Somerset House at Mr. Lee's, perfumer, No. 544, Strand, near the corner of Catherine Street; till the 4th of May, it will remain on Exhibition at No. 64, Newman-street, Admission 1s.

This advertisement appeared four more times before May 2, and a similar advertisement appeared in the May 8 *Times*.

Cromek's promotion of the *Canterbury Pilgrims* painting and engraving received major impetus about a month later, when John Hoppner permitted his letter of May 30, 1807 to the dramatist Richard Cumberland to be published in the June 6 *Artist*, edited by Prince Hoare. In it, Hoppner describes the painting in some detail and praises it lavishly. The "most happy discrimination of character" in each of the pilgrims shows that Stothard has "studied the human heart with as much attention, and not less successfully, than the Poet." The "charm of colouring . . . is strong, and most harmoniously distributed throughout the picture." The painting "is wholly free from that vice which painters term *manner*" and "bears no mark of the period in which it was painted, but might very well pass for the work of some able artist of the time of Chaucer." It has "a primitive simplicity, and the total absence of all affectation, either of colour or penciling." With obvious irony, Hoppner ends his letter by pointing out the "one great defect" of the painting: "The picture is, notwithstanding appearances, *a modern one*. But, if you can divest yourself of the general prejudice that exists against contemporary talents, you will see a work that would have done honour to any school, at any period."

Hoppner stresses that this original rendition authentically reproduces the medieval world of Chaucer's pilgrims. He also argues that the painting does not attempt any exaggerated effect, but instead portrays the pilgrims in a candid, natural way. Mannerism was a pejorative word at the time.

Hoppner's letter contains no mention of Cromek, and indeed William Mudford, Cumberland's biographer, asserts that he wrote it in response to Cumberland's "unsolicited exertion in behalf of my friend Mr. Cromek's picture of *Chaucer's Pilgrims*." Mudford adds, "In all that Cumberland did on this occasion, he acted purely from a desire to befriend the progress of the fine arts; and as it was no less unexpected than unasked." At this time, however, Cumberland and Cromek maintained close ties; during the entire month of July 1809, Cumberland was Cromek's houseguest. Hoppner wrote to Prince Hoare of his letter, "My eye is not quick enough to detect any error, if there be one. Cromek, I believe has copied my nonsense accurately enough, if not my memory is not equal to detect him, and I have no copy."[21]

Hoppner's letter was noticed by, among others, the engraver John Landseer, who wrote in his *Review of Publications of Art* that Hoppner, "with the usual sportive, but sarcastic, brilliancy of his pen, has written some shrewd remarks on dilettante pretension, and in discrimination of beauty from fashion, and a very liberal critique on Mr. Stothard's Procession of Chaucer's Pilgrims."[22] Hoppner's letter was prominently featured in all Cromek's advertisements for the *Canterbury Pilgrims* engraving during the next several years.

Other commentators followed Hoppner's approach to Stothard's painting, even to the extent of repeating his words and phrases. One wrote:

> In a word, we do not hesitate to say, that the present picture is by far the best that ever proceeded from the pencil of Mr. Stothard, and would have done honour to the most distinguished modern or ancient Artist. . . . It is the particular merit of this Piece that the story is immediately brought home to the spectator; he becomes instantly one of the groupe, and sees them move before him, marked by their distinctive habits, characters, and sensations, in the same manner as Chaucer has drawn them—the idea of the Poet is impressed at the first view,–a humour unforced, agreeable and comic.[23]

By April 1807, Cromek was making plans to travel outside London in quest of more subscribers, much as he had the previous year for subscribers to the *Grave*.[24] His first stop was to be in Edinburgh. On April 25, his neighbor, the landscape painter George Arnold of 36 Newman Street, wrote a letter of introduction to the Edinburgh editor and critic Robert Anderson: "A Mr. Cromeck[s:c] of Newman Street, will shortly be at Edinburgh to exhibit a Singularly fine picture of the Procession of Chaucers Pilgrims, Painted by *Stothard R. A.* to have a print engraved from it by Subscription—if you would be so obliging as to mention this, in your connection, it might be of service to him, he is a very respectable character."[25]

Cromek arrived in Edinburgh in June, writing to his wife on June 11, "I have this moment unpacked the picture. It is perfectly safe."[26] If Anderson advanced Cromek's interests, however, his efforts were ineffective, since after two weeks Cromek had not collected a single subscription. According to a later account, it took the intervention of Francis Jeffrey (1773-1840), the editor of *The Edinburgh Review* and perhaps the most imposing critic of the time, to turn the visit into a success. Jeffrey arranged a breakfast party "and the subject of the Subscription [was] introduced, when the names of all present, and ultimately, to the number of forty, more or less, followed from people of the first rank and consideration in Edinburgh."[27] Once again, a commanding authority led others to join an ever-growing procession.

One subscriber was Walter Scott, who wrote:

> Mr. Walter Scott begs Mr. Cromek will take the trouble to put down his
> name & that of Thomas Thomson Esquire Register Depute of Scotland for
> two proofs of the print from Stodarts [*sic*] painting. Mr. Scott would wish
> very much to have his copy tinted after the picture & would cheerfully pay
> any advance of price for a circumstance which would give the print so much
> value to an antiquary.[28]

Cromek carried Stothard's painting to Manchester in August and
Liverpool in September. There he met the young artist, architect, and
critic William Paulet Carey, who shortly thereafter wrote a *Critical
Description* of Stothard's painting "respectfully addressed, by permission, to John Leigh Philips."[29] Carey's description delineates the portraiture of each pilgrim in glowing terms. Cromek, who had arranged
publication of Carey's extensive puff with Cadell & Davies, wrote
Carey from Wakefield on November 21, 1808 that he intended to give
the *Critical Description* "to each of the principal Members of the Royal
Academy, and to the leading characters of the British Institution."[30]
The publication also sold for two shillings.

Although the August 1, 1807 *Artist* still designated Bromley as the
engraver of Stothard's *Canterbury Pilgrims* in its "List of Engravings
in a State of Progress," the Prospectus at the end of *The Grave*, published in July 1808, trumpets that Louis Schiavonetti, the engraver of
Blake's *Grave* designs, will also engrave Stothard's painting.

Early in 1809, Cromek made a final trip with Stothard's painting
first to Bristol, then to Bath. He wrote from Bath on February 4 to
William Tartt that he had little to show for his four weeks in Bristol:
"With all my activity I could not procure more than 25 Subscribers to
the Pilgrims at Bristol. What I shall do at Bath I know not. This City
swarms with *Quality*: It is a perfect Fair of Fashion! I sadly fear its visitors are too foolish and too volatile to be attracted by the good sense
& good humour of Stothard's Picture."[31] Cromek had not included
Bath during his peregrinations around the provinces collecting *Grave*
subscribers during 1806 and 1807.

Part IV

Any discussion of Stothard's *Canterbury Pilgrims* must include
some mention of William Blake's competing painting.[32] Blake, of
course, maintained that the idea to paint the procession was his and

Cromek stole it. There is no way to verify this claim, although Cromek certainly was capable of such theft. Cromek's claim of the painting's origin, as elaborated in the "Biographical Sketch of Robert Hartley Cromek" in the 1813 *Grave*, is, to say the least, fanciful:

> On his return to London [in January 1808] from this journey [to Scotland] he was under the necessity of passing a few hours in Halifax, to wait for a further conveyance. To while away the time, he resorted to books, his usual amusement, and picked up in a bookseller's shop a copy of Chaucer. On perusing the CANTERBURY TALES, he was so struck with the picturesque description of the pilgrims, that he conceived the idea of embodying the whole procession in a picture.[33]

Apart from this convenient explanation, the date of this epiphany is some ten months after Cromek began exhibiting the painting in his home.

Whether the idea to paint the pilgrims came first to Blake or to Cromek, there is no evidence to support Blake's claim that he started his first. The earliest mention of Blake and the *Canterbury Pilgrims* comes in Cromek's vituperative response of May 1807 to Blake's demand of four guineas for his drawing intended to illustrate his dedicatory poem to *The Grave*, "To the Queen." Cromek's phrasing makes very clear that he is answering Blake's criticism of Stothard's painting and that, at this point, Blake does not have his own painting for comparison with Stothard's:

> Why sh[oul]d you so *furiously rage* at the success of the little picture of 'The Pilgrimage?' 3,000 people have now *seen it and have approved of it*. Believe me, yours is '*the voice of one crying in the wilderness!*'
> You say the subject is *low*, and *contemptibly treated*. For his excellent mode of treating the subject the poet has been admired for the last 400 years! The poor painter has not yet the advantage of antiquity on his side, therefore w[it]h some people an apology may be necessary for him. The conclusion of one of Squire Simkin's letters to his mother in the Bath Guide will afford one. He speaks greatly to the purpose:
>
>> I very well know,
>> Both my subject and verse is exceedingly low:
>> But if any *great critic* finds fault with my letter,
>> *He has nothing to do but to send you a better*.[34]

It seems very likely that Cromek's taunt to Blake to paint a better *Canterbury Pilgrims* than Stothard is the genesis for Blake's rival project. Blake's own Public Exhibition featuring his *Canterbury Pilgrims* was announced to open May 15, 1809, but, as Bentley notes, it may not have opened until September 1809.[35]

Alexander Gilchrist's landmark biography of Blake, published in 1863, paints Cromek a villain of the first rank. But Cromek had his defenders. Among them was Tartt, who wrote in his review of Gilchrist's biography that he "greatly wrongs" Cromek.

> We met Cromek in 1808, as the guest of Mr. Roscoe at Allerton, and knew him afterwards; and we do not believe him to have been the mercenary in literature or art that he is here described. In his dealings both with Blake and Stothard he gave them what they required for the works he purchased; he faithfully fulfilled his engagements; and if he knew better than they did how to attract the attention of the public, he had a right to use such knowledge for his own advantage. It was only in this way that he made more by their works than they could have made themselves.[36]

Part V

Near the end of 1809 Cromek began paying Schiavonetti as he neared completion of the engraving. On November 23, Cromek gave Schiavonetti a bill payable in two months for seventy-five pounds "on account of the Pilgrimage," and on December 12 Schiavonetti wrote a receipt to Cromek for two hundred pounds "in part of 840£ for Engraving Stothard's Picture of the Canterbury Pilgrims."[37] On November 27 Cromek began delivering proofs of Schiavonetti's etching to a select group of artists, engravers, printsellers, and connoisseurs, including Stothard, Hoppner, and Roscoe; by December 9 he had distributed seventeen proofs. The December 3 *Examiner* announced Schiavonetti's progress:

> Mr SCHIAVONETTI has made a most masterly Aqua-fortis of the Plate he is engraving from Mr. STOTHARD's celebrated painting from *Chaucer's Pilgrims*. It is one of the best if not the best ever made exhibiting the energie [*sic*] character of the original, with knowledge of drawing and rich playfulness of line for which this engraver is so eminent. The tasteful reader shall have a minute description of it when finished. (p. 783)

Cromek wrote the wood engraver Thomas Bewick on December 20, "Schiavonetti has completed an *Etching* of the *Canterbury Pilgrims*, which has produced an effect among both *Painters* and *Engravers* that it would be in vain for me to describe. It is really a *Painter's* Etching,

with an Engraver's skill superadded. . . . Six days ago I paid Mr.
Schiavonetti 300 Guineas (in part of 800 [*sic*]) for the Etching, and my
wing has been plucked, in consequence, that I have scarce a single
feather to fly with."[38] On New Year's Day, 1810, Cromek sent William
Roscoe a proof of Schiavonetti's etching, mentioning in his letter that
it has "considerably increased my list of Names."[39] In a letter written
at about this time, George Cumberland, Jr. reported to his father, "Mr
Blake has nothing but the remarks on his Chaucer—have you seen the
etching of Mr Stothard['s] Pilgrims[?] [I]t is finished[.]"[40]

Before Schiavonetti could complete his work on the engraving,
however, he fell ill. The April 29, 1810 *Examiner* reported that his illness would delay the publication of the *Canterbury Pilgrims* print:

> It is unfortunate for the progress of Art that its eminent votaries are often
> snatched away in the maturity of their powers, and, that by too sedulous an
> exercise of them, become martyrs of their profession. The property of genius
> is to impel to excellence by an intenseness of application frequently beyond
> the strength of the human frame to sustain. The distinguished Engraver, Mr.
> LOUIS SCHIAVONETTI, has been attacked by a severe pulmonary com-
> plaint, accompanied with alarming bilious symptoms, the consequence of
> unremitting study and industry. . . . The admirers of superior Engraving
> exhort him "to have a revered care" of it [his health]; for his rapid profes-
> sional advancement has already raised him to a station few would be com-
> petent to succeed to. Many of his finished productions prove this, and espe-
> cially the Engraving of Mr. STOTHARD's celebrated cabinet picture of *The
> Canterbury Pilgrims*, the completion of which is delayed by his illness. The
> Etching, just published, is in itself a chef-d'ouvre, and the Subscribers will
> cheerfully accede to the delay when they consider how difficult it would
> have been for an Artist of even equal ability, to perfect what he had begun.
> He is indeed peculiarly qualified for the undertaking, as he unites the vigorous
> splendor of AUDRAN with the grace and delicacy of BARTOLOZZI. (p. 269)

Just over a month later, on June 7, Schiavonetti died. An account of
his funeral was published in the June 17 *Examiner*, and Cromek's
"Account of Louis Schiavonetti" appeared in the July 1 *Examiner* (pp.
412-414). Of Schiavonetti's *Canterbury Pilgrims* engraving,
Cromek wrote:

> It would have raised Mr. Schiavonetti as the founder of a new and superior
> School of Engraving, and would have mainly contributed to rescue the Art
> from the bad taste which now so universally degrades it. In the present state
> of this etching, considered with reference to the peculiar circumstances of
> the case, perhaps no better mode could be devised of paying an impressive
> and lasting tribute to his memory, and one in which all his admirers could

participate, than by giving it to the public as he left it,–a consecrated monument of his genius. At the same time, to alleviate, as much as possible, the general disappointment of those who are interested in its fate, the publisher of the print will feel it his pride and his duty to have it finished in the ablest manner, with the most careful attention to produce in the execution a congeniality of spirit and effect with the original design.

Both alternatives, of course, were certain to benefit Cromek financially. In his letter of June 13 to the publisher Archibald Constable he wrote, "Under all circumstances I am extremely fortunate to be left in possession of the finest *Etching* that ever the Art produced. I shall publish it with a Little description of the Artist, & that it was his *great Work* &c. print 100 or 150 *only*, & I am certain they will sell for *5 Guineas each*."[41] Cromek apparently never acted on these intentions, however. Instead, he engaged William Bromley, the person who originally was to engrave Stothard's painting, to finish Schiavonetti's engraving, announcing this arrangement in the September 2 *Examiner*. In addition, in order to hasten the process, Cromek announced that "I have undertaken to labour jointly" with Bromley on the plate (p. 554).[42]

It is unlikely, however, that Cromek did any significant work on the engraving, and Bromley's progress also was severely limited. Cromek engaged yet another engraver, Francis Engleheart (1775-1849), to work on the plate between September 20 and the end of 1810, paying him a total of forty-four pounds and one shilling for twenty-four days' work.[43] Cromek seems to have withheld payments from Bromley, however, for the simple reason that he did little, if any, work on the plate. On August 23, 1811, Cromek wrote his wife from Wakefield, "As to Bromley, I have received a second letter from him, *promising* his best exertions and I don't know what, but not a word of comfort about commencing. *Entre nous*, I shall pay him no money without you or Raimbach see[ing] the plates but I hope my illness will take a turn and enable me to superintend the progress of the Plate, myself."[44]

Cromek, suffering from the advanced stages of consumption, was in Wakefield in order to benefit from the presumably healthful atmosphere there. While Cromek was trying desperately to have the engraving of the plate completed, he was able to sell Stothard's painting for a profit of one hundred and ninety pounds. The diarist Joseph Farington records in his entry of June 26, 1810 the circumstances of that sale:

Mr. [Hart] Davies [of Bristol and Bath] sd. that having now nearly completed His collection of pictures by Old Masters He should make a collection of pictures by the best modern Artists & wished [Benjamin] West to inform

[him] of any productions in which any of those eminent might be thought to have excelled. In consequence West yesterday at Mr. Knight's mentioned Stothard's picture from Chaucer of the procession to Canterbury, & said the price which had been mentioned for it was £200. Mr. Davies immediately sd. Purchase it for me at £250.[45]

Cromek's greatest obstacle to completing the Canterbury Pilgrims project, however, was his own rapidly declining health. From late 1810 on, consumption weakened him more and more. The inevitable conclusion arrived on March 4, 1812. Cromek was dead at forty-two, leaving a widow and two children. At his death, the *Canterbury Pilgrims* plate still remained unfinished, more than five years after he had begun promoting it.

Cromek's widow, Elizabeth Cromek, undertook the task of finding yet another engraver to complete the work. She first engaged Schiavonetti's brother, Niccolo Schiavonetti, who, according to Stothard, requested 330 guineas to finish the engraving in fifteen months.[46] Her father, Samuel Hartley of Wakefield, grudgingly lent her the money and even charged her interest on the loan. Then, in 1813, before he had been able to make any significant progress, Niccolo Schiavonetti died. The engraving finally was finished by James Heath and Heath's assistant, W. H. Worthington, on October 1, 1817.[47] Elizabeth Cromek then delivered the prints to the numerous subscribers, often personally, a gesture many of them remembered long afterwards.[48] A dozen years later, on February 4, 1829, she sold the plate, copyright, and remaining proofs to the printsellers Boys and Graves for four hundred pounds.[49]

Part VI

The furor between Cromek and Blake apparently had no effect on Cromek's relationship with Stothard. On June 29, 1809, Cromek and Stothard left London together to spend the next two months visiting Burns country in Scotland, where Stothard drew characteristic scenes. Cromek engraved a dozen of them during 1811, and they were included in Cadell and Davies' 1813 edition of Burns' *Works*.

According to Bray, at the time of Cromek's death, he still owed Stothard forty pounds of the one hundred for the painting. Stothard, however, charitably did not press Cromek's widow for this balance. Stothard's son Alfred noted that Mrs. Cromek gave Stothard "a number of impressions of the plate of the Pilgrims" in lieu of the debt.[50]

Stothard, however, secured compensation on his own by making three copies of the painting and selling them to J. Benson of Doncaster, Samuel Rogers, and Samuel Boddington.[51] The original passed into the Miles Collection, then was acquired for the National Gallery. It now is in the Tate Gallery.

Part VII

Stothard's painting has fallen into neglect for more than a century now; Blake's painting and engraving have long since eclipsed it. Such are the vagaries of taste and fashion. But perhaps without the engine of Cromek's persistent, incessant promotion, marshalling legions of prominent artists and members of the aristocracy to advance notice of the design, Stothard's most successful work might never have risen above nominal notice. The measure of his success can be noted in a poem published in the October 1821 *European Magazine*, fourteen years after Stothard painted the *Canterbury Pilgrims* and nine years after Cromek's death:

> Methinks I hear their horses capering head,
>   And now the merry group full blythe I see;
> Genius, thou Sorcerer wild! by thee I'm led,
>   And my heart leaps with heavenly ecstasy.
> First comes the brawling Host, the rest close join,
>   Pressing the greensward, Hark! they troup with glee,
> Next Chaucer view–Behold the Bard divine!
>   Lock'd in bright mental thought, how sweet looks he;
> Oh! would I were a horseman by the side,
>   Of you fair Nymph, prancing so courteously,
> Or I should like with you blythe Friar to ride
>   His dewy eye full of rich roguery;–
> Stothard! a peerless wreath thou here hast won,
>   And Painting hails thee as her matchless son.[52]

Notes

[1] Letter to T.H. Cromek, September 12, 1862; "Memorials of R. H. Cromek" (1863), unpublished MS in the possession of Mr. Paul Warrington.

[2] Letter to T.H. Cromek, January 7, 1862, University of Edinburgh Library.

[3] *Life of Thomas Stothard, R.A.* (London: John Murray, 1851), 138.

4 *Life of Stothard*, 134. Most of Stothard's sketches are now in the National
Gallery, London.

5 Bray, 136. Charles Stothard (1786-1821) by this time had developed his interests
in medieval English dress and fashion. Four years later, in 1811, he published the
first volume of his *Monumental Effigies of Great Britain*, "a work designed to portray the changes in English costume from the twelfth century to the reign of Henry
VIII," according to *DNB*. He was elected a Fellow of the Society of Antiquaries
in 1818.

6 Bowden, "Transportation to Canterbury: The Rival Envisionings by Stothard
and Blake," *Studies in Medievalism* 11 (2001), 102.

7 Bray, 130. The "Biographical Sketch" in the 1813 *Grave*, however, states, "The
multifarious engagements of [Stothard] at times suspended the accomplishment of
the work; but nothing could retard or discourage the perseverance of Mr.
Cromek[.]"

8 Letter to an unidentified correspondent (probably Rev. Mr. Markham of Bolton
Percy, a patron of Stothard's), quoted in Bray, 142. The letter is undated, but internal evidence suggests it was written in 1813.

9 British Museum Department of Prints and Drawings; quoted in Shelley M.
Bennett, "Thomas Stothard, R.A." (diss. University of California, Los Angeles,
1977), 226. The names of the Antiquarian Society members who Cromek claims
helped Stothard are unknown.

10 According to Thomas Gullick and John Timbs' *Painting Popularly Explained*
(London: Kent and Co., 1859), 18, "Cabinet pictures are so named because they are
so small in size as to be readily contained in a cabinet" (quoted by *OED*). The
dimensions of Stothard's painting, $12^{1/2}$ inches by $36^{2/5}$ inches, would seem to
strain the limits of that definition.

11 *Works of Geoffrey Chaucer*, ed. F.N. Robinson, 2nd ed. (Boston: Houghton
Mifflin, 1961). All references to *The Canterbury Tales* are to this edition.

12 The *General Prologue* places the Reeve at the back of the procession: "And
evere he rood the hyndreste of oure route" (I.622). The Miller's placement is less
clear. Chaucer states, "A baggepipe wel koude he blowe and sowne,/And therwith-
al he broughte us out of towne" (I.565-566). Some depictions therefore show the
Miller leading the other pilgrims. But the Miller could be playing from the middle
of the procession. From the *General Prologue* and the links one may infer groupings of pilgrims (e.g., Cook and the Five Guildsmen who have engaged him), but
the order of procession remains unspecified.

13 John Dryden, *Fables Ancient and Modern; Translated into Verse from Homer,
Boccace, & Chaucer; with Original Poems* (London, 1700). The quoted part of the

preface is in *The Works of John Dryden*, ed. Vinton A. Dearing (Berkeley: University of California Press, 2000), vol. 7, 37.

[14] Betsy Bowden, "Visual Portraits of the Canterbury Pilgrims 1484(?)-1809," *The Ellesmere Chaucer: Essays in Interpretation*, ed. Martin Stevens and Daniel Woodward (San Marino, California: Huntington Library; Tokyo: Yushodo Co., 1997), p. 193.

[15] Bray, *Life of Stothard*, 138.

[16] "Transportation to Canterbury: The Rival Envisionings by Stothard and Blake," *Studies in Medievalism* 11 (2001), 73-111.

[17] Article of March 21, 1807 from an unidentified newspaper, in the Whitley *Scrapbooks of Printed Material on British Artists,* British Museum Department of Prints and Drawings; quoted by Bennett (1977), 226.

[18] In the possession of Mr. Paul Warrington.

[19] Sheffield City Libraries (SLPS 36-95).

[20] Sheffield City Libraries (SLPS 36-76); quoted in G.E. Bentley, Jr., "Blake and Cromek: The Wheat and the Tares," *Modern Philology*, 71 (1974), 372.

[21] G. E. Bentley, Jr., *Blake Records* (Oxford: Clarendon, 1969), 190-91; first printed in "Blake, Cromek and Hoppner," *TLS* (October 7, 1926), 680. Hoppner's letter is undated.

[22] *Review of Publications of Art* (1808), 9.

[23] Anonymous newspaper or magazine article in the *Royal Academy Collection of Engravings by Thomas Stothard, R. A.*, collected by W. E. Frost (London, 1861); quoted by Bennett, *Thomas Stothard: The Mechanisms of Art Patronage in England circa 1800* (Columbia: University of Missouri Press, 1988), 46.

[24] See Dennis M. Read, "Cromek's Provincial Advertisements for Blake's *Grave*," *Notes & Queries*, n.s. 27 (1980), 73-76.

[25] National Library of Scotland. I am indebted to the scholarly generosity of G. E. Bentley, Jr. for a transcription of this document. Arnold (1763-1841) was elected an Associate of the Royal Academy in 1810 and was landscape painter to the Duke of Gloucester.

[26] "Memorials," f. 10.

[27] "On the Genius of Stothard, and the Character of His Works," *Arnold's Magazine of the Fine Arts*, n.s. 3 (1834), 439. The anonymous author may be Allan Cunningham or, less likely, Bray.

[28] Library of Congress Department of Manuscripts, n.d. Cromek dined with Scott on June 14. 1807. In *Autobiography of Sir Walter Scott* (Philadelphia: Carey & Lea, 1831), 288, it is noted that "Stothard's Canterbury Pilgrims are on the mantelpiece" of Scott's den.

[29] *Critical Description of the Procession of Chaucer's Pilgrims to Canterbury* (London, 1808). Carey published a second edition in 1818. John Leigh Philips, of Mayfield, Manchester, was a connoisseur of the arts and the father of the painter and engraver Nathaniel George Philips (1795-1831).

[30] "Memorials," f. 18. Cromek was introduced to Carey by William Roscoe, who, Cromek states in this letter, "subscribed [to the engraving] at my house in London *before the picture was completed.*" Roscoe wrote Montgomery on January 21, 1809 that "The latter part of his [Carey's] stay in Liverpol was wholly devoted to the society of Chaucer's pilgrims[,] a circumstance which I should regre[t] the more if it had not produced one [of] the best critiques that ever was written on a work of art" (Sheffield City Libraries, SLPS 36-149).

[31] National Library of Scotland, 3112/221. Cromek had met Tartt, a young poet, in Roscoe's home in 1808.

[32] Bentley, *The Stranger from Paradise: A Biography of William Blake* (New Haven: Yale University Press, 2001), 291-304 provides a summary of Cromek's , Stothard's and Blake's positions. For more fully argued studies see Dennis M. Read, "The Rival *Canterbury Pilgrims* of Blake and Cromek: Herculean Figures in the Carpet," *Modern Philology* 86 (1988-89), 171-90; Aileen Ward, "Canterbury Revisited: The Blake-Cromek Controversy," *Blake: An Illustrated Quarterly* 22 (1988-89), 80-92; and Bentley, "'They take great liberty's': Blake Reconfigured by Cromek and Modern Critics–The Argument from Silence," *Studies in Romanticism* 30 (1991), 657-84.

[33] *The Grave* (London: R. Ackermann, 1813), xlviii.

[34] Bentley, *Blake Records*, 186-187. The lines of verse are from Christopher Anstey, *The New Bath Guide* (London, 1804), 38-39.

[35] Bentley, *Blake Records*, 219, n.2.

[36] Tartt, *Essays on Some Modern Works, Chiefly Biographical* (London: Tinsley Brothers, 1876), II, 200.

[37] Both documents in the possession of Mr. Paul Warrington.

[38] "Memorials." Cromek's date and figures do not agree with the surviving receipt cited in the previous endnote. December 12 was eight days earlier, and Cromek had paid Schiavonetti two hundred pounds.

[39] Letter in the Liverpool Public Library.

[40] BM Add. MSS 36515, ff. 84-85; *Blake Records*, 220.

[41] National Library of Scotland (670/367).

[42] On the last two pages of his *Remains of Nithsdale and Galloway Song*, published in December 1810, Cromek printed an advertisement dated August 15, 1810 which states that the print "is now engraving in the line manner, by Mr. Bromley, and R. H. Cromek."

[43] "Memorials," Appendix No. 3, f. 54.

[44] "Memorials." Abraham Raimbach (1776-1843), a line engraver, lived on Warren Street, Fitzroy Square, Cromek's previous locale before moving to Newman Street.

[45] *The Diary of Joseph Farington,* ed. Kathryn Cave (New Haven: Yale University Press, 1984), 2675. "Mr. Knight" is probably Richard Payne Knight (1750-1824) of Soho Square. A less likely possibility is Charles Knight (1743-1827), a Hammersmith stipple engraver.

[46] Bray, p. 141.

[47] Heath complained to Landseer that Worthington "spoiled the plate." (Farington, 5160)

[48] See, for instance, John Holland and James Everett, *Memoirs of James Montgomery* (London: Longman, Brown, Green & Longmans, 1854), II, 180. In his *Diary* entry of February 17, 1818, Farington gives the total number of subscribers as seven hundred. (Farington, 5160)

[49] Memorandum of Agreement, in possession of Mr. Paul Warrington. Later in 1829 the firm became Moon, Boys & Graves. I am indebted to Robert N. Essick for information relating to these printsellers.

[50] Bray, 143.

[51] Bennett, *Stothard* (1988), 96, suggests the Rogers copy is now in the collection of Pierre Jeamnerat, London. The Boddington copy was last sold April 25,1975 at Christie's to an unknown buyer. A smaller copy ($11^{1/2}$ by 41 cm.) is in the Stanford University Art Gallery (8.206). Bennett notes Stothard also made several watercolor versions. One was sold June 18, 1980 at Christie's (4 by $13^{1/2}$ in., lot 108).

[52] "Sonnet on Stothard's Painting of the Canterbury Pilgrims" by Enort, copied into the extra-illustrated edition of Bray's *Life of Stothard*, Boston Public Library.

Chapter 7

Victorian Illustrations to Chaucer's
Canterbury Tales

Judith L. Fisher and Mark Allen

T his essay attempts to fill a gap of some ninety years between the 1807 Stothard and 1809 Blake paintings of Chaucer's pilgrims and Morris's Kelmscott Chaucer of 1896. There are, in fact, a surprising number of illustrated editions, free-standing paintings, and independent projects such as decorative murals, a fresco in the new Houses of Parliament, and a now-lost window in Poet's Corner in Westminster Abbey (see Appendix 1868). We have not been able to trace all of these or identify all that was produced, but we have appended a list of illustrations as an invitation for readers to supplement and revise our findings. Depictions of Chaucer's pilgrims and *The Canterbury Tales* from approximately 1812 with Henri Fuseli's paintings to Burne-Jones in the 1890s prompt a two-fold analysis: the illustrations and paintings reflect artists' responses to the demands of literary-narrative-historical painting and, in turn, help to establish the specialized characteristics of Victorian medievalism. Below we posit two varieties of pictorial medievalism, which we hope will clarify how literature, art, and history combined to shape Victorian representations of Chaucer's best-known work.

Martin Meisel in his study of narrative painting and the relation between the verbal and visual in Victorian art divides the familiar category of "illustration"—a visualization derived from a verbal text— into "realization" and "illustration." A "realization," derived from theatrical tableaux, is a literal recreation of a section of a text. As Meisel defines it, "to move from mind's eye to body's eye was realization, and to add a third dimension to two was realization, as when words became picture, or when picture became dramatic tableau."[1] Realizations give

"concrete perceptual form to a literary text" (Meisel 32). An "illustration," on the other hand, embellishes the text, offering a visual version
that "tends to explain or throw light upon the text" (31). This "interpretive re-creation," to use Meisel's phrase (32), is most easily exem-
plified by George Cruikshank's illustrations to *Oliver Twist* or
Thackeray's illustrations to his own *Vanity Fair*, both of which extend
the metaphoric implications of the written texts (Meisel 32). Painters
realizing or illustrating narrative texts had the particular problem of
freezing a moment of narration. While artists working for a particular
edition, such as Edward Henry Corbould when illustrating *The
Canterbury Tales* for Routledge's British Poets in 1854, had the advantage of the text present, they, like painters of free-standing literary
paintings, still had to imply large parts of the whole story in clear narrative moments and render those moments effectively so as to evoke an
immediate emotional response. Thus nineteenth-century literary narrative art developed as "readable" art, profuse with clues about what has
happened and what will happen in the narrative as well as the appropriate moral interpretation of the immediate scene. But these clues are
not simple Hogarthian objects that comment upon the scene satirically;
nor are they Christian icons that identify a moral or spiritual quality.
Victorian "clues" tend to derive from contemporary culture, including
a vocabulary of physiognomy based on theatrical types. Even the basic
techniques of composition, color, and lighting become means of evok-
ing an "effect," defined by Meisel as the immediate feeling of the
whole before analysis (71). The existing model for artists was the theatre, and painters readily adopted and adapted theatrical devices to their
two-dimensional stages. Foreground figures were set against backdrops, chiaroscuro imitated the gaslight of the stage, the narrative
moment became a dramatic situation in which the relation among the
figures, and their sometimes exaggerated and often stereotypic features
and gestures, clearly told the audience how to read the moment.
Victorian narrative painting at its best was a skillful blending of the recognizable, the "real," with the theatrical, paradoxically, a composition
of life. The demand for "realism" can be understood as the viewer's
expecting the painting to convey the illusion of "accident," a moment
in time caught by the artist. If a painting were too symmetrical or harmonious (by repeating forms), it could be criticized as too "studied,"
whereas the variation of forms suggested a dynamism or vitality to the
audience. The Victorian audience looked for all the details to be clearly delineated in fore-, middle-, and back-grounds.

Historical painting, of course, added the particular problem of composing and conveying the life of the past. Stereotypic features and gestures from conventions of contemporary culture combined with historicizing details of costume and architecture, also often derived from the stage. Moreover, depictions of Chaucer's or Shakespeare's works, and other familiar historical literature, demanded not only accurate portrayal of their historical periods but also fidelity to the literary texts. Chaucer's authentic fourteenth-century voice and his eye for particularizing detail (especially in the "General Prologue") made his texts obvious sources for a generalized Victorian notion of historical accuracy, which has its roots in eighteenth- and early nineteenth-century antiquarian research. One of the most important of the antiquarians, according to Roy Strong, was Joseph Strutt, born in 1749.[2] Using manuscripts of the British Museum, Strutt produced elaborate collections of illustrations of medieval dress and customs such as *The Regal and Ecclesiastical Antiquities of England* (1773), *Honda Angel-cynnan or A Compleat View of the Manners, Customs, Arms, Habits, etc. of the Inhabitants of England* (1774-76), *A Complete View of the Dress and Habits of the People of England* (1796-99), and *Sports and Pastimes of the People of England* (1801) (Strong 50). These books became sources for theatrical productions and for history painting. For example, in his *Chaucer Reading the Legend of Custance* (1851; color plate 35), Ford Madox Brown modeled his headdresses on those in Strutt and used "the Westminster tomb effigy of the King . . . drawn almost certainly from [Charles Alfred] Stothard's *Monumental Effigies*" [*of Great Britain*, (1811-33)] (Strong 58). Strong points out that "by 1860 inaccuracy had become a crime against art, and art had been led hard along the sterile path of pedantic historical reconstruction" (54). Given the visual detail of Chaucer's descriptions of his pilgrims, it is easy to see how *The Canterbury Tales* became sources for "living" scenes of the fourteenth century.

Strutt's work exemplifies one variety of medievalism, stemming from Thomas Percy's 1765 publication of *Reliques of Ancient English Poetry*. This "antiquarian medievalism" took seriously its business of recovering the past, anticipating the development of history, art history, and literary history as academic disciplines. There is a gradual move from antiquarian collections of coins and curios to the publication of illustrations of dress, habits, and poetry to the professional study of Middle English and Chaucer in the Early English Text Society and the Chaucer Society. This specialized medievalism in turn diffuses into two visually-oriented medievalisms designed for the lay audience. Characterized by Brown's work or Edward Burne-Jones's wedding present to William and Jane Morris of a chest decorated with scenes from the "Prioress's Tale," "aesthetic" medievalism is a romantic, expressive, often decorative mode, interested in the lyric possibilities of the stories or the poetic possibilities of the history [color plate 36]. "Conventional" or "popular" medievalism combines a concern for Chaucer's historicity with nineteenth-century conventions of didacticism and pictorial representation. The illustrated editions and most of the free-standing paintings are products of this "conventional" medievalism.

Both illustrated editions and free-standing art work derived from *The Canterbury Tales* met the demand for familiarity characteristic of conventional medievalism by fusing antiquarian detail with dramatic composition, drawn or painted in a contemporary vocabulary of style, including facial types, body types, and poses. Historical accuracy in this general sense is neither authentic nor inauthentic in a strict sense, but rather conventional or stereotypical. A man in chain mail, for example, equals a medieval knight; a crown and long robe signifies a king. Consequently, these pictorial versions of *The Canterbury Tales* can look like a contemporary theatrical scene or a fancy-dress ball. But easy as it is to denigrate such generalities, it is more accurate to see them as attempts, more or less successful, to *vivify* the Middle Ages in ways that made Chaucer's world seem a familiar precursor to that of the nineteenth century. William Vaughan has called this conventional art "historicist," defined as giving "a vivid and anecdotal treatment of the past, strongly influenced by the historical novels of Sir Walter Scott and the popular history paintings of [the English painters'] French contemporary, Paul Delaroche. Their paintings were the costume dramas of the day."[3] Free-standing paintings and illustrations to Chaucer's *Tales* also strove to emulate the details of dress and appearance familiar to a literate audience—the Merchant's forked beard, the Miller's bagpipes, and the Pardoner's lanky blond hair are three of the most commonly reproduced characteristics. So a painter or illustrator of Chaucer had to present a dramatic scene that implied the whole narrative and that also suggested both the general historical period of the fourteenth century and Chaucer's specific characterizations and narrative details.[4]

All varieties of the medieval during the Victorian period share a basic conservative outlook either explicitly or implicitly. Alice Chandler, Georg Lukács, John Robson, and most recently David

Matthews have discussed this at some length.[5] Simply put, the nos-
talgic backward-glance toward Chaucer and his times resulted from a
desire for a recognizable order and stable class hierarchy. From Percy,
who sought aristocratic patronage by means of his *Reliques*, to Scott,
Cobbett, Carlyle, Disraeli, Pugin, and Ruskin, "medieval" poetry,
houses, work ethics, and daily life embodied the yearning after a lost
order and tranquility sanctified by an omnipresent spirituality. For
Cobbett the Middle Ages meant material comfort for the peasants; for
Carlyle it meant the yoking of strength to reason. Implicit in all the
varieties of medievalism, and certainly in the visualizations of Chaucer,
was a basic nostalgia for a stable, knowable order of things and people.
As analysis of depictions of Griselda and the gatherings of the pilgrims
will show, Chaucer was used to evoke a period in specifically English
history where "English liberty" meant the comfortable subjoinment of
class to class with each satisfied in its rights and obligations.

    There seems to be relatively little interest in *visualizing* Chaucer in
the Victorian public popular press and art-market until the 1840s, when
the decoration of the new Houses of Parliament excited fresh interest
in Britain's past.[6] However, his work would have already been familiar to the literate audience by his presence in earlier "library sets" like
S. W. Singer's 1822 *The British Poets: Including Translations* in which
the works of Chaucer comprise the first six volumes. In 1845 William
Pickering published the Aldine Edition of the British Poets of which
The Poetical Works of Chaucer again occupy the first six volumes. This
edition was re-issued in 1866 by Richard Morris (Matthews 170). In
the mid-Victorian period, Robert Bell published an *Annotated Edition
of Chaucer* as volumes 1-8 in his *Annotated Edition of the English
Poets* (1854-56). All these editions used Tyrwhitt's text and presented
Chaucer as the "father" of English poetry.[7] None of them were illustrated. David Matthews points out that until Thomas Wright's edition
of the *Canterbury Tales* in 1847-51, Chaucer was seen as closer to the
moderns, separated from "Middle English," because he himself strug-
gled with a "barbaric language" (164, 167-68). As early as 1805,
George Ellis distinguished Chaucer's beauty and accuracy (Matthews
73) from most medieval literature, which was "regrettably, inferior, but
[was] useful to its depictions of customs and manners" (Matthews 80).
The illustrated editions of *The Canterbury Tales*, the free-standing
paintings from the *Tales*, and the illustrated children's editions all support Matthews's contention that Chaucer grew to be important for the
Victorians in search of their history because he could fill the slot of "the

The Mirror

OF

LITERATURE, AMUSEMENT, AND INSTRUCTION.

No. 624.]   SATURDAY, SEPTEMBER 21, 1833.   [PRICE 2d.

THE CANTERBURY PILGRIMS, AND THE TABARD INN, SOUTHWARK.

Fig. 1 - "The Canterbury Pilgrims and the Tabard Inn, Southwark"

author" of the period and also could be used to illustrate manners and customs (173). The two earliest illustrated editions are pedagogical. The first, Charles Cowden Clarke's *Tales from Chaucer in Prose* (1833; rpt. 1870) is selected for young people. John Saunders's *Canterbury Tales, from Chaucer* (1845-47; rev. 1870) also has a didactic purpose directed toward adults unfamiliar with Chaucer or the Middle Ages.

Chaucer's omnipresence made him an ideal means to return to a past that was a golden age of social relations. His comfortable familiarity is evident in the fact that art critics easily referred to him as "old Dan Chaucer."[8] In 1833, essayist H. Innes felt on such easy terms with "the venerable Dan" that he and his friends could gather in the Tabard on the site of the "Pilgrim's Room" and participate in a "public lecture on the genius of Chaucer."[9] In 1834, Innes gleefully wrote to *The Mirror* that it "was a novel experiment, and we flattered ourselves that we were the second pilgrim gathering."[10] In his earlier contribution to *The Mirror*, in a topographical survey of London, Innes authenticates his history by means of an anonymous sketch of the pilgrims before the Tabard (figure 1). The backdrop is almost certainly an adaptation of an etching from John Urry's 1721 edition of Chaucer's *Works*; the pilgrims are derived from Stothard, and the sign is from Blake. That this engraving is a pastiche of three earlier engravings does not make this representation "unrealistic" to Innes; the tenor of his prose presents the engraving as a perfectly normal rendition of "one of the most interesting localities of the metropolis" (1833:178). The fact that the Tabard still existed in 1833, known as the Talbot, plus the "minute and critical manner in which [Chaucer] illustrates the personal appearance, the habits, the moral and social qualities of the pilgrims . . . scarcely leaves a doubt but that they were faithful transcripts from existant originals" (1833:178-9). To reinforce that point, Innes inserted Chaucer himself in the fore-left (in nearly Napoleonic dress) reviewing "the train as it passes before him" (1833:179).[11]

Chaucer became didactic history for Charles Knight, the editor and publisher of the pictorial history, *Old England: A Pictorial Museum* (1845).[12] Robert Buss, who drew the designs for the engravings in Knight, illustrated the habits and dress of the fourteenth century and arranged the pilgrims from *The Canterbury Tales* in groups of two and three to identify specific social classes. Buss follows Chaucer in grouping the Knight and the Squire (figure 2), the Summoner and the Pardoner, and the five Guildsmen, for example. Yet other groupings reflect what can be seen as nineteenth-century notions of gender,

Fig. 2 - "Knight and Squire"

vocation, and class-the Wife of Bath with the Prioress, for example, the Lawyer and Doctor, and the Parson and Clerk. Paradoxically, these rearrangements reflect nineteenth-century social alignments at the same time that the accompanying text praises Chaucer for "availing himself of the opportunity [the pilgrimage] offered for the mingling of different ranks (we need hardly say that such unnatural and pernicious extreme social divisions as mark our time were unknown in Chaucer's)" (Knight 322).[13] The text also admires Chaucer as one of "the few supreme master spirits" (322) and prizes him for his realism. Indeed, Chaucer's "history" was better than Froissart's, according to the text, because his descriptions "went so much deeper beneath the surface, that he at the same time described human nature under a thousand varying aspects; the consequence is, we turn with ever-fresh instruction to his pages" (323). Buss's engravings of Chaucer's pilgrims are interspersed with illustrations of medieval dress taken from manuscripts, thus implying Buss's own historical authenticity. Each grouping conveys the social "place" of the group within a dramatic scene. The "Monk and the Friar" (figure 3) for instance, caught in a moment of collusive gossip, are properly libidinous Catholics from a nineteenth-century Protestant point of view. (Knight was a major publisher for the Society for the Diffusion of Useful Knowledge, an eminently Protestant and didactic organization). The "Sumpnour and Pardoner" exemplify "the ecclesiastical abuses" of Chaucer's day (330). The text for *Old England* quotes the appropriate description from Chaucer's prologue, then uses the Chaucerian character to exemplify a particular class of citizen, such as "knight" or "London merchant," including a general description of that socio-economic identity conflated with nineteenth-century ideology. The Wife of Bath, for example, has a "masculine disposition" and "gay temper"; she is not truly womanly because her "rovings, often without any, or very inadequate protection, were likely to injure the growth of true womanly qualities" such as exhibited by the "exquisite gentlewoman," the Prioress (327). The engravings belong both to the antiquarian school of medievalism in their historicizing detail and to the

conventional school in their use of contemporary facial types and coiffures.
Buss's engravings remain faithful to
selected details from Chaucer (e.g., the
Squire's flute and embroidered flowers,
and the Monk's hunting hounds) even as
they adapt his characters to nineteenth-
century conventions of male and female
appearance (e.g., the Squire's dandified
posture). Chaucerian accuracy becomes
historical accuracy in this work, while the
past is linked to the present through typing
and topographical continuity asserted by
the inclusion of three images of the Tabard,
dated 1720, 1780, and 1841.

Fig. 3 - "Monk and Friar"

A later-century version of *The
Canterbury Tales* as history centers on the
social and ethical utility of the work. Mary Haweis's *Chaucer for
Children, A Golden Key* (1876), written to introduce the Father of
English Poetry to children, presents Chaucer as the founder of "our
present National Tongue," and argues that Chaucer is "a thoroughly
religious poet, all his merriest stories having a fair moral." This book
claims that there "is no clearer or safer exponent of the life of the 14th
century, as far as he describes it, than Geoffrey Chaucer."[14] Haweis
dismisses the difficulties of Middle English, stating that this language
"appears easy to children, whose crude language is in many ways its
counterpart" (ix). Haweis balances two goals. The first is to make
Chaucer's poetry accessible to children, and not just accessible, but
enjoyable. Her text offers a facing-page translation with a glossary in
the margin, and her preface includes a simple guide to pronunciation.
Her claim is not just for poetic beauty but for textual accuracy of both
words and images:

> I have adhered generally to [Richard] Morris's text (1866), being both
> good and popular, only checking it by his Clarendon Press edition, and by
> Tyrwhitt, Skeat [1872?], Bell, &c,. when I conceive force is gained. . . .
>   In the pictures I have been careful to preserve the right costumes,
> colours, and surroundings, for which I have resorted to the MSS. of the time,
> knowing that a child's mind, unaided by the eye, fails to realize half of what
> comes through the ear. (Preface xii)

KNIGHT.   SQUIRE.   BOY,   WIFE OF BATH. PRIORESS. CHAUCER (A CLERK).   FRIAR.   MINE HOST.
                                      MONK,   SUMMONER.   PARDONER.   SECOND NUN. FRANKLIN

Fig. 4 - "The Canterbury Pilgrims"

The frontispiece exemplifies her quest for Chaucerian accuracy as historical accuracy while meeting the contemporary demand for narrative incident (figure 4, and see Appendix, 1876, Haweis). The drawing is Haweis's own, although the ultimate source of her Chaucer, whom she characterizes as "a clerk," is Thomas Hoccleve's portrait of Chaucer in *The Regement of Princes* (107). Like most of the free-standing paintings (see below), the general composition is a pyramid, with Chaucer and the Wife presiding at the top-the author and his most popular character. Six distinct subgroups provide moments of a "story." The characters are arranged in a frieze with the suggestion of a backdrop, medievalized by the crenellated city walls, church and castle towers. The outstretched arm of "Mine Host" on the right and the Knight on the left point toward Chaucer, while the boy's arms connect the two sides of the painting. The Wife gossips with Chaucer; the Monk flirts with the Prioress; the Summoner, complete with pustules, scowls at the Host; the Franklin makes jovial conversation with the Nun. The scene is lively and crowded; even the horses seem to know that something unusual is going on. In her "Notes on the Pictures" Haweis painstakingly establishes the historical accuracy of her illustrations, citing manuscripts and providing a bibliography that includes Samuel Meyrick's

Antient Armour, Skeat's *Chaucer*, William Fairholt's *Costume in England*, and Froissart's *Chronicles*. The notes on this illustration concentrate on the authenticity of her costumes. While she adheres to the "chain-mail equals knight" convention (here plate armor), she points out that it is a convention of representation: "[t]he attire of the Knight is open to criticism, for the amount of armour he wears is certainly more than he need wear on so peaceful an errand; but a portion of the well-used plate may be permitted to distinguish the man of war from the numerous men of peace in the train" (107). She proceeds to justify her version by saying, "The numerous miniatures of mailed knights journeying for no sinister purpose, appear to me to prove that it was very constantly worn" (107).

If Haweis's frontispiece and notes offer a clear "illustration" of Chaucer's pilgrims departing, the painting of the Miller by Henry Stacy Marks is a purer "realization" of a single pilgrim (figure 5). Probably

Fig. 5 - The Miller

THE MAN OF LAW'S TALE.

" On the fourth day Constance, with a deadly pale face, went toward the vessel; and, kneeling down upon the strand, she said, ' Lord ! ever welcome be thy decree.' "

Fig. 6 - "The Man of Law's Tale"

related to the enormous canvases Marks painted for a commission by the Duke of Westminster for Eaton Hall, and exhibited as studies in 1875, this Miller is clearly nothing but Chaucer's particular Miller, with his white coat, blue hood, bagpipes, sword and buckler, a "stout carl" (strong fellow), with a red beard and a wart on his nose.[15] But most depictions of Chaucer's text mix specific details of description with what can be called "narrative" accuracy, that is, re-presenting an identifiable moment in recognizable fashion. All of Charles Cowden Clarke's realizations for his 1833 edition, for instance, depict precise moments in their tales, abstracted from the tale, placed at the beginning and identified by appropriate lines of text.[16] For example, Custance, of the "Man of Law's Tale," is shown holding her son, kneeling on the shore, and accepting the will of Christ (figure 6, "Man of Law's Tale" 4.823-26). The quoted lines combine with Custance's theatrical gesture, the pathos of the baby on her arm, and the constable's emblematic keys of authority to locate the scene clearly, but the details overwhelm its particularity. The stern of the ship to the left might be thought Anglo-Saxon in some general way and thereby appropriate to Chaucer's setting of the scene before the Christianization of England. But Custance's crown and gown are strictly conventional, and the constable's keys, staff, robe, and baldpate do more to suggest general spiritual authority than the secular authority he has in Chaucer's tale as keeper of a sixth-century castle.

Corbould's *Canterbury Pilgrims Assembled in the Yard of the Tabard Hostelry* (1872) mixes both historical and Chaucerian accuracy, presenting Chaucer as emblematic of the fourteenth century (color plate 37).   Corbould, of course, had much practice envisioning Chaucer, having illustrated the Routledge Chaucer in 1854. In the later work, the seated Chaucer-figure on the right, holding a book, looks toward a full array of the pilgrims arranged in narrative "bites" that suggest Chaucer's characterizations. One first sees the center of the painting showing the women in light dresses, then following upwards to the twins (?), who wave to the two women in the gallery of the Tabard. But one may also "read" this painting from left to right, seeing the procession of pilgrims that Chaucer is creating; this view gives us Chaucer as the realist novelist. Corbould used the conventions of generic historical accuracy with some details from Chaucer's texts to match his scene with his title. The Knight on horseback is accompanied by his entourage of Squire and Yeoman, who wears his characteristic green hood; his bow lies at his feet, just as the Miller is next to his bagpipes, ready to lead the pilgrimage (see "General Prologue," 1.103-104, 565-66). The Wife is recognizable (by her broad hat), as are the feasting Monk and lank-haired Pardoner. The Knight's armor and the Squire's mail and crusader's cross are generic, but the Norman hounds'-tooth archivolt in the back right of the scene and the many other architectural details reflect effort towards historical particularity. On horseback, the Friar chucks the chin of the Prioress, while an unidentifiable figure flirts with the Wife. The Monk exudes gluttony at the table. Another unidentifiable figure sits beside him, flirting with the two serving women—one pouring him beer and the other standing between his legs. The "Tabard" sign and the proprietor's sign that reads "Harry Bailee" clearly mark this as Chaucerian. The entire painting projects a jolly, lively image of "merrie olde England," accentuated by the golden wash that harmonizes the figures into a unit. The details provide hints of authenticity for the viewer in the know, but it is not necessary to have any familiarity with *The Canterbury Tales* to understand this historical narrative. Corbould's free combination of historical and Chaucerian detail seemingly did not detract from his authenticity for his audience.   He was appointed "Instructor of Historical Painting" to the Royal Family in 1851.[17]

All the pictures of the pilgrims gathered together, whether in the courtyard of the Tabard or inside around the table, depict the pilgrims as a harmonious, jolly gathering, but these pictures maintain subtle lines of social distinction through arrangement and composition. For instance, in Buss's engraving for *Old England* and in F. W. Fairholt's engraving reproduced in the *Art Journal* in 1849 (11:[111]), the female pilgrims, Prioress, Nun, and Wife, are safely sequestered from the Miller and the Cook. Thus, despite the fact that the Wife is "unwomanly" according to *Old England*, as a female she is to be protected. The reconceptualization of *The Canterbury Tales* into nineteenth-century cultural ideals is, in fact, most clearly seen in the Victorians' imposition of their own gender ideology upon the figures of Griselda and Emily. Versions of the Griselda story in particular demonstrate the power of Victorian history painting to connect the past to the present because they recreate the past as an exemplary representation of nineteenth-century gender-class concerns. By doing so, these representations are more illustrations than realizations, to return to Meisel's distinction, using their fidelity to Chaucer's text to hold an idealizing mirror up to the present.

Richard Altick notes in *Paintings from Books* that "[a]llusions to [Griselda] abound in novels of the time, and she and her latter-day counterparts were the actual subject of novels and poems from Maria Edgeworth's *The Modern Griselda* (1840) to Edwin Arnold's *Griselda: A Tragedy* (1856). Some twenty versions of several scenes of the story are recorded."[18] The image of long-suffering Griselda fit Victorian mores of courtship, the realities of the middle-class female, and ideals of female behavior and nature. In the mid-nineteenth century, in fact until 1870, British women, like Griselda, had no civil or legal existence while they were minors or after they were married. A woman had no right to property (even if it was her earnings) or to her children. Two favorite scenes taken from "The Clerk's Tale" were the marriage moment, showing Griselda passing safely from her father to her husband, and the "First Trial," as it was named by the Victorians, showing Griselda suffering the loss and, as she thinks, death of her firstborn. As Griselda was changed by marriage, so in the nineteenth century, "it was the man's position which . . . defined the course of the rest of his wife's life."[19] And this course was not always strewn with roses. Richard Redgrave's paintings of *The Patience of Griselda* (1837) and *The Trial of Griselda's Patience* (1838)—both exhibited at the Royal Academy—would have surely resonated with the case of Caroline

Norton, then notoriously public. Her husband George, having failed to get a guilty verdict in a specious accusation of "criminal conversation" between Caroline and Lord Melbourne, cruelly took Caroline's young sons away from her, forbidding her to see or communicate with them. Caroline, already a well-known writer, put her case before the public in a pamphlet, *Separation of Mother and Child by the Custody of Infants Considered*, published in 1837. Her friend Serjeant Talfourd lay before Parliament the Infant Custody Bill in 1838, which passed in 1839, allowing mothers of children under seven at least to petition for a custody hearing.[20]

Redgrave returned to the subject of Griselda in 1850 (see below) after his depictions of her in the 1830s launched his reputation as a painter of the mournful female victim: Ophelia, his famous "Governess" and "Seamstress" paintings, and Olivia from the *Vicar of Wakefield*. The 1837 Griselda was Redgrave's first version of his many images of long-suffering female virtue. Susan Casteras notes that after this painting he produced "a string of vignettes of female tribulation and testing . . . some of them couched in terms of romantic distress and others in terms of class differences."[21] Redgrave, although not the first to present such scenes, "was a pioneer in his persistence" (Casteras, *Redgrave*, 12). The Griselda motif would have fit in with Redgrave's self-perceived moral mission; he wrote in 1850, the year he exhibited *The Marquis having chosen patient Griselda for his wife, causes the Court ladies to dress her in her father's cottage*, that

> [i]t is one of my most gratifying feelings that many of my best efforts in art have aimed at calling attention to the trials and struggles of the poor and the oppressed. In the "Reduced Gentleman's Daughter," "The Poor Teacher," "The Sempstress," "Fashion's Slaves," and other works, I have had in view the "helping them to right that suffer wrong" at the hands of their fellow men.[22]

In the 1840s and early 1850s, when Charles West Cope was working on his version of the *First Trial of Griselda* as a fresco in the Upper Waiting Room of the new Palace at Westminster (and exhibited as a color study in 1852), women's rights were again in the air. Debates about women's property rights would culminate in the first Property Bill of 1857; during 1854-1855, Thackeray was publishing *The Newcomes* in which Clara Newcome would lose her children because she eloped with another man.

Obviously, Griselda was not a fallen woman like Clara Newcome. In fact, it was just her innocence that made her an ideal woman to become ideal victim for the Victorians. Muriel Whitaker points out that Griselda's virtues of obedience and patience were not specifically gendered for Chaucer's audience, reflecting instead the good Christian's submission to the will of God.[23] For the Victorians, however, Griselda's virtues are more specifically and necessarily feminine. As the art critic in the *Athenaeum* observed, "[t]he tale has been ever popular: the moral of the endurance and the virtue it inculcates are ever to be cherished."[24] This idealization crystallized in the marriage moment, a scene depicted in remarkably similar ways by Richard Redgrave (1850), Alfred Elmore (1850), Charles West Cope (1852), Frederic George Stephens (1850?), and in the editions illustrated by Charles Cowden Clarke (1833), R. W. Buss for John Saunders' *Chaucer* (1845), Edward Henry Corbould (1854), and Mary Haweis (1876). All these depictions conflate the ideal of female purity with the class tensions crucial to the tale and endemic in class-conscious Victorian society. In all of them, conventional sentiment overwhelms historical particularity, while the specific scene evokes tension—dramatic tension because the viewers expect the fruition of this moment. The temporal present of the paintings is precisely the shift from her humble past to her long-suffering but ultimately successful future, and this moment and movement are embedded in the compositions of the paintings. The critic for the *Art Journal*, describing Redgrave's composition, points inadvertently to the social transformation that is taking place:

> In this composition the figures are numerous. Griselda is the nucleus of this assemblage; she is in profile, seated, and one of the ladies is busied in dressing her hair; some are preparing her attire, others are idly gossiping, the envied Griselda being pointedly the subject of this discourse. In the features of the principal figures there are, variously expressed, sarcasm and contempt. The humble abode of the father of Griselda contrasts strongly with the rich dresses of the ladies, although the figures are so numerous that little of the cottage is seen. The Marquis is seated just within the cottage-door, a curtain separates him from the dressing room of Griselda, and outside appear his attendants, mounted and in waiting.[25]

Both Cope's and Elmore's paintings are similar "moment[s] of poise" (Meisel 35), suggesting that this marriage moment was the narrative epiphany of the story for its Victorian audience.

Charles West Cope's *The Marques of Saluce Marries Griselda,* exhibited in 1852, attempts some kind of historical accuracy with its house and chickens, background castle and fancy dress. But the period seems to combine fairy tale with the Bible, emphasizing the moral and social implications of the scene (color plate 38). Griselda is the epitome of Victorian maidenly modesty and the Marquis is the respectful lover in fancy dress, his modernity indicated in his typically mid-century hair and moustache. Griselda is dressed like a Scottish peasant from a David Wilkie painting or a Scott novel. This version of the tale re-presents the moment as Prince Charming proposing to Cinderella, whose lovely modesty has earned her the elevation in station. The painting emphasizes the change by its division into halves. The right side shows a sheltered Griselda, protected by her father and the stone walls of her cottage. The chickens, dog, and egg basket proclaim her homely background, while the jug reminds a literate viewer of the earlier scene when the Marquis first sees her at the well. The left side suggests the perils of the ornate, open future Griselda enters with her marriage. We look through the throng of courtiers up a hill to the castle, her future home. The courtiers evince surprise, wariness, and disdain; they will test her refinement just as the Marquis will test her moral worthiness. One lady holds a bridal gown that suggests the sexual and social transformation that is to come, perhaps capitalizing on the emblematic value of clothing and dress that recurs throughout Chaucer's "Clerk's Tale" (e.g., 4.375-78, 890-91, 913, and 1114-17). As Marquise she will become subject to the public gaze, beginning already as people peer around the corner and crowd into the background. And her future home, the castle on the hill, offers a subtle contrast to her humble cottage. The transfer is already in process: Janicula holds one hand while the Marquis grasps the other, signifying that Griselda passes from father to husband as virgin.

The boundary of Griselda's world is also the center of the painting, marked not only by the wooden pier but also by the two impish pages offering rich gifts and the rather somber background figure holding a coronet indicative of her future state. This saturnine figure, garbed more like a Victorianized Hebrew prophet than a medieval courtier, seems to suggest, in his dark coloring and downward glance, the danger beneath the superficial fairy tale. The critics noticed the fairy-tale motif:

> The aged father of the fair rustic sits under his shed. His mean air and expression—an aggregate of the bedesman, the miser, and the pauper—contrast with those of his maiden daughter;—one of those peasants who, bred and

born in a hovel, coarsely fed and housed, and hardly worked, yet always-in operas and fairy tales-surpass in delicacy of form, fair hands, and feet, as in purity of soul, the real princess reared in the hothouse atmosphere of luxury and refinement.[26]

This *Athenaeum* critic finds fault with the painting, calling the attitudes "laboured,—the faces and flesh unreal, conventional,—and life-lacking, a family nose and nostrils belong to all,-the draperies are cramped and wanting in breadth" even though "[t]he minor accessories—the poultry, dog, pitcher, rafters, and so forth—are excellently studied and treated. The general result is, a failure. The straining is evident,—and Mr. Cope has yet to learn that the one grand point in Art is, the art to conceal it" (583). To this critic, the theatricality of the scene overrides the narrative interest, eliminating any illusion of "accident." However, the *Illustrated London News* finds "considerable merit" in the painting and singles out Griselda as an icon of the ideal female: "[t]he gentle heroine blushes with true rustic bashfulness, as she still clings to her aged father's hand, and looks inquiringly into his face, as the dazzling proposal is made to her."[27]

Elmore's painting is simply called *Griselde* (1850) and is accompanied by the lines "And as she wolde over the threshwold gon, / The Markis came and gan for to call, / And she set down hire water-pot anon, / Beside the threswold gin and oxe's stall" (color plate 39, "Clerk's Tale," 4.288-91). The scene conflates two moments from the "Clerk's Tale." Griselda is setting down her water jar, but her father is already there; missing is the sequence when she falls on her knees before the Marquis and then fetches her father at his request. Elmore's Italianate setting—in the architecture, "banditti" style peasant dress of Griselda, and vine leaves over the stucco arch—suggests Chaucer's setting in Saluces (modern Saluzzo). Unlike Cope, Elmore has no court ladies waiting to dress Griselda, but like Cope's, this painting is organized with a left-right structure. The humble peasantry is noted by the cow byre; the woman with the distaff suggests Griselda's spinning as well as her readiness for marriage; her fecundity is perhaps indicated by the peasant woman and child in the lower center. The most significant difference between Cope and Elmore is suggested in the composition. While both paintings offer this as a moment of social transition, Elmore depicts the scene as a pyramid, with Griselda at the apex. His emphasis is on her: we see her full face as she looks warily at the marquis; she stands above him, and the white blouse and full lighting

THE CLERK'S TALE.

" The Marquis turned to this gentle and very faithful creature, and said:—
'Griselda, it pleases your father and myself that I should take you to be my wife;
and I think you will not reject our wishes.' "

Fig. 7 - "The Clerk's Tale"

draw the viewers' eyes to her very typical Victorian beauty. Elmore emphasizes Griselda as a female icon in her "innocent and guileless bearing,"[28] and her typicality was such that this same figure appeared in a later engraving as "Rebekah at the Well."[29]

The other images of the marriage moment include the same thematic, iconic emphases. Like Cope, Charles Cowden Clarke gives us a Griselda in a conventional peasant dress with very contemporary hair.[30] Clarke's illustration is less historically particular than Cope's painting, and Griselda's father is rather comic. Yet the emphasis is still on demure Griselda being passed from father to husband (figure 7). Mary Haweis also depicts the transference as a physical exchange from father to husband: one of Griselda's hands is held, just by the fingertips, by her father (figure 8). She places her other hand in the Marquis's. Her station is indicated by her rags, the chicken, cow, and just a glimpse of the water jug, while Walter's class is suggested by the castle behind him. Frederic George Stephens' version, *The Proposal*, is the least Chaucerian (color plate 40). Only the tell-tale chickens and water jug suggest her humble status. In fact, our attribution is based upon Richard Altick's supposition that the scene is Chaucerian at all (340) and on the Tate's subtitle of the painting, "The Marquis and

Fig. 8 - "Griselda's Marriage"

Griselda." Griselda could as easily be a vicar's daughter as a peasant. The background, the beamed house, the wooden shutter, the red-tiled floor, and the feather in the Marquis's cap may suggest an Italian setting appropriate to Saluces, and the open door points to her escape from her lowly surroundings. Yet the details are very difficult to read historically. Walter's shoes and the chair behind Griselda may be medieval, but little else suggests a particular time. The three hats seem to clash, as do Griselda's dress and Walter's leggings. The linen on which Walter sits is unusual at best.

These various marriage moments evidently appealed to the nineteenth century through their transparency. As Walter is older than Griselda so were 73% of husbands older than their wives by at least 4.3 years between 1780 and 1850.[31] In the tale as in these scenes, the entire courtship is beyond reproach. Walter goes through the father to the daughter; there are no trysts, no flirtation, no courting, nothing that would impugn Griselda's purity (unlike the elaborate games of courtship played out in Victorian novels such as Thackeray's *Adventures of Philip* and Eliot's *Middlemarch*, or in many contemporary paintings). Except in Stephen's *Proposal*, she passes untouched from father to husband. In fact, the inclusion of the water jug in these

Fig. 9 - "Griselda as Shepherdess"   *Fig. 10 - "Griselda as Walter's Wife"*

pictures emphasizes her virginity; it is a comment on the "cruche cassé" motif familiar in eighteenth-century painting, the "broken" jug or jar symbolizing the loss of virginity. John Saunders's version of Griselda emphasizes the seamlessness of this transfer from father to husband in his mirror images (Figures 9-10).[32]   In the first we see Griselda in the field with her sheep, spinning, and placed before a patriarchal father. He looms over her, protecting this demure human lamb. Saunders's excerpted text on the facing page emphasizes Griselda's obedience, diligence, and reverence to her father; he includes adaptations of the "Clerk's Tale," 4.218-52. The next illustration (pp. 190-91) shows exactly the same composition, only this time the sheep are exchanged for whippets, and the looming male is Walter, who carries a spear instead of a shepherd's crook; here the facing text emphasizes Griselda's social ascendancy, adapting lines 4.394-427. Griselda's hands are now empty, her idleness indicative of her elevation in class. And instead of hills in the background, there is a castle. Visually, the illustrations corroborate the text, and corroborate also that Griselda's

GRISELDA'S SORROW.
'And as a lamb sche sitteth meeke and stille,

Fig. 11 - "Griselda's Sorrow"

social ascendancy results from her obedience to her father and her sub-ordination to her new husband, another form of obedience consistent with Victorian middle-class gender politics.

It seems an odd choice, but when awarded the decoration of the Upper Waiting Hall in the new Palace, Charles West Cope chose "Griselda's First Trial," from the general topic of "Chaucer." The fresco itself soon deteriorated, but it survives in a colored study Cope exhibited in 1849 (color plate 41).[33] In 1876 Mary Haweis chose this moment for one of her illustrations in a *A Golden Key*, another odd choice, given her youthful audience (figure 11). Both Cope and Haweis depict the moment when the Marquis's servant takes the child. They convey the servant's "cheere / As though he wolde han slayn it er he wente" ("Clerk's Tale," 4.535-36) by means of a bushy mustache, flowing hair, and his threat to the child with a knife. Certainly Cope's is the more melodramatic image, with one serving lady in agony and Griselda swooning in grief on the floor as her panic-stricken baby reaches wildly toward his mother. Yet Cope's Griselda is supine on the floor (Chaucer has "sitteth meke and stille" [4.538]), a collapsed woman as an image of grief rather than stoic endurance. Walter watches her from the window above. Griselda for Haweis is an icon of patient endurance. The scene is entitled "Griselda's Sorrow," and is accompanied by the lines "And as a lamb sche sitteth meeke and stille, / And let this cruel sergeant doon his wille." Her arms hang listlessly by her side, and her fingers are open in resignation. Her face is sorrowful but placid, and the headrest of her chair acts as a nimbus, turning her into a Madonna. The etching emphasizes her; we see only the back of the child, and the servant recedes into the background. The lighting and composition in Cope's painting emphasize the child more than the mother and put the viewer in the mother's position of seeing her child taken. However, Walter, whom Griselda does not see, adds an ambiguous note to both scenes. Are we to be comforted because we know this is just a test, or are we to condemn Walter for

THE CLERKES TALE.

Fig. 12 - "Ye Clerkes Tale"

his unnecessary cruelty? Does his hand over his mouth in Haweis's version suggest that he is speechless in cruelty or amazement?

Depictions of Griselda in the illustrated editions also show her as an exemplary icon. Two scenes from the "Clerk's Tale" in Corbould's Routledge edition and Saunders's 1845 edition share compositional styles. In both, the figures are set in the foreground against a backdrop. That is, there is no middle-ground to lead the eye to the horizon. The effect is of a theatrical scene instead of figures in an interior or a landscape. This theatricality emphasizes the iconicity of Griselda, as does the static pyramid composition in Saunders's depiction of the reunion of Griselda with her family from the end of the "Clerk's Tale" (opposite p. 178, and significantly, the frontispiece of the tale). There is no hint of Griselda's swoon or any criticism of Walter's harshness; in fact, Walter as paterfamilias dominates this scene, his arms enveloping wife and children alike. Corbould also emphasizes the power of the male in his scene of Walter on one of his hunting excursions "happening" to see a rather voluptuous although demure Griselda in her habitual practice of picking roots and herbs to bring home [opposite p. 216, Figure 12]. She herself seems ripe for the plucking, to paraphrase Susan Casteras's description of the common maiden-in-the-garden motif in Victorian paintings and *Annual* engravings (*Images* 86). This Griselda is very much in the Keepsake beauty tradition, particularly in the buxom shoulders and bosom. An obvious question the composition evokes is how she can possibly be oblivious to Walter and his horse, which seems to be not more than a foot from her. However, her modest, downcast eyes are necessary to counterpoint her voluptuous figure. Walter's mount, hawk, and pseudo-medieval dress denote his upper-class status, echoed by the glimpse of the castle behind him. Griselda's status is apparent in her placement beneath him, her lowly occupation, and the cottage behind her. With unintentional irony, Corbould's composition could as easily illustrate the impending rape in the "Wife of Bath's Tale," as it does impending marriage in the "Clerk's Tale."

The popularity of the "marriage moment" and the consensus that Griselda was ideal in her modesty and obedience suggest that she can be read as a social icon as well as an ideal of gender. Given that medievalism idealized class relations, Griselda herself embodies the "correct" subordination to her better. She is female and peasant, subjecting herself to the will of her lord because her nature and status dictate that subordination. In one important respect she differs from Cinderella, also a popular subject for genre paintings: while Cinderella has been disinherited by her wicked stepmother, Griselda is a peasant by birth. She is raised to ruling status only because she submits completely to the will of her ruler. The Marquis, however, is not simply acting from *noblesse oblige*; he is also acting out the Disrealian chivalric ideal of the high caring for the low. One of Carlyle's primary emphases in *Past and Present* is the necessity that the aristocracy care for those in their charge. Alice Chandler points out that, to Carlyle, the Victorian nobility had forgotten their "duty to assure [their] tenants and workers of the simple justice of 'a fair day's-wages for a fair day's-work.'"[34] The gender/class structure of the Victorian Griselda paintings automatically suggests this bond of rule and service—or mutually dependent asymmetrical relations so unlike the contemporary agitations for Reform, Unions, and Women's Property Rights. And the "marriage moment" focuses on the emotional appeal of the Middle Ages, disguising social hierarchy in sentiment (Chandler 153). Griselda's peasant status embodies the subordination of the Victorian working class. Her naiveté, purity, and modesty say that she accepts her role and thus the dominant role of the Marquis. The justness which the art critics see in this story suggests that they also accept the underlying social relations. Griselda's passivity, recurrently emphasized by her downcast eyes, makes her a parable for a conservative view of class relations. Subordinating class to gender in the figure of Griselda, which emphasizes her "natural" worth as her beauty, avoids overt class antagonism. Her gender-typing conveys this story as one of a "natural" hierarchy, embodying

> two major aspects [of medievalism] in the eighteenth and nineteenth centuries. One is its naturalism—its identification with nature and the past and thus with simpler and truer modes of feeling and expression and nobler and more heroic codes of action. The other is its feudalism—its harmonious and stable social structure which reconciled freedom and order by giving each man an allotted place in society and an allotted leader to follow. The bridge between these two aspects is chivalry, which made the spontaneous generosity of the natural man the guiding principle of man in society and which compensated for human frailty by having the strong protect the weak. (Chandler 195)

Griselda's appearance *is* her nature, and it is this nature that invites Walter's chivalric proposal. His trial of her endurance wins her a place in high prosperity.[35] Class tension would be unavoidable if the gender roles were reversed and Griselda were a male being raised up by a female, an occurrence at the opening of Chaucer's "Franklin's Tale" (see 5.734-42), a scene nowhere depicted in nineteenth-century art to our knowledge. In Victorian England, such a reversal would be impossible except as a parody in the pages of *Punch*.

Corbould's Emily in the "Knight's Tale" is a similar female icon whose class status emphasizes the ideal of pre-marital purity. Emily does not draw water or pick wort, i.e. work. She is decorative like the flowers she picks and is herself a flower ripe for the plucking as she plucks roses in her garden (figure 13, frontispiece). The female in the garden is a familiar figure in Victorian genre painting and derives directly from medieval traditions of the *hortus conclusus*. According to Susan Casteras, "[t]he bequest of the medieval walled garden as an attribute

THE KNIGHTES TALE.

Fig. 13 - "Ye Knightes Tale"

FAIR EMELYE GATHERING FLOWERS.
'The fairnesse of the lady that I see
Yonde in the gardyn romynge to and fro.'

Fig. 14 - "Fair Emelye Gathering Flowers"

of feminine purity, a sacred space where the modern madonna inhabited an insular sanctuary of artificial maidenhood, was a critical one" (Casteras, *Images*, 87). Interestingly, however, Emily was not as popular a figure as Griselda as far as we can ascertain; she does not, for example, appear in any free-standing paintings that we know. Both Corbould and Haweis present her as a prize, a rare treasure to be won. Corbould's Emily picks roses, a symbol of love, in her walled garden, while Palamon, far away up in his prison, looks on. Her long unbound hair signifies her maiden purity, and her face is a typical *Keepsake* beauty. Haweis's highly romanticized "Fair Emelye Gathering Flowers" appears to be simply an image of the Aesthetic stunner (figure 14). However, Haweis takes pains to historicize her image and rationalize Chaucer's text. According to Haweis's "Notes," Emelye wears a dress "common to the thirteenth and fourteenth centuries," and the halo is also an accurate natural phenomenon:

> It will be remembered that Palamon mistook Emelye at first sight for a goddess; Arcite perceived her to be human. I have endeavoured to give the two men's views of her—each quite possible according to her position in the garden. Palamon may have caught sight of her just at a turn where the dazzle of sunrise behind the tree would be certain to lend a kind of halo to the outline of a head against it. An instant afterwards Emelye may have moved aside, the false halo disappearing, and she would seem what she truly was, simply an attractive maiden. (108)

Mary Haweis draws Emily as an icon of female purity but discusses her as a person. That is, Haweis saw Emily as a symbol and as real. And, as we have argued, the various depictions of Griselda offer her story simultaneously as fiction, history, and contemporary emblem.

Such multi-layered representation is central to the most familiar image of the Victorian period associated with *The Canterbury Tales*, Ford Madox Brown's *Chaucer Reading the 'Legend of Custance' to*

Edward III, and his Court, at the Palace of Sheen, on the anniversary of the Black Prince's forty-fifth Birthday (color plate 42). Brown combines mimetic and metaphoric perspectives with historical accuracy to achieve an intensely personal vision of Chaucer within his Middle Ages. As the title of the earliest version of this work, *The Seeds and Fruits of English Poetry*, indicates, Brown conceived of his subject as an emblem. *The Seeds and Fruits* is a triptych, an altarpiece to English literary heritage. Brown was inspired by a sentence from Sir James Mackintosh's history of England written for Dionysius Lardner's *Cabinet Cyclopaedia* (1829-49).

> In the summer of [18]45 I went to the British Museum to read Sir James Mackintosh's history of England, having heard that it was of a phylosophical [sic] nature, with a view to select some subject connected with the history of this Country of a general and comprehensive nature. . . .
>   In this mood, glancing over the pages of the above named history I fell upon a passage to this effect as near as I can remember[:] "And it is scarcely to be wondered at, that the English about this period should have become the judicial language of the country, ennobled as it had recently been by the genius of Geoffrey Chaucer." This at once fixed me, I immediately saw visions of Chaucer reading his poems to knights & Ladyes fair, to the king & court amid air & sun shine.[36]

Brown's reminiscence suggests that he was caught by the emblematic importance of Chaucer as the Father of English Poetry as well as with the poetic and romantic possibilities of his "scene." *The Seeds and Fruits* and the later, finished, *Chaucer Reading* communicate both ideas through what can be called "aesthetic medievalism." The two versions are contained within arched frames that emphasize their status as "paintings." The viewer outside the frame has little sense of a spontaneous accidental viewing. Despite the vitality of the scenes, these are set, composed pieces. *Chaucer Reading*, like *Seeds and Fruits*, modeled on the composition of Daniel Maclise's design of *Chivalry* for the Houses of Parliament, subdues the decoration of the latter, but the three-tiered structure, luxuriant color, and frieze-like composition align it with Pre-Raphaelite aestheticism.

However, Brown's historicity equaled his sense of decoration. In the February 1850 *Germ*, the magazine of the Pre-Raphaelite Brotherhood, Brown wrote that an aspiring historical artist should "make himself thoroughly acquainted with the character of the times, and habit of the people, which he is about to represent; and next, to consult the proper authorities for his costume, and such objects as may fill his canvass; as the architecture, furniture, vegetation or landscape, or accessories, necessary to the elucidation of his subject."[37] Contemporary art critics easily saw the historical within the aesthetic. The *Athenaeum*, in fact, criticized the "learning" of the painting as "antiquarian rather than artistic."[38] In addition to drawing upon Joseph Strutt's work, tomb effigies, and Knight's *Old England* for details such as the lectern, Brown dressed his models in accurate medieval costumes (Bennett 53; Strong 72-73) and was meticulous in matching color and style to personage (*Diary* 4-10). In fact, Roy Strong focuses on Brown as a pre-eminent painter of the "Artist-Antiquarian phase" (102). Describing *Seeds and Fruits* in the catalogue for his 1865 one-man show, Brown stressed the historical situation of all his major characters, to place this scene, Chaucer reading from the "Man of Law's Tale," at precisely 1375, the year of the Black Prince's forty-fifth birthday, although Brown mistakes his calculations:

> Edward III. is now old, Phillippa being dead; the Black Prince is supposed to be in his last illness. John of Gaunt, who was Chaucer's patron, is represented in full armour, to indicate that active measures now devolve upon him. . . . Edward the Black Prince, now in his fortieth year [sic], emaciated by sickness, leans on the lap of his wife Joanna, surnamed the Fair Maid of Kent. There has been much opposition to their union, but the Prince ultimately had his way. To the right of the old King is Alice Perrers, a cause of scandal to the Court. . . . Two *dilettante* courtiers learnedly criticizing; the one in the hood is meant for the poet Gower.[39]

The *Art Journal* observed that "[e]very figure of the composition evinces research and unwearied study."[40] To the *Illustrated London News*, the scene is presented "much as it probably occurred," but this realism is also "chivalric" and "poetic."[41] The romance of history is created by the vibrant color and graceful arrangement of the figures. The harmony of the drapery coincides with the parallel ascending figures-in shadow in the fore-left and right with a river of light running up from the fore-ground pavement over the figures (illuminating the face of Julia Wild, a professional model), landing on the base of the lectern. This pyramid of light balances the painting while the pairs of heads in animated conversation keep the scene from being static. We feel both the enthrallment and excitement of Chaucer's poetry.

The lines from the "Man of Law's Tale" that Brown imagines Chaucer to be reading connect this fourteenth-century scene to the sentiments of the Victorian audience:

Hire litel child lay weping on hir arm,
  And, kneling pitously to him she said,
Pees litel sone, I wol do thee no harm!
  With that hir couverchief of hir hed she braid
And over his litel eyen she it laid,
  And in hir arme she lulleth it ful fast,
And unto the hevens hir eyen up she cast.
    (Bendiner, 132; *Man of Law's Tale* 2.834-40)

That Brown chose these lines despite the fact that there is no hint of the tale in the painting aligns him with Victorian sentimentality.

The detail is antiquarian; the conception and composition are aesthetic; and the narrative moment and sentiment are conventional. Brown's successful combination of these three medievalisms contribute to the *Art Journal*'s estimate of *Chaucer Reading* as "a truly magnificent essay, it has an abundance of every quality necessary to constitute excellence in Art" (1851:157). And yet the contemporaneity of the painting is personal for Brown, for he dressed his friends as Chaucer's court. Walter Deverell, a friend of the Pre-Raphaelite Brotherhood, is Thomas of Woodstock, the young man flirting on the bottom left. John Marshall, a surgeon and Brown's friend, was the jester. Emma, soon to be Brown's wife, was Philippa Roet in the red headdress on the middle-left as well as the Fair Maid of Kent on the top right. Brown's daughter Lucy from his first marriage was her small child. Dante Gabriel Rossetti sat for Chaucer. The troubadour was William Michael Rossetti, and the lady with the red sleeves, clasping her hands, may have been Elizabeth Siddal.[42]

Chaucer Reading is thus a statement of Brown's personal relationship with the Middle Ages as well as an expression of the communal feeling and the sense of ownership that characterized Victorian medievalism. The painting is both intimate and theatrical, both informal and regal. It is a visualization of "old Dan Chaucer" as the "Father of English Poetry" as well as a "dream of community," both historical and contemporary, as Alan Gaylord puts it.[43] In visual language, *Chaucer Reading* shows us why Chaucer was so important and has survived so well. Brown was so inspired by Chaucer's linguistic importance that he imagined Chaucer reading-the poet is shown to us reading his tale that mesmerizes his audience, who is also the nineteenth-century audience mesmerized by Chaucer now. Paradoxically, *Chaucer Reading* is a painting that evokes an abiding literary genius. Gaylord has described this painting as a "scene of speaking [that explores] a space where the audience at once confirms the powers of the poet and confers status on him in its own right" (219). As Brown wrote in his catalogue, "Spelling, and a few of the minor proprieties apart, after a lapse of five hundred years, his delicate sense of natura-listic beauty and his practical turn of thought . . . comes home to us as naturally as the last volume we hail from the press" (Bendiner 132). Brown's sensibility brings us full circle, back to David Matthews's point that Chaucer was felt to be "modern" by the nineteenth century. Thus, visualized in every English pictorial vocabulary, Chaucer became the encyclopedia of the Victorians' past-personal, historical, and iconic.

Notes

[1]   Martin Meisel, *Realizations. Narrative, Pictorial, and Theatrical Arts in Nineteenth-Century England* (Princeton: Princeton UP, 1983), 30.

[2]   Roy Strong, *Recreating the Past. British History and the Victorian Painter* (London: Thames and Hudson, 1978), 50.

[3]   William Vaughan, "'God Help the Minister who Meddles in Art': History Painting in the New Palace of Westminster," in *The Houses of Parliament. History, Art, Architecture*, Christine Riding and Jacqueline Riding, eds. (London: Merrell, 2000), 232.

[4]   The Victorians' flexibility-and inflexibility-when it came to historical verisimili-tude can be illustrated in an example from Charles West Cope's experience. While Cope was at work on his fresco *Edward the Black Prince Receiving the Order of the Garter from Edward III* for the new Palace of Westminster, he wrote Robert Peel in September, 1844, that Sir Harris Nicholas, the historian of the Orders of Knighthood, had told him that no such event ever occurred. At first Peel wrote that this posed a serious problem because, after all, this fresco was to be an historically accurate decoration for the seat of English government. But after deliberation (and Nicholas's refusing to back down), Peel and then Prince Albert told Cope to contin-ue work. After all, wrote Peel to Charles Locke Eastlake, the artist on the Fine Arts Commission, the event *might* have happened: "The Order was founded by his father. It was finally established after Military Exploits in which the Black Prince took a conspicuous part." Albert wrote to Eastlake, "That there is no record of a historical act, which must once have taken place, does not constitute the representa-tion of that act in painting 'an historical absurdity,'" which was Nicholas's term for Cope's subject (18 October 1844). See David Robertson, *Sir Charles Eastlake and the Victorian Art World* (Princeton: Princeton UP, 1978), 67.

5   Alice Chandler, *A Dream of Order. The Medieval Ideal in Nineteenth-Century English Literature* (Lincoln: U of Nebraska P, 1970); Georg Lukács, *The Historical Novel* (London: Merlin, 1962); John Robson, "Social Change and Political Accommodation" in *The Mind and Art of Victorian England*, Josef L. Altholz, ed. (Minneapolis: U of Minneapolis P, 1976); David Matthews, *The Making of Middle English, 1765-1910*. Medieval Cultures, vol. 18 (Minneapolis: U of Minnesota P, 1999).

6   As Francis Bonner makes clear, one reason that *The Canterbury Tales* were not illustrated until mid-century despite the numerous editions of Chaucer's works (nine between 1775-1845) and the interest in his life (nineteen "lives" were published in that same period) is that Chaucer's reputation derived not from *The Canterbury Tales* but from apocryphal works that allowed the Romantics to type him as one of their own. He was depicted as "a vigorous and bitter satirist of the Catholic Church, a close friend and follower of Wycliff, a religious reformer. . . . [and] as one of the great nature poets of England." If one felt as did Isaac D'Israeli that "the 'Canterbury Tales' are but the smallest portion of Chaucer's works!," it is not surprising that no publisher contracted with artists to present illustrated editions or that artists did not produce free-standing versions of scenes from the tales or of pilgrims (qted. in Bonner 21). See Francis Bonner, "Chaucer's Reputation during the Romantic Period," *Furman Studies* 34 (Winter 1951):1-21.

7   Thomas Tyrwhitt, ed., *The Canterbury Tales of Chaucer*, 4 vols, and supplement (London: T. Payne, 1778). Unlike many of his predecessors and followers, Tyrwhitt based his text on manuscripts, rather than previous editions, producing a more accurate version.

8   "Fine Arts. Exhibition of the Royal Academy," *Illustrated London News* 16 May 1875, 470.

9   H. Innes, "Chaucer's Canterbury Pilgrims," *The Mirror* 22 (1833):178.

10 "Chaucer's Tomb," *The Mirror* 23 (1834): 97.

11 The same etching was adapted in 1886 for *London Society* to illustrate Mark Lemon's article, "Up and Down the London Streets" 9 (1866): 79-96, where it is identified as "drawn by J. A. Pasquier."

12 Charles Knight, *Old England. A Pictorial Museum*. 1844-45. Rpt. New York: Bracken Books, 1987. This folio picture book-cum-history was originally published by Knight in two volumes, then republished as two volumes in one in 1847 by James Sangster. Robert William Buss's engravings from *The Canterbury Tales* in *Old England* were reprinted in John Saunders, *Cabinet Pictures of English Life*, also published by Knight in 1845.

13 For a more detailed discussion of the social structure implied by *Old England*'s use of Chaucer's pilgrims, see Judith L. Fisher, "*The Canterbury Tales* in Charles Knight's *Old England*: Conservative Reform in Popular Publishing," *Poetica* 39 (1994): 155-77.

14 Mrs. H. R. (Mary Eliza) Haweis, *Chaucer for Children. A Golden Key* (London: Chatto & Windus, 1876), x.

15 See Henry Stacy Marks, *Pen & Pencil Sketches* (London: Chatto & Windus, 1894), 1:215-16. *The Illustrated London News* notes the studies as by "far the most important work of the kind the artist has yet undertaken" ("Associates of the Royal Academy," *Illustrated London News*, 8 May 1875, 446). For Chaucer's "General Prologue" description of the Miller (1.545-66), see John H. Fisher, ed. *The Complete Poetry and Prose of Geoffrey Chaucer* (Dallas: Harcourt, 1987). All references to Chaucer's works are from this edition, although our quotations follow the illustrated editions where appropriate.

16 Charles Cowden Clarke, *Tales from Chaucer in Prose* (London: Effingham Wilson, 1833).

17 "Edward Henry Corbould (British, 1815-1905)," Art Magick. March 12, 2002. <http://www.artmagick.com/artists/corbould/asp>.

18 Richard D. Altick, *Paintings from Books. Art and Literature in Britain, 1760-1900* (Columbus: Ohio State UP, 1985), 340.

19 Susan P. Casteras, *Images of Victorian Womanhood in English Art* (Cranbury, NJ: Associated UP, 1987), 27.

20 Micael M. Clarke, *Thackeray and Women* (DeKalb: Northern Illinois UP, 1995), 37.

21 Susan P. Casteras "'Social Wrongs': the Painted Sermons of Richard Redgrave," Susan P. Casteras and Ronald Parkinson, eds. *Richard Redgrave 1804-1888* (New Haven: Victoria and Albert and Yale Center for British Art, 1988), 9-28, esp. 12.

22 "Autobiography of Richard Redgrave, A.R.A.," *Art Journal* 12, n.s., 2 (1850): 49.

23 "The Artists' Ideal Griselda," Muriel Whitaker, ed. *Sovereign Lady: Essays On Women in Middle English Literature* (New York and London: Garland, 1995), pp. 85-114, 86.

24 "Royal Academy," *Athenaeum* 25 May 1850, 559.

25 "The Royal Academy. The Eighty-Second Exhibition-1850," *Art Journal* 12, n.s., 2 (1850): 169.

[26] "Fine Arts," *Athenaeum* 22 May 1852, 583.

[27] "Royal Academy Exhibition.," *Illustrated London News* 8 May 1852, 369.

[28] "Royal Academy," *Athenaeum* 25 May 1850, 560.

[29] The engraving, done by Francis Holt, was published as a companion print to William Holl's *The Gleaner*. Alfred Elmore, E.104-1970, Case 9, Drawer (1), Print Library, Victoria and Albert Museum, London. Whitaker suggests that the distaff and water jug are "Marian" images that establish Griselda as a type, not a specific character; see Whitaker, as in note 22, pp. 89 and 99.

[30] *Tales from Chaucer in Prose, Designed Chiefly for the Use of Young Persons* (London: Effingham Wilson, 1833), 196.

[31] Leonore Davidoff and Catherine Hall, *Family Fortunes. Men and Women of the English Middle Class, 1780-1850* (Chicago: U of Chicago P, 1991), 326-27.

[32] John Saunders, *The Canterbury Tales from Chaucer*, 2 vols. (London: Charles Knight & Co., 1845), 1.184-85.

[33] Whitaker did not find Cope's study, but in her discussion of T. J. Gallickson's 1865 description of it she notes that it was papered over in 1897. Cope recorded in his diary that the fresco started to deteriorate within four years. See Whitaker, as in note 22, pp. 97-98.

[34] Thomas Carlyle, *Past and Present. Complete Works of Thomas Carlyle*, 1896-99 (Rpt. New York: AMS Press, 1980),10:19. Quoted in Chandler, *Dream of Order*, p.139.

[35] Eleanora Hervey published a poem "Griseldis" in the *Athenaeum* in 1850 in which Griselda blames herself for Walter's behavior. Her obedience to Walter contravenes her duty as a mother in this poem, and she envisions her children blaming her for their supposed death. Once the children magically re-appear, Griselda can hold no grudge, "If heaven smile thus I cannot see the blackness of the wrong!" ("Griseldis," *Athenaeum* 1 June 1850, 583-84).

[36] Ford Madox Brown, *The Diary of Ford Madox Brown*, Virginia Surtees, ed. (New Haven: Yale UP, 1981), 1-2. There is some confusion about the actual Mackintosh source. Surtees identifies it as a contribution to Lardner's *Cyclopaedia*, while Mary Bennett identifies it as Mackintosh's *History of England* in *The Pre-Raphaelites* (London: Tate Gallery, 1984), 52.

[37] Ford Madox Brown, "On the Mechanism of a Historical Picture. Part I. The Design," *The Germ*, no. 2 (February 1850) in *The Germ. A Pre-Raphaelite Little Magazine*, Robert Stahr Hosman, ed. (Coral Gables, FL: U of Miami P, 1970), 70.

38 [Soloman Hart], "Fine Arts," *Athenaeum* 24 May 1851, 560.

39 Ford Madox Brown, "The Exhibition of Work, and other Paintings," Appendix 3 in Kenneth Bendiner, *The Art of Ford Madox Brown* (University Park, PA: Pennsylvania State UP), 132. Roy Strong erroneously identifies the figure in armor as the Black Prince (58).

40 "The Royal Academy. The Eighty-Third Exhibition-1851," *Art Journal* 13, n.s., 3 (1851): 157.

41 "Royal Academy Exhibit. Second Notice," *Illustrated London News* 17 May 1851, 416.

42 Mary Bennett makes all but the last two of these identifications in *The Pre-Raphaelite Brotherhood*, 54. The *Athenaeum* makes these identifications and adds W. M. Rossetti and Siddal, "Fine Arts. Exhibition of the works of Ford Madox Brown at the Grafton Gallery," *Athenaeum* 13 February 1897, 220.

43 Alan T. Gaylord, "Imagining Voices: Chaucer on Cassette," *Studies in the Age of Chaucer* 12 (1990): 219.

Appendix

Illustrations of Chaucer's *Canterbury Tales* between William Blake's *Chaucer's Canterbury Pilgrims* (1809) and William Morris and Edward Burne-Jones's *Kelmscott Chaucer* (1896)

This checklist is certainly incomplete. We encourage additions, expansions, and corrections. References to Hammond below are to Eleanor Prescott Hammond, *Chaucer: A Bibliographical Manual*. London: Macmillan, 1908. Reprinted. New York: Peter Smith, 1933. References to Altick are to Richard Altick, *Paintings from Books*. Columbus: Ohio State UP, 1985.

1812
Fuseli, Henry. *Der Ritter findet die ihm angetraute Greisin in ein schönes junges Weib ver wandelt* (The Knight Discovers that the Old Lady Betrothed to him Changed into a Beautiful Young Woman). Oil canvas. $35^{3/4}$ X 27in. 1812? Petworth House. B&W reproduction in Witt Library, Courtauld Institute, London, and in Altick, plate 253.
From the *Wife of Bath's Tale*. Transformed loathly lady as reclining nude. Knight in bed-shirt parts the canopy. Small fairy (?) looks out from under the bed.

Stothard, Thomas. *Canace with the Enchanted Ring*. Oil on canvas. Mentioned in Altick, p. 340, including reference to *The Examiner* 31 May 1812, p. 346.
Not seen. From the *Squire's Tale*.

1821
Fuseli, Henry. *The Devil and the Sompnour*. Drawing; study for painting(?). Dated 8 July 1821. B&W reproduction in Peter Tomory, *The Life and Art of Henry Fuseli*. New York

and Washington: Praeger, 1972, p, 127, plate 161.

From the *Friar's Tale*. The demon, holding pan, seizes the summoner from his horse; the widow gestures below. Perhaps inspired by an engraving of John Hamilton Mortimer's parallel scene.

1833

"The Canterbury Pilgrims, and the Tabard Inn, Southwark." Cover illustration for essay by H. Innes, "Chaucer's Canterbury Pilgrim's." *The Mirror* 22 (1833): 177-79.

Engraving of pilgrims (after Stothard) in Tabard yard (after illustration in John Urry's 1721 edition of Chaucer's *Works*?). Figure 1.

Clarke, Charles Cowden. *Tales from Chaucer in Prose, Designed Chiefly For the Use of Young Persons*. London: Effingham Wilson, 1833. [For children; Hammond, p. 229.] Fourteen woodcuts by W. H. Mott and S. Williams: 1) "The Procession of the Pilgrims to Canterbury" (frontispiece); 2) "Arms of Geoffrey Chaucer" (titlepage); 3) "Gateway to Donnington Castle, the last country residence of Chaucer"; 4) Chaucer's tomb 5) "The Clerk's Tale" [Walter's pledge to Griselda before her father]; 6) "The Squire's Tale" [the lion-drawn cart from Spenser's continuation, *The Faerie Queene*, 4.3]; 7) "The Cook's Tale of Gamelin" [spurious; Gamelin attacks with his staff]; 8) "The Knight's Tale" [the Queen and Emily weep before Theseus]; 9) "The Man of Law's Tale" [Custance at the ship before departing Northumbria;]; 10) "The Nun's Priest's Tale" [Chaunticleer crows; Russell lies in wait]; 11) "The Pardoner's Tale" [the rioters and the old man]; 12) "The Prioress's Tale" [the abbot blesses the clergeon in his tomb]; 13) "The Canon-Yeoman's Tale" [the canon dupes the priest at the furnace]; 14) "The Wife of Bath's Tale" [the knight meets the loathly lady].

In the 2d edition (London: C. Lockwood, 1870), 'The Procession of the Pilgrims to Canterbury" appears between 2) and 3) above, and a Portrait of Chaucer (after Hoccleve portrait) is added as a frontispiece. Clarke's *Riches of Chaucer*, 2 vols. (London: Effingham Wilson, 1835; later editions and reprints), includes two additional illustrations to *The Canterbury Tales*: 1) "The Friar's Tale" [the summoner confronts the old lady; demon as monk?]; 2) "The Franklin's Tale" [Aurelius pleads with Dorigen]. This edition also replaces 6) above: "The Squire's Tale" [Canacee speaks with hawk in the tree]. Volume 2 of *Riches* includes five illustrations of works besides *The Canterbury Tales*. Figures 6 and 7.

1837

Redgrave, Richard. *The Patience of Griselda*. Exhibited at Royal Academy, 1837.

Unseen. Referred to in Susan P. Casteras and Ronald Parkinson, eds. *Richard Redgrave 1804-1888*. New Haven, CT: Victoria and Albert and Yale Center for British Art, 1988, p. 12.

1838

Redgrave, Richard. *The Trial of Griselda's Patience*. Exhibited at British Institution, 1838.

Unseen. Referred to in Susan P. Casteras and Ronald Parkinson, eds. *Richard Redgrave 1804-1888*. New Haven, CT: Victoria and Albert and Yale Center for British Art, 1988, p. 12.

1840

Leslie, Charles Robert. *Griselda*. Oil on oval panel. 10 X 8in. Victoria and Albert Museum London, no. FA128. B&W reproduction and description in Ronald Parkinson. *Victoria and Albert Museum. Catalogue of British Oil Paintings 1820-1860*. London: HMSO, 1990, p.173, and in Altick, plate 252; Altick dates the painting 1836.

--- Bust of Griselda, from the *Clerk's Tale*, intended as companion piece to Leslie's "Portia." The Victoria and Albert also has an enamel copy on porcelain, signed and dated "T[homas] Allen. 1853." and an impression of an engraving by an unknown artist.

1843

Le Jeune, Henry. *Griselda*. Oil on canvas (?). Exhibited at Royal Academy, 1843.
Unseen. Description from anonymous review "The Royal Academy," *Art Union* [later the *Art Journal*] 5 June 1843:159-78, esp. 168: Walter on horseback approaches Griselda, who holds an earthen jug, at doorway.

1845

Brown, Ford Madox. "The Seeds and Fruit of English Poetry." Oil on canvas. $13^{3/8}$ X $18^{1/8}$in. Ashmolean Museum, Oxford. Designed 1845-51; colored 1853. Exhibited at Liverpool Academy, 1853. Color reproduction and discussion in Alastair Grieve, and others. *The Pre-Raphaelites*. London: Tate Gallery and Penguin, 1984, pp. 52-53.

--- Study for Brown's "Geoffrey Chaucer Reading. . ." (1851 below).
Chaucer reading to court in central panel. Left panel depicts Milton, Spenser, and Shakespeare; right panel, Byron, Pope, and Burns. Other literary figures indicated in medallions and cartouches.

Knight, Charles, ed. *Old England: A Pictorial Museum of Regal, Ecclesiastical, Municipal, Baronial, and Popular Antiquities*. 2 vols. London: Charles Knight, 1845-46. 2 vols. in 1, London: James Sangster, 1847. Reprinted. New York: Portland House, 1987.
Volume 1:300-05 includes sixteen engravings, numbered 1114 through 1134; artists and engravers include John Jackson, Robert William Buss, Sly (?), and others: 1114) "Portrait of Chaucer"; 1115) "The Tabard" [table scene before the hearth, designed as a frontispiece]; 1116) "The Tabard. (from Urry's edition of Chaucer, 1720)"; 1117) "The Tabard. (From a Drawing about 1780)"; 1118) "The Talbot, 1841"; 1119) "The Knight and the Squire"; 1120) "The Sergeant at Law and the Doctor of Medicine"; 1123) "The Monk and the Friar"; 1124) "The Parson and the Clerk of Oxenford"; 1125) "The Prioress and the Wife of Bath"; 1126) "The Franklin and the Merchant"; 1130) "Miller, Manciple, and Reve"; 1131) "The Ploughman and Shipman"; 1132) "Carpenter, Haberdasher, Weaver, Dyer, and Tapestry maker"; 1133) "The Host and the Cook"; 1134) "Sumpnour and Pardoner." For discussion, see Judith L. Fisher, "*The Canterbury Tales* in Knight's *Old England*: Conservative Reform in Popular Publishing." *Poetica* (Tokyo) 39-40 (for 1993): 155-77. Figures 2 and 3.

Saunders, John. *Cabinet Pictures of English Life: Chaucer*. Knight's Weekly Volumes. London: [Charles Knight], 1845. [Hammond, p. 231]
Adapts the engravings from Knight above, retaining six (numbers 1116, 1119-20, 1123-24, and 1133 above) and retouching several to produce ten portraits of individual pilgrims or groups of pilgrims (numbers 1125-26, 1130, and 1132-34).

--- *Canterbury Tales, from Chaucer*. 2 vols. London: Charles Knight, 1845-47. 2nd ed. 1870. [modernization; Hammond p. 230.] See Saunders (1889) below.
Ten framed illustrations by John Jackson (with asterisk * below) and twenty unsigned illustrations (perhaps by Robert William Buss). Volume 1: 1) death of Arcite* (frontispiece to Knight's Tale); 2) Palamon in temple of Venus; 3) Arcite in temple of Mars; 4) perjurer's death at Alla's court* (frontispiece to Man of Law's Tale); 5) Custance with baby in boat; 6) Alla as pilgrim; 7) knight and loathly lady at Queen's court*

(frontispiece to Wife of Bath's Tale); 8) knight on horseback; 9) loathly lady and fairies; 10) demon on horseback seizes Friar's summoner* (frontispiece to Friar's Tale); 11) summoner pays archdeacon; 12) summoner accuses old lady; 13) reunion of Walter, Griselda, and children* (frontispiece to Clerk's Tale); 14) Griselda as shepherdess, with her father; 15) Griselda as aristocrat, with her husband. Volume 2: 16) steed arrives at court of Cambuscan* (frontispiece to Squire's Tale); 17) disarming of the visiting knight; 18) Canacee (with maidens) finds the fallen falcon; 19) Arveragus and Dorigen lament* (frontispiece to Franklin's Tale); 20) Dorigen at the rocks; 21) Aurelius importunes Dorigen; 22) Death and the rioters* (frontispiece to Pardoner's Tale); 23) child serves the rioters in the tavern; 24) rioters and the old man; 25) widow feeds Chaunticleer and the chickens (frontispiece to Nun's Priest's Tale); 26) Russell flatters Chaunticleer*; 27) barnyard chase scene; 28) canon dupes priest at furnace* (frontispiece to Canon's Yeoman's Tale); 29) the Canon and his Yeoman talking; 30) the Canon and his Yeoman at the furnace. Figures 9 and 10.

1848

Stephens, Frederic George. *Dethe and the Riotours*. Pen and black ink over pencil indications. $9^{7/8}$ X $16^{1/8}$in. Composed 1848; drawn 1852. Bryson Bequest (293). Ashmolean Museum, Oxford. B&W reproduction and discussion in David Brown, "Pre-Raphaelite Drawings in the Bryson Bequest to the Ashmolean Museum," *Master Drawings* 16.3 (1978), pp. 287-93, plate 38.
From the *Pardoner's Tale*. Rioters before the old man at the stile.

1849

Cope, Charles West. *A "Coloured Study" for "Griselda's First Trial," a Fresco in the House of Lords*. Oil on panel. $19^{3/8}$ X $9^{3/8}$in. Privately owned. Exhibited at Royal Academy, 1849, no. 117. Color reproduction from Christie's Sale Catalog in Witt Library, Courtauld Institute, London.
The fresco was painted in 1849 in Upper Waiting Hall of House of Lords, but destroyed by damp soon afterwards. A cartoon for the fresco was exhibited at Royal Academy, 1848, no. 903 (?). The Witt Library holds an undated etching by W. Thomas of the scene in 'Coloured Study' (color plate 41).

Fairholt, F. W. "The Tabard Inn; The Night Before the Pilgrimage to Canterbury." "Passages from the Poets." *Art Journal* 11 (1849): [111].
Drawing by Fairholt; engraved by J. Bastin. Canterbury Pilgrims at table before a fireplace. Twenty-three pilgrims identified (of twenty four) in bottom margin, with quotation from *General Prologue* 1.23-26.

1850

Elmore, Alfred W. *Griselde*. Oil on canvas. 40 X 60in. Exhibited at Royal Academy, 1850, no. 312. Color reproduction from Christie's Sale Catalog in Witt Library, Courtauld Institute, London.
Walter approaches Griselda at a well next to a stable outside city walls, following scene of *Clerk's Tale* 4.288-91. Janicula (?), with shepherd's staff and boy, sits nearby. Other spectators: Walter's page, woman and child, woman with distaff (color plate 39).

Redgrave, Richard. *The Marquis having chosen patient Griselda for his wife, causes the Court ladies to dress her in her father's cottage*. Oil on canvas (?). Exhibited at the Royal Academy, 1850.

Unseen. Description from anonymous review "The Royal Academy. The Eighty-Second Exhibition-1850." *Art Journal* 12, n.s., 2 (1850): 165-78, esp. 169: interior scene; Griselda dressed by opulent ladies of the Marquis.

Stephens, Frederic George. *The Proposal (The Marquis and Griselda)*. Oil on canvas. 33 X 21in. 1850? Tate Britain, 4633. B&W reproduction in Altick, plate 252.
Interior scene; a proposal of an aristocrat to a maiden in her humble cottage; her father sits in back right. Doorway to back left. Altick (p. 340) suggests this "may or may not be" a Griselda painting that Stephens submitted to the Royal Academy under an assumed name.

1851

Brown, Ford Madox. *Geoffrey Chaucer Reading the 'Legend of Custance' to Edward III and his Court, at the Palace of Sheen, on the Anniversary of the Black Prince's Forty-fifth Birthday*. Oil on canvas. $146^{1/2}$ X $116^{1/2}$in. Art Gallery of New South Wales, Sydney. Exhibited at the Royal Academy, 1851. Replica by Brown, 1867-68. Oil on canvas. $48^{1/2}$ X 39. Tate Gallery, London. B&W and color reproductions and discussion in Alastair Grieve, and others. *The Pre-Raphaelites*. London: Tate Gallery and Penguin, 1984, pp. 14 and 53-55. [Hammond, p. 283]
Chaucer at bookstand before Edward III, his court, and numerous spectators. Study begun in 1845; see Brown above (1845). We include both in this list for their importance and because the title specifies that Chaucer reads from the *Man of Law's Tale* (color plate 35).

1852

Cope, Charles West. *The Marquis of Saluce Marries Griselda*. Oil on canvas. $50^{1/2}$ X 69in. Collection of Cary M. Maguire. Exhibited at Royal Academy, 1852, no. 171. Color reproduction from Sotheby's Sale Catalog in Witt Library, Courtauld Institute, London. Collection of Cary M. Maguire.
Walter and his court at entrance to Janicula's house. Walter holds Griselda's hand, addressing Janicula, seated, who holds Griselda's other hand (color plate 38).

1854

Corbould, Edward Henry. Illustrations to *The Canterbury Tales . . . From the Text and the Notes and Glossary of Thomas Tyrwhitt, Condensed and Arranged Under the Text*. New edition. Routledge's British Poets. London: G. Routledge, 1854. Reprinted frequently. British Library catalog lists an edition of 1853 (unseen). [See Hammond, pp. 139 and 324].
Eight illustrations by Corbould; engraved by Dalziel Brothers: 1) "Y^e Knightes Tale" (frontispiece) [Emelye gathering flowers before the prison tower window]; 2) "The Reves Tale" [horses in fen; mill in background]; 3) "Y^e Wif of Bathes Tale" [knight on horseback approaches peasant maid carrying vegetable (?) basket]; 4) "Y^e Clerkes Tale" [Walter on horseback approaches Griselda gathering herbs]; 5) "Y^e Squieres Tale" [Canacee with hawk in her lap]; 6) "Sire Topas and ye gret Giaunt Oliphant" [Thopas on horseback approaches Oliphant; sundry fairies] 7) "Y^e Monkes Tale" [Samson asleep in Dalilah's lap]; 8) "Y^e Nonnes Priestes Tale" [traveller prepares to sleep in "oxes stalle"]. Corbould's illustrations also appear in Routledge's editions of Chaucer's *Works* and various editions of *The Canterbury Tales*, sometimes with 6) above as frontispiece. Figures 12 and 13.

1858

Burne-Jones, Edward. *The Chaucer Wardrobe*. Oil on wood. 7 X 4 X 2ft. (approx.).
Ashmolean Museum. Oxford. Presented by Burne-Jones to William and Jane Morris on
the occasion of their marriage, 1859.
Painted wooden wardrobe, decorated with scenes from the *Prioress's Tale*, quotations
from the tale, and depiction of Chaucer as artist. Primary scene on front panel: Mary
placing grain on tongue of clergeon (in stylized grave), with village and dwellers in
background; also Mary with angelic choir, and Chaucer with book and quill. See Burne-
Jones, *The Prioress's Tale* below (1865-98) (color plate 36).

1865-98

Burne-Jones, Edward. *The Prioress's Tale*. Gouache on paper. $40^{9/10}$ X $24^{4/5}$in. 1865-98.
Samuel and Mary Bancroft Collection. Delaware Art Museum, Wilmington. Color
reproduction and description in Russell Ash, *Sir Edward Burne-Jones*. London:
Pavilion; New York: Harry N. Abrams, 1993, pl. 40.
Parallels the primary scene of Burne-Jones's *The Chaucer Wardrobe* above (1858),
although the background village is redone here as a city scene. The illustration facing
page 61 in *The Kelmscott Chaucer* (1896) is reminiscent, although an interior scene.

1866

"The Canterbury Pilgrims and the Tabard Inn, Southwark." Engraving (p. 91) accompanies
an essay by Mark Lemon, "Up and Down the London Street." *London Society* 9 (1866):
79-96.
Table of contents of *London Society* volume 9 (p. iv) says drawn by J. A. Pasquier; a
reproduction of the engraving by the same title above (1833).

1868

Waller, J. G., design. *The Chaucer Memorial*. Stained Glass Window. South Transept (Poet's
Corner), above Chaucer monument, Westminster Abbey. 1868. B&W photograph in
Muniment Room & Library, Westminster Abbey. Etching and description in Frederick
James Furnivall. "Appendix III. The Chaucer Window in Westminster Abbey." *A
Temporary Preface to the Six-Text Edition of Chaucer's Canterbury Tales*. Chaucer
Society Publications, Second series, no. 3. London: Trübner, 1868, pp. 133-36.
Destroyed by bomb blast 19 September 1940. From top to bottom: upper medallions in
tracery: portraits of John Wyclif, Ralph Strode, Edward III, Chaucer (center), Phillippa
Chaucer, John Gower, and John of Gaunt. Spandrils: arms of Chaucer. Borders: arms of
England, France, Hainault, Lancaster, Castile, and Leon. Top of two lancets: Lady of the
Floure and Lady of the Leaf (from spurious "The Floure and the Leafe"). Two central
medallions: Chaucer and others receive commission from Edward III to the Doge of
Genoa. Doge receives the commission. Bottom of two lancets: Pilgrims departing:
Reeve, Manciple, Chaucer, Knight, Yeoman, Squire, Serjeant at Law, Shipman,
Physician. Pilgrims arriving: Summoner, Pardoner, Parson, Monk, Prioress, Second
Nun, Franklin, Plowman, and Clerk. At bottom of window is Chaucer's name and death
year, 1400, with four lines (1-2, 15-16) from Chaucer's lyric, *Truth* (*Balade de Bon Conseil*).

1871

Burne-Jones, Edward. *Dorigen of Bretaigne longing for the safe return of her husband*.
Watercolor. Victoria and Albert Museum. 1871. Transparency slide, CAI 10.
[Hammond, p. 314]
From the *Franklin's Tale*. Interior view with Dorigen at low, rectangular window look-
ing out to rocks at sea. Decor includes foot of bed, small organ, and books.

1872

Corbould, Edward Henry. *The Canterbury Pilgrims Assembled in the Yard of the Tabard Hostelry.* $43^{3/4}$ X $72^{1/2}$in. Inscribed on backboard and dated 1872; signed and dated with monogram 1892. Perhaps exhibited at Royal Academy, 1874, no. 930. Exhibited at London, Earls Court, The Victorian Era Exhibition. Historical and Commemorative Section, 1897, no. 1. Color reproduction from Sotheby's Sale Catalog in Witt Library, Courtauld Institute, London.

Thirty-four figures (many identifiable as Chaucer's pilgrims, including Chaucer himself) assembling in a busy inn yard. Two signs: one indicates the Tabard; the other Harry Bailly's proprietorship. Church with Norman style arch in background. Many details (color plate 37).

1875

Boughton, George Henry. *Pilgrims Setting Out for Canterbury—Time of Chaucer.* Oil on canvas (?). Exhibited at Royal Academy, 1875.

Unseen. American artist. Description from anonymous review, "Fine Arts. Exhibition of the Royal Academy. Third Notice." *Illustrated London News* 16 May 1875, pp. 470-71: road through a spring landscape, with town in background. Pilgrims on road, except for two at shrine in foreground and two filling water bottles at a well, assisted by village maidens.

Marks, Henry Stacy. Two paintings of the Canterbury Pilgrims. Designs exhibited at Royal Academy, 1875. Paintings on canvas completed 1878; installed at Eaton Hall, Chester, 1882.

Unseen. Marks discusses the project in *Pen and Pencil Sketches*. London: Chatto & Windus, 1894. 1:212-17, describing the two canvases as over thirty-five feet long (1:216).

--- "The Miller from Chaucer's 'Canterbury Tales'." $78^{3/4}$ X 69in. Color reproduction from Christie's Sale Catalog in Witt Library, Courtauld Institute, London.

Miller in profile on horseback; playing bagpipes. Apparently related to Marks's paintings of Canterbury Pilgrims at Eaton Hall, above. Figure 5.

1876

Haweis, Mrs. H. R. [Mary Eliza]. *Chaucer for Children, a Golden Key.* London: Chatto & Windus, 1876. [Hammond, p. 234]

Embossed cover represents five scenes adorned by daisies, followed by an explanatory key: 1) Palamon and Arcite at battle, beset by Cupid's arrows; 2) Aurelius offers his flaming heart to Dorigen; 3) Friar's summoner on horseback, led away by demon; 4) Pardoner's rioters overlooked by skull and crossbones; 5) one of Griselda's babies (?). Eight color pictures: 1) "Pilgrim's Starting" (frontispiece); 2) "Dinner in the Olden Time"; 3) "Lady Crossing the Street in Olden Time"; 4) "Fair Emelye Gathering Flowers"; 5) "Griselda's Marriage"; 6) "Griselda's Sorrow" [Walter's sergeant threatens her child] ; 7) "Dorigen and Aurelius in the Garden" [sporting court figures and rocks in background]; 8) "The Rioter" [third rioter returning with poisoned vessels]. Figures 4, 8, 11, and 14.

A steel engraving "Geoffrey Chaucer" [reversal of Hoccleve portrait]. Twenty-eight woodcuts, including a tournament, maps of Old and Modern London, clothing, etc., and portraits of Canterbury pilgrims: Knight, Squire, Yeoman, Prioress, Monk, Friar, Merchant, Clerk, Serjeant-of-Law, Franklin, Doctor of Physic, Wife of Bath, Parson, Ploughman, Summoner, Pardoner, and Host, accompanying adaptations/quotations of the descriptions from the *General Prologue*. The Appendix (pp. 107-11) includes "Notes on the Pictures" and "Notes on the Woodcuts," discussing details, especially garb, and identifying manuscripts after which the illustrations are modeled.

1881

Corbould, Edward Henry. "The Canterbury Pilgrims." 29 X 59$^{1/2}$in. B&W reproduction from Sotheby's Sale Catalog in Witt Library, Courtauld Institute, London.
Signed and dated 1881. Canterbury pilgrims on horseback, traveling right to left; several pilgrims identifiable. City(?) in background.

1889

Saunders, John. *Chaucer's Canterbury Tales. Annotated and Accented, with Illustrations of English Life in Chaucer's Time*. New and revised edition. London: Dent, 1889. Reissued 1894. Same text as Saunders (1845) above; uses Ellesmere pilgrims as models for color illustrations.

Before 1897

Sewell, Robert Van Vorst. *The Canterbury Pilgrims*. Oil on canvas frieze. 7 X 84ft. Great Hall in the Mansion of Georgian Court College. Lakewood, N. J. Commissioned by George Jay Gould for his estate [Hammond, p. 324]. Description and 3 b&w details in M. Christina Geis, R.S.M., *Georgian Court: An Estate of the Gilded Age*. Philadelphia: Art Alliance; London and Toronto: Associated University Presses, 1982, pp. 164-71; color detail facing p. 132. Described by Sewell in his booklet "The Canterbury Pilgrimage: A Decorative Frieze." New York, n.d.
Pilgrims in procession, perhaps in Tabard inn yard; 24 figures: (east wall) Cook, Manciple, Chaucer, Host, Clerk, Sergeant at Law; (north wall) Haberdasher, Merchant, Shipman, Doctor, a humble wayfarer, Yeoman, Knight, Squire, Wife of Bath, Friar, Summoner, Pardoner; (west wall) Miller, Monk, Second Nun, Prioress, Parson, Reeve.

Undated

Corbould, Edward Henry. "The Canterbury Pilgrims." B&W engraving from Hampstead Public Libraries Local Collection (H. J. Cornish Collection. 1929) in Witt Library, Courtauld Institute, London.
Pilgrims departing from the Tabard, with spectators. Several pilgrims identifiable. Two signs: one depicting a tabard and reading "Henry [?] Bailey"; one reading "Tabard Herberwe.
Farme and herbergage for folke and hors." Gables of the inn in background.

Fig. 1 - Kelmscott Chaucer; title page

Chapter 8

The Kelmscott Chaucer

Duncan Robinson

Part I

The illustrated edition of *The Works of Geoffrey Chaucer* (figure 1) published by William Morris at his Kelmscott Press in 1896 marked the culmination of an artistic partnership formed almost half a century earlier. 'When Morris and I were little chaps at Oxford, we should have just gone off our heads if such a book had come out then,' Edward Burne-Jones wrote just before its publication, 'but we have made at the end of our days the very thing we would have made then if we could.'[1]

During their lifetimes, both men achieved the status of eminent Victorians, one a poet, the other a painter, and together, as directors of Morris and Company, the founding fathers of the Arts and Crafts movement. They met as undergraduates at Exeter College, Oxford, in January 1853. A few weeks later, Burne-Jones recalled that 'I was reading in my room when Morris ran in one morning bringing the newly published book with him, so everything was put aside until he read it all through to me.'[2] The book in question contained John Ruskin's essay on Pre-Raphaelitism: 'If they adhere to their principles,' he wrote of the Pre-Raphaelite Brotherhood, 'and paint nature as it is around them, with the help of modern science, with the earnestness of the men of the thirteenth and fourteenth centuries, they will, as I said, found a new and noble school in England.'[3]

In the same year, Book II of *The Stones of Venice* appeared, with its chapter on 'The Nature of Gothic' which Morris described as 'one of the very few necessary and inevitable utterances of the century,':

'Understand this clearly: you can teach a man to draw a straight line, and to cut one; to strike a curved line, and to carve it; and to copy and carve any number of given lines or forms, with admirable speed and perfect precision; and you find his work perfect of its kind: but if you ask him to think about any of those forms, to consider if he cannot find any better in his own head, he stops; his execution becomes hesitating; he thinks, and ten to one he thinks wrong; ten to one he makes a mistake in the first touch he gives to his work as a thinking being. But you have made a man of him for all that. He was only a machine before, an animated tool.'[4]

For Morris, those words constituted a call to arms on behalf of both art and society; a call which he answered with a lifelong commitment to improving both. And like his mentor, Ruskin, he turned for both ideas and inspiration to the Middle Ages.

As students at Oxford, Burne-Jones and Morris abandoned their intentions of taking holy orders. Burne-Jones left Oxford without a degree after two years, in order to attach himself as a pupil to the Pre-Raphaelite painter Dante Gabriel Rossetti (1828-82), while Morris completed his degree before joining the Oxford office of the Gothic Revival architect George Edmund Street (1824-1881). In December 1856 the two friends moved into Rossetti's former rooms at no.17 Red Lion Square, London. They set about furnishing their apartment according to their new-found principles, with 'tables and chairs like incubi and succubi,'[5] as Rossetti described Morris's first attempts as a furniture designer. Austere by comparison with most contemporary, high Victorian manufacture, the plain surfaces of these massive, domestic fittings provided Burne-Jones with the opportunity to develop his talents as a decorator. Inevitably his subjects were drawn from the literature of the Middle Ages in which both men were steeped. Major influences included Malory's *Morte d'Arthur* and, above all, the poetry of Geoffrey Chaucer, whom Morris apostrophied in the *Jason* sequence of his *Golden Legend* in 1867:

> Would that I
> Had but some portion of that mastery
> That from the rose-hung lanes of woody Kent
> Through these five hundred years such songs have sent
> To us, who meshed within this smoky net
> Of unrejoicing labour, love them yet.
> And thou, O Master! – Yes, my Master still,
> Whatever feet have scaled Parnassus' hill,
> Since like thy measures, clear and sweet and strong,

Thames' stream scarce fettered drave the dace along
Unto the bastioned bridge, his only chain-
O Master, pardon me, if yet in vain
Thou art my Master, and I fail to bring
Before men's eyes the image of the thing
My heart is filled with.

To decorate the doors of the wardrobe in Red Lion Square (Victoria and Albert Museum, London), Burne-Jones chose the 'miracle' from *The Prioresses Tale*, and devised a composition he was to repeat, thirty-five years later, in one of his illustrations for the Kelmscott Chaucer (figure 2).

At Oxford, Morris was encouraged by Ruskin and Rossetti to study the medieval manuscripts in the Bodleian Library. In 1856 he tried his own hand at writing and illuminating manuscript pages, a practice which he continued throughout his prodigiously active life. As his daughter May put it, 'it is a pretty thing to think of the illuminator's patient art blossoming under the hand of so impetuous and eager a man.' In 1870 he completed *A Book of Verse* (Victoria and Albert Museum, London), the first of four manuscripts he wrote and decorated for Burne-Jones's wife, Georgiana, comprising twenty-five of his

Fig. 2 - The Prioresses Tale, finished drawing

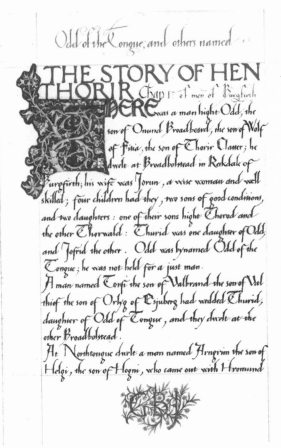

Fig. 3 - The Story of Hen Thorir

own poems. Four years later, he gave her another manuscript, containing three of the sagas he and Eirikr Magnússon translated from the Icelandic (figure 3). Meanwhile, with the help of Burne-Jones, he had embarked upon the most ambitious of his calligraphic projects, an illuminated *Æneid*, for which he developed a 'Roman' script of his own, based on sixteenth-century handwriting manuals of which he was able to acquire copies for his own library, including Ludovico Arrighi's *La Operina* and Giovantonio Tagliente's *La Vera Arte de Scrivere*. In 1874 Burne-Jones wrote to Charles Eliot Norton, 'Every Sunday morning you may think of Morris and me together – he reads a book to me and I make drawings for a big Virgil he is writing', an activity he predicted would 'put an end to printing.'[6]

He could not have been more mistaken. The *Æneid* remained unfinished,[7] long after Morris turned his attention to the reformation of the printer's art. On November 15, 1888, he attended a lecture on printing

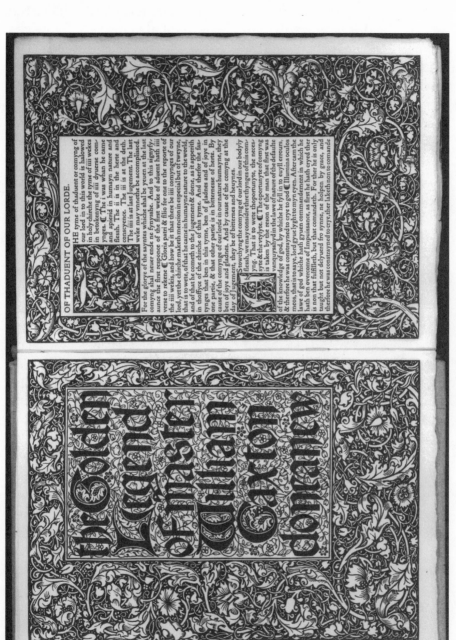

Fig. 4 - The Golden Legend, title page

given by his friend Emery Walker to the Arts and Crafts Exhibition Society. Walker used words which could not fail to resonate for Morris when he argued that 'type and paper may be said to be to a printed book what stones or bricks and mortar are to architecture. They are the essentials; without one there can be no book in the one case, and no architecture in the other.' For Morris that meant, inevitably, a return to first principles, and just as he had felt obliged to scrutinize every stage in the manufactures of Morris and Company, from the supplying of raw materials to the retailing of the products, so he turned his attention to ink and paper (and vellum), as well as refining his own skills as a typographer and graphic designer. At first he thought of printing only, but from 1893 onwards he added the title of publisher to his other list of achievements.

Between 1891 and 1896, Morris planned the production of fifty-two works at the Kelmscott Press: sixty-six volumes in all, sixteen of which were issued after his death on October 3, 1896. The list of titles reflects a lifetime of literary and artistic loyalties; he planned original-ly to launch his Press with an edition of William Caxton's translation of Jacobus de Voragine's *Golden Legend*, but impatience got the better of him and instead of those three volumes in large quarto, which appeared at the end of 1892 (figure 4), he was able to issue 200 copies of his own *Glittering Plain*, in small quarto on May 8, 1891. However, his subsequent tributes to Caxton as the father of English printing included a new edition of the first book printed in English, *The Recuyell of the Historyes of Troy*, 1892, and *The History of Godefrey of Boloyne and of the Conquest of Iherusalem*, 1893. *Beowulf* and Malory were joined by Morris's contemporaries and friends: Ruskin's *Stones of Venice*, poems by Rossetti and Swinburne and Wilfrid Scawen Blunt and his own works, including his translations of the Icelandic sagas. But no book could match the size, scope or embellished detail of *The Works of Geoffrey Chaucer*.

Part II

The first public announcement of a Kelmscott edition of Chaucer's works, illustrated 'with about sixty designs by E. Burne-Jones,' was made in December 1892. By then, according to Georgiana Burne-Jones, 'the friends [had] sat down dutifully to read Chaucer over again before beginning their work,'[8] Morris reading aloud to Burne-Jones as he had done at Oxford and during the preparation of the *Æneid* in 1874.

The text itself was prepared by Frederick S. Ellis, after Morris had cleared permission with the Oxford University Press 'to use Professor [Walter W.] Skeat's Chaucer' and 'to avail myself of the corrections of errors which Professor Skeat's learning and acumen are making public.'[9]

To an order of the contents of the book in Morris's hand Burne-Jones added the number of illustrations projected for each poem,[10] and on the cover of a rough sketchbook in the Fitzwilliam Museum, comprising twelve sheets of Burne-Jones's earliest ideas for the illustrations, he noted: 'There are 48 planned here, / but I may add to the Knight's / Tale? & and the early part? / there may be 60 in all if I like.' This turned out to be an underestimate; on another rough sheet the total has crept up to '72 all / and he [presumably Morris] won't have more'.

Morris accepted the inevitable increase. He issued a letter to his subscribers on November 14, 1894 to inform them that: 'It has been found necessary for the due completion of the above work to add considerably to the number of woodcuts designed by Sir Edward Burne-Jones.[11] There will now be upwards of seventy of these.' He took the same opportunity to announce an increase in the number of copies to be printed, from 325 to 425. Six months later, during the summer of 1895, Burne-Jones wrote to Lady Leighton: 'Yesterday I began the last ten that will decorate the last poem, Troilus and Cressida. Seventy I have done – ten more to do – and in three or four weeks I can breathe and look back on a longish task.'[12] The final number of illustrations was eighty-seven. They were finished just before Christmas in 1895, but Morris remained nervous in case his collaborator should want to add still more; when a visitor to Hammersmith admired proof sheets of some of the later designs, in which the illustrations appear side by side on double pages, Morris retorted: 'Now don't you go saying that to Burne-Jones, or he'll be wanting to do the first part over again; and the worst of that would be, that he'd want to do all the rest over again, because the other would be so much better, and then we should never get done.'[13]

In deciding what to illustrate Burne-Jones showed a clear preference for the more chivalric and courtly elements in Chaucer's work. His early sketches contain marginal notes such as 'no picture to Miller / no picture to Reeve / no picture to Cook's Tale'.[14] All of these, with their bawdy, native humour characteristic of at least half of *The Canterbury Tales*, proved too strong for the delicate feelings of the artist. In a letter to Swinburne he confessed: 'I have abstained from

Fig. 5 - Troilus and Criseyde, rejected design

Fig. 6 - Troilus and Criseyde, woodcut illustration

decorating certain of the Canterbury Tales … Morris has been urgent with me that I should by no means exclude these stories from our scheme of adornment – especially he had hopes of my treatment of the Miller's Tale, but he ever had more robust and daring parts than I could assume.'[15] In fairness it should be added that Morris himself concentrated on the romance aspect of Chaucer's poetry. Whatever his private views, his own work showed a restraint altogether in line with Victorian standards of expression. His *Earthly Paradise* was recommended by the *Saturday Review* of May 30, 1869 'for conveying to our wives and daughters a refined, although not diluted version of those wonderful creations of Greek fancy.'

Even among the finished drawings there are examples of censorship. For the rendezvous between Troilus and Cressida, Burne-Jones designed them initially in seductive embrace in her bedchamber, Troilus kneeling beside the seated Cressida with hands clasped at the point of intersection between his groin and her knee (figure 5). Either he or Morris rejected this idea, however, and the scene was redrawn to show the couple in a more decorous standing pose. The antechamber was enlarged to push the curtained bed further back into the room and an ornate vase filled with flowers was added somewhat vacuously to the left foreground (figure 6).

'Any condemned design was done over again, and again after that if necessary,' Lady Burne-Jones recorded. She quotes her husband as saying: 'I want to shew Morris the new Chaucer designs; he tells the truth always, and I shall know if he likes them.'[16] Even so, among the finished drawings that survive only a small number record unused designs. In most cases Morris must have approved both the choice of subject and its treatment. Other changes, where they occur, can be laid squarely at the artist's own door. For the illustration to *The Romaunt of the Rose* that appears on p.273, for instance, Burne-Jones originally drew just the two figures of the Lover and Danger barring his way (figure 7). His preliminary notes show that he was not altogether satisfied 'by the Tree itself — & Danger beside it — perhaps/the other 2,' and went on to design the much livelier figure group that appears in the book: 'Shame with hand [over] her face / Slander with coat / full of tongues', and 'Bialacoil/ a lusty bachelor of good height.'[17] (figure 8) Both versions rely heavily upon the text, the final one illustrating the lines:

Fig. 7 - The Romaunt of the Rose, rejected design

Fig. 8 - The Romaunt of the Rose, woodcut illustration

> He was not sole, for ther was mo;
> For with him were other two
> Of wikkid maners, and yvel fame.

They show how closely Burne-Jones observed Chaucer's words and how the change he made, for the sake of pictorial interest, was if anything closer to the letter of the text.

'In the book I am putting myself wholly aside,' Burne-Jones wrote, 'and trying to see things as [Chaucer] saw them; not once have I invaded his kingdom with one hostile thought.'[18] Even so he could not help exercising a degree of scientific rationalism in his interpretations of Chaucer's descriptions. The arrival of a strange knight at Cambuscan's court provides a dramatic focal point in 'The Squieres Tale' and Burne-Jones naturally chose to illustrate it:

> In at the halle-dore, al sodeynly,
> Ther cam a knight upon a steede of bras,
> And in his hand a brood mirour of glas.
> Upon his thombe he hadde of gold a ring,
> And by his side a naked swerd hanging;
> And up he rideth to the heighe bord.
> (Kelmscott Chaucer 153-154)

The artist takes up each detail in turn and tackles the design of the metal horse with all the practical ingenuity of a maker of mechanical toys. It had to be articulated to give credibility to its movements for the benefit of the nineteenth-century reader (figure 9). For Chaucer the miraculous does not need the same amount of explanation. Occasionally the pictorial interpretations verge on the absurd. In *The Hous of Fame*, for instance, where Chaucer writes:

> And al this hous, of whiche I rede,
> Was made of twigges, falwe [yellow], rede,
> And grene eek, and som weren whyte,
> Swiche-as men to these cages thwyte [whittle],
> Or maken of these panniers,
> Or elles hottes or dossers [types of wicker baskets][.]
> (ibid., 468)

What appears in the illustration is a kind of lobster-pot, cited in the *Memorials* as an example of 'perfect obedience to those words.'[19] It fails because the artist has tried to give pictorial form to an image that

Fig. 9 - The Squieres Tale, finished drawing

Fig. 10 - The Romaunt of the Rose, finished drawing

the poet evokes but does not describe. From the hint that such 'twigges' are used to make baskets, Burne-Jones constructed a straw palace that does little justice to his imagination, or to that of the poet. The note for one of the illustrations to *The Romaunt of the Rose* – 'Venus. (make her naked never mind Chaucer)'[20] – strikes a rare, an exceptional note of independence (figure 10).

There are other cases of elusive imagery that frustrated the artist intent upon 'trying to see things as he saw them.' The rhetorical device of ekphrasis, of bringing a picture fully to life, is used to good effect in *The Romaunt of the Rose* when Chaucer describes in great detail the painted allegories of vice, discussing even the texture of a gown.

> Wel coude he peynte, I undertake,
> That swiche image coude make.
> (ibid., 243)

Burne-Jones put it another way as he made his way through the long descriptions: 'I wish Chaucer could once for all make up his unrivalled and precious mind whether he is talking of a picture or a statue'[21] (figure 11).

Fig. 11 - The Romaunt of the Rose, finished drawing

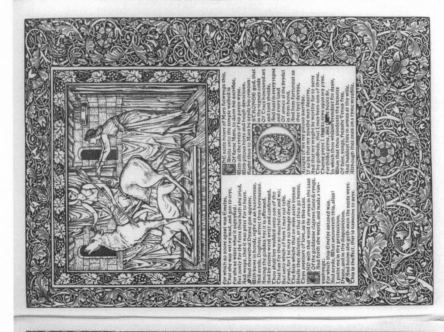
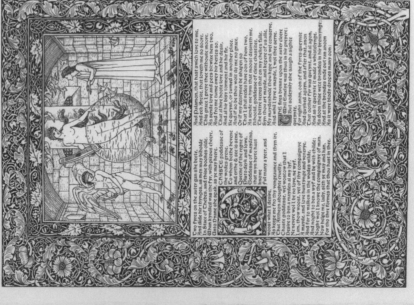

Fig. 12 - The Knyghtes Tale

A similar problem was raised, and solved, in 'The Knyghtes Tale', the first and one of the more chivalrous of the Canterbury Tales, heavily illustrated in the Kelmscott edition. Burne-Jones chose to depict each of the three temples visited by Emelye and her two suitors respectively. The text is highly descriptive of the shrines, each one containing a statue of its deity:

> The statue of Venus, glorious for to see,
> Was naked, fletynge in the large see,
> And fro the navele down all covered was
> With waves grene, and brighte as any glas.
> A citole in hir right hand hadde she,
> And on hir heed, ful seemly for to see,
> A rose gerland, fresh and wel smellynge,
> Above hir heed hir dowves flickerynge.
> Biforn hire stood hire sone Cupido,
> Upon his shuldres wynges hadde he two;
> And Blynd he was, as it is ofte seene;
> A bowe he bar and arwes brighte and kene.
>
> (ibid., 19)

Burne-Jones paid his usual attention to every detail (figure 12). The rose garlands, the flickering doves, the citole (stringed instrument, resembling a zither) and blind Cupid, they are all there. So too, ingeniously represented as a transparent sphere, is the sea, covering Venus downwards from the navel with its waves, just as the poet stipulated. An early sketch for the scene suggests that Burne-Jones began by trying to design a shallow trough before he hit upon the idea of showing the statue in a liquid orb. On another sheet the lower half of the figure is redrawn at an angle, to enable Venus to float (figure 13). This helps to reinforce the pictorial device because the pose of the figure is now dependent upon the water for its support. It also brings the representation closer still to the letter of the text.

There is a precedent for the 'large see' in Burne-Jones's earlier drawings. It appears, appropriately, as an attribute of Neptune, in one of the decorations he prepared for Morris's hand-written *Æneid* in 1874. A neat, emblematic solution to the problem of depicting a marine figure, it may derive from a specific medieval source. There are innumerable pictorial examples from the fourteenth century onwards of the *orbis mundi*,[22] of which Burne-Jones's kingdom of the sea is a collateral descendant. Burne-Jones was also familiar with panel painting of the early Renaissance. The rocky desert in which Griselda wanders

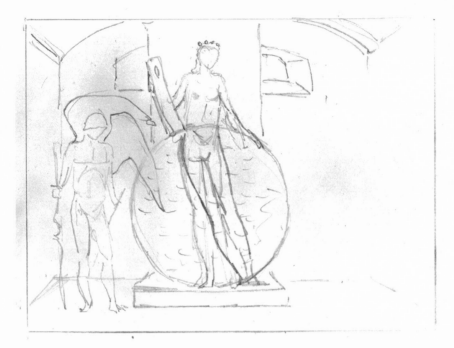

Fig. 13 - The Knyghtes Tale, preliminary sketch

in one of the preliminary drawings for 'The Tale of the Clerk of Oxenford' is strongly reminiscent of the wilderness in which Domenico Veneziano placed St John in one of the predella panels of the St Lucy altarpiece.[23] The stony path winding among rocky foothills bears comparison also with the work of Sienese painters such as Sassetta and Sano di Pietro, which Burne-Jones could have seen during his visit to Siena in 1873.

We know, from a surviving sketchbook which records that journey,[24] that Burne-Jones copied pictures in the gallery there. 'When I get back I want to write much about Siena, which has captivated my heart,' he confided to Charles Eliot Norton. 'I drew there a great deal before I fell seedy, chiefly from the old floor of the Duomo, and left Murray there settling at work at the Pax in the Palazzo Pubblico.'[25] His drawings of the biblical scenes inlaid in black and white marble on the cathedral pavement reveal an appreciation of line for its own sake. Apart from the obvious significance this had for the future designer of woodcut illustrations, continuous flowing lines, often in the form of billowing draperies, became a characteristic of Burne-Jones's graphic work from 1873 onwards.[26] In Siena he also made sketches of the medieval town itself (figure 14). They are delicate and crisp little records of the old buildings and narrow streets that delight every tourist. For Burne-Jones they also served another purpose. As Troilus takes his leave of Cressida on her way to the Greek camp, he does so against the background of Troy, and Burne-Jones's Troy is heavily reminiscent of a medieval town in central Italy, with its archways built into the city's walls, its towers, turrets and crenellations (figure 15).

In a letter to the Graham daughters who were visiting Florence in 1876, Burne-Jones wrote: 'I want to see Botticelli's Calumny in the Uffizi dreadfully, and the Spring in the Belle Arte.'[27] His designs for pp. 256-7, illustrating the dance in *The Romaunt of the Rose*, suggest an affinity (figure 16). The poised elegance of Burne-Jones's dancing figures, their long, slender bodies draped in high-waisted, heavily folded garments, are late descendants of the Primavera, and the Venus that appears in *The Hous of Fame* is equally related to Botticelli's other masterpiece.

Fig. 14 - View of Siena

As we know from Burne-Jones's correspondence, Mantegna was another of the fifteenth-century Italian artists whose work he studied. 'If ever they would look at me as I have looked at Mantegna, what a well-rewarded ghost mine would be,' he wrote to Mrs. Horner about the generation of aspiring artists after one of them had made the pilgrimage to the Grange to visit him.[28] His knowledge of Mantegna's detailed, classical architectural settings is reflected in an early drawing for page 315 of the *Chaucer* to illustrate the passage in *The Parlement of Foules* in which:

> This forseid African me hente [seized] anoon,
> And forth with him unto a gate broghte
> Right of a parke, walled with grene stoon;
> And over the gate, with letters large ywroghte,
> Ther weren vers ywriten.

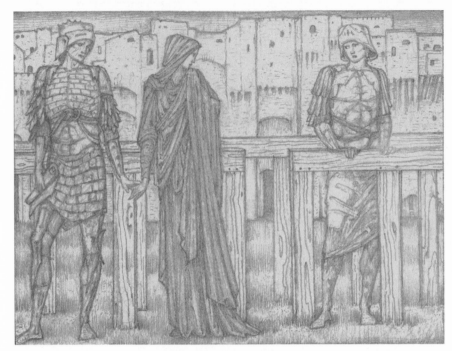

Fig. 15 - Troilus and Criseyde, finished drawing

Fig. 16 - The Romaunt of the Rose, finished drawing

The decorated gateway is reminiscent of the triumphal arch in front of which St James is martyred in Mantegna's fresco, formerly in the Church of the Eremitani in Padua.

Not all Burne-Jones's pictorial sources lay in the Middle Ages or the early Renaissance. In one of the early studies for the 'steede of bras' on which the strange knight rides into Cambuscan's court in 'The Squiere's Tale,' the horse's head is drawn in profile, strictly based upon the Parthenon frieze. Inevitably the artist also made use of his own earlier inventions. The adaptation for the book of his illustration of 'The Prioresses Tale' on the cabinet he painted for Morris is so direct that it amounts to repetition (figure 2).

Burne-Jones also drew from nature. The studies of birds made for *The Parlement of Foules* are directly and sharply observed before being worked into the finished design. He employed models, from which he drew in the studio, both for figures and for their principal attributes. It is well known that he went to great lengths to achieve accuracy with the armour worn by the king in his painting *King Cophetua and the Beggar Maid*, completed in 1884 (now in the Tate Gallery). A detailed sketch survives for Troilus' helmet and breastplate as they appear, with the addition of the broadsword, beside his couch on page 500.

If we study the preparatory drawings that survive, it is surprising to see how rarely they record changes in the overall composition of the Chaucer illustrations. As we have seen, a finished drawing might be rejected in favour of a different treatment of the subject, but in that case the earliest sketches of the second version include the principal features of the composition in roughly the right place. This is true of the designs for the temple of Diana in 'The Knyghtes Tale.' An early pencil sketch illustrates Chaucer's description of the appearance of the goddess to Emelye after she has kindled the sacrificial flames:

> And therwithal Dyane gan appeere,
> With bowe in honde, right as an hunteresse.
> (ibid., 23)

This design was abandoned after it had been worked up with inks and Chinese white (figure 17). Instead of illustrating the actual appearance of the goddess to Emelye, Burne-Jones turned to the dramatically less important but pictorially richer description of the shrine given about three hundred lines earlier in the poem:

Fig. 17 - The Knyghtes Tale, rejected design

This goddesse on an hert ful hye seet,
With smale houndes al aboute hir feet ....
                                    (ibid., 20)

Once again an early sketch shows the principal features of the second
composition established (figure 18). Above it, on the same sheet, the
artist tackles the pictorial problem posed by Chaucer's description:

And undernethe hir feet she hadde a moone
Wexynge it was, and sholde wanye soone.
                                    (ibid.)

It proved too awkward and he finally omitted it from his illustration.
On another sheet he studied in greater detail the anatomy of the 'hinde'
on which the goddess is seated.

Intermediate sketches served in this way to polish the details of particular illustrations. For that of Theseus deserting Ariadne a rough
sketch indicates the overall composition, and in the separate figure
studies beneath, Burne-Jones investigates the reclining pose of the
grief-stricken Ariadne.

The statue of Mars in 'The Knyghtes Tale' is conceived from the start within the shrine, though as a standing male nude (figure 19). As such he is closer to the text than the seated warrior in the finished illustration (figure 20), but Burne-Jones had to lift him up from the base line of the picture to leave room for

A wolf ther stood biforn hym at his feet
With eyen rede, and of a man he eet.
(ibid., 19)

This is the detail studied in a number of smaller sketches on another sheet, together with drawings for the censer on a tripod base (figure 21).

In fact Burne-Jones seems to have devised, consciously or unconsciously, a series of formu-

Fig. 18 - The Knyghtes Tale, preliminary sketch

lae for the Chaucer illustrations. We have already seen the similarities that exist between the treatment of each of the temples in 'The Knyghtes Tale,' with their relatively shallow, centralized perspective reminiscent of that used by fifteenth-century Tuscan painters. The same construction underlies most of the interiors depicted. The magician's cell to which Aurelius goes in 'The Frankeleynes Tale' is a variation of the same composition as are the bedchambers of Troilus (figure 22) and Boethius. Each emphasizes the flat back wall of the room, often recessed, with a gently curved vault and pierced further with either a window or a door. The side walls are short, leaving a wide band of floor space on which the figures can be arranged. The palace interior into which Griselda welcomes Walter and her children, in 'The Tale of the Clerk of Oxenford', is constructed on the same principles. A banquet table replaces the bed or couch against the end wall and there is the familiar horizontal window with an arched top that in this case looks out on to the same stony landscape as the one in which Griselda was shown wandering three pages earlier.

Fig. 19 - The Knyghtes Tale, preliminary sketch

Fig. 20 - The Knyghtes Tale, finished drawing

The recognition of a formula should not encourage us to underestimate the subtlety with which Burne-Jones was capable of handling it. In 'The Tale of the Wife of Bath' Chaucer takes great delight in the knight's discomfort as he

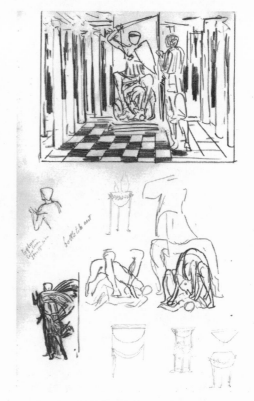

Constreyned was,
    he nedes moste hire wedde;
And taketh his olde wyf,
    and gooth to bedde.
               (ibid., 115)

Burne-Jones obviously shared the poet's relish; beside one of his preliminary drawings of the scene, he sketched an improbable and delightful little Peeping Tom. More significant are the changes he made to his standard bed-chamber design (figure 23). Instead of placing the bed cen-

Fig. 21 - The Knyghtes Tale, preliminary sketch

trally at the back of the chamber he arranged it along the left-hand wall. This leaves the centre of the room empty, apart from the few roses strewn forlornly on the boards of the floor. The knight stands well to the right, turned away from his haggard bride, clearly preferring the look of the hard narrow bench that complements on his side of the composition the bed from which her stern allurements issue:

Greet was the wo the knight hadde in his thoght,
Whan he was with his wyf abedde ybroght.
He walweth [writhes], and he turneth to and fro.
               (ibid.)

In the center of the end wall an archway leads out of the room on to a landing from which stairs descend. With this simple device the artist responded to the psychological tensions that exist in the poetry. The knight's honour, as well as his life, is at stake in his obligations to an unattractive spouse. His revulsion separates them:

Fig. 22 - Troilus and Criseyde, finished drawing

Fig. 23 - The Tale of the Wife of Bath, finished drawing

> Thou art so loothly, and so cold also,
> And therto comen of so lough a kynde,
> That litel wonder is, thogh I walwe and wynde [turn].
>
> (ibid.)

And yet he must submit to her demands of his own free will before the story can have a happy ending. The archway stands bleakly open, a reminder that he can, but must not, flee from his commitment. That Burne-Jones made a special effort in this case to match the subtlety of the poetry is confirmed by an earlier drawing of the scene that he rejected. It is predictably much closer to his standard bedchamber design, but fails to characterize the particular nature of the confrontation.

In one case the bedchamber formula is employed at the expense of a whole series of expressive preliminary drawings. In a couple of studies for *The Legend of Good Women* Burne-Jones assembled the familiar components of Lucretia's chamber, in which he showed her in the final design remorsefully about to take her own life. It remains a mystery as to why he rejected at least thirteen earlier figure drawings (figures 24-26) of her falling, stabbed, into her brother's arms, of them swearing vengeance over her corpse and of her carried

Fig. 24 - The Legende of Goode Wimmen: Lucrecie, preliminary sketch

Fig. 25 - The Legende of Goode Wimmen: Lucrecie, preliminary sketch

Fig. 26 - The Legende of Goode Wimmen: Lucrecie, preliminary sketch

Fig. 27 - The Legende of Goode Wimmen: Lucrecie

...

...on a bere
Through al the toun, that men may see & here
The horrible deed of her oppressioun.

(ibid., 416)

They are far more vigorous; in none of them is there more than a hint of the architectural setting that dominates the finished drawing (figure 27).

The standard interior composition could also be adapted for street scenes. For 'The Prioresses Tale' Burne-Jones illustrated the Jewish quarter through which the widow's son passed each day on his way to school. Chaucer conveys the impression of a community sealed within its own labyrinthine ways of wickedness and vice:

Ther was in Asye [Asia], in a greet citee,
Amonges cristene folk, a Jewerye,
Sustened by a lord of that contree
For foule usure, and lucre of vileynye,
Hateful to Crist and to his compaignye;
And thurgh the street men myghte ride or wende
For it was free, and open at eyther ende.

(ibid., 59)

To represent it Burne-Jones conceived an effective inside-outside composition, based upon a pierced back wall and opposite side walls, in this case exterior to the crowded buildings of the ghetto.

For his arrangement of figures within an outdoor setting the artist often devised a three-layer composition, using a wall or battlements to divide the picture plane horizontally. It appears in the illustration to *A Treatise on the Astrolabe* where the astronomer and his son look out over a parapet and above the dune-like landscape beyond to the starry sky. The composition is similar on page 482, where Cressida is shown to the right of the foreground, watching Troilus return from doing battle with the Greeks, against a background occupied by the turreted buildings of fortified Troy. The list of examples can be lengthened: on page 437 Ariadne brings the ball of string to the imprisoned Theseus in the foreground; beyond the crenellated parapet the circular maze occupies the middle ground and behind that the familiar townscape closes the composition. In the first illustration to 'The Knyghtes Tale' Arcite and Palamon are shown behind bars at the back of the composition, while Emelye occupies a garden containing a fountain in the middle of the picture, her full length revealed through the open gate in the low wall that fills the foreground (figure 28). A glance at the text shows how closely Burne-Jones observed the details within his well-tried formula for the composition:

Fig. 28 - The Knyghtes Tale, finished drawing

> Yclothed was she fresshe, for to devyse;
> Hir yelow heer was broyded in a tresse
> Bihynde hir bak a yerde long, I gesse.
> And in the gardyn at the sonne upriste,
> She walketh up and doun ....
> The grete tour, that was so thikke & stroong,
> Which of the castel was the chief dongeoun, ...
> Was evene joynant to the gardyn wal[.]
>
> (ibid., 11)

Emelye's garden is just one version of the *hortus conclusus* that occurs throughout Chaucer's poetry, as it does throughout romance literature generally. The front page of the Kelmscott *Chaucer* is another example (figure 1). The poet is shown standing in a fenced garden beside a well, quill in hand, in the throes of composition; a more sophisticated version of the image of the dreaming poet which he drew in the early 1860s (Birmingham City Museum and Art Gallery). In both, the horizontal lines of a fence divide the composition into bands. The garden in which Pandarus finds Cressida is still more enclosed and suggests that Burne-Jones knew medieval representations of the *hortus conclusus* such as those in the Cluny tapestries.[29] The high viewpoint, which enables the spectator to look down into the enclosure, is typical of late Gothic designs, and was used by the artist for his illustration to 'Womanly Noblesse' on p.240 of the *Chaucer*. There the poet stands before his

> lady of pleasaunce,
> Soveraine of beautè, flour of wommanhede

in a complete enclosure, an Elysian field. The poem does not mention the setting; it was Burne-Jones's decision to place them in the enchanted garden.

The symbolism attached to the garden receives its fullest exploration in Chaucer's works in *The Romaunt of the Rose*, his translation of the thirteenth-century French poem by Guillaume de Lorris and Jean de Meun. It treats the lover's quest for his ideal and his attempts to enter the garden of love and gain access to the Rose. It is rich in romantic allegory and its appeal for Burne-Jones can be seen in designs such as that for page 312, where the lover kneels outside the circular palisade and gazes in at the Rose herself (figure 29). It was one of his most popular designs and was adapted for tapestry weaving at Morris's

Fig. 29 - The Romaunt of the Rose, finished drawing

Fig. 30 - The Book of the Duchesse, finished drawing

Merton Abbey works. Finally the drawing for *The Book of the Duchesse* deserves mention. Once again the text does not offer a specific setting for the game of chess played between the story-teller and Dame Fortune. Burne-Jones chooses to put them into a circular enclosure, and following the hint that

> So turneth she hir false whele
> Aboute, for it is nothing stable,
> (ibid., 390)

he puts a large wheel of fortune, on end like a millstone, into it (figure 30). Besides the figures he includes the chessboard and, with the embroidered backcloth stretched from top to bottom and the rocky landscape in the distance, manages to convey just the right degree of uncertainty about the reality of the situation. As an illustration it successfully captures the mixture of dream and fantasy that permeates the whole book.

Part III

While Burne-Jones was revising and redrawing his ideas for the illustrations, the production of Chaucer presented Morris with a series of problems, which derived from its size and complexity as an illustrated book. Initially he planned to set the text in the Troy type which he designed in 1891 and named for the edition of Caxton's translation of *The Recuyell of the Historyes of Troy* which he published in 1892. Based on a close study of fifteenth-century prints by Günther Zainer of Augsburg, Anton Koburger of Nuremberg and above all Peter Schoeffer, the printer of the Mainz Bible of 1462, it was the face with which Morris hoped to 'to redeem the Gothic character from the charge of unreadableness which is commonly brought against it.' But when he set two trial pages, one from 'The Cookes Tale' and one from 'Chaucers Tale of Thopas,' it became clear that Troy was too large to print and bind the Chaucer in a single volume. As a result Morris commissioned his punch cutter Edward Prince (1846-1923) to produce a *pica* version which was cast by Sir Charles Reed & Son and was ready for use by July 1892, when Morris approved a specimen page from 'The Knyghtes Tale' set in double columns of fifty-eight lines in what he named the Chaucer type.

In 1891, Morris suffered a severe illness from which he never made a full recovery. His response to his own physical decline was characteristically one of impatience; but as his son-in-law and biographer J.W. Mackail wrote, 'The amount of work he had already done, in literature, in art, in politics, in handicraft, was enough to fill not one, but many lives; and the machinery that had been working at continuous high pressure for so long began to show signs of permanent weakening.'[30]   Even so, he set about the task of designing the borders, initial words and decorated capitals with typical resourcefulness and energy. His working method is captured in a description by his disciple W.R. Lethaby: 'He would have two saucers, one of Indian ink, the other of Chinese white. Then, marking the slightest indications of the mainstreams of the pattern he had in mind, with pencil, he would begin at once his finished final ornament by covering a length of ground with one brush and painting the pattern with the other.'[31] In this way, Morris produced designs for fourteen borders, eighteen frames to surround the illustrations, twenty-six large initial words and, one of his final efforts, the title page. Although the first page of the book, with Burne-Jones's image of the pen-poised poet beside the well-head of inspiration, and Morris's elaborately foliated border, was exhibited as a specimen at the Arts and Crafts exhibition in October 1893, further progress was slow. Both the size of the book and the scale of the task were reflected by Burne-Jones in the letter he wrote to Charles Eliot Norton on December 8, 1894: 'When the book is done, if we live to finish it, it will be a little like a pocket cathedral. My share in it is that of the carver of images at Amiens, and Morris' that of the Architect and Magister Lapicida.'[32] A year later in 1896 Burne-Jones admitted that 'I am getting very anxious about Morris and about the Chaucer. He has not done the title-page yet, which will be such a rich page of ornament, with all the large lettering. I wish he would not leave it any longer.'[33]

The printing of the Chaucer began on August 8, 1894. Like all Kelmscott books it was hand-printed on the Albion presses which Morris installed at No. 14 Upper Mall, Hammersmith, a laborious process albeit one which was firmly in line with Morris's principles of craftsman-based manufacture. In January 1895 a third Albion press was acquired so that not one but two machines could be dedicated to the production of the Chaucer. By that expedient, Morris hoped to complete the book by the following winter. Although that estimate proved to be an optimistic one, he was assisted as usual by a talented group of collaborators. Emery Walker, whose lecture in 1888 had done so much to stimulate his initial interest, persuaded him to overcome his aversion for electrotypes and to use them as a means of duplicating blocks for initial letters and recurrent ornaments. This process reduced considerably the task of William Harcourt Hooper and the other wood-block cutters. Walker's intervention was even more crucial in devising a way of transferring Burne-Jones's illustrations to woodblocks. Unlike the black and white designs which Morris supplied to Hooper, Burne-Jones's delicate pencil drawings with their soft contours and extensive use of shading did not translate easily into the kind of linear shorthand required by block-makers. After a number of time-consuming and ultimately unsuccessful attempts to cut blocks directly from the drawings, Walker used photography to introduce an intermediate stage into the process. From each of the drawings he made a pale, photographic print, or platino as he called it, actual size (figure 18). This then became a sort of expendable cartoon on which the outlines of the drawing could be replicated with Indian ink and Chinese white. Initially, the gifted artist, collector and *marchand-amateur*, Charles Fairfax-Murray (1849-1919), tried his hand at this extraordinarily difficult (and self-effacing) task before it was entrusted to Robert Catterson-Smith (1853-1938). He explained the whole process in considerable detail, including the constant referrals to Burne-Jones as well as 'sometimes work by Albert Durer ... to see how he had dealt with passages,' adding 'I only claim to have made myself as complete a tool for Burne-Jones as I could.'[34] Finally, when both the artist and the craftsman were satisfied with the result, Walker photographed the design again, this time directly on to the woodblock which Hooper and his associates then engraved.

While all of these technical difficulties were being resolved, Morris turned his attention to designing pigskin bindings for the *de luxe* edition of the Chaucer. Of the four he advertised, he completed only one design which was produced to order, eventually, by the Doves Bindery. On March 21, 1896 the last three woodblocks were delivered to the press, just before the Easter holidays which Morris described as 'four mouldy Sundays in a mouldy row, the press shut and Chaucer at a standstill.'[35] On May 6, he approved a proof of his title page and two days later, the printing of the Chaucer was complete, exactly twenty-one months after it began. The Kelmscott edition of *The Works of Geoffrey Chaucer*[36] was published on June 26, 1896, although two advance copies were delivered to Morris and Burne-Jones on June 2, bound to Morris's design by Douglas Cockerel. On the following day, Burne-Jones gave his copy as a birthday present to his daughter Margaret, inscribing it: 'I want particularly to draw your attention to the fact that there is no preface to Chaucer, and no introduction, and no essay on his position as a poet, and no notes, and no glossary; so that all is prepared for you to enjoy him thoroughly.'

Morris died four months later, on October 3, 1896. 'There was not a part of him that was not thoroughly worn out,' according to Fairfax-Murray or, as one doctor put it, 'I consider the case is this: the disease is simply being William Morris, and having done more work than most ten men.'[37] It fell to the survivor of that most enduring and productive of all artistic partnerships to point out that 'remembering those early years and comparing them with the last in which I knew him, the life is one continuous course. His earliest enthusiasms were his latest.'[38] Of that truth, and the common cause between Morris and Burne-Jones, there is no greater proof than their Kelmscott Chaucer.

Note: The text of this essay has been adapted from the author's *Companion Volume to the Kelmscott Chaucer* which appeared alongside the facsimile of the Chaucer published by the Basilisk Press, London, in 1975. It was re-issued as *William Morris, Edward Burne-Jones and the Kelmscott Chaucer* by Gordon Fraser, London, in 1982. All reproductions of drawings are by kind permission of the Syndics of the Fitzwilliam Museum, Cambridge.

Notes

[1]   Quoted in Georgiana Burne-Jones, *Memorials of Edward Burne-Jones*, 2 vols., London, 1964, II, p.278

[2]   Ibid., I, p.99

[3]   John Ruskin, *Pre-Raphaelitism*, London, 1851; E.T. Cook and A. Wedderburn (eds.), *The Works of Ruskin*, Library edition, XII, London, 1904, p.398n.

[4]   Ibid., X, London, 1904, pp.191-2

[5]   Letter from D.G. Rossetti to William Allingham, December 18, 1856.

[6]   Quoted in G. Burne-Jones, op.cit., II, p.56

[7]   Formerly in the Estelle Doheny Collection, St John's Seminary, Camarillo, California, USA. See Anna Cox Brinton, *A Pre-Raphaelite Æneid*, Los Angeles, 1934. The Manuscript was sold at Christie's (New York), May 19, 1989, lot 2370, bought by Andrew Lloyd Webber; offered for sale by Christie's (London), November 27, 2002, lot 10.

8 G. Burne-Jones, op.cit., II, p.217

9 William Morris to the Secretary of the Delegates of the Oxford University Press (autograph draft, n.d.). Now in the Pierpont Morgan Library, New York, gift of John M. Crawford Jr.

10 MSS, Fitzwilliam Museum, Cambridge

11 Burne-Jones became a baronet in 1894.

12 G. Burne-Jones, op.cit., II, p.259

13 J.W. Mackail, *The Life of William Morris*, 2 vol., London, 1899, II, p.322

14 Sketch-pad with plans of layout etc. for the Kelmscott *Chaucer*, 12 pp., Fitzwilliam Museum, Cambridge

15 Letter dated August 3, now in the Brotherton Collection, Leeds

16 G. Burne-Jones, op.cit., II, p.260

17 Sheet of notes, Fitzwilliam Museum, Cambridge

18 G. Burne-Jones, op.cit., II, p.217

19 Ibid., II, p.217

20 Sheet of notes, Fitzwilliam Museum, Cambridge

21 G. Burne-Jones, op.cit., II, p.217

22 For example in the *Très Riches Heures* of the Duc de Berri, illuminated by the Limbourg Brothers, before 1416.

23 Painted for the Church of Sta Lucia dei Magnoli in Florence, between 1442 and c.1448. *The Baptist in the Wilderness* is now in the National Gallery of Art, Washington, DC.

24 Sketchbook, 29 pp. sheet size 179 x 254 mm, Fitzwilliam Museum, Cambridge

25 G. Burne-Jones, op.cit., II, pp.36-7

26 For a further discussion of the Sienese copies made by Burne-Jones and Fairfax Murray, see Duncan Robinson, 'Burne-Jones, Fairfax Murray and Siena', *Apollo*, CII, No. 165, November 1975, pp.348-51

27 G. Burne-Jones, op.cit., II, p.64

28 Ibid., II, p.226

29 Late fifteenth-century or early sixteenth-century. The tapestries hung in the Chateau de Boussac, in the Creuse district, from 1660 until they entered the Musée de Cluny in 1882.

30 Mackail, op.cit., II, p.255

31 Quoted by H.H. Sparling, *The Kelmscott Press and William Morris, Master Craftsman*, London, 1924, p.67

32 Edward Burne-Jones to Charles Eliot Norton, December 8, 1894. Pierpoint Morgan Library, New York. Gift of John M. Crawford, Jr.

33 G. Burne-Jones, op.cit., II, p.227

34 R. Catterson-Smith in a letter to the *Daily Chronicle*, responding to a review of S.C. Cockerel, *A Short Description of the Kelmscott Press ... and an Annotated List of the Books Printed thereat*, London, 1898, which appeared on November 17,1898. A silver-worker and member of the Art Workers' Guild, Catterson-Smith became an Inspector of Art Schools for the London County Council, then Head of the Victoria Street School, Birmingham and finally, until his retirement in 1920, Principal of the Birmingham School of Art.

35 Mackail, op.cit., II, p.323

36 THE WORKS OF GEOFFREY CHAUCER. Edited by F.S. Ellis. Folio. Chaucer type, with headings to the longer poems in Troy type. In black and red. Borders 20a to 26. Woodcut title and 87 woodcut illustrations designed by Sir E. Burne-Jones. 425 on paper at twenty pounds, 13 on vellum at 120 guineas. Dated May 8, Issued June 26, 1896. Published by William Morris.

37 Mackail, op.cit., II, p.336

38 Ibid., II, p.336

Chapter 9

Rockwell Kent's Canterbury Pilgrims

Jake Milgram Wien

T he publication of the lavishly produced *Canterbury Tales* in 1930 heralded the wedding of Geoffrey Chaucer and Rockwell Kent. It was one of many unions that took place during the craze for expensive, limited editions that were conceived in America in the years leading up to the stock market crash of 1929. Bookstores oversubscribed all 999 sets of the two folios comprising the 1930 Covici-Friede edition of *Canterbury Tales* well before they went to press.[1] These sets, which featured a new verse translation by William Van Wyck as well as twenty-five full-page pen, brush, and ink drawings of medieval pilgrims by Kent,[2] made their way into well-appointed public and private libraries. They were followed in the next several years by tens of thousands of copies of the one-volume trade edition with the J.U. Nicolson translation of 1934. These trade editions and subsequent reprintings, all of which reproduced Kent's pilgrims (as well as his head and tail pieces), may have provided more readers with a visual introduction to Chaucer than any other printed interpretations before or since.

Kent's drawings for *Canterbury Tales* updated Chaucer for an ever-widening twentieth century audience. As he did with Casanova, Voltaire, Melville, and later with Whitman, Shakespeare, Goethe, Boccaccio, and other world-class writers, Kent produced illustrations that persuasively melded his intelligence and artistry with the spirit of the text at hand. Kent's reputation among distinguished book publishers became legendary for his ability to depict dramatically unfolding events involving multiple characters and dynamic compositions. Stanley Morison, the influential English type designer, book artist, and historian of printing and typography, considered the publishing debut of Random House, the 1928 *Candide*, filled with Kent's sprightly pen, brush, and ink drawings, to be "the most important illustrated book to have been made in America."[3] Among the finest, and most critically acclaimed of Kent's accomplishments in the book arts were his pen, brush, and ink drawings for the monumental three-volume Lakeside Press edition of *Moby Dick or the Whale*, also published in 1930. They reflected Kent's ongoing commitment to research extensively the particulars of his literary classic; in the case of *Moby Dick or the Whale*, the challenge included nineteenth century rigging and whaling. Kent's twenty-five Canterbury pilgrims, however, are portraits of individuals-something that prompted one graphic art historian to comment that they are, in a strictly technical sense, "barely illustrative."[4] Though Kent did complete his pilgrims with relative dispatch and constancy in conception, he nevertheless sustained them in ways that subtly inform the reader and rise to the lofty spirit of the text.

Sublime, indeed, is how those responsible for updating Chaucer's *Canterbury Tales* deemed Kent's visual interpretations. Upon seeing the first ten of Kent's twenty-five portraits, Pascal Covici considered them "magnificent."[5] Unmitigated praise also came from the book's translator, William Van Wyck, who received the volumes immediately upon publication. Van Wyck, a wealthy prodigy living in elegance in Paris at the time,[6] congratulated Kent for his illustrations, describing them as "big, vital things" that capture "every possible nuance of the spirit of Chaucer. The sculptural quality literally takes my breath away," he wrote. Van Wyck also approved of Kent's "very intelligent head and tailpieces which also breath [sic] the spirit of the tales." Van Wyck's favorite portraits were the Miller (figure 1), the Friar (figure 2), the Shipman (i.e., the Sailor), and the Wife of Bath (figure 3). Originally concerned about the selection of Kent as illustrator, Van Wyck was all the more thrilled upon seeing the resulting set of folios. Fearing he might not interpret the Chaucer spirit, Van Wyck proclaimed, "Good God! Interpret the Chaucer spirit! Man alive, old Geoffrey couldn't have interpreted the Chaucer spirit any better than you have done. Were he alive, he would be hugging himself over his luck in having you for his illustrator." He added in an emphatic postscript, "Your manner of doing *hands* and *feet* is *too marvellous for words*."[7]

What excited Kent's publishers, and particularly the translator, was the entirely modern sensibility with which Kent conjured up his pilgrims, substantially differing, for example, from their portrayal in the

Fig. 2 - The Friar

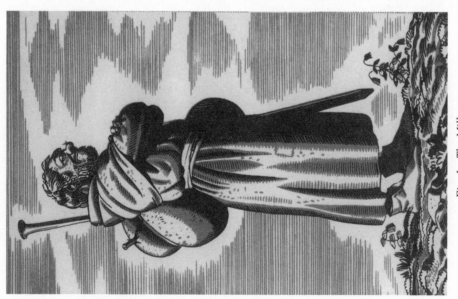

Fig. 1 - The Miller

Fig. 3 - The Wife of Bath

early nineteenth century tempera painting by William Blake
(color plate 33), whom Kent admired. Blake's pilgrims set forth on
horses, whereas Kent's pilgrims are stationary and without their
mounts. As one who was sympathetic to the workingman and the
underprivileged throughout his life, Kent provided a new approach to
visualizing the social hierarchy of Chaucer's times. By situating the
pilgrims on the earth (or on tree stumps or rocks), Kent accentuated
their shared humanity and leveled the playing field by blurring class
distinctions. The absence of animals from Kent's portraits also provided for decorative unity, and most certainly, for simplicity of his
effort both in research and design. The featureless backgrounds—skies
constructed solely with horizontal lines—provided commentary
beyond their faux-Italian Renaissance woodcut design that recalled
Titian's *St Roch*, for example. Kent occasionally illuminated his pen,
brush, and ink illustrations with lines emanating diagonally from
above, thereby creating a sense of awe and religiosity, if not divinity.
He notably refrained from so anointing his Canterbury pilgrims, rendering them less pious, in alignment with the Chaucerian spirit.

In yet another way, Kent broke with conventional portrayals of
Chaucer's pilgrims. In a very real sense, Kent rendered the pilgrims as

Chaucer conceived them—bearers of fascinating stories and individuals capable of inhabiting various roles. In Kent's imagined world they became *dramatis personae*—actors on the stage of life, rendered as though taking commands from a director or posing for the camera. As an amateur photographer in Greenland who stood behind a hand-held moving camera in the months leading up to completing *Canterbury Tales*, Kent had long cultivated an appreciation of the stage and screen. His creative life was enriched by the theatrical impulse, particularly during the 1930s when he tried to make a role for himself in Hollywood. Though he did not succeed in making the Hollywood movie of his dreams (which he hoped to film during his second winter sojourn in Greenland), he did invest his drawings, watercolors, and paintings from those years with theatricality and even a cinematic vision.[8] Kent's twenty-five pilgrims prefigure the full-length portraits of Greenlanders he drew between 1932 and 1935, portraits that approximate character studies for a prospective movie.[9]

Also particularly modern was the way Kent's pilgrims appeared on the printed page—strangely looking as though pulled from a Renaissance woodblock. Kent hoped to "enrich the appearance" of his pilgrims with the addition of a color (he originally suggested gray), and Covici immediately approved, wanting to implement Kent's designs and ideas "to the letter."[10] The effect of the resulting coloration—black, brown, and white of the paper—not only enhanced the dimensionality, character, and design of the pilgrims, it strongly suggested a link to the age of Chaucer (or shortly thereafter) through the evocation of the chiaroscuro woodcut. The playful spirit with which Kent drew and colored his pilgrims was in keeping with the way he often cast his twentieth century vision in a classical mold.[11] Kent also subjected his signature technique—a consuming linearity established through precise, successive strokes and ornamental restraint—to the incongruities of geometric abstraction. Myriad highly irregular geometries in brown and black emerge primarily within the borders of the costumes, and additional abstract highlights are provided by the white of the paper. The resulting confluence of techniques—art deco and geometric abstraction with Renaissance classical—generated visual intrigue in the same knowing, charming way that Chaucer enlightened through the inner ironies of his tales.

Modern as well as unabashed were Kent's overt references to theories of behavior propounded by Freud. Kent, an incorrigible playboy of the Western world, found Freudian analysis amusing, if less than

Fig. 4 - The Monk

compelling. More than occasionally Kent brought Freud to task with his suggestive compositions in pen, brush, and ink,[12] and he found ample room for play with his Canterbury pilgrims. Witness the presence, size, and generally vertical placement of such medieval weapons as the lance which Sir Thopas clutches with both hands; the sword and scabbard of the Knight; and the swords of Melibeus, the Reeve, the Miller, the Monk (figure 4), and the Yeoman. Kent subjected the masculinity and virtue of these pilgrims to his good-natured assault—an obvious artistic ploy but perhaps excusable in light of the dead-end he claimed to have reached when investigating medieval costume. He recalled quitting his research for *Canterbury Tales* after the chief librarian of Copenhagen informed him "of all periods within the Christian era the Fourteenth Century in England is possibly the most lacking in pictorial representation."[13] Kent surmised, "in [the] last analysis, Chaucer's own words are the best extant authority for what was worn in Chaucer's day."[14] Consequently, he relied on his undergraduate training as an architect at Columbia University, which had prepared him to reconstruct buildings graphically from written descriptions. Confident that he did the best job he could do with the limited visual resources at hand, Kent mused, "[A]s to credit for the merits or defects of the Chaucerian costumes as I have shown them, it may always be a toss-up between Geoffrey Chaucer and R. Kent."[15]

In many instances, Kent set aside Chaucer's explicit details of costume and personal effects for details of his own imagining. For example, he omitted the sharp spurs on the Wife of Bath's feet (perhaps because she was no longer atop her nag) as well as the soft boots of the Monk (he wore sandals instead). Kent also omitted the lap box of the Pardoner (perhaps because he was not sitting) and placed a scroll in his right hand.

This exercise of artistic license demonstrated Kent's proclivity to supplant, and at times to disregard, the Chaucerian text. When supplying marks of physical distinction, Kent frequently followed Chaucer's lead. The Miller's marvelous nose wart with its tuft of hairs, the forked beard of the Merchant and the tangled beard of the Sailor, the bandaged open sore on the shin of the Cook, and the flamboyant shoulder-length curls of the Pardoner were all persuasively handled by Kent. But Kent chose not to display the famous gap between the teeth of the Wife of Bath, opting for other descriptive measures to convey the same sexual innuendo—a round face and accentuated wide hips. The Monk in facial profile shows off his extraordinary proboscis, not alluded to by Chaucer, who instead mentioned his bulging eyes and corpulence. And as already noted, Kent altered Chaucer's vision by dismounting the pilgrims.

Kent's mastery at satiric portraiture is most evident in his deft handling of character nuances such as posture, gesture, and facial expression. The Lawyer, for example, has his back turned to the reader, thereby rendering inscrutable his countenance. Kent mocked effeminacy in the Pardoner by rendering limp the wrist that holds his cross set with stones, as he skewered delicacy in the Nun's Priest by presenting him with hands plaintively crossed over his heart, with feet that are slightly pigeon-toed, and one knee bent. The Manciple is drawn with fists clenched, and scowling face to reflect his consuming passion for fiscal gain. Bodily strength and fortitude are suggested in the stances of the Plowman (figure 5) and the Sailor, both of whom eye the reader with the directness indicative of rectitude.

Among Kent's characteristic flourishes is the fluttering bird apparently fascinated with the Wife of Bath, the bird positioned curiously in sight of her ample bosom revealed through an open blouse. A careful reader will notice the tiny face of bearded Jesus (a vernicle or veronica) sewn on the cap of the Pardoner—a most unlikely pilgrim to bear

Fig. 6 - The Cook

Fig. 5 - The Ploughman

such an artifact. Kent made sure to include it in his portrait, and it hints at the artist's iconoclasm with respect to the Church and its mystical doctrine. Other personal touches are found in characters with which Kent probably identified, including the Cook (figure 6) and the Friar. Bald, rather short, and sexually precocious as a mature adult, Kent, who occasionally engaged his pen, brush, and ink in deprecating self-portraiture, probably saw elements of his past in the Cook whom he rendered essentially hairless, bug-eyed, and spent. Musically inclined and with a daughter who played the violin, Kent may also have identified with the Friar, affectionately partnered with his fiddle, and distinctively sporting a tonsered crown. Gracing the dust jacket of many trade editions is the Friar, who lends a musicality to the entire text.

Subjecting Chaucer's pilgrims to the inventive artistry of Rockwell Kent demonstrated Covici-Friede's conviction that the writer and artist might be cut from a similar cloth. Though judgmental, dogmatic, and frequently unforgiving in life, Kent the writer was, like Chaucer, an assiduous student of humanity and an accomplished observer. Indeed, each was unsentimentally in love with the world and its inhabitants, and concerned about improving the social order. Kent (through his drawings rather than his paintings) and Chaucer alike took great delight in the practical joke and exhibited a proclivity toward irony in their artistry and genius for sympathetically conveying the pretenses and foibles of their fellow man. More importantly, each mirrored a world in disorder—Chaucer, the declining and uncertain world of Christianity, and Kent, the transitional society of modernizing post-WWI America. By the time he confronted Chaucer's pilgrims head on, Kent was nearly fifty years old, a world traveler himself who had long abandoned the religiosity of his early youth for a secular humanism that would mold his life's work.

Pascal Covici and Donald Friede recognized in Kent a kindred spirit who held the beauty of the printed book in high regard. Kent was a committed bibliophile who was deeply influenced by the visionary writings and drawings of William Blake, and a proponent of the achievements of William Morris and his Kelmscott Press. Following their aesthetic lead, Kent took part in the design and layout of the books he wrote and illustrated as well as of the commissions that came to him, advising even on the choice of paper and typeface that would best complement his artistry. Kent worked with Covici and Friede both in the design and the layout of *Canterbury Tales*, helping Covici realize his publishing ambition to make their illustrated edition of Chaucer's classic "the most beautiful book" Covici-Friede had ever done.[16]

Fig. 7 - The Wife's Extended Family

Covici and Friede probably appreciated Kent for yet another of his many talents – his piquant drawings in ink that raised many an eyebrow in the 1920s. For more than a decade (1916-1926), Kent pursued a parallel career as the pen-and-ink humorist "Hogarth, Jr.," creating astonishingly fluid and decisively modern-spirited drawings that landed on the desks of Manhattan's finest editors including *Vanity Fair*'s dapper Frank Crowninshield. As early as 1916, Crowninshield published Kent's light-hearted, irreverent drawings, pairing them with the raucous verse of Dorothy Parker and the urbane satire of George S. Chappell. *Harper's Weekly, Puck, Life*, and the Sunday *New York Tribune* gave Kent additional exposure both during and after World War I. Like his contemporary Miguel Covarrubias, Kent undertook assignments requiring the drawings of types of individuals. In May and June of 1922, for example, *Vanity Fair* published two series of caricatures by Kent celebrating bohemian painters and poets – eccentric types native to Greenwich Village and the Bronx. In March of the same year, the Sunday *New York Tribune* published six small drawings by Kent (figure 7) that accompanied a humorous article about the sorry preeminence of the wife's family (one in a series of humorous articles Kent illustrated, under the heading "A Handbook for Husbands").[17]

On ten of its covers in 1927, the semimonthly pulp magazine *Adventure* featured Kent's brush drawings in ink and tempera of stalwart individual outdoorsmen, including a pirate, gunslinger, big game hunter, Crusader, cowboy, explorer, and Native American on the warpath. These drawings demonstrated Kent's extraordinary facility at rendering character types, a natural ability that would ultimately chart him on a course toward the twenty-five "types" he encountered in *Canterbury Tales*.

Friede first proposed that Kent prepare one full-page illustration for each tale, as well as separate drawings as frontispieces for each of the two volumes with each drawing depicting all the pilgrims whose tales appear in that volume.[18] This conceptual framework gave way, in the next several months, to the contract entered into, which provided for twenty-five full-page drawings of the pilgrims, with the deluxe editions (defined below) accorded five separate panels depicting them in groups of five. Kent was required to submit a maximum of ninety-six head and tail piece drawings for the various tales and prologues by October 1, 1929. In February 1929, the deadline was moved forward to June 1, a few weeks before Kent would set sail for Greenland. This accelerated schedule proved unrealistic, primarily because of Kent's outstanding obligations to complete his drawings for *Moby Dick or the Whale* and the time-consuming preparations required for the month he would spend in a boat without motor or radio.

The publisher's anxiety about project completion heightened when news of Kent's harrowing mid-July shipwreck appeared on the front page of *The New York Times*. Though Covici and Friede were relieved to find Kent had survived, they were nervous about being able to fill in a timely manner the orders already outstanding. By December, Kent had returned to his upstate New York farm via Copenhagen, with partially completed canvases in hand—sea and landscapes of Greenland painted with brushes he salvaged from the shipwreck. Once back in his studio, he focused on his commission to illustrate Chaucer, submitting ten full-length portraits in early February 1930, and the remaining fifteen by early March. Kent executed these drawings with pen, brush, and black ink over graphite (image size $11^{1/8} \times 6^{7/8}$ inches) on paper laid down on Whatman artist's board (15 x 11 inches). Same size proofs of the drawings were printed by Offset Printing Plate Company of New York, and in early April Kent completed hand coloring the proofs in brown (or bistre) and submitted the head and tailpieces.[19]

Both Kent and Covici recognized the appeal of color in the modern world of publishing. An attractive flourish on an otherwise staid printed page, color had just gained Kent critical recognition, after he (with studio assistants) applied a rainbow of watercolors to the dozens of his pen, brush, and ink drawings reproduced in the first 95 of 1470 copies comprising the 1928 limited edition of *Candide*. Carl Van Doren regarded these hand-colored volumes of *Candide* as the most beautiful of any edition of the book since its appearance in 1759. In the hand-colored *Candide*, Kent perhaps came closest in his career to approximating the overall beauty of William Blake's hand-colored engraved texts and illustrations. Kent's well-stocked library contained much by Blake, including a nineteenth-century facsimile edition of the marvelously hand-colored *The Marriage of Heaven and Hell*. Just as Blake may have inspired Kent to hand color *Candide*, so an artist like Lucas Cranach or Ugo da Carpi may have inspired Kent to color his Canterbury pilgrims. The chiaroscuro woodcut of the Renaissance— with its classical coloration of black, brown, and white of the paper— may have served as Kent's visual template.

After coloring the printer's proofs, Kent fulfilled his obligations to Covici-Friede at the end of the summer when he added his signature to the five horizontal panels reproducing five pilgrims each, and to the "limit" page at the back of the second volume in each of the 999 sets of folios. Those copies numbered 1-75 (the "deluxe edition") were printed on Crane's Olde Book paper, bound in pigskin, and housed in a box which contained a cloth slipcase for the five signed panels. Those copies numbered 76-999 were printed on Worthy Number Two Rag paper and bound in gilt titled linen covered boards. All pages in the limited edition measured 15 x 10 inches and had top edges gilt. Unlike the successor trade editions, which contained only the modern translation, the limited edition presented both the Chaucerian text and its new verse translation in parallel columns.

Each of the five panels contained in the deluxe edition slipcase measured approximately 15 $3/8$ x 39 $3/4$ inches. The images were the same as in the two folios, with additional touches seamlessly weaving the ground foliage together—facilitated by the uniformly low horizon lines throughout the twenty-five portraits—to create the illusion that the five pilgrims stand (or sit, as the case may be) next to one another. Kent cleverly placed at panel left those pilgrims looking to their left, and at panel right those pilgrims looking to their right, with the exception of the Lawyer, whose back is turned. The central figures—the Plowman, the Second Nun, the Prioress, the Wife of Bath, and the Yeoman—generally direct their attention at the reader. The inclusion of these signed panels in the deluxe edition accounted in large part for the price differential between it and the ordinary limited edition ($250 to $50). This original valuation differential of 5:1 has escalated to about 20:1 in 2003.

The 1930 limited edition sets printed each of Kent's twenty-five Canterbury pilgrims on a full page, without text or title, with the reverse side blank. The drawings were reproduced by way of an innovative, highly accurate process conceived by Hugo Knudsen, general manager of Offset Printing Plate Company of New York. The Knudsen process involved, very generally, the creation of lithographic plates for printing that are produced photographically and without ruled screens.[20] Each pilgrim is situated directly opposite the beginning page of his or her tale, except for the Plowman, who tells no tale and becomes the frontispiece. In order of appearance, those pilgrims in Volume I are: the Plowman, the Knight, the Miller, the Reeve, the Cook, the Lawyer, the Sailor, the Prioress, Sir Thopas, Melibeus, the Monk, the Nun's Priest, and the Physician. Those pilgrims in Volume II are: the Pardoner, the Wife of Bath, the Friar, the Summoner, the Clerk, the Merchant, the Squire, the Franklin, the Second Nun, the Canon's Yeoman, the Manciple, and the Parson.

In 1934, Kent's Canterbury pilgrims proliferated in trade editions published by Covici-Friede and Doubleday & Co., each situating the full-page illustrations in the body of the tales themselves, mostly on facing pages with the reverse side blank. The Covici-Friede trade edition reproduced in blue a newly minted drawing by Kent of a jester's hat, with Sir Thopas as the fontispiece. The successor Doubleday trade edition reproduced the pilgrims in the same order, with the following exception: the drawing of Melibeus was renamed "Chaucer" and used not in sequence as specified above, but as the frontispiece. The Doubleday edition rectified ambiguities created by the Covici-Friede trade edition by titling each portrait with the identity of the pilgrim, and at the bottom of the page inserting a quotation from the text describing the pilgrim. Beneath the drawing of Chaucer, for example, was the title "Chaucer" and beneath that the quotation, "I will relate a little thing in prose/That ought to please you, or so I suppose. . . ." Illustrations in the trade editions were reduced in size by about forty percent, from $9 \ ^{3/4}$ inches to, generally, $5 \ ^{1/2}$ inches. Compromising severely the beauty and detail of Kent's original portraits, the illustrations reproduced to such small scale in the trade editions have not served Kent well, though they have increased the accessibility of Chaucer in the twentieth century. Only the privileged few have seen Kent's Canterbury pilgrims in the fullness of their original incarnation as published in the lavish two-folio sets.

Notes

I am grateful to the following individuals who assisted in the realization of this essay: John G. Deedy, Jr., Jerry Kelly, Robert Rightmire, Will Ross, Eliot H. Stanley, and Richard V. West.

1   Letter from Donald S. Friede to Rockwell Kent (in Copenhagen), dated September 4, 1929. Archives of American Art, Rockwell Kent Papers, Smithsonian Institution, Washington, D.C, microfilm roll 5172, frame 782 (hereinafter referred to as the "Rockwell Kent Papers").

2   Kent's studio drawings in India ink were frequently executed with a finely tipped brush. He probably used a combination of pen and ink with brush and ink to render his drawings for *Canterbury Tales*.

3   Letter from Elmer Adler (in London) to Donald Klopfer, dated May 20, 1928, cited in Kenneth A. Lohf, "The Candide Collaboration: A Pair of Gifts", Columbia *Library Columns*, February 1976.

4   Fridolf Johnson, *The Illustrations of Rockwell Kent* (New York: Dover Publications, Inc., 1976), p. xii. Johnson failed to mention that the scope of Kent's assignment for Covici-Friede was the limited presentation of the pilgrims, and not the more laborious and time-consuming portrayal of characters and events presented in the pilgrims' tales.

5   Pascal Covici to Rockwell Kent, letter dated February 6, 1930. Rockwell Kent Papers, microfilm roll 5172, frame 789.

6   Ward Ritchie, "When Life was the Future: a Memoir", *Coranto*, Number 24 (1988), pp. 39-41.

7   William Van Wyck to Rockwell Kent, letter dated September 25, 1930. Rockwell Kent Papers, microfilm roll 5172, frame 814.

8   This thesis is first presented in my article "Rockwell Kent and Hollywood", Archives of American Art *Journal*, Volume 42, nos. 3-4, 2002, forthcoming.

9   Kent's Greenlanders were painted with watercolor, drawn on lithographic stone, or drawn directly on paper with conté crayon. The conté drawings were published in *Salamina*, Kent's 1935 Greenland book.

10 Rockwell Kent to Pascal Covici, letter dated January 2, 1929 [1930]. Rockwell Kent Papers, microfilm roll 5172, frame 767. Pascal Covici to Rockwell Kent, letter dated January 8, 1930. Rockwell Kent Papers, microfilm roll 5172, frame 786.

11 As an experienced printmaker, Kent had addressed related visual issues with equal aplomb. For example, his chiaroscuro zinc engraving, *Wayside Madonna*, imitated the classically colored woodcut print, though its content was highly irreverent and contrary to classical notions of piety. Created in 1927 for the holiday cards of *Vanity Fair* editor Frank Crowninshield, Kent's engraving portrayed the Virgin Mary playfully balancing the baby Jesus on her shoulders. By adding the colors brown and grayish-green to his composition, Kent highlighted the area where the full-length skirt meets the right thigh to create the illusion that the Virgin's skirt were dramatically slit.

12 Little has been written about the influence of Freud on Kent. As early as 1919, Kent's second print, *Blue Bird*, a woodengraving, reflected the artist's perverse interest in Freudian theory.

13 Rockwell Kent, *It's Me O Lord* (New York: Dodd, Mead & Company, 1955), p. 443. Kent began his research into Chaucer while a guest of Knud Rasmussen, the Danish Arctic explorer and ethnographer, whom Kent met on the steamer sailing from Greenland. It was Rasmussen who introduced Kent to the chief librarian of Copenhagen.

14 Ibid.

15 Ibid.

16 Pascal Covici to Rockwell Kent, letter dated January 8, 1930. Rockwell Kent Papers, microfilm roll 5172, frame 786.

17 The types reproduced in figure 7 are the wife, the grouchy rich uncle, gloomy distinguished brother, boring but brilliant nephew, dissolute cousin, and spoiled child. These drawings were published in the *New York Tribune*, March 5, 1922. Collection of Richard V. West.

18 Donald S. Friede to Rockwell Kent, letter dated August 22, 1928. Rockwell Kent Papers, microfilm roll 5172, frame 758.

19 Four of the twenty-five drawings surfaced in the marketplace in February 2003. The four—ex-collection Dexter G. Cook, signed by Kent lower right and titled lower left in ink—were of identical size. Presumably, all twenty-five of Kent's Canterbury pilgrims conformed to this 11 $^{1/8}$ x 6 $^{7/8}$-inch format.

20 See, for example, A.C. Austin, "An Outline of the Knudsen Process", in *The Penrose Annual: Review of the Graphic Arts* (R.B. Fishenden Ed., London, Lund and Humphries & Co. Ltd.), Vol. 40, 1938, pp. 121-123.

Fig. 1 - Eric Gill, title page of Prologue

Chapter 10

The Golden Cockerel Press, *The Canterbury Tales* and Eric Gill: Decoration and the *Mise En Page*

Peter Holliday

The Golden Cockerel Press edition of Chaucer's *The Canterbury Tales* was published in four volumes between February 1929 and March 1931, one volume for each day of the pilgrimage. Eric Gill was commissioned to do the wood engravings by his friend and fellow-engraver, Robert Gibbings, who owned the Golden Cockerel Press and determined its publishing agenda.

The Canterbury Tales has two hundred and ninety-eight wood engravings in all. Only one, the title page, is a full-page illustration. There are twenty-six half-page illustrations, one for each of the title pages of the Tales, and three others. The remaining illustrations are border decorations, tail-pieces and line fillings. In addition, there are over sixty initial letters, some printed in red and blue. Chaucer's prose sections (*The Tale of Melibeus* and *The Maunciples Tale*) are not illustrated.

Gill's work depended on the creative rapport he enjoyed with Robert Gibbings at the Golden Cockerel Press. Gibbings' interests as a printer and publisher followed from his own earlier pursuits of wood engraving and book illustration. And, like Gill, he was also a writer. Their '*Canty. Tales*', as Gill nicknamed the book in his diary, was the outcome of their shared thought and their practical collaboration. Gill had already illustrated five smaller books for Gibbings, including Chaucer's *Troilus and Creseyde*, in 1927. His work on *The Canterbury Tales* began immediately after, in mid-1927. In concept the two books have much in common. Gill's collaboration with Gibbings was to continue in 1931 with *The Four Gospels*, the crowning achievement of the Press. These two companion volumes, flanking *The Canterbury Tales* before and after, have a certain bearing on our study.

Gibbings used the Chaucer text that was edited by the Rev. Walter W. Skeat, the doyen of Anglo-Saxon studies, in 1894-97. It had been published by the Oxford University Press and used by William Morris. (This raises the question as to the ease with which Gill read the text, a consideration to be taken up later.) Five hundred copies of *The Canterbury Tales* were hand-printed; fifteen of these were on vellum and the remainder were on hand-made Bachelor paper, containing the Cockerel watermark. Significantly, Gibbings set the book in Caslon Old Face type, using 18 point, which is comfortably large on the page size of 12.2 by 7.2 inches. Caslon Old Face will feature importantly in our discussions. Allowing top and bottom margins of 1.5 and 3.5 inches and generous leading, Gibbings printed thirty lines to the page. (The colophon credits the printers and compositors at the Press but, oddly, does not state that Gill was the illustrator.)

Gill's New Departure: Decoration and the *Mise en Page*

The first of Eric Gill's wood-engraved illustrations combines with the title of The Prologue—HERE BEGINNETH THE BOOK OF THE TALES OF CANTERBURY. A nude, putto-like figure clasps the

Fig. 2 - Eric Gill, Frankeleyns Tale

initial letter H (Fig. 1). Into this composition Gill introduces a chanti-cleer, which is the emblem of the Golden Cockerel Press. While no longer golden, he is refulgent still, though now in printer's black. Thereafter, Gill furnishes every page with a wood engraving. The work is prodigious. Looking through the book one senses the presence of a new artistic departure, quite remote from the Pre-Raphaelite illustrations provided by Burne-Jones for the Kelmscott Chaucer that William Morris printed in 1896.

The Golden Cockerel Press edition appeared only thirty-odd years later than the Kelmscott Chaucer. In common with its magisterial predecessor, it reveals a unity of design across the page-openings. Text, image, and margins harmonise flawlessly to serve the printed text. A fine example of Gill's mastery of these elements occurs in Book Four where the page opening shows the tailpiece of *The Squieres Tale* opposite the title page of *The Frankeleyns Tale* (Fig. 2). Here, as elsewhere, it is the double page—flat and mirror-imaged—which is paramount. But now, in contrast to the design of the Kelmscott tome, light, space and arabesques prevail. A distinct *joie de vivre* has entered in.

Gill embellished virtually every page of the Tales with decorative accompaniments. They are frieze-like compositions, where figures intertwine with the motif of trailing leafy stems. But Gill does not indulge in these to create a tendrilled moody languour. Instead, his drawing is taut, the lines cut crisp by the graver tool. The effect is an objective detachment. Is this not a form of classicism renewed, Gill's pages frescoed, as it were, like the villas of Pompei? Stylised, devoid of 'sentiment'—to use Gill's own term—his scenes have more to do with decoration than with illustration. When this was pointed out, he responded:

> As to my lack of emotional display I think that the business of engravings is very much like the business of typography....—my engravings are, I admit, only a kind of printer's flowers'. As to my lack of historical sense, it is true, I have none.[1]

Throughout *The Canterbury Tales*, Gill is concerned exclusively with the *mise en page*. While he takes account of the text and pays a token respect to its historical period, his intention is to rejoice in the Tales rather than to retell them. In a discussion with Herbert Furst about printing wood engravings he wrote: 'the engraving is part of the typography'.[2] This is the starting point for Gill. If image and printed text are integral, then they need to be designed as an entity. This view-point was reinforced by his own tract, *An Essay on Typography*, which was gestating at this very time and was to be designed and printed by Gill himself in his own typeface, Joanna, in 1931.[3] (Underway, too, was another typeface, which Gill designed for Gibbings' Press between 1929 and 1931, to be called 'Golden Cockerel'.) Gill's preoccupation at this time was typography. It could be said that in *The Canterbury Tales* he was thinking as a typographer's illustrator.

From the design of its pages it is clear that a particular variety of English Modernism was being born. Gill's achievement raises the question as to the traditions and influences which nourished it, for the origins of his involvement in wood engraving explain much about this achievement. These contextual considerations will play an essential part in our enquiry.

Wood Engraved Illustration:
The Aesthetic and Social Context

Wood engraving (with its earlier sister process the woodcut) relies on letterpress printing.[4] When it is used as book illustration, the block is printed in the same operation with the text. It is simply clamped into the printer's forme in conjunction with the lead type. Image and text become an integral unit on the page and can be visualised as such by the artist-designer. It therefore has a particular advantage over intaglio printing (such as etching) or planar printing (such as lithography) where this combination is not possible. This was its appeal to William Morris, who first revived the artist's wood engraving in order to illustrate his Kelmscott Press books. That Morris called himself an 'architect' of books was not lost on Gill.

Nor were Morris's deeper aesthetic and social reasons for using wood engraving. Gill inherited from Morris the notion that the artist-craftsman had had restored to him a responsibility for, and a control over, his handwork. Gill was highly critical of the commercialisation—and in his view, the corruption—of wood engraving in the nineteeth century. He wished to return it to a pristine state, as practised by Thomas Bewick, who perfected the technique and had brought it to a high level as a mode of book illustration in the 1790s.

That these aesthetic and social issues especially engaged Gill is shown in a lecture entitled 'The Artist and Book Production' that he gave in 1926 (just three years before the *The Canterbury Tales* project) to the Double Crown Club in London, an exclusive dinner club attended by luminaries of the printing, publishing and typographic world for the purpose of discussing ideas on good printing. Members would meet to award a double crown to the two finest examples of printing of the past year and to listen to a discourse by their designer. In 1926, the winning book was *Sonnets and Verses* by Enid Clay, who happened to be Gill's sister. The press was the Golden Cockerel Press and its six wood engravings were by Gill—his first commission, in fact, for Robert Gibbings. In his discourse, Gill was ready, as ever, to propagate his ideas.

A contentious streak in Gill, born of his convictions, would readily break out from the religiously austere routines of his life. From the very outset of his address Gill taunted most of his audience (and probably amused the rest) by casting himself as 'a miner in the company of mandarins'. (The elevated audience to whom he spoke included Emery Walker, Francis Meynell of the Nonesuch Press, Frank Sedgwick of Jackson Publishers and Michael Sadleir of Constable & Co.) The theme that Gill developed was, by that date, a stock-in-trade one in his repertoire. Art, in the most basic sense, he argued, is the practice of skill, and a work of art is therefore 'a thing well made'. A book, then, is 'a thing well made or ill, an artistic book is one well made: it is a work of art, it is the work of an artist.' Gill thereby aligned himself against the fraternity of what he dismissively called 'book producers', whose motivation he perceived to be little more than profitable gain and who began, Gill claimed, not with the book itself, but with its distribution and sale. To their exasperation, Gill, the wood engraver, portrayed himself as a maker—the humble 'miner' (of coal?)—midst a company of businessmen turned cynical by the lure of profit.[5]

The antipathy to commerce which Gill flaunted before the Double Crown Club was the resistant core of an ideology he had first imbibed as a student at the Central School of Arts and Crafts, the pedagogic bastion of the Arts and Crafts movement. Gill's entire artistic life was to be orientated by his teacher there, the calligrapher and lettering artist Edward Johnston. Born in 1872, Johnston was just ten years older than Gill. The impact of his artistic integrity on Gill is recalled in Gill's *Autobiography* of 1940 with poignant eloquence.[6] While Johnston's calligraphy and Gill's wood engraving may appear quite disparate, the connection between them is straightforward, and more so given that Gill studied lettering with Johnston before he took up wood engraving. In a word, Johnston's philosophy of design was transferable from lettering to all crafts.

These developments, which led Gill to take up engraving images in wood, explain much about the rationale behind *The Canterbury Tales*. Playing a part, too, was an aesthetic preference for the Caslon type face —first designed in the 1720s and appreciated once again by the Arts and Crafts movement as a highly legible face.[7] The revival of Caslon is a theme inseparably bound up with the revival of wood engraving in books. These strands of influence come together in Gill's engraving work for *The Canterbury Tales*. It is illuminating of Gill's position, therefore, to explore in the following excursus how they developed (in a little more detail).

Gill and the Tradition of the Arts and Crafts Movement: An Excursus

An understanding of what prompted Gill to take up wood engraving is the prerequisite to appreciating its role in *The Canterbury Tales*. The English School of 'autograph' (or artists') wood engraving emerged from around 1905, born of the Arts and Crafts movement. Gill had the closest of links with key figures in this School and movement; indeed, at the outset of his artistic career he was part of them. In this regard, it was not a wood engraver whose influence was crucial but, instead, Gill's teacher of lettering, Edward Johnston. Gill's concept of wood engraving was informed by his experience as a lettering artist - his cutting of inscriptions in stone or wood and his designing of typefaces. All these skills were related facets of Gill's imagination in carving in line. Instruction in wood engraving itself was given by Johnston's fellow-teacher, Noel Rooke, who stimulated the revival of the craft. These two teachers held the view that the craftsman's tools are the essential determinant of form. Additionally, they imparted ideas first developed by William Morris which sought to integrate the book illustration with the printed text. This relates to what Sister Elizabeth Brady called 'allusive' typography in her study of Gill's book design, an interpretation which will be touched on in the conclusion.[8]

If Gill was the child of Edward Johnston, Johnston himself had come to prominence through his own mentor, the architect and educator William Lethaby. Lethaby, born in 1857, had a deep interest in the history of art and the crafts, and, as a consequence, had insights into the spiritual impoverishment that followed the industrialising of British society—the degradation of the urban environment, the misshapen nature of design, the misconceptions of art education. At this point in his thinking he was, in effect, the *alter ego* of William Morris. As an education inspector for the London County Council, Lethaby in 1896 helped establish a new institution for the LCC, to be called the Central School of Arts and Crafts. It was here that Lethaby in 1899 appointed Johnston, only twenty-seven years old, to organise and teach a course on lettering and illumination. Although concerned with the writing and decoration of hand-written manuscripts, Johnston saw clearly that the principles underlying these skills applied equally to the printed book.

Johnston was modest, clear thinking and independently minded. He was especially interested in the historical development of the techniques of lettering—how a script was made rather than the text written in it. He focused on the methods of the medieval scribes and, crucially, on the preparation and holding of the quill. Understanding the connections between form and technique entailed intense comparative inspection of specimens of medieval scripts. In spite of the work of palaeographers, such an analysis of medieval calligraphy had not been undertaken before. His findings became the basis of his teaching at the Central School. Johnston insisted on the use of the broad-edged (or chisel-edged) quill or pen, since he discerned that it was this, rather than the pointed one, which determined the letterforms of medieval scripts. The consequences of Johnston's analysis were unbounded. His classes became the fulcrum of a quiet but profound revision of the lettering and the book arts in Britain. Johnston taught respect again for the broad tradition of the Roman letter, its proportions, its forms, its spacing and the application of these elements to the printed page. He considered that they had become debased in the nineteenth century by crass commercialism.

However, in pioneering these changes Johnston built on the work of others. A number of his pupils in those early classes were considerably older than their teacher. Among these were some highly accomplished craftsmen and connoisseurs of the arts. These adult pupils became Johnston's companions and, with others in the circle in which he moved, they shared and encouraged him in his beliefs. In different ways, they shaped the beliefs of the Arts and Crafts movement—and thereby formulated Gill's own.

Moreover, they mostly lived close to one another, clustering into loosely-grouped craft communities. Johnston, ever eager for discourse, was a prime mover in this. He first lived in Holborn, sharing an apartment in Lincoln's Inn Fields with Gill. On getting married in 1903 Johnston moved to Gray's Inn, where he was the neighbour of Lethaby.

In 1905 he moved to a house on the riverside in Hammersmith Terrace, West London. Close by, on Upper Mall, was Kelmscott House, Morris' former house where his daughter, May Morris, still lived. This stretch of the river (together with its more important institutions, the Art Workers' Guild and the Arts and Crafts Exhibition Society) was the Mecca of the Arts and Crafts movement.

Largely as Johnston's protégé, Gill crossed the threshold into this privileged (and, for the most part, well-heeled) circle. When he enrolled in Johnston's lettering class in 1900 he was eighteen years old. He had already studied at the Technical and Art School in Chichester, where his aptitude for accurate drawing was revealed by his renderings of Chichester's Georgian architecture and its cathedral. Following this training, Gill served as an assistant in the office of the London-based ecclesiastical architect W. D. Caroë. Thereafter, Johnston became his enduring inspiration. After his marriage he followed Johnston in 1905 to Hammersmith. His workshop there was in a lane just off Hammersmith Terrace. Their lives continued to be closely intertwined.

Skirting the fringe of this group was Sydney Cockerell. Born in 1867, he had formerly been William Morris' secretary and, on Morris' death, had brought the Kelmscott Press to a well-organised close. Like Morris, he was a collector of medieval manuscripts and early books and later became the director of the Fitzwilliam Museum, Cambridge. Cockerell is perhaps best thought of as the ever-benevolent eminence grise of the Arts and Crafts movement. Prompted by Lethaby, he showed Johnston certain manuscripts at the British Museum and encouraged him to study the style of their scripts, notably that of the celebrated Harley MS. 2904. This late tenth-century Gospels was written in an English Carolingian script of exceptional clarity. Moreover, the symmetry of its layout derives from the lettering of Roman inscriptions. (Fig. 3).

Fig. 3 - Harley MS 2904

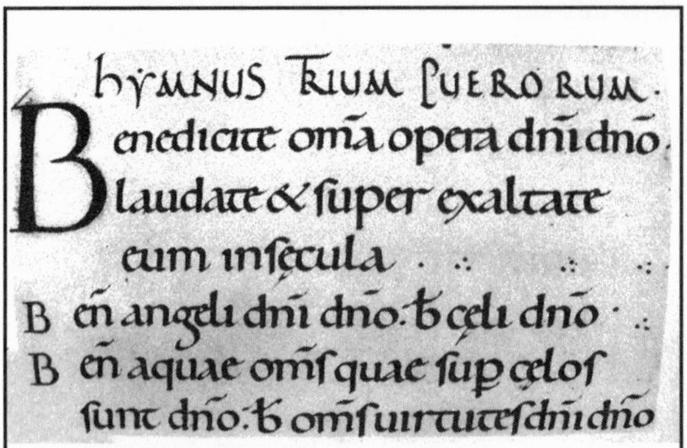

Johnston adopted MS. 2904 as the model for his own formal script, calling his modernised version his 'Foundational hand'. He favoured it over older half-uncial scripts in imparting to his students the qualities which he considered essential in the new calligraphy, naming these 'sharpness' (of the letterforms drawn with a well-sharpened quill), 'unity' (of the ensemble of letters, making for a flowing line of writing), and 'freedom' (of expression of the calligrapher, no longer hidebound by the exemplars).

One of Johnston's first pupils was Thomas James Cobden-Sanderson, a retired lawyer, born in 1840. His considerable wealth was lavished on aesthetic pursuits. In 1900 he had set up his private Doves Press, first in Hammersmith Terrace and then on Upper Mall. Cobden-Sanderson's ideas regarding the book appeared in his tract which he printed in 1900 entitled *The Ideal Book, or Book Beautiful*. He advocated that the design of a book should be guided by the conventions of medieval calligraphy. This, he understood, was the praxis of the very first printers. Johnston was profoundly inspired by *The Book Beautiful*, and at Cobden-Sanderson's request, he calligraphed copies of it. In 1903 Cobden-Sanderson printed the five volumes of the celebrated *Doves Bible*, which became an exemplar for the entire private press movement—and therefore a point of departure for the Golden Cockerel Press. Johnston designed initial letters for the Doves Press, some of which Gill (with Noel Rooke) transferred to engraved wood blocks.

A third figure of this generation was Emery Walker, born in 1851, who also lived in Hammersmith Terrace. Walker is crucial to an account of Gill's wood engravings because he advocated the revival of wood engraving for book illustration. A specialist in printing (he owned a photo-engraving 'process' works on Upper Mall) he also had a technical interest in the early book at a time when its history was scarcely thought about. On 15 November 1888 he lectured on the incunabula book to the Arts and Crafts Exhibition Society. This became a legendary occasion because by listening to Walker, William Morris finally decided to take up printing himself. Walker became Morris' adviser about his Kelmscott Press, helping him with the design of his types. Walker's relationship with Cobden-Sanderson was even closer. He became a business partner in the Doves Press and the designer of the Doves type—based, incidentally, on those of the sixteenth-century Venetian printer, Nicholas Jenson. Gill came to know Emery Walker well, and visited him in later years to talk about colour printing.

The impact of this circle of bookmen on Gill was profound. Their ideas as to how books were made in the past and how they should appear in the future helped stimulate Johnston to write a tract himself. Conceived in 1902 at the suggestion of Lethaby, it was finally published in 1906. Johnston called it, with scrupulous care, *Writing & Illuminating, & Lettering*.[9] Needless to say, it was set in Caslon type. In an important sense, therefore, his handbook was the outcome of an amalgam of experience and became one of the seminal utterances of the Arts and Crafts movement. Gill was closely involved with its making and therefore knew it intimately.

While Johnston's handbook is mainly concerned with the primacy of the broad-edged pen or quill, an important section deals with the principles of calligraphic design as applied to the printed book. On page 368, Johnston quotes from Cobden-Sanderson's *The Book Beautiful*:

> The passage from the Written Book to the Printed Book was sudden and complete.   ...The Printer carried on into Type the tradition...of the Calligrapher at his best. It is [now] the function of the Calligrapher to restore the craft of the Printer to its original purity of intention and accomplishment. ...The great revival of printing which is taking place under our own eyes is the work of a Printer who before he was a Printer was a Calligrapher and an Illuminator, WILLIAM MORRIS.

The topic of the 'illumination'—and here Johnston included the illustration—of books brought up the issue of wood engraving. It led him to quote from Emery Walker's discourse to the Arts and Crafts Exhibition Society in 1888 where Walker spoke of a book's overall design. The impact of Johnston's observation is to be seen in Gill's work on *The Canterbury Tales*:

> Next in importance to the type are the ornaments, initial letters, and other decorations which can be printed along with it. These...should always be designed and engraved so as to harmonise with the printed page as a whole. Hence, illustrations drawn only with reference to purely pictorial effects are entirely out of place in a book, that is, if we seriously desire to make it beautiful.[10]

Cobden-Sanderson, Walker, and Morris, followed by Johnston, exhorted the maker of books to regard the double page of text and illustrations as a whole. Like Morris, Walker preferred wood-engraved illustrations printed by letterpress alongside the text in the same operation. Such historicism characterised the period. Walker, influencing Morris, had in mind those early printed books which had used woodcuts.[11] Here was the origin of Gill's own preference for the wood engraved illustration.

The exemplar Johnston most commended was the wood-engraved vignettes which graced the naturalist books of Thomas Bewick (1753-1828). Johnston praised Bewick in his *Writing & Illuminating, & Lettering* and reproduced two full-page illustrations from Bewick's masterpiece, *History of Quadrupeds, (*1791), commenting (in a note on his page 221): 'these are suggested as examples of drawing—of plants and animals—suitable for book decoration' (Fig. 4). Under the section 'Special Subjects' (page 364), Johnston paid tribute to Morris:

Fig. 4 - Thomas Bewick Woodcut

> Of all the 'processes' wood engraving agrees best with printing. The splendid effect of Title and Initial pages engraved in wood may be seen in the books of the Kelmscott Press.

Johnston was true to his own advice and sought the help of his colleague, Noel Rooke. A lesser-known figure than Johnston or Gill, Rooke is of pivotal importance in the revival of wood engraving in England. Born in 1883, he had been brought up in an artistic ambience, his father being a watercolour painter who depicted scenes for John Ruskin and had at one point been an assistant to Burne-Jones. Noel Rooke studied at the Slade School before joining Johnston's class at the Central School in 1900, with Gill and Cobden-Sanderson. Almost exactly Gill's contemporary, he was of a scholarly frame of mind, undertaking for both Johnston and Lethaby work in 'various libraries and collections'. In his unpublished memoir, 'The Qualifications and Experience of Noel Rooke', he recalled:

> Inspired by the thought of Johnston's calligraphy I started in 1905 to make engravings on the same basis as calligraphy, that is designing and producing in terms of the strokes of the brush or pen or pencil. The change of principle was a cause of regret to the older engravers. Gill followed next. From that start came the group of engravers on 'Autographic' principles which flourished between the wars.[12]

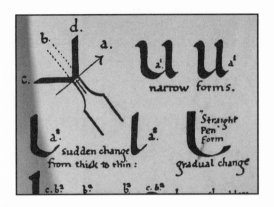

Fig. 5 and 6 - Two examples of Noel Rooke's engraving

This memoir provides a crucial link from Johnston's calligraphy to wood engraving.

By 1905 Rooke was also teaching a class called 'Book Illustration, Lettering, Black and White, etc' at the Central School. Johnston asked him to provide for his handbook a set of wood-engraved illustrations of the calligrapher's hand positions when correctly preparing and holding the quill or pen. Johnston's own hands were Rooke's model (no book has more portraits of the author's hands than *Writing & Illuminating, & Lettering*). Rooke also engraved the specimens of lettering Johnston showed in the handbook[13] (Figs. 5-6).

Writing & Illuminating, & Lettering had a profound effect on Gill, who, it must be said, was not left out of Johnston's project. Johnston invited him to contribute an entire section, Chapter XVII, 'Inscriptions in Stone'. He also enlisted his help in the rush to get the copy to the printers in 1906 and to revise the second edition in 1908.

Gill's induction into wood engraving was two-fold. First, he was captivated by Johnston's own interest to try it out. Both Johnston and Gill meticulously kept diaries, or work books. Johnston's work book for 16-18 November 1906 records: 'Bt. Wood Engraving matls'; 'My first Wood Engraving'; '2nd Wood Engraving 3rd Wood Engraving'. On 20 November he recorded: 'Gill abt. 9pm to 2am (21st) (trying engraving) (EJ's 4th wood engraving)'[14] Their experiment is corroborated by Gill's diary for the 20th November: 'Tried wood Engraving a little in evening'.[15]

Gill's second induction was through Rooke. Just one year after the experiment with Johnston, on 16 November 1907, Gill recorded in his diary taking classes with Rooke in Clapham at 10.30 am on Tuesdays. Given that wood engraving had become Rooke's speciality, it is safe to assume these 'classes' were, indeed, in wood engraving.

While Rooke was Gill's instructor, the key to Gill's artistry lay in Johnston's method. Just as the letterforms of the 'Foundational hand' were the natural outcome of the pen, so 'autograph' wood engraving was dependent on the primacy of the engraver's tool. The assortment of gravers became the determinant of form; it was the natural shapes of their incisions alone which built up the image. Johnston's concept of 'Sharpness, Unity and Freedom' was equally applicable to the discipline imposed by the engraver's tools—and the liberation these could offer when properly used.

That Johnston's teaching was fundamental to Rooke's teaching is indicated by the lecture, *Woodcuts and Wood Engravings*, that Rooke gave (to the Print Collector's Club) on 20 January 1925. Therein is a direct echo of the wood-engraved diagrams he made for *Writing & Illuminating, & Lettering*. Using three diagrams he shows the variety of cutting edges of the graver and the marks made by them. A fourth shows how these marks make up an image typical of this kind of work. (Figs. 7a-d). Furthermore, he began his lecture by saying it set out to explore 'the origin of the modern movement in wood cutting and wood engraving, printed in the European method, as a means of direct artistic expression'.[16]

The notion of 'artistic expression' also ties Noel Rooke in with Johnston's critique of commercialism—and with Gill's fulminations at the Double Crown Club. Rooke took up 'autograph' wood engraving out of a disillusionment with the commercial photo-mechanical 'process' reproduction of illustrations. He had endured a spell of employment in 1900 at Emery Walker's 'process' works at The Upper Mall, Hammersmith, where he prepared pen drawings and diagrams for reproduction in books. He also worked for a spell at the LCC School of Photo Engraving at Bolt Court. His memoir describes this experience:

> Drawing for 'process' was unsatisfactory and disheartening work, and one used to be told on all hands that the future held no store. So of necessity it had to be in a sporting spirit that one put to the test one's faith in the future of an art which was to arise out of the ashes of a dead craft.[17]

Rooke's misgiving is rooted in the Arts and Crafts shibboleths of 'truth to materials' and mistrust of commercialism. His lecture of 1925 continued in an entirely Johnstonian vein: 'There is only one way of getting a thoroughly satisfactory engraving, the designer and engraver must be one and the same person.' (And, like Johnston, he then turned for inspiration to Thomas Bewick). Rooke paid homage where it was due:

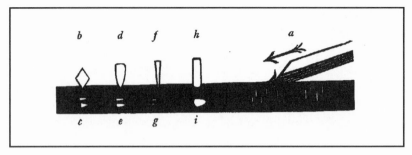

Fig. 7a - Diagram of engraving tool

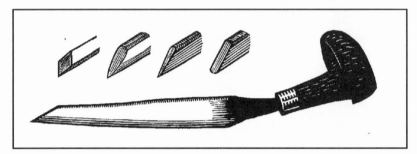

Fig. 7b - Diagram of engraving tool

Three people should be mentioned who gave encouragement when it was most needed: Mr Edward Johnston the scribe; but for him not so many people would have become engravers as is the case; Professor Lethaby; and Geoffrey Whitworth, who tried very hard to persuade his firm to break into new ground.'[18]

The firm in question was the commercial publishing house, Chatto and Windus. But, the new opportunity for wood engraving was provided not by commercial publishers but by the private press movement. The first initiative had already come as early as 1904 from the anglophile German, Count Harry Kessler, on behalf of the Insel Verlag Press, and then for Kessler's own private Cranach Presse which he set up in 1911. Gill designed and engraved lettering on wood for Count Kessler, notably for the Cranach Presse editions of Homer's *Die Odyssee* and Virgil's *Eclogues*. Gill's *Autobiography* records that 'this lettering work then led to pictorial engraving and all my future work'.[19]

A second private press (started by Hilary Pepler in Ditchling in 1916 and initially called The Ditchling Press) also needed such 'pictorial engraving'. Pepler was Gill's (and Johnston's) close friend. Like them, he had lived in Hammersmith Terrace, where, as a Quaker social

Fig. 7c - Diagram of engraving technique

worker and writer on social issues, he became convinced that craft activity could play a therapeutic role in social work. Gill moved to Ditchling in 1907; he was followed by Johnston in 1912 and by Pepler in 1915. Collaborating on various projects, they amounted, *de facto,* to a tiny craft community. In 1909 Gill helped Johnston by engraving on wood a Caslon alphabet for his portfolio, *Manuscript and Inscription Letters.* (It was published in 1909 at 13, Paternoster Row, London, by a little-known but pivotal figure John Hogg). Other pieces of wood-engraved work followed, as did a trilogy of books concerned with craft which Pepler was inspired to publish.[20]

This publishing venture prompted Pepler to learn printing himself. On 19 January he tried his hand with a hand-operated Albion press. Johnston was present to help. The following day Gill experimented,

too. His diary for 20 January reads: 'Did my first piece of printing. Supper at Sopers.' (Sopers was Gill's first house in Ditchling, then occupied by Pepler.) On January 31 he noted: 'Sabin, printer, (staying at Pepler's) came to lunch and I walked back to D.[itchling] with him after and had instruction in printing wood-blocks.'[21]

Between 2 and 4 February Gill printed onto a Japanese paper seven of the engravings from Pepler's satire, *The Devil's Devices.* He bound up fifteen copies of this rare volume, signed and numbered, entitling them *Emblems.*[22] Pepler converted to Roman Catholicism in 1917. In 1918,

Fig. 7d - Rooke's wood-engraving

he and Gill became novices of the third order of St. Dominic, at which point the press was renamed S. Dominic's Press. With the formation in 1920-21 of the craft-based Guild of St. Joseph and St. Dominic at Ditchling, Gill provided many wood-engraved illustrations for the S. Dominic's Press.

While the S. Dominic's Press was a jobbing business, the third private press to commission Gill, the Golden Cockerel Press, had far loftier ambitions. It is in this new episode in Gill's career that the various threads explored in the foregoing excursus come together. It is to the collaboration between Gill and Robert Gibbings and to the wood engravings for their project, of *The Canterbury Tales*, that our study can now more profitably turn.

Gill and Gibbings: Shared Concepts and the Golden Cockerel Press

Between Gill and Gibbings there was a natural affinity. Gibbings was a painter and writer. He attended the Slade School in 1911-12 where, like Gill, he came into touch with modernist tendencies. In 1912 he also attended the Central School, where he learned wood engraving from Rooke. He learned much there, too, about the setting of type from John Mason, who ran the School of Book Production and who, incidentally, had been a pupil with Johnston and had been the chief compositor for the *Doves Bible*. One half of Gibbings, so to speak, was therefore cast in the mould of Johnston and Cobden-Sanderson. Gill and Gibbings first knew of each other in March 1920 as founding members (with Rooke, Philip Hagreen, Lucien Pissarro, and others) of the Society of Wood Engravers. They both exhibited in the Society's first exhibition at the Chenil Gallery in Chelsea in November of that year.

But more propitious was 1924, when Gill's friendship with Hilary Pepler in Ditchling broke down. Gill put it frankly in his *Autobiography* (page 210): 'I fled from the beloved Ditchling of my childhood and found refuge in a hidden valley in the Black Mountains'. With his move to Capel-y-ffin, an abandoned Benedictine monastery in the Ewyas valley in mid-Wales, Gill stopped wood engraving for the S. Dominic's Press forever. He acquired his own printing press and began to print wood engravings for himself. It was in this new situation, in 1924, that Gibbings and Gill became close personal friends.[23]

Also, in 1924, Gibbings bought and took over the direction of the Golden Cockerel Press. The immediate casualty of Gill's departure from Ditchling was Pepler's intention to print Enid Clay's *Sonnets and Verses* at the St. Dominic's Press. The first thing Gibbings did was to rescue that book. Gibbings' and Gill's creative ventures as book artists started because they were brought together by its publication in 1925. Gill provided six wood-engraved illustrations—soon to be praised by the Double Crown Club.

The Golden Cockerel Press had been started by Harold Midgely Taylor in 1920 and named after Diaghilev's ballet, *Le Coq d'Or*.[24] By a significant coincidence, Taylor and his wife had learned about printing by spending part of that year with Hilary Pepler at the S. Dominic's Press on Ditchling Common—where he may have met Gill. The Golden Cockerel Press was located at Taylor's home, Elms Cottage, in the village of Waltham St Lawrence, in Berkshire, where it remained after Robert Gibbings took it over. Gibbings rethought its purpose, making it a private press that was more concerned with 'the aesthetic than the commercial aspect of book production'. Gibbing's preference was for books illustrated with wood engravings and printed, therefore, letterpress and on hand-made paper. Furthermore, his preference was for Caslon Old Face type, a stock of which he had bought with the Press, though he no doubt extended its range. Gibbings then continued a tradition which had been inherited by Taylor from Hilary Pepler at the St. Dominic's Press.

Pepler, in his turn, had freely acknowledged that his typography owed much to Johnston. In his teaching portfolio, *Manuscript and Inscription Letters,* Johnston had championed the Caslon type design which had first been revived by Morris and Walker. And, as if to complete the circle of coincidence, it was Gill who had engraved the Caslon alphabet for Johnston's portfolio. Gibbings appreciated that a refined boldness in wood engraving suited the Caslon design, just as Pepler had done at the S. Dominic's Press.

It stood to reason, therefore, that Gill and Gibbings shared that aesthetic of book design developed at the Central School by the three mentors—Johnston, Rooke and John Mason. Legibility of type, combined with a Carolingian harmony of margin ratios and clarity of layout, were its hallmark. Caslon type apart, these had already been put into practice at the Doves Press. To this Gill and Gibbings now added wood engraving. Gill called this combination the 'making of a collation'.[25] There is a striking similarity among the various statements they made about this subject. These were voiced in a number of statements between 1920 and 1957, and are traced below. They show that Gill (with Gibbings) brought strongly held pre-conceptions to *The Canterbury Tales* project that precluded him from illustrating slavishly the Chaucer text. He was an independent-minded player.

Gill first outlined his ideas about wood engraving in 1920 when he announced in *The Architect* the formation of the Society of Wood Engravers. He stressed the antipathy of wood engraving to the 'imitation of nature' and its value, therefore, to decorate, rather than illustrate, with line:

> Membership of the Society is confined to those who use the European method of wood engraving. This method, distinguished from the Japanese…method by the fact that prints are obtained by means of the printing press, is more suitable to the tradition and temperament of European artists, and is of greater utility in connection with book production and decoration.
>
> Decoration (a word formerly prefixed by the word 'mere') is now returning to its right place at the head of artistic activities. In a decoration the artist is forced to consider the actual beauty of his work, and only secondly the beauty of the story or scene depicted. And as the bootmaker, however useful he may be as a voter, is as a workman primarily a maker of footwear, so the artist, however useful he may be as a storyteller, is, as an artist, primarily a maker of things of beauty and not of sentiment.
>
> The modern world has been led to attach an absurd beauty to mere representation, and to judge all works from a mere imitation of natural form. There is, however, at the present time, by the mercy of God, a tendency to realise again the intrinsic value of works of art as opposed to their extrinsic or sentimental value, and, in this matter, wood engraving is especially valuable, from [sic] the exact imitation of nature, which, in paint or etching is comparatively easy and natural, is, in wood engraving, both difficult and unnatural. The wood engraver is forced by his material to have some respect for the thing in itself and to place an absolute value upon the art of drawing.[26]

In 1920, Gill also wrote the introduction to John Ralph Beedham's handbook, *Wood-Engraving*, published by Pepler at his S. Dominic's Press). Gill pours vitriol over corrupting social relations: 'The factory system is a servile system in which personal responsibility is denied.' Commercial 'line' block engraving, Gill held, is part of this system. Autograph wood engraving, by contrast, 'places responsibility upon the shoulders of the workman. The workman who draws, engraves and prints his own blocks is master of the situation.' But Gill then turns to a new notion: the specificity of engraving. It is a necessarily detached medium, even abstract. Here Gill is closer to Gibbings, though Gill doesn't yet consider type:

...wood engraving forces upon the workman some respect for the thing in itself and makes it impossible for him to place a merely relative value upon the art of drawing. Mere likeness to nature is much more easily achieved by drawing, whether in line or wash, on paper. The graver and the wood both of them make their own demands and make mere imitation of nature almost impossible. The workman is compelled to consider his work primarily as an engraving and only secondarily as a representation.... He must be prepared to start with the wood and the graver and his sense of what is beautiful in itself and not strain after effects.... A zig-zag pattern such as a child would engrave is better than the most expert imitation of a sunset.[27]

In 1923 the new Society of Wood Engravers organised a talk at the Art Workers' Guild on the theme of 'The Relation of Typography to Woodcuts and Wood Engravings in Book Decorations', with which Gill, no doubt, was closely involved. Its title indicates the focus which Gill was developing, though no record survives of what was actually said.

In 1927 Gibbings wrote a piece, 'The Golden Cockerel Press', for the first issue of *Woodcut*, a new magazine devoted to wood engraving and edited by Herbert Furst. Gibbings had just finished the *Song of Songs* with Gill, and they were embarking on Chaucer's *Troilus and Creseyde*. Gibbings agreed with Gill about the specificity of wood engraving but now began to theorise about the image in relation to the type. The weight, style, and 'colour' of the type (its overall lightness, or greyness, or darkness on the page) are what Gibbings newly—and usefully—calls the 'unit of texture':

> The artists who design for the Press are chosen on account of their work considered as Art.... They are encouraged to work in close touch with the compositors, and many of them spend days at the Press while their books are being printed.... It is paradoxical that wood engravings, which are pre-eminently suitable as book decoration, should today be the most difficult of illustrations to combine with type; and this is the fault of the artists, and in many cases the critics....
>
> If engravings are to harmonise with type, they must in some way approximate to its fusion. Wood engravings for books are not ends in themselves, they are ornaments for the Book, and on this account a more rigorous discipline on the part of the artist is necessary. Very few contemporary engravers have considered what may be known as the unit of texture....
>
> Type when properly printed requires a very nicely adjusted quantity of ink per square inch: a fraction too much, and it fills up; a fraction too little and it prints grey. It must be obvious that a block set amongst type must, for success, approximate to the texture of the type, otherwise one or other must suffer in printing—there is need that the unit of texture [of the wood-block]

should in some degree approach the unit of texture of the type. A few coarse lines left standing on the block may print well with small types, but they will not look well. Something of the relationship of the thick and the thin of type must be observed in the block. One might almost suggest that it would be a good rule only to use gravers of a size which might conceivably have been used for engraving the type, but that is perhaps a little severe. An entirely successful example of harmony between blocks and type may well be found in Mr. Gill's engravings for the *Song of Songs*, recently published for the Press. Of work in hand, the two volumes which might approximate to what people call 'important' are Chaucer's *Troilus and Creseyde*, with engravings by Gill, and Lucian's *True History* decorated by the writer. In the first, the engravings are in the form of very delicate borders almost identical with the weight of the type, so that the page is of an entirely even texture picked out here and there with the accents of rubrication and coloured initials'.[28]

In 1929, Gill's friend, Douglas Cleverdon, published a volume, *Engravings by Eric Gill: A Selection*. Gill wrote a lengthy preface in which he anticipates the very issues with which his critics took exception when *The Canterbury Tales* came out: namely, his 'formal' and 'objective' (as opposed to 'naturalistic') figure drawing and the 'collation' of image and type. Gill's claim is the Johnstonian one that, first, there is a 'thing' to make. Only then may it be art:

> When I started wood engraving in 1906 or 1907, it was for the sake of lettering…. The problem presented itself to me not at all as a problem of how to get things like 'nature', but how to get them to 'go with' type. Whatever may be said of my earlier wood engravings [those for *Sonnets and Verses* by Enid Clay, 1926] as being too black to go with the type, it remains that they are in nature typographical. A printed letter is a thing and a wood engraving is a thing and not a representation of a thing…. I am not saying here that what is called naturalism is necessarily inimical to art. I am saying simply that as a wood engraver I have…never been concerned with it…. A technically expert lettercutter and engraver of lettering—hating the accidental and undecided—I could not bring myself, when it came to the human figure, to 'go in for effects'. If I had to carve an eye, it must be a real stone eye all there, and not something which, at a certain distance, looked like an eye— moreover it must be an eye which went with the lettering—it must be, so to say, a letter eye. However naturalistic I set out to be willy nilly the material and the occasion (the wood and the book) led me to the formal and the objective….[29]

In 1934 Gill wrote another, shorter, preface to a follow-up volume of prints published by Faber & Faber called *Engravings 1928-33, by Eric Gill*, quoted from earlier. It responds unflinchingly to the criticism levelled at *The Canterbury Tales* (and *The Four Gospels* of 1931):

Some critics have complained that my engravings are cold & unemotional, lacking in the warmth of human affection. Others have complained that I make no distinction between what is suitable to accompany the poetry of Chaucer & what is suitable for the decoration of a book of the Gospels—that I have no sense of history or illustration.

As to my lack of emotional display I think that the business of wood engraving is very much like the business of typography. I think tenderness and warmth in such things are not to be looked at except in the workman- ship. You do not want the designer of printing types to wear his heart on his sleeve—my engravings are, I admit, only a kind of printer's flowers.

As to my lack of historical sense: it is true I have none. The world is the same for me—today, yesterday, tomorrow—there is neither ancient nor modern.

In fact, it seems to me, to act Hamlet in Elizabethan costumes is to degrade Shakespeare to the level of a sort of journalism. To build 'gothic' churches in the 20th century is to make religion a pastime for leisure; and to make for the Gospels a different sort of picture than you would make for Chaucer or James Joyce is as foolish as having one code of morals for Saturday and another for Sunday, one code for men and another for women. Lettering that is right for the closet is right for the cloister; both are holy or neither are.[30]

In 1939 a discussion took place between Gill and Herbert Furst about the printing of 'black line' wood engraving (defined in footnote 4). Touching on this, some lines of Gill's letter to Furst read:

In conjunction with letter press it seems clear there is a good reason [for black line engraving] namely that the letter press surface and the engraving surface are of the same nature and therefore give the printer a straightfor- ward homogeneous job—in fact the engraving is part of the typography.[31]

Gibbings' article, 'Memories of Eric Gill', is the fullest account he left of their working relationship. Printed in the *Book Collector* in 1953, the article distinguished between an earlier and a later phase of their working together. Though Gibbings focuses on *The Four Gospels*, he makes it clear that he is speaking equally of *The Canterbury Tales*:

In the printing of *Sonnets and Verses* [by Enid Clay] there was little that could be called planning between artist and printer. The author sent me her manuscript, Eric sent me his blocks, and I put them together as best I could; and in the books that followed soon after, such as *The Song of Songs* and *The Passion*, decorated for me by Gill, there was not close co-operation that came later.... In none of these volumes was there any real marriage of wood and metal. The blocks and the type had little more than a brotherly-sisterly relationship; that is to say the designing and cutting of the wood did not await the setting of the type. Apart from the title pages of *The Canterbury Tales*, there was little of the ideal partnership that was achieved in *The Four Gospels*.

Eric Gill was the perfect collaborator. He was always ready to accept a suggestion, as he was always capable of carrying it to a wonderful fruition....

Those were idyllic days. It was my boast then, and I am still happy to think of it, that I never had a formal agreement with an artist or an author who worked for me, and I never had a disagreement. With Eric in particular the collaboration worked smoothly. He was tremendously conscientious about delivery, and when he gave me a date for a block I could answer the postman's knock on that particular morning with the assurance that there would be put into my hand a parcel addressed in Eric's precise calligraphy.[32]

In 'Thoughts on Wood' written in 1957 for *The Saturday Book*, Gibbings reminisced rather than theorised. The craft of wood engraving, as taught by Noel Rooke, '...provided a discipline of thought'. Gibbings realised that '...slowly a love of the wood came upon me'. He dwells further on the nature of the engraver's line and its natural bias towards decoration. His view of his own wood engraving as achieving a balance of illustration and decoration could, perhaps, pass as a description of Gill's own:

I began to appreciate the cleanness of the white line that [the graver] incised: even the simplest silhouettes had an austere quality, a dignity, that could not be achieved by other means. Clear precise statement, that was what it amounted to. I began with simple patterns of black and white, trying to co-ordinate them, as it were in terms of music.... A world of rich textures awoke under my hand!

Now, with the years, I incline to austerity of outline in combination with formalised texture. I would like my engravings to partake somewhat of the quality of the low relief stone carvings from Assyria in the British Museum: illustration and decoration combined to perfection within the limits of their medium—'near enough' to realism as illustration, as decoration 'just right'.[33]

Gill's Wood Engravings for *The Canterbury Tales*: An Appraisal

Gill started the wood engravings for *The Canterbury Tales* in mid-1927 and finished them in November 1930. But in fact many of the border designs were re-used from those he had already engraved for *Troilus and Creseyede*. Work began for these at Capel-y-ffin. A letter Gill wrote to Desmond Chute (his friend and fellow Catholic from

Ditchling) on 11 March 1927 mentions: 'I am getting on with the *Troilus* blocks. But it is a long job. About sixty different borders to do! as well as 5 full-page pictures and some initials.'[34] Another letter to Chute on 10 June 1928 shows the new commission to be well under way:

> Frightfully busy doing engravings for *Canty. Tales*. Yes, I can do engravings on my own of course, but G.C.P. is the only press, & I am to give them the refusal of other engravings. Item: Denis [Tegetmeier] v. well & helping me scorp *Canty. Tales* bks.'[35]

Work continued when Gill stayed at Salies-de-Béarn, France, during 1928. In October 1928 he moved to Pigotts, near High Wycombe in Buckinghamshire—and not far from Gibbings at Waltham St. Lawrence—where most of Gill's work was done.[36] Considerable help in the donkey-work of scorping the woodblocks was given him by his friend, Ralph John Beedham.[37] Gill had his drawings transferred photographically to the blocks by T.N. Lawrence.[38]

The fact that many border engravings were recycled from *Troilus and Creseyde* is indication enough that Gill conceived them to be decorative. So, too, is his repetition of fresh engravings executed especially for the Tales. (Each image is used approximately two or three times through six hundred and sixty-seven pages.) The imagery is not determined by Chaucer's poem. Rather, its function is to frame the text areas on the page. Being verse, the lines are necessarily uneven on the right-hand side. In typographic terms this is 'unjustified' type, or 'ranged ragged right'. (This convention was recommended by Gill in his *Essay on Typography* for all typesetting since it enabled an evenness of the word spacing which would otherwise be compromised.) Gill's border decorations of the margins on the right-hand pages are closely tailored to the text area. In his article, 'Memories of Eric Gill', Gibbings recalled that the typeset proofs of the text were sent to Gill, who then designed the engravings to match. The guiding principle, it seems, was for the gauge of the engraved line to match the 18 point size of the type. Gibbings spoke of 'very delicate borders almost identical with the weight of the type.' This was his notion of the 'unit of texture' put into practice. Initially it was envisaged that these lines would be engraved in copper, a skill with which Gill had recent experience through his making the illustrations for the Golden Cockerel Press edition of *Procreant Hymn*, by Powys Mathers (1926). This idea gave way, however, to wood engravings.

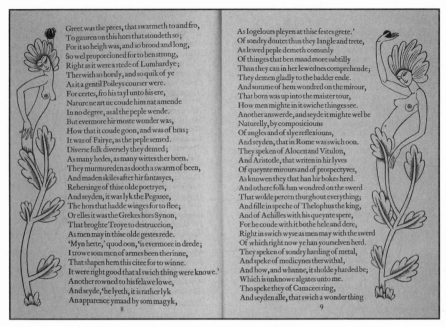

Fig. 8 - Eric Gill, Squieres Tale

Gill's organising principle is masterful. A leafy stem, heraldic-like, is allotted to each page, rising up the height of the text. (Figs. 8-10). The different shapes of the text areas prompted many variations in these designs. Moreover, the stems, with their leaves and fruits, are also varied though they have no particular botanical identity. They flow from page to page to support a whole theatre of figures which either recline on, cling to, or spring from this foliage.These figures are reminiscent of an illuminated medieval text but only in a general sense. Gill possibly recalled medieval sculptures or the wood-carved misericords he had formerly seen in the cathedrals he visited at Chichester, Chartres and elsewhere.

Gill depicts a *comédie humaine* of figures which are historical and mythological, religious and fanciful and which are presented in a range of poses and combinations. Paired figures face each other across the pages: a Pan-figure clinging to a stem is opposite a winged dragon; a horse rears opposite its rider; two snakes oppose each other; there are two pairs of lovers, one set vertically on the stems, the other set within its fork; two naked female figures metamorphose from the foliage. Elsewhere there is no correspondence at all: a bishop is opposite a cock and a hen with chicks; a clothed crouching skeleton is opposite a tunic-clad figure with a pipe. Other figures are not twinned. There is a solitary king figure. Elsewhere there are three hanged men.

All these figures are medievalised in a general way, too. Their accoutrements (including clothing, headgear, footwear, coiffures) vaguely signal Chaucer's period, as do their weapons and tools and goblets. Gill's inventiveness is not unlike the playfulness displayed by medieval scribes in their illuminated manuscripts. The figures are variously droll, graceful, vivacious, pathetic, sensual, or erotic. Randomly interspersed among them are stems supporting different animals: two kinds of ape, for example, or different kinds of birds—a dove, a swallow—and two kinds of fox. Vignettes from life are played out in these borders, though not in the manner of Chaucer's text.

In 1927, John Rothenstein, Director of the Tate Gallery, made what amounted to an anticipated critique of these border designs (though he was actually referring to *Troilus and Creseyde*), saying that they are 'infinitely remote from the spirit of Chaucer'.[39] At times, Gill appears almost to have lost interest in the commission, for some of his designs are slight, even perfunctory. (A case in point is his title page for the Tale of Sir Topas in Book Two.) One wonders whether Gill read the entire *Canterbury Tales*. But what escaped Rothenstein's gaze is Gill's primary concern and his greatest strength—the typographical integrity of the double page spread of printed text.

Fig. 9 - Eric Gill, Squieres Tale

Fig. 10 - Eric Gill, Squieres Tale

Gill rings the changes on the inexorable task he gave himself with the border decorations by using a range of graphic devices. One plays on the mass of black and white contained within the imagery, set cleverly against the tonal range of the density of the type on the page—its 'weight' or 'colour'. Gill devised three variations to achieve this interplay. Some of Gill's border decorations lighten the page by his use of essentially white figures. (Fig. 8). Others, by contrast, give more weight to the page with figures printed in black silhouette. (Fig. 9). And others achieve a combination of these two. (Fig. 10). A dialectic is thus set up which alternated the predominance of either black or white, but which Gill invariably resolved by restoring a balance between them. Overall, the mass of black of the wood engravings equates with the density of the type. This balancing may have been intuitive on Gill's part. It is possible, however, that he made this equality a desideratum on account of the earlier response from the printers at The Golden Cockerel Press that his engravings (for *Sonnets and Verses*) were too black to go with the type.

Gill addressed this issue. In 1924 he wrote to his sister, Enid Clay, explaining that his view of wood engraving encompassed more than just the text. 'You see, engravings are as much a part of *book making* as of *illustration*. They don't merely illustrate the text, they also decorate the book. Therefore the engraver and printer must be one firm'.[40]

Gibbings indicated that such collaboration with Gill began only with the twenty-six title pages which introduce the Tales. One senses that Gill was somewhat better motivated in this work, which was less unrelenting. The title pages are compositionally similar to the border decoration, but they also incorporate the lettering of the text. In most of the half-page designs Gill opted to link a capital letter of the text with a figure from the illustration or with the stem's foliage that encompassed it. (Figs. 11a-e). Its effect is to stabilise the illustration on the page, the flatness of which is thereby reinforced. (Gill was to bring this device to heights of virtuosity in *The Four Gospels* of 1931.) Never is the reader's eye drawn into the illusion of a space beyond the page's surface in which a scene takes place. Gill's designs are diametrically opposed to that mode of *trompe l'oeil* illustration in which the book artists of fifteenth-century Italy so excelled—their vellum pages opening up into distant vistas. Neither does Gill emulate the kind of perspectival box stage spaces in which Burne-Jones locates many of his illustrations for the Kelmscott *Chaucer*. The physicality of the page and its purpose to convey type is never compromised. This is the enduring principle—and the consummate achievement - of Gill's designs for a trio of Golden Cockerel Press books—*The Canterbury Tales,* with *Troilus and Creseyde* as its precursor and *The Four Gospels* as its glorious successor.

This priority is upheld by Gill's approach to the imagery of his twenty-six title pages. As is to be expected, these relate specifically to the story line of the Tales and come closer, therefore, to decorative illustration. Nevertheless, Gill eschews the portrayal of the dramatic details from the Tales in preference for more general representation. His scenes are low key. They lead us into the story rather than show their *dénouement*. In this way he avoids recourse to those pictorial devices usually associated with drama—striking perspectives, for example, or unusual angles of view, or contrasting lighting and modelling, all of which tend to rupture the flatness of the page. Gill's continued use of the enveloping foliage motif reinforces this strategy.

A telling example occurs immediately with the title page of The Prologue. (Fig. 12). Gill opts to show Thomas à Becket's murder in Canterbury Cathedral, even though Chaucer does not write of this at all. In spite of his skill in topographical drawing, Gill avoids both the gore of the act and the spot in the cathedral where it took place. Instead, he shows the quiet moments prior to the deed. The knight-assassins, wearing tunics reminiscent of ancient Rome, stand in a

Fig. 11a   *Fig. 11b*   *Fig. 11c*

rhythmic frieze. Their swords are poised at an angle above their shoulders, echoing exactly the angle of their empty scabbards. A graphic, abstract pattern prevails. The scene is devoid of dark purpose. In short, Gill has sidestepped expectations of text, creating instead a static, decorative tableau. Moreover, while the figures are in profile, there is no illusion of depth. And, as in so many of his border decorations, the distribution of white and black in the figures balances the density of the type that occupies the lower part of the page.

A second instance where Gill uses a low-key approach, so as not to detract from the text on the page, will suffice. The Nonne Prestes Tale from Book Two tells the story of a chanticleer. Lured by a fox hidden in the cabbage patch, he drops his guard and is caught, but contrives his own release (Fig. 13). Like many of Chaucer's Tales, this one has an allegorical purpose. But instead of presenting the drama of the chanticleer's capture, or even his subsequent escape, Gill has chosen to

Figs. 11a to 11e -

Examples of Gill's initial letters from Canterbury Tales

Fig. 11d   *Fig. 11e*

The text within the illustration reads:

And palmers for to seken straunge strondes
To ferne halwes, couthe in sondry londes;
And specially, from every shires ende
Of Engelond, to Caunterbury they wende,
The holy blisful martir for to seke,
That hem hath holpen, whan that they were seke.
Bifel that, in that seson on a day,
In Southwerk at the Tabard as I lay
Redy to wenden on my pilgrimage
To Caunterbury with ful devout corage,
At night was come into that hostelrye
Wel nyne and twenty in a companye,
Of sondry folk, by aventure yfalle
In felawshipe, and pilgrims were they alle,
That toward Caunterbury wolden ryde;
The chambres and the stables weren wyde,
And wel we weren esed atte beste.
And shortly, whan the sonne was to reste,
So hadde I spoken with hem everichon,
That I was of hir felawshipe anon,
And made forward erly for to ryse,
To take our wey, ther as I yow devyse.
But natheles, whyl I have tyme and space,
Er that I ferther in this tale pace,
Me thinketh it acordaunt to resoun,
To telle yow al the condicioun
Of ech of hem, so as it semed me,
And whiche they weren, and of what degree;
And eek in what array that they were inne:
And at a knight than wol I first biginne.
3

WHAN that Aprille with his shoures sote
The droghte of Marche hath perced to the rote,
And bathed every veyne in swich licour,
Of which vertu engendred is the flour;
Whan Zephirus eek with his swete breeth
Inspired hath in every holt and heeth
The tendre croppes, and the yonge sonne
Hath in the Ram his halfe cours yronne,
And smale fowles maken melodye,
That slepen al the night with open ye,
So priketh hem nature in hir corages:
Than longen folk to goon on pilgrimages
2

Fig. 12 - Eric Gill, Second title page of Prologue

show the opening of the story. The chanticleer is crowing on his perch before his mistress and her two daughters. The scene has a benign charm, and the design is straightforward, decorative, even banal.

Elsewhere Gill shows another aspect of his graphic inventiveness. The rendering of The Man of Lawes Tale in Book Two is perhaps the crowning achievement of his designs for *The Canterbury Tales*. (Fig. 14). The story concerns Constance, the Christian daughter of the Roman Emperor, who is cast out by her husband from Syria in an open boat to wander the high seas. Like Burne-Jones in the Kelmscott *Chaucer*, Gill shows her in the boat, but instead of carrying a crucifix, she cradles her child in her arms. The child appears only later in the Tale, so again Gill has taken licence in his rendition by giving his illustration a Catholic—in truth, a Marian—overtone.[41] This scene is an excellent example of Gill's running with the natural propensity of wood engraving for line. The fusion of the curved timbers of the boat with the swirling waves of the sea and with the surrounding decorative foliage is artistically intense and convincing. They intertwine to form a homogenous and decorative design in which the sea has no horizon and thus the picture plane has no recession. Moreover, it is hooked by one of the leaves into the initial letter O of the text, confirming its presence on the surface. Gill's illustration is emblematic rather than realistic. And like the title page for The Prologue, the disposition of white and black balances the density of the type. By these devices, as usual, the integrity of the page is maintained.

Gill handles the problem of perspective equally adroitly wherever he portrays buildings or other structures. Just two examples, The Reves Tale from Book One and the Monkes Tale from Book Two, will suffice. In the Reves Tale (Fig. 15), Gill shows the baby's cradle, which has been misplaced by the mischievous apprentice in front of his own bed. But Gill avoids the trap of foreshortening the bed, and therefore the illusion of depth, by presenting the scene frontally. Both ends of the bed (with the cradle at its foot) are in virtually the same plane. The figures themselves—the two apprentices, the cheating miller and his love-lorn wife—are equally flat. Dressed in diaphanous robes they appear almost transparent. The surrounding foliage and the hooking device also emphasise that the illustration is on the same plane as the printed text. In the Monkes Tale (Fig. 16) Gill has chosen the scene of Samson's destruction of the temple. Again, the architecture is depicted frontally, with Samson astride the narrowest of picture planes set between two rows of pillars.

Fig. 13 - Eric Gill, Nonnes Prestes Tale

The dreynte Leander for his Erro;
The teres of Eleyne, and eek the wo
Of Brixseyde, and of thee, Ladomea;
The crueltee of thee, queen Medea,
Thy litel children hanging by the hals
For thy Iason, that was of love so fals!
O Ypermistra, Penelopee, Alceste,
Your wyf hod he comendeth with the beste!
But certeinly no word ne wryteth he
Of thilke wikke ensample of Canacee,
That lovede hir owne brother sinfully;
Of swiche cursed stories I sey "fy";
Or elles of Tyro Apollonius,
How that the cursed king Antiochus
Birafte his doghter of hir maydenhede,
That is so horrible a tale for to rede,
Whan he hir threw upon the pavement.
And therfor he, of ful avysement,
Nolde never wryte in none of his sermouns
Of swiche unkinde abhominaciouns,
Ne I wol noon reherse, if that I may.
But of my tale how shal I doon this day?
Me were looth be lykned, doutelees,
To Muses that men clepe Pierides—
Metamorphoseos wot what I mene:—
But nathelees, I recche noght a bene
Though I come after him with hawe bake;
I speke in prose, and lat him rymes make.'
And with that word he, with a sobre chere,
Bigan his tale, as ye shal after here.

4

O HATEFUL harm! condicion of poverte!
With thurst, with cold, with hunger so confounded!
To asken help thee shameth in thyn herte;
If thou noon aske, with nede artow so wounded,
That verray nede unwrappeth al thy wounde hid!
Maugree thyn heed, thou most for indigence
Or stele, or begge, or borwe thy despence!

5

Fig. 14 - Eric Gill, Man of Lawes Tale

In pursuance of this ornamental naturalism, Gill in creating his wood engraved figures drew heavily on his sculptural practice, especially his work in bas-relief. In his fourteen panels of the Stations of the Cross (1913-18) for Westminster Cathedral, Gill developed a flat linear style for his figures which largely empties them of emotion.[42] These panels bring to mind again two of his statements, one from 1920 in the magazine *The Architect*, the other from 1929 in *Engravings by Eric Gill*. In the former Gill wrote, 'An artist [is] primarily a maker of things of beauty not of sentiment. The modern world has been led to attach an absurd beauty to mere representation and to judge all works from a mere imitation of natural form'.[43] And in the latter he declared, 'The problem presented itself to me...not how to get things like 'nature', but how to get them to go with type.... It remains that my [wood engravings] are in nature typographical'.[44]

Critics saw in Gill's bas-relief style a Byzantine, or an Assyrian, or an Egyptian tendency. Gill transposed this style, no doubt unconsciously, into his wood engravings. Speaking of these, Herbert Furst wrote tartly of Gill's 'persistent affectation of ascetic Byzantine mannerisms'. Yet Gill did not have any specialist knowledge of Byzantine work. To these assertions he replied:

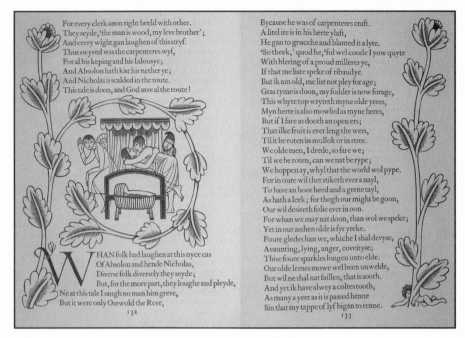

Fig. 15 - Eric Gill, Reves Tale

Fig. 16 - Eric Gill, Monkes Tale

> I gather...that it is generally supposed that I am endeavouring to imitate some bygone style. Critics always say that I am a person who attempts to be Egyptian or Syrian or something or other. That is simply not the case. I am working in the only style in which I can work. I am not a learned antiquarian who can work in any style at choice.[45]

An early example of this process is the wood engravings he made in Ditchling in 1917 from the drawings for the Stations of the Cross (with scorping by Ralph Beedham). The figures in the wood engravings are schematic and depersonalised. Here Gill also drew from his experience as a letter cutter. The stylistic connection among Gill's three forms of 'carving' is generic. His wood engravings relate conceptually to his lettering. In the Introduction to *Engravings by Eric Gill: A Selection*, he wrote:

> An apprenticeship to architecture...and years devoted to lettering...has [sic] weaned my mind from the common notion that art is primarily representation.... A printed letter is a thing; and a wood engraving is a *thing* and not a representation of a thing.... M. Maurice Denis said: 'What I ask of a painting is that it shall look like paint'....and however much a painter desires flesh, he would, it seems to me, be wrong if he made paint to look like it.[46]

Historical accuracy was not part of Gill's artistic thinking. He rationalised this view in the Preface to the collection, *Engravings 1928-1933*: 'The world is for me the same—today, yesterday and tomorrow —there is neither ancient nor modern'.[47]

In The Prologue, Chaucer provides descriptions of the pilgrims. Elsewhere, however, details about the characters are scant. Nor are those details particularly visual ones. Though Gill had little need of such information, he was, by this token, thrown back on his own devices and relied, therefore, on what was already familiar to him. Gill's papers—his diary, his *Autobiography*, his letters—say nothing of what he thought of *The Canterbury Tales*. Gill was not necessarily inspired by personal conviction about *The Canterbury Tales*; he regarded his work on this project as a jobbing commission. He simply accepted Chaucer's Christian purpose, as expressed in 'Chaucer's Retraction': 'For our Book says 'all that is written is written for our doctrine'.

Gill's detachment from the letter of the text links to his detachment from the letter of historical appearance. His title page for the Seconde Nonnes Tale, in Book Four (Fig. 17) shows the martyr, Cecilia, and her executioner in vaguely late antique (or early Roman Christian) dress, which happens to be redolent, too, of Gill's 'Byzantine or Egyptian tendency'. Conveniently, this style approximated the visual treatment he gave to the figures in his wood engravings of the Stations of the Cross. Compositionally, too, the title page is generic; its frieze-like quality relates closely to that of the title page for The Prologue (Fig. 12).

Lastly, there is the motif of the leafy stem foliage, the workhorse of both the title pages of the Tales and the page-by-page borders. It is a ubiquitous but an underrated trope of Gill's graphic resources. Not unlike the action of a current, its fluidity enabled Gill to loosen up the rigidity of the blocks of text, which are the visual *terra firma* of the Chaucer Tales, and so enliven the entire *mise en page*. The stems flow round each page and make inroads, as it were, into the margins' contours, which are left open-ended (or 'ragged') by the poem's unequal lines. They connect page-opening to page-opening, dissolving the book's underlying structures, and thus invite the reader on. This subtle undulation of the page is, it would seem, what Sister Elizabeth Brady had in mind when speaking of Gill and 'allusive' typography. The visual momentum which Gill sets up across the page openings is suggestive —subliminally, no doubt—of the flow of the narrative and also, one might conjecture, of the four days of journeying to Canterbury.

Conclusion

In the Golden Cockerel Press edition of *The Canterbury Tales*, Gill absorbed the experience of his own origins in the Arts and Crafts movement in the orbit of Johnston, Cobden-Sanderson, Count Kessler, and others of the Hammersmith craft community, and then extended his range far beyond it. He recalled in his *Autobiography* having engraved wood blocks for lettering at the outset of his career in 1904-06 for Count Kessler: 'He had a Press of his own at Weimar and I used to do engraved title-pages and initial letters for him, in fact it was largely by his encouragement...that I took up the engraving of letters on wood...'.[48]

Those pages of austere perfection which are the achievement of Kessler's Cranach Presse and Cobden-Sanderson's Doves Press now gave way to more fluid, and more engaging, structures. The *mise-en-page* of the Golden Cockerel *Canterbury Tales* is at once more dynamic and endearing. In the 'marriage of wood and metal', Gill (with Gibbings) reached, it seems, that state of 'freedom' once taught him by

Fig. 17 - Eric Gill, Seconde Nonnes Tale

Johnston. But no doubt it is the reader who is best placed to tell. Turning the pages, it is as if one can now visualise *The Canterbury Tales* as well as listen to Chaucer's telling it. The eye is fascinated. One is encouraged to linger, to explore, or to travel on. Gill, as a typographer's illustrator, evolved a fresh approach to book design which, by empathising with the text, draws the reader in.

Modernist typography discarded the established notion that the *mise en page* should be merely the vehicle to carry the text. This ideal had lingered in Britain, enshrined as a late flowering, in 1932, in Beatrice Warde's metaphor of the page as a finely-fashioned but transparent 'crystal goblet'.[49] Moving ahead, typographers in Europe came to think of the page as a visual analogue actively communicating the text. This position was implicit in Jan Tschichold's tract, *Die neue Typographie*, which burst upon the typographical world in Germany in 1928.[50] Gill, himself a free-spirited pilgrim on the journey of the *avant garde*, gave Chaucer a new, post-William Morris outlook. With *The Canterbury Tales* he established a distinctly English genre of 'conservative' Modernism.

Notes

The author of this chapter wishes to thank Ray Watkinson, Alison Wilkinson, and Geoffrey Toy for their help with reading and proofreading.

1   Eric Gill, Preface to *Engravings, 1928-1933* (London: Faber & Faber, 1934), v.

2   Letter to Herbert Furst (the editor of *Woodcut* and *Apollo*), February 1939. In *Letters of Eric Gill* (London: Jonathan Cape, 1947), 415-16.

3   Eric Gill, *An Essay on Typography* (London: Sheed and Ward, 1931). The tract was actually written in 1930.

4   It needs to be mentioned that wood engraving relies on the incisions of the graver tool to form an image on the end grain, or the cross-section, of a block of wood. This has to be hard and close-grained, and is usually boxwood—'a close-fibred material', wrote Gibbings, 'that is hard almost as metal' ('Thoughts on Wood', *Matrix* No. 9 [1989]: 8). Lines as fine as in a copper engraving can be achieved—'there is no let or hindrance from the grain', continued Gibbings. The size of the image is necessarily restricted by the relatively small size of the block, given that the girth of the boxwood tree never grows very large, perhaps six inches at maximum, though this difficulty can be overcome by joining separate blocks together—'by rite of glue or batten'. The image stands in relief, and is therefore printed by letterpress. The raised image is inked by a leather dabber or a roller, and is therefore the part which prints. The areas intended to be white are those which are cut away. When these are extensive a scorper is used, leaving 'black line' engravings, a variant which Gill used in *The Canterbury Tales*.

The woodcut pre-dates the wood engraving and is distinct from it by using the long grain, or the side of the plank of wood. The image can therefore be larger and the grain of the wood can be used as a texture in the blacks of the image. Its tool is the knife. The woodcut is, needless to say, a letterpress process.

5   Quotation from Eric Gill, 'The Artist and Book Production', with editorial comment by John Bidwell. *Fine Print* 8, no. 3 (1982): 96 et seq. Francis Meynell was especially put out by Gill's mindset, by then somewhat behind the times. Using Morris' own simile, he also saw himself as 'an architect of books not a builder'. His Nonesuch Press, he believed, entirely lived up to Gill's criterion of 'art'—and at prices that a widening circle of people could afford.

No doubt to the bewilderment of Francis Meynell, Gill's avowed belief in the value of making things by hand was matched by an increasing involvement in industrial design. Imaginative new projects in this field compelled him forward. Thus, while pontificating in 1926 before the Double Crown Club on the shortcomings of commercialism, he was by that date already well engaged in commercial work, of a sort, for the Monotype Corporation, typefounders. Monotype invited him to provide two type designs for their new type-composing machine. Overcoming his diffidence, he accepted the Monotype challenge; the two typefaces, Perpetua and

Gill Sans, are among his most enduring monuments. And not so far in the future, in 1930, Gill was to set up with his son-in-law, René Hague, at Pigotts, as a commercially-based printer-publisher. (Hague had learned printing by working at The Golden Cockerel Press). Using hand-operated presses, 'Hague and Gill, Printers' applied to their job printing the principles that Gill expounded in his celebrated manifesto, *An Essay on Typography*.

6   Eric Gill, *Autobiography* (London: Jonathan Cape, 1940), 118-31 and 130-132.

7   The Caslon type design is classified as 'Old Face', the provenance of which goes back to French designs of the sixteenth century. It is essentially calligraphic, with even swelling curves of its letterforms—unlike the contrast of thick and thin strokes which characterise the 'modern' designs, such as Didot, of the nineteenth century. For this reason it was favoured by Edward Johnston, as a calligrapher. Its excellence, to his mind, precluded the necessity to design a new typeface.

8   Elizabeth A. Brady, *Eric Gill: Twentieth Century Book Designer* (Metuchen, NJ: Scarecrow Press, 1974).

9   *Writing & Illuminating, & Lettering* (London: John Hogg, 1906), and many editions thereafter.

10 Johnston quoted from William Morris and Emery Walker, 'Printing' in *Arts and Crafts Essays* (London: Rivington, Percival and Co., 1893 and later editions), 111, et seq.

11 This revivalist inspiration (rather than imitation) also affected Johnston and became an essential part of his teaching. In his Preface to *Writing & Illuminating, & Lettering* (page xvi) he wrote: 'Developing, or rather re-developing, an art involves *the tracing in one's own experience of a process resembling its past development*'.

12 'Qualifications and Experience of Noel Rooke', cited in Justin Howes, 'Noel Rooke: the Early Years', *Matrix* 3 (1985): 118-125. Also in E. Johnston, *Lessons in Formal Writing*, ed. Heather Child and Justin Howes (London: Lund Humphries, 1986), 88. The manuscript is in private hands.

13 Noel Rooke made one other significant, if small, contribution. Johnston's chapter called '"Design" in Illumination' incorporates a note by Rooke referring to Bewick: 'The intricacies of a natural scene (...after Bewick) may be simplified when rendered in such a simple medium as pen drawings.... Students should practise themselves by translating figs. 132, 133 [the Bewick illustrations] into fine Quill-pen drawings.—(N. R.)'. In *Writing & Illuminating, & Lettering*, page 227.

14 Johnston's workbooks. The Craft Study Collection and Archive, Surrey Institute of Art and Design University College, Farnham campus, Johnston Archive.

[15] Eric Gill's diary. MS. at the William Andrews Clark Memorial Library, University of California at Los Angeles and a microfiche copy at Tate Britain. Additionally, in November 1906 Johnston gave a lecture at the Leicester Municipal School of Art when he encouraged students to do wood engravings for book illustration, rather than rely on 'process' zincography, saying: 'I commend wood engraving to you for its simplicity & its direct educational value... you will find that the wood and the graver will teach you at once things about form that are new to you and wonderful....' In E. Johnston, *Lessons in Formal Writing*, 96-7.

[16] N. Rooke, *Woodcuts and Wood Engravings* (London: Print Collector's Club, 1926), 11. (The diagrams are Rooke's figures 3, 5, and 6, on pages 28-29.)

[17] 'Qualifications and Experience of Noel Rooke', cited in Justin Howes. 'Noel Rooke: the Early Years', *Matrix* 3 (1985): 122. The MS. is in private hands. Rooke's memoir further confirms his link to Johnston: 'After learning all I could about wood-engraving and process reproduction I concluded that wood-engraving offered the best means of book decoration and illustration for the future, but on condition that it was done from a new point of view.' *Matrix* 3 (1985): 122.

By 'dead craft' Rooke was referring to two aspects of the same commercial problem. In the post-Bewick period, wood engraving was used for the 'facsimile' reproduction of illustrations prepared by artists - and soon by photographers - for burgeoning newspapers and magazines, of which *The Penny Magazine* and *The Illustrated London News* were examples. While there were undoubted masters of this craft, during the period 1850-90 it degenerated into a routine of lifeless copying, due in part to the demand for engravers outstripping their supply of skill. The 'death' was compounded further by the arrival of photo-mechanical 'process' engraving which rendered the wood engraver redundant. But even when so employed, as Noel Rooke's lecture of 1925 so devastatingly shows, the devices natural to the artist's pen could not be translated faithfully by the graver. Rooke cited the artist's practice of modelling by cross hatching: '... this makes the whole mental process of engraving black line different from that of drawing it. The draughtsman with pen and brush who draws naturally will make a drawing that engraves unnaturally. From the point of view of vitality, the facsimile engraving is doomed before it is begun.' N. Rooke, *Woodcuts and Wood Engravings*, 21-22.

[18] N. Rooke, *Woodcuts and Wood Engravings*, 25 (quote in text) and 27 (indented quote).

[19] Eric Gill, *Autobiography*, 179.

[20] In approximately 1911 Gill engraved a bookplate made to a design by Johnston for Pepler's son, Steven. In 1913 a letter from Johnston to Count Kessler includes a request that Kessler send wood engraving tools to his sister, adding: 'I should have sent her mine, but that I have lent most of them to Gill.' Letter dated 25 November 1913 held at the University Library, Cambridge. Cited in Christopher Skelton, *Eric Gill: The Engravings* (London: Herbert Press, 1990): 14, Footnote 9. In 1915, Gill

engraved a logo of a hog and wheatsheaf for Pepler's *A Statement of Aims* of his Hampshire House Workshops. In 1915 Pepler commissioned Gill to do twelve wood-engraved illustrations for his social satire, *The Devil's Devices, or Control versus Service*. Printed at the Westminster Press, it is an early sign of the emergent new school of English wood engraving. Pepler also published in 1915 the two other related books of this trilogy, William Cobbett's *Cottage Economy* and Johnston's *A Carol and other Rhymes*, both of which had Gill wood engravings, though of diagrams rather than illustrations.

21 Eric Gill, Diary. MS. at the William Andrews Clark Memorial Library, University of California at Los Angeles and a microfiche copy at Tate Britain.

22 Eric Gill, *Emblems*. Printed in Ditchling by Douglas Pepler and Eric Gill on the Feast of the Purification, 1916.

23 Their relationship has been explored by Fiona McCarthy in her biography Eric Gill: *A Lover's Quest for Art and God* (London: Faber & Faber, 1988) and in her article, 'Gill and Gibbings: Arcady in Berkshire', *Matrix 9* (Winter 1989): 27 et seq. Her point that the sensual, indeed homosexual, joy of the friendship between Gill and Gibbings flowed into Gill's illustrations is more applicable to *Song of Songs* of 1925 than to *The Canterbury Tales* of 1929-31, by which time the relationship had calmed. Gill wrote of Gibbings in a letter to Desmond Chute, dated 5 May 1926, as 'the dearest creature ever known', while also recording in his diary the ménage à trois involving Gibbings' wife, Moira. In the letter to Desmond Chute Gill refers to the engravings for the *Song of Songs* and mentions, bawdily, 'Robt. Gibbings (Golden Cock! Press)'.

24 Taylor's idea was for young authors without publishers to use the press to do their own printing co-operatively under his direction. But in due course he had to engage Arthur Cooper as pressman and Frank Young and Harry Gibbs as compositors. The printing methods at the Golden Cockerel Press in Gibbings' day were recorded in detail by Albert Cooper. See A.C.Cooper, 'Notes on the Printing Methods of the Golden Cockerel Press' in Christopher Sandford's article, 'A Note on the Golden Cockerel Type', *Matrix* 2 (1982): 19-22. The following few sentences are a summary of his account. A Columbian hand-press was used for proofing sheets to check the copy and for proof printing engravings. A heavy Phoenix platen press, power operated, was used to print the books. The hand-made Bachelor paper was dampened overnight and flattened in a copying press, prior to printing. The books were bound by Sangorski & Sutcliffe in London. Cooper's account goes on to explain that from 1931 Gibbings also used the Golden Cockerel typeface, designed by Gill and cast by the Caslon type foundry, especially for the Press. Christopher Sandford, who bought the Press in 1932 on its financial collapse in the Depression and who largely compiled its bibliographies, wrote of the typeface: 'The "Golden Cockerel" type undoubtedly fulfilled Gill's intention for it to combine most charmingly with surface printing from wood-blocks'. Christopher Sandford, 'A Note on the Golden Cockerel Type', *Matrix* 2 (1982): 24.

[25] 'In fact the only thing I have ever gone in for with complete and undiluted enthusiasm is the making of a collation—the putting of things together in what seem to me their proper places....' *Engravings by Eric Gill: A Selection.* (Bristol: Douglas Cleverdon, 1929. Printed for Douglas Cleverdon in London by the Fanfare Press, 1929), 1.

[26] Eric Gill, 'The Society of Wood Engravers', *The Architect* 104 (1920): 300.

[27] E. Gill, Introduction to R.J. Beedham, *Wood-Engraving* (Ditchling: S. Dominic's Press, 1920), re-appearing in *Art Nonsense.* (London: Cassell & Co., 1929), 100. Gill's interest, nevertheless, in commercial 'line' block engraving is reflected in his *Autobiography* (pages 160-61, footnote 1), where he recounts a description told to him by a sculptor-modeller, Stirling Lee, of a process engraver's workshop in St. John's Wood, London, in the 1860s.

[28] Robert Gibbings, 'The Golden Cockerel Press', *Woodcut* No. 1 (1927): 13 et seq.

[29] E. Gill, Introduction, *Engravings by Eric Gill: A Selection*, 4 et seq.

[30] Eric Gill, Preface to *Engravings, 1928-33.* (London: Faber and Faber 1934), v-vi.

[31] *Letters of Eric Gill*, (23rd February 1939). Edited by Walter Shewring. (London Jonathan Cape, 1947), 415.

[32] Robert Gibbings, 'Memories of Eric Gill', *The Book Collector* 2. No. 2 (1953): 95 et seq.

[33] Robert Gibbings, 'Thoughts on Wood', *The Saturday Book* 17 (1957), reprinted in *Matrix* 9 (1989): 10.

[34] *Letters of Eric Gill* (11th March 1927), 217.

[35] *Letters of Eric Gill* (10th June 1928), 233.

[36] Pigotts was formerly a farm. Gill adapted the outhouses as workshops for himself and his small community of fellow-craftsmen, until his death in 1940. (The community comprised his two sons-in-law, Denis Tegetmeier, married to Petra, and René Hague, married to Joanna. Others included Gordian Gill, David Jones, Brocard Sewell, David Kindersley, Donald Potter). Gill had his wood engraving workshop in the house, however, which also served as his office and library. In the broadsheet, 'The Eric Gill Workshops', Gordian Gill wrote: 'Gill's aim was that Pigotts should become the enduring home of craftsmanship'. Gordian Gill and others, *The Eric Gill Workshops* (Pigotts, North Dean, High Wycombe: The Hague and Gill Press, 1940.

[37] Ralph Beedham was an instructor in wood engraving in the LCC School of Photo-Engraving at Bolt Court, London and author of a handbook *Wood Engraving,*

illustrated and introduced by Gill and printed by Hilary Pepler at the S. Dominic's Press, Ditchling, in 1920.

[38] T.N. Lawrence also ran a business supplying wood blocks in Bleeding Heart Yard, off Hatton Garden, London. His premises became the Mecca for wood engravers.

[39] A review by John Rothenstein in *Bibliophile's Almanack for 1928* (London: Fleuron, 1928).

[40] Letter from Eric Gill to Enid Clay, Ist March 1924. William Andrews Clark Memorial Library at the University of California at Los Angeles. Cited from Fiona McCarthy, 'Gibbings and Gill: Arcady in Berkshire', *Matrix* 9 (Winter 1989): 27.

[41] I am indebted to Mr. Ray Watkinson, the William Morris scholar, for this insight and for many others, offered so imaginatively.

[42] In 1917 Gill made a book of small wood engravings from his designs for the fourteen sculptured bas-relief panels of the Stations of the Cross for Westminster Abbey. John Ralph Beedham helped him. *The Way of the Cross*. Printed and published by Douglas Pepler, in Ditchling, Sussex, in 1917. Gill exhibited them alongside his drawings for the Stations of the Cross panels at the Alpine Club Gallery, in London. The catalogue was printed by Hilary Pepler at the S. Dominic's Press and has an introduction written by him. (It does not address the wood engravings specifically.) *Catalogue of Drawings and Engravings by Eric Gill* (London: Alpine Club Gallery. 5th-14th May AD 1918, and printed in Ditching. 1918).

[43] Eric Gill, 'The Society of Wood Engravers', *The Architect* 104 (1920): 300.

[44] *Engravings by Eric Gill: A Selection*, 4.

[45] 'Mr. Gill's reply to the critic,' *The Observer* (17th October 1915): 16. Cited from Judith Collins, *Eric Gill Sculpture* (London: Lund Humphries, 1992), 37.

[46] E. Gil, Introduction. *Engravings by Eric Gill: A Selection*, 1 et seq.

[47] E. Gill, Preface, *Engravings 1928-33*.

[48] Eric Gill, *Autobiography*, 178-9.

[49] Beatrice Warde, 'Printing Should be Invisible', an address to the British Typographer's Guild at St. Bride's Institute, London 1932, printed in Beatrice Warde, *The Crystal Goblet* (London: The Sylvan Press, 1960), 11 et seq.

[50] Jan Tschichold, *Die neue Typographie* (Berlin: Bildungsverband der Deutschen Buchdrucker, 1928). Reprinted in an English translation by Ruari McLean with an introduction by R. Kinross, as *The New Typography: A Handbook for Modern Designers*. (Berkeley and Los Angeles: University of California Press, 1995).

Appendix 1

From *A Descriptive Catalogue of Pictures, Poetical and Historical Inventions, Painted by William Blake in Water Colours, Being the Ancient Method of Fresco Painting Restored: And Drawings, for Public Inspection, and for Sale by Private Contract.* London: Printed by D. N. Shury . . . for J. Blake, . . . 1809

Number III.

Sir Jeffrey Chaucer and the nine and twenty Pilgrims on their journey to Canterbury.

The time chosen is early morning, before sunrise, when the jolly company are just quitting the Tabarde Inn. The Knight and Squire with the Squire's Yeoman lead the Procession; next follow the youthful Abbess, her nun and three priests; her greyhounds attend her –

> Of small hounds had she, that she fed
> With roast flesh, milk and wastel bread.

Next follow the Friar and Monk; then the Tapiser, the Pardoner, and the Somner and Manciple. After these "Our Host," who occupies the center of the cavalcade, directs them to the Knight as the person who would be likely to commence their task of each telling a tale in their order. After the Host follow the Shipman, the Haberdasher, the Dyer, the Franklin, the Physician, the Plowman, the Lawyer, the poor Parson, the Merchant, the Wife of Bath, the Miller, the Cook, the Oxford Scholar, Chaucer himself, and the Reeve comes as Chaucer has described:

> And ever he rode hinderest of the rout.

These last are issuing from the gateway of the Inn; the Cook and the Wife of Bath are both taking their morning draught of comfort. Spectators stand at the gateway of the Inn, and are composed of an old Man, a Woman, and Children.

The landscape is an eastward view of the country, from the Tabarde Inn, in Southwark, as it may be supposed to have appeared in Chaucer's time, interspersed with cottages and villages; the first beams of the Sun are seen above the horizon; some buildings and spires indicate the situation of the great City; the Inn is a gothic building, which Thynne in his Glossary says was the lodging of the Abbot of Hyde, by Winchester. On the Inn is inscribed its title, and a proper advantage is taken of this circumstance to describe the subject of the Picture. The words written over the gateway of the Inn are as follow: "The Tabarde Inn, by Henry Baillie, the lodgynge-house for Pilgrims, who journey to Saint Thomas's Shrine at Canterbury."

The characters of Chaucer's Pilgrims are the characters which compose all ages and nations: as one age falls, another rises, different to mortal sight, but to immortals only the same; for we see the same characters repeated again and again, in animals, vegetables, minerals, and in men; nothing new occurs in identical existence; Accident ever varies, Substance can never suffer change nor decay.

Of Chaucer's characters, as described in his Canterbury Tales, some of the names or titles are altered by time, but the characters themselves for ever remain unaltered, and consequently they are the physiognomies or lineaments of universal human life, beyond which Nature never steps. Names alter, things never alter. I have known multitudes of those who would have been monks in the age of monkery, who in this deistical age are deists. As Newton numbered the stars, and as Linneus numbered the plants, so Chaucer numbered the classes of men.

The Painter has consequently varied the heads and forms of his personages into all Nature's varieties; the Horses he has also varied to accord to their Riders; the costume is correct according to authentic monuments.

The Knight and Squire with the Squire's Yeoman lead the procession, as Chaucer has also placed them first in his prologue. The Knight is a true Hero, a good, great, and wise man; his whole length portrait on horseback, as written by Chaucer, cannot be surpassed. He has spent his life in the field; has ever been a conqueror, and is that species of character which in every age stands as the guardian of man against the oppressor. His son is like him with the germ of perhaps greater perfection still, as he blends literature and the arts with his warlike studies. Their dress and their horses are of the first rate, without ostentation, and with all the true grandeur that unaffected simplicity when in high rank always displays. The Squire's Yeoman is also a great character, a man perfectly knowing in his profession:

> And in his hand he bare a mighty bow.

Chaucer describes here a mighty man; one who in war is the worthy attendant on noble heroes.

The Prioress follows these with her female chaplain:

> Another Nonne also with her had she,
> That was her Chaplaine, and Priests three.

This Lady is described also as of the first rank, rich and honoured. She has certain peculiarities and little delicate affectations, not unbecoming in her, being accompanied with what is truly grand and really polite; her person and face Chaucer has described with minuteness; it is very elegant, and was the beauty of our ancestors, till after Elizabeth's time, when voluptuousness and folly began to be accounted beautiful.

Her companion and her three priests were no doubt all perfectly delineated in those parts of Chaucer's work which are now lost; we ought to suppose them suitable attendants on rank and fashion.

The Monk follows these with the Friar. The Painter has also grouped with these the Pardoner and the Sompnour and the Manciple, and has here also introduced one of the rich citizens of London: Characters likely to ride in company, all being above the common rank in life or attendants on those who were so.

For the Monk is described by Chaucer, as a man of the first rank in society, noble, rich, and expensively attended; he is a leader of the age, with certain humorous accompaniment in his character, that do not degrade, but render him an object of dignified mirth, but also with other accompaniments not so respectable.

The Friar is a character also of a mixed kind:

> A friar there was, a wanton and a merry.

but in his office he is said to be a "full solemn man": eloquent, amorous, witty, and satyrical; young, handsome, and rich; he is a complete rogue, with constitutional gaiety enough to make him a master of all the pleasures of the world.

> His neck was white as the flour de lis,
> Thereto strong he was as a champioun.

It is necessary here to speak of Chaucer's own character, that I may set certain mistaken critics right in their conception of the humour and fun that occurs on the journey. Chaucer is himself the great poetical observer of men, who in every age is born to record and eternize its acts. This he does as a master, as a father, and superior, who looks down on their little follies from the Emperor to the Miller; sometimes with severity, oftener with joke and sport.

Accordingly Chaucer has made his Monk a great tragedian, one who studied poetical art. So much so, that the generous Knight is, in the compassionate dictates of his soul, compelled to cry out:

> "Ho," quoth the Knyght, - "good Sir, no more of this;
> That ye have said is right ynough I wis;
> And mokell more, for little heaviness

> Is right enough for much folk, as I guesse.
> I say, for me, it is a great disease,
> Whereas men have been in wealth and ease,
> To heare of their sudden fall, alas,
> And the contrary is joy and solas."

The Monk's definition of tragedy in the proem to his tale is worth repeating:

> Tragedie is to tell a certain story,
> As old books us maken memory,
> Of hem that stood in great prosperity,
> And be fallen out of high degree,
> Into miserie, and ended wretchedly.

Though a man of luxury, pride and pleasure, he is a master of art and learning, though affecting to despise it. Those who can think that the proud Huntsman and Noble Housekeeper, Chaucer's Monk, is intended for a buffoon or burlesque character, know little of Chaucer.

For the Host who follows this group, and holds the center of the cavalcade, is a first rate character, and his jokes are no trifles; they are always, though uttered with audacity, and equally free with the Lord and the Peasant, they are always substantially and weightily expressive of knowledge and experience; Henry Baillie, the keeper of the greatest Inn of the greatest City; for such was the Tabarde Inn in Southwark, near London: our Host was also a leader of the age.

By way of illustration, I instance Shakspeare's Witches in Macbeth. Those who dress them for the stage, consider them as wretched old women, and not as Shakspeare intended, the Goddesses of Destiny; this shews how Chaucer has been misunderstood in his sublime work. Shakspeare's Fairies also are the rulers of the vegetable world, and so are Chaucer's; let them be so considered, and then the poet will be understood, and not else.

But I have omitted to speak of a very prominent character, the Pardoner, the Age's Knave, who always commands and domineers over the high and low vulgar. This man is sent in every age for a rod and scourge, and for a blight, for a trial of men, to divide the classes of men; he is in the most holy sanctuary, and he is suffered by Providence for wise ends, and has also his great use, and his grand leading destiny.

His companion, the Sompnour, is also a Devil of the first magnitude, grand, terrific, rich and honoured in the rank of which he holds the destiny. The uses to Society are perhaps equal of the Devil and of the Angel, their sublimity, who can dispute.

> In daunger had he at his own gise,
> The young girls of his diocese,
> And he knew well their counsel, &c.

The principal figure in the next groupe is the Good Parson; an Apostle, a real Messenger of Heaven, sent in every age for its light and its warmth. This man is beloved and venerated by all, and neglected by all: He serves all, and is served by none; he is, according to Christ's definition, the greatest of his age. Yet he is a Poor Parson of a town. Read Chaucer's description of the Good Parson, and bow the head and the knee to him, who, in every age, sends us such a burning and a shining light. Search, O ye rich and powerful, for these men and obey their counsel, then shall the golden age return: But alas! you will not easily distinguish him from the Friar or the Pardoner; they, also, are "full solemn men," and their counsel you will continue to follow.

I have placed by his side the Sergeant at Lawe, who appears delighted to ride in his company, and between him and his brother, the Plowman; as I wish men of Law would always ride with them, and take their counsel, especially in all difficult points. Chaucer's Lawyer is a character of great venerableness, a Judge, and a real master of the jurisprudence of his age.

The Doctor of Physic is in this groupe, and the Franklin, the voluptuous country gentleman, contrasted with the Physician, and on his other hand, with two Citizens of London. Chaucer's characters live age after age. Every age is a Canterbury Pilgrimage; we all pass on, each sustaining one or other of these characters; nor can a child be born, who is not one of these characters of Chaucer. The Doctor of Physic is described as the first of his profession; perfect, learned, completely Master and Doctor in his art. Thus the reader will observe, that Chaucer makes every one of his characters perfect in his kind; every one is an Antique Statue; the image of a class, and not of an imperfect individual.

This groupe also would furnish substantial matter, on which volumes might be written. The Franklin is one who keeps open table, who is the genius of eating and drinking, the Bacchus; as the Doctor of Physic is the Esculapius, the Host is the Silenus, the Squire is the Apollo, the Miller is the Hercules, &c. Chaucer's characters are a description of the eternal Principles that exist in all ages. The Franklin is voluptuousness itself, most nobly pourtrayed:

> It snewed in his house of meat and drink.

The Plowman is simplicity itself, with wisdom and strength for its stamina. Chaucer has divided the ancient character of Hercules between his Miller and his Plowman. Benevolence is the plowman's great characteristic; he is thin with excessive labour, and not with old age, as some have supposed:

> He would thresh, and thereto dike and delve
> For Christe's sake, for every poore wight,
> Withouten hire, if it lay in his might.

Visions of these eternal principles or characters of human life appear to poets, in all ages; the Grecian gods were the ancient Cherubim of Phoenicia; but the Greeks, and since them the Moderns, have neglected to subdue the gods of Priam. These gods are visions of the eternal attributes, or divine names, which, when erected into gods, become destructive to humanity. They ought to be the servants, and not the masters of man, or of society. They ought to be made to sacrifice to Man, and not man compelled to sacrifice to them; for when separated from man or humanity, who is Jesus the Saviour, the vine of eternity, they are thieves and rebels, they are destroyers.

The Plowman of Chaucer is Hercules in his supreme eternal state, divested of his spectrous shadow; which is the Miller, a terrible fellow, such as exists in all times and places for the trial of men, to astonish every neighbourhood with brutal strength and courage, to get rich and powerful to curb the pride of Man.

The Reeve and the Manciple are two characters of the most consummate worldly wisdom. The Shipman, or Sailor, is a similar genius of Ulyssean art; but with the highest courage superadded.

The Citizens and their Cook are each leaders of a class. Chaucer has been somehow made to number four citizens, which would make his whole company, himself included, thirty-one. But he says there are but nine and twenty in his company:

> Full nine and twenty in a company.

The Webbe, or Weaver, and the Tapiser, or Tapestry Weaver, appear to me to be the same person; but this is only an opinion, for full nine and twenty may signify one more or less. But I dare say that Chaucer wrote "A Webbe Dyer," that is, a Cloth Dyer:

> A Webbe Dyer, and a Tapiser.

The Merchant cannot be one of the Three Citizens, as his dress is different, and his character is more marked, whereas Chaucer says of his rich citizens:

> All were yclothed in o liverie.

The characters of Women Chaucer has divided into two classes, the Lady Prioress and the Wife of Bath. Are not these leaders of the ages of men? The lady prioress, in some ages, predominates; and in some the wife of Bath, in whose character Chaucer has been equally minute and exact, because she is also a scourge and a blight. I shall say no more of her, nor expose what Chaucer has left hidden; let the young reader study what he has said of her: it is useful as a scare-crow. There are of such characters born too many for the peace of the world.

I come at length to the Clerk of Oxenford. This character varies from that of Chaucer, as the contemplative philosopher varies from the poetical genius. There are always these two classes of learned sages, the poetical and the philosophical. The painter has put them side by side, as if the youthful clerk had put himself under the tuition of the mature poet. Let the Philosopher always be the servant and scholar of inspiration and all will be happy.

Such are the characters that compose this Picture, which was painted in self-defence against the insolent and envious imputation of unfitness for finished and scientific art; and this imputation, most artfully and industriously endeavoured to be propagated among the public by ignorant hirelings. The painter courts comparison with his competitors, who, having received fourteen hundred guineas and more, from the profits of his designs in that well-known work, Designs for Blair's Grave, have left him to shift for himself, while others, more obedient to an employer's opinions and directions, are employed, at a great expence, to produce works, in succession to his, by which they acquired public patronage. This has hitherto been his lot – to get patronage for others and then to be left and neglected, and his work, which gained that patronage, cried down as eccentricity and madness; as unfinished and neglected by the artist's violent temper; he is sure the works now exhibited will give the lie to such aspersions.

Those who say that men are led by interest are knaves. A knavish character will often say, 'of what interest is it to me to do so and so?' I answer, 'of none at all, but the contrary, as you well know. It is of 'malice and envy that you have done this; hence I am aware of you, because I know that you act, not from interest, but from malice, even to your own destruction.' It is therefore become a duty which Mr. B. owes to the Public, who have always recognized him, and patronized him, however hidden by artifices, that he should not suffer such things to be done, or to be hindered from the public Exhibition of his finished productions by any calumnies in future.

The character and expression in this picture could never have been produced with Rubens' light and shadow, or with Rembrandt's, or anything Venetian of Flemish. The Venetian and Flemish practice is broken lines, broken masses, and broken colours. Mr. B.'s practice is unbroken lines, unbroken masses, and unbroken colours. Their art is to lose form; his art is to find form, and to keep it. His arts are opposite to theirs in all things.

As there is a class of men whose whole delight is in the destruction of men, so there is a class of artists, whose whole art and science is fabricated for the purpose of destroying art. Who these are is soon known: "by their works ye shall know them." All who endeavour to raise up a style against Rafael, Mich. Angelo, and the Antique; those who separate Painting from Drawing; who look if a picture is well Drawn, and, if it is, immediately cry out, that it cannot be well Coloured – those are the men.

But to shew the stupidity of this class of men nothing need be done but to examine my rival's prospectus.

The two first characters in Chaucer, the Knight and the Squire, he has put among his rabble; and indeed his prospectus calls the Squire the fop of Chaucer's age. Now hear Chaucer:

> Of his Stature, he was of even length,
> And wonderly deliver, and of great strength;
> And he had be sometime in Chivauchy,
> In Flanders, in Artois, and in Picardy,
> And borne him well, as of so litele space.

Was this a fop?

> Well could he sit a horse, and faire ride,
> He could songs make, and eke well indite
> Just, and eke dance, pourtray, and well write.

Was this a fop?

> Curteis he was, and meek, and serviceable;
> And kerft before his fader at the table[.]

Was this a fop?

It is the same with all his characters; he has done all by chance, or perhaps his fortune, — money, money. According to his prospectus he has Three Monks; these he cannot find in Chaucer, who has only One Monk, and that no vulgar character, as he has endeavoured to make him. When men cannot read they should not pretend to paint. To be sure Chaucer is a little difficult to him who has only blundered over novels, and catchpenny trifles of booksellers. Yet a little pains ought to be taken even by the ignorant and weak. He has put The Reeve, a vulgar fellow, between his Knight and Squire, as if he was resolved to go contrary in everything to Chaucer, who says of the Reeve:

> And ever he rode hinderest of the rout.

In this manner he has jumbled his dumb dollies together and is praised by his equals for it; for both himself and his friend are equally masters of Chaucer's language. They both think that the Wife of Bath is a young, beautiful, blooming damsel, and H—says, that she is the Fair Wife of Bath, and that the Spring appears in her Cheeks.[1] Now hear what Chaucer has made her say of herself, who is no modest one:

But Lord when it remembereth me
Upon my youth and on my jollity
It tickleth me about the heart root,
Unto this day it doth my heart boot,
That I have had my world as in my time;
But age, alas, that all will envenime
Hath bereft my beauty and my pith
Let go; farewell: the Devil go therewith,
The flower is gone; there is no more to tell
The bran, as best I can, I now mote sell;
And yet to be right merry will I fond, —
Now forth to tell of my fourth husband.

She has had four husbands,[2] a fit subject for this painter; yet the painter ought to be very much offended with his friend H—, who has called his "a common scene," "and very ordinary forms," which is the truest part of all, for it is so, and very wretchedly so indeed. What merit can there be in a picture of which such words are spoken with truth?

But the prospectus says that the Painter has represented Chaucer himself as a knave, who thrusts himself among honest people, to make game of and laugh at them; though I must do justice to the painter, and say that he has made him look more like a fool than a knave. But it appears in all the writings of Chaucer, and particularly in his Canterbury Tales, that he was very devout, and paid respect to true enthusiastic superstition. He has laughed at his knaves and fools, as I do now. But he has respected his True Pilgrims, who are a majority of his company, and are not thrown together in the random manner that Mr. S– has done.[3] Chaucer has no where called the Plowman old, worn out with age and labour, as the prospectus has represented him, and says that the picture has done so too. He is worn down with labour, but not with age. How spots of brown and yellow, smeared about at random, can be either young or old, I cannot see. It may be an old man; it may be a young one; it may be any thing that a prospectus pleases. But I know that where there are no lineaments there can be no character. And what connoisseurs call touch, I know by experience, must be the destruction of all character and expression, as it is of every lineament.

The scene of Mr. S–'s Picture is by Dulwich Hills, which was not the way to Canterbury; but perhaps the painter thought he would give them a ride round about, because they were a burlesque set of scare-crows, not worth any man's respect or care.

But the painter's thoughts being always upon gold, he has introduced a character that Chaucer has not; namely, a Goldsmith; for so the prospectus tells us. Why he has introduced a Goldsmith, and what is the wit of it, the prospectus does not explain. But it takes care to mention the reserve and modesty of the Painter; this makes a good epigram enough:

> The fox, the owl, the spider, and the mole,
> By sweet reserve and modesty get fat.

But the prospectus tells us, that the painter has introduced a Sea Captain; Chaucer has a Ship-man a Sailor, a Trading Master of a Vessel, called by courtesy Captain, as every master of a boat is; but this does not make him a Sea Captain. Chaucer has purposely omitted such a personage, as it only exists in certain periods: it is the soldier by sea. He who would be a Soldier in inland nations is a sea captain in commercial nations.

All is misconceived, and its mis-execution is equal to its misconception. I have no objection to Rubens and Rembrandt being employed, or even to their living in a palace; but it shall not be at the expence of Rafael and Michael Angelo living in a cottage, and in contempt and derision. I have been scorned long enough by these fellows, who owe to me all that they have; it shall be so no longer.

> I found them blind, I taught them how to see;
> And, now, they know me not, nor yet themselves.

Notes

1   The artist John Hoppner.

2   Actually five.

3   Thomas Stothard.

Appendix 2

Edited by Maria McGarrity

William Paulet Carey, *Critical Description of the Procession of Chaucer's Pilgrims to Canterbury, Painted by Thomas Stothard, Esq., R.A.* 2nd ed. (London: W. Glindon, 1818).

Introduction

William Paulet Carey's (b. 1759, d. 1839) *Critical Description of the Procession of Chaucer's Pilgrims to Canterbury, Painted by Thomas Stothard, Esq., R.A.* offers much to modern audiences of Chaucer's work and Stothard's interpretation of that work. Carey's *Critical Description* is just that, an assessment and portrait of Stothard's visual interpretation of Chaucer's famed *Canterbury Tales*. The relationship between Chaucer's *Canterbury Tales* and the visual arts is long and has been well discussed in other areas of this volume. Carey's project, originally published in 1808 and reprinted in 1818, was intended to publicize and celebrate the work commissioned by the art dealer Robert H. Cromek, Stothard's *Canterbury Pilgrims*. Carey's work becomes instructive as art criticism and literary interpretation reflecting the cultural perspectives of the early nineteenth century.

Carey, a Dublin-born painter and engraver who turned to writing criticism, takes a self-deprecating tone throughout his *Critical Description* as he continually moves among three central concerns of his work: the description of the Pilgrims and their horses (the importance and detailed discussion of the horses may surprise modern audiences),[1] a comparison of Stothard's visual interpretation and Chaucer's language, and ultimately a discussion of the artistic merits of the composition itself. Throughout his discussion, he references literary and artistic precedents from the ancients to the relatively contemporary Alexander Pope as sources of comparative insight. He finds links between Stothard's *Pilgrims* and the exquisite forms of Rubens. He suggests that Stothard's Wife of Bath, perhaps Chaucer's best-known character, allows "the most fastidious Moralist [to] forget…his severity on a view of her aspect" (60).[2] Carey's description, above all else, is characterized by its interest in accuracy. It is this very interest in the accuracy of textual comparison that separates Carey's art criticism from that of his contemporaries. He compares Chaucer's text with Stothard's vision and applauds Stothard's interpretation for its illumination of the original. He confesses to having in his possession at writing only "the Bible, Johnson's Dictionary, Montgomery's Poems, and Chaucer's Works" (54). Carey needs nothing else to distract him from his own vision. Carey's interest in the accuracy of Stothard's work becomes most clear when he pronounces ultimately that "the drawing is correct" (74).

Carey's largely conservative outlook can be placed within the antiquarian movements of the late eighteenth and early nineteenth centuries. Though his art criticism was later rebuked as a "parcel of sad stuff" by John Constable,[3] his celebration of Stothard's work has a certain resonance for modern viewers even if what remains with us is not the accuracy of Stothard's depiction but his "shadowy splendor" (75). What Carey's *Critical Description* offers to us, as a modern audience, is a portrait of both Stothard's reception and interpretation as it was in the early part of the nineteenth century, a portrait characterized by its formalism and enthusiasm for Stothard and Chaucer in particular and creative expression in general.

Maria McGarrity
Long Island University, Brooklyn

Notes

[1] For a further discussion of the importance of horses for Carey, see Betsy Bowden's "Transportation to Canterbury: the Rival Envisionings of Stothard and Blake," *Studies in Medievalism* XI, 2001, pages 73-111.

[2] All quotations and transcript are from William P. Carey's *Critical Description of the Procession of Chaucer's Pilgrims to Canterbury, Painted by Thomas Stothard, Esq., R.A.,* 2nd ed. (London: W. Glindon, 1818).

[3] Constable was specifically commenting on a series of articles Carey wrote for the *Worcester Guardian* in 1835. See C.R. Leslie's *Memoirs of the Life of John Constable, R.A.,* London, 1843, page 246.

In the following appendix, endnotes with roman numerals refer to the original text, whereas endnotes with numbers refer to the editor's notes of this book.

Critical Description, *&c. &c.*

Many have expressed a surprise that the *Procession of Chaucer's Pilgrims* was not earlier selected by some of our distinguished Artists. But difficulties exist in the subject sufficient to deter the generality of minds from the undertaking.

In historical composition the Artist has many advantages in pointing of grouping and disposition. By placing his principal figure, or main action, any where near the centre, he is enabled to introduce his subordinate agents with all due variety of direction, movement and attitude. He can represent them in well contrasted groups; some sitting, some standing, others pressing forward, or retiring; all tending to give effect and force to the main incident and to give superior consequence to his principal character.

On the contrary, in the *Procession of the Pilgrims*, the difficulty of exhibiting the characters with a sufficient variety of outline and action, is extremely discouraging. The very idea of a Procession on canvas is connected with a view of a number of figures, *all formally directed one way*. Any attempt to introduce variety, unless accounted for by incidents obviously arising out of the business of the Procession, must have a burlesque effect. It would exhibit the Pilgrims in a sort of pantomime, riding one way and looking another.

But this is not the only difficulty. When we survey a general composition from sacred or profane history, we have some important event to excite our interests and exercise our sensibility. Our passions kindle over unmerited sufferings; and we exult as Virtue triumphs, or Vice is overthrown. Thus, we participate in the acute feelings of Jeptha and his daughter. We glow with Mutius Scevola in the camp of Porsenna.[1] We catch the phrensy of the Conqueror, or we groan over the desolating career of Ambition, on a view of the battles of Alexander, by LeBrun.[2]

But the *Procession of the Pilgrims* exhibits no historical event, and unfolds no catastrophe. Abstractly considered, it neither involves nor excites any individual interest. The Painter must depend upon the resources of his own mind to enrich it with incident, to charm our attention, and to give it value as an imposing spectacle, and a superior work of Art.

Before Mr. Stothard undertook the subject, it presented a difficulty like that of Columbus's egg.[i] Every one felt, and no one knew how to overcome it. Since his picture has appeared, the difficulty is no longer remembered. Connoisseurs talk only of the beauties of the composition, and of the triumph of the Artist.

As the same dresses are all copied from authentic originals in different Museums, the Picture is a very valuable record, and must every day rise in value. It possesses some singular features of advantage. It includes a variety of characters; each is of a distinct class, and each is the head of the class to

which it belongs. The scene is laid in England, and the time in a remote age.
From Chaucer's minute description, the Artist has drawn each as a Portrait in
the English costume of the 14th century. Of its importance in this point of
view, a judgment may be formed from the following declaration of Mr.
Douce,[3] in his ["]*Illustrations of Shakespeare,* and *of Ancient Manners*:"
"Mr. STOTHARD, with every claim to superior merit, has recently finished
a Painting of the *Procession of Chaucer's Canterbury Pilgrims*, which may be
classed among the *choicest morsels of its kind*. The *attention* to *accuracy of
costume* which it displays, has *never been exceeded*, and *but very seldom so
well directed*."

    To its merits, as *a superior work of art*, Mr. HOPPNER[4] has borne most
liberal testimony. All that the discriminating eye of Genius could seize at a
single view, and compress in a rapid digest, will be found in the following
masterly letter.

    To RICHARD CUMBERLAND, *Esq.*

                                                                    30th MAY, 1807.

        Dear Sir,
        You desire me to give you some account of the Procession of Chaucer's
Pilgrims*, painted by Stothard, and the task is a pleasing one; for the praise
called forth the merits of a living artist, from a rival in the pursuit of fame, is, I
feel, like mercy, twice blessed-*

        "It blesseth him that gives, and him that takes."

        *The Painter has chosen that moment for his Picture when the Pilgrims may
be supposed to have disengaged themselves from that multitude that bustle in
the environs of a great metropolis, and are collected together by Harry Baillie,
their guide and host. The scene is therefore laid in that part of their road from
London that commands a view of the Dulwich hills, where, it may be supposed,
the host could, without fear of interruption, proclaim his proposal of drawing
lots, to determine who should tell the first tale. He is represented standing in his
stirrups, and appears to exalt in the plan he has formed for their mutual enter-
tainment You see the group gently passing forward-all are in motion,- yet too
well satisfied with each other to be eager for their journey's end. The features
of each individual are touched with the most happy discrimination of character,
and prove the Painter to have studied the human heart with as much attention,
and not less successfully, than the Poet.*
        *This intelligent group is rendered still more interesting by the charm of
colouring, which, though simple, is strong, and most harmoniously distributed
throughout the picture. The landscape has a deep-toned brightness, that accords
most admirably with the figures; and the painter has ingeniously contrived to
give a value to a common scene and very ordinary forms, that would hardly be
found, by unlearned eyes, in the natural objects. He has expressed too, with
great vivacity and truth, the freshness of morning, at that season, when nature*

herself is most fresh and blooming-the spring; and it requires no great stretch of fancy to imagine we perceive the influence of it on the cheeks of the Fair Wife of Bath, and her rosy companions, the Monk and Friar.

In respect of the execution of the various parts of this pleasing design, it is not too much praise to say, that it is wholly free from that vice which the painters term manner; *and it has this peculiarity beside, which I do not remember to have seen in any picture ancient or modern, that it bears no mark of the period in which it was painted, but might very well pass for the work of some able artist of the time of Chaucer. This effect is not, I believe, the result of any association of ideas connected with the costume, but appears in a primitive simplicity, and the total absence of all affectation, either of colour or pencilling. Having attempted to describe a few of the beauties of this captivating performance, it remains only for me to mention one great defect-the picture is, notwithstanding appearances,* a modern one. *But if you can divest yourself of the general prejudice that exists against contemporary talents, you will see a work that would have done honour to any school, at any period.*

> *I am, Dear Sir, &c.*
> JOHN HOPPNER

It is delightful to fly swiftly over the field of description, and to paint the great and striking features of Nature. The present is a different task, but also very pleasing. It is an attempt to paint excellence in *detail;* to describe a variety of individual Characters, so minutely distinguished by the Poet and Painter, that *the description to be faithful must also be minute.* To effect this, the boldest wing must descend to earth, and the most ardent Fancy move from particular to particular, with the slow pace of a tortoise. This is attended with a great difficulty; that of giving the reader some general idea of the light, shadow, colouring and composition of a picture, which he has not seen.

THE MILLER.

The cavalcade is led by the Miller, playing on his favourite instrument.

> A Baggepipe wel coulde he blowe and soune,
> And therwithall he brought us out of toune.

The expression of his face is that of sottish carelessness. It appears that, before he quitted the *Tabard,* he had taken care to slake his thirst pretty freely:

> Our Host saw that he was *dronken* of ale.

Contrary to the practice of many persons so overtaken, the honest Miller himself acknowledged the fact, in reply to the Host, before he commenced his tale;-

> But first I make a protestatioun
> That I am *dronke; I* know it by my soun:
> And therfore if that I misspeke or say,
> Wite it the *ale* of *Southwerk,* I you pray.

He rides without a bridle. The halter hangs loose upon his horse's neck. The knot near the end, and the three thongs into which it is divided from thence, show that it is occasionally applied to the double purpose of a stay and a whip. There is a piece of sheep-skin spread under him on an ordinary saddle.   A bald white face, hanging lip, broken look, dull, jogging pace, and dark gray coat, all give effect to the heavy jade upon which he is mounted. The domestic drudge is in as perfect agreement with the carlish rider, as *Rozinante* with *Don Quixotte,* or *Dapple* with *Sancho Pancha,* in Coypell's[5] admirable series of designs from Cervantes.[6]

There is not the slightest tendency to coarseness or caricatura in the appearance of the rider. The good sense of the Artist has not gone beyond truth in any part of his habiliments, features, or person. His sword and buckler hang at his side: his wallet depends from his saddle. His white coat, blue cap and hood, short breeches and buskins, with his half naked leg and thigh, are peculiarly appropriate.

He leans or rather topples forward in his seat, wholly inattentive to the company behind. His back is bent, and the action of managing the musical instrument is accurately delineated. The paleness of intoxication, noted by Chaucer:-"The Miller *that for* dronken *was* all pale."- contrasted with his foxy hair and beard, his heavy eye, large bottle-nose, wide nostril, and the whimsical contour of his profile, form altogether with his dress, a picture of common life, the humour of which acquires a double force from its simplicity.

THE MILLER'S DOGS,

the one white, the other mottled, gambol along by the off side of his horse. The head of the near one is seen in profile, somewhat from behind. The mouth is turned up, playfully snapping at its companion, whose jaws are extended over it, with a picturesque variety and reciprocal vivacity of action. The white one skims like an arrow over the ground, to which its fore feet are descending, while the hind fly up. The mottled, in contrast, springs upon its hind legs, and flourishes the fore with a sort of sparring sprightliness, as it runs. Owing to the breadth of light and silvery flow of tint with which these nimble little animals are painted, they relieve from the tender green of the banks behind, and from the yellow soil of the road, with peculiar richness: they also assist to relieve the Miller's horse from the back ground. In lightness of pencil they equal Teniers,[7] in his best time: in correctness and spirit they are superior[ii] to any dogs which I have seen from the hand of that eminent painter.

Dr. Johnson's remark upon the style of Goldsmith may be applied in some measure to the younger Teniers. That justly-admired artist painted almost every object in rustic life; and communicated a charm to every other object which he painted. But it appears that, in drawing dogs, he copied only one species, the long-bodied, short-legged, shepherd's cur, with a large head, which makes an awkward object in a picture. It is also very remarkable that, in designing dogs, he was a mannerist of the lowest order. He generally introduced them in one action, and nearly in the same view, running, with the head turned back. He has even frequently copied this view from one of his pictures into others. This fact any person may ascertain, who is in possession of the admirable engravings by Major[8] and Le Bas,[9] from the best pictures of that distinguished master.

Philip Wouverman's,[10] Berghem,[11] and Peter de Laer,[12] painted every species of domestic animals with great truth and spirit. Yet, I think, that the most zealous of their unprejudiced admirers will find it difficult to view these two dogs without feeling a warm sense of the British Artist's excellence.

THE HOST

is the next seen, riding as the guide before the Pilgrims. His person is a front view; his face a profile; but in an opposite direction to that of the Miller. He is represented at the moment when he *"began his horse arest,"* standing up in the stirrups, looking back, and addressing the company. One of his arms is extended to them, holding up the lots by which they are to decide who is to relate the first story.

> A semely man our Hoste was withalle,
> For to han ben a marshal in an halle,
> A large man he was, with eyen stepe;
> A fairer burgeis [tradesman] is their non in Chepe [Cheapside].
> Bold of his speche, and wise, and wel ytaught.
> And of manhood him lacked righte naught.
> Eke therto, was he a right mery man.

It will be easily understood, from the above extract, that this was no common Host, but one of high respectability in his class. We may fairly judge of the estimation in which he was held, from the freedom with which he addressed the company, and the complaisance with which they conceded to his proposition.

To represent such a character upon canvas requires no small share of skill and judgment. The painter has to convey an idea of ordinary occupation; and his representation must not only be free from any traits of vulgarity, but it must possess a due degree of decorous importance. The imagination can with a degree of comparative ease define the extremes of character; but it cannot be denied that this, to which I advert, is a task of difficult accomplishment.

The artist has nevertheless succeeded completely in his full-length portrait of Harry Baillie. He has united the Host and the respectable individual in the same person.

In conformity with the text, he is a tall, portly figure, in his prime; of a fresh and pleasant countenance. There is a look of good cheer about him. His action is unrestrained. He is well mounted; and his dress is that of a person in easy circumstances. He is bonnetted in dark olive silk; habited in a scarlet cloak; girdled, and well booted. A *Sheffield Whittel*[13] hangs at his breast.

There is no void in the composition between him and the preceding figure. They are so judiciously disposed as to form agreeable links of one great chain, or group. The head and breast of his horse intercept the flank of the Miller's jade from view. The Host's is strong, but not large-sized; of a reddish brown, or deep transparent, burnt terra-sienna colour, mellowed in the shades. This vigorous mass unites well with the scarlet of his drapery, and the warm hues of the scenery: it also forms a brilliant but chaste opposition to the clear blue of the sky.

COMPOSITION OF THE FIRST GROUP

The next six Pilgrims are the DOCTOR OF PHYSIC, the MERCHANT, the SERJEANT AT LAW, the FRANKLEIN, the KNIGHT, and his Son, the YOUNG SQUIRE. They ride nearly side by side, in a picturesque, negligent line, following the HOST so near, that there is no open space between him and them. The heads of the three furthest horses group well under his extended arm; and the outline of their breasts is intercepted by the hinder part of his Roadster. His situation may be likened to that of a Captain of Cavalry on a march, so close to the centre of the front rank, that as his men move *irregularly* forward, some of their horses appear to touch upon his.

It will be obvious to the reader, from this, that there is no unseemly chasm in this part of the procession: it is a chain in motion. The Miller is the first link, the Host the second of this group; and, by it, they are connected with the succeeding groups of the composition.

This arrangement is that of a master, who felt the difficulty of advantageously disposing a number of figures advancing together to the same goal. If order, contrast, and richness of grouping, constitute so large a portion of the excellence of composition, it might have been supposed that there existed in this subject an insuperable obstacle to that excellence. An ordinary mind would have robbed the procession of its picturesque beauty, by a too frequent recurrence of the same contour and action. It must be confessed that, amidst all the grandeur and beauty of the Antique Remains, preserved by the masterly point of Bartoli,[14] the eye is at times sensible to this fatiguing sameness.[iii] Let me not be too severely censured for having hazarded this profane reflection. I too am an idolater; an *adorer* of images. In the presence of Grecian and Roman Art, my spirit is lifted up, as the soul of the worshipper of the sun, in the temple of his deity.

If it be the wisdom of feeble minds to court facility, and shine in tame properties, it is the pride of Genius to grapple with impediment and overcome it. In adopting the subject of the *Procession of the Pilgrims*, the Painter closed with a difficulty. In the outline traced by his invention, the difficulty of arrangement vanished. By the diagonal direction which he gave to the first line of the Pilgrims, he was enabled to exhibit each character in the most advantageous point of view; and to give life, variety, and dignity, to his composition.

THE DOCTOR OF PHYSIC,

a diminutive, elderly personage, is the most distant figure, or *pivot-man*, of the first rank or group; and necessarily, from its diagonal direction, the most advanced upon the road. His professional cap and gown are silk, of what the London drapers term a morone or dusky orange colour.

> In sanguine [red], and in perse [blue], he clad was alle,
> Lined with taffata, and with sendalle [kind of silk].

His profile is sharp, and in a varied direction from that of the Host. His chin is bare, his complexion a dingy brown, his countenance morose, and apparently indicative of night-watching and study. Chaucer has recorded his intense application, and profound acquaintance with medical authorities,

> Wel knew he the old Esculapius,
> And Dioscorides, and eke Rufus,
> Old Hippocras, Hali, and Gallien,
> Serapion, Rasis, and Avicen,
> Averrois, Damascene, and Constantin,
> Bernard, and Gatisden, and Gilbertin.

His eye wanders away, somewhat like that of Rembrandt's *Doctor Faustus*; and from the absence of his look it may be supposed that his mind is buried in the perplexities of astral calculation, or the mysteries of natural magic.

THE MERCHANT.

As the Artist avoided a sameness of view in the preceding *profiles* by varying their direction, he has presented a contrast to them by drawing the following characters in three-quarter view. The first is the Merchant, with a "forked *berd*." He rides close beside the Doctor, but is so much less advanced on the line as to admit the face and breast of the latter to be seen. His indented brow is confident, shrewd, and speculative; his eye fixed earnestly upon the Host, with a look of self-sufficiency.

> His resons spake he ful solempnely,
> Souning always the increase of his winning.

His person is robust and above the ordinary stature. He is in the vigor of life. His visage is manly, and sun-burnt; he wears a black high-crowned "Flaundrish *bever* hat," and a coat of "*mottelee*," pale mixed blue, in the fashion of his time, and station.

THE SERJEANT AT LAW

rides immediately next the preceding Pilgrim, but forms a striking variety of character. He is low, spare, more advanced in years. His complexion is pale, but not sallow or unhealthy: his chin close shaven. His forehead high. His countenance thin, but its expression mild and agreeable; calm and intellectual.

> -ful riche of excellence.
> Discrete he was, and of gret reverence;
> He semed swiche; his wordes were so wise.

He wears his professional cap and collar; and his vest, like that of the Merchant, is a pale mixed blue.

THE FRANKLEIN

rides next, and is, in his person and countenance, a direct contrast to the preceding. In this man the animal propensities predominate. But it is a gentlemanly view of a "*foul feeder*." He was a Country Justice and Knight of the shire. He had also been Sheriff, and there is a sort of a true old English Harry-the-eighth consequence about him. His coat is of a pale violet colour; his bonnet a figured silk: his beard cut short, round, and white "as is the dayesie." He is full bodied, and past his prime, but hale and florid. His countenance denotes content and good living.

> Of his complexion he was sanguin;
> Wel loved he by the *morwe* a *sop* in *win*.
> To liven in delit was ever his wone;
> For he was Epicure's owen sone,
> That held opinion, that plein delit

Was veraily felicite parfite.
His brede, his ale, was always after on;
A better envyned man was no wher non.
Withouten bake mete never was his hous,
Of fish and flesh, and that so plenteous,
It snewed in his hous of mete and drinke,
Of alle deintees that men coud thinke.

The expression of his features is open and chearful. He and the Serjeant at Law listen with a smile of pleasure, to the discourse of Harry Baillie. I do not allude in the preceding, to the manners of an after-age, that of Harry the Eighth; but to the countenance and figure of that monarch, as they are to be seen in the best portraits.

THE KNIGHT.

The two next Pilgrims are the Knight, and his Son, the Young Squire, who is the nearest to the eye in the first rank, and occupies a distinguished place upon the fore-ground. From their oblique direction, the Reve is seen between them, although he rides on the off side of the Knight, somewhat apart, and more in the middle ground of the picture.

The Artist has here again successfully exerted himself to avoid all appearance of sameness in designing his heads. In opposition to the three-quarter view of the characters immediately preceding, the three following are drawn in diversified profile. Another variety here occurs. The Doctor, the Merchant, the Serjeant at Law, and the Franklein are seen, in different degrees, no lower than the breast. All beneath is concealed by each other, or by the high stately head and neck of the Knight's Charger. On the contrary, the person of the Knight is drawn at full length. If there be no character so difficult for the Poet, the Painter, and the Actor, to exhibit, as that of the finished gentleman, certainly some praise is due to the Artist, for having had the courage to attempt, and the talents to succeed in, a conspicuous display of that character.

It cannot be denied, that Chaucer's description of the Knight is very marked in all its details, and very perfect. It unites the minute accuracy of Albert Durer's *St. Hubert* with the fine colouring and dignity of Holbein in his most *Titianesque* portraits. After having set forth his noble bearing, his courage, and his victories in different countries, he dwells, with a feeling of delight, on the gentler qualities of his mind, and the polished suavity of his manners;

-in the Grete See,
At many a noble armee had he be;
At mortal battailles hadde he ben fiftene,

> And foughten for our faith at Tramissene;
> In listes, thries-and ay slain his fo."
>
> * * *
>
> And though that he was worthy, he was wise;
> And of his port as meke as is a mayde:
> He never yet no vilaine ne sayde
> In alle his lif, unto no manere wight.
> He was a veray parfit gentil Knight.

The author's intimacy with the Courtiers of Edward III. probably furnished him with the most prominent features of the original. Men of strong genius may succeed in painting the *passions* with a powerful effect, but they are rarely so successful in the nicer gradations of colour, the finer shades, which mark the *manners* of the great. It is true, but in a different sense from [Alexander] Pope's obvious meaning, that "It is from *high life, high characters* are drawn;"[15]-and , on comparing Shakspeare with Chaucer, in this particular, we may find in the former a faculty, which enabled him to paint the manners of Kings and courts, without having had an opportunity of studying the realities.

Stothard's Knight is of a middle size, and well proportioned: his age between forty and fifty: his beard pointed, trimmed pretty close, and of a silver gray: his complexion, "fallen into the sere," but "that not much."-An aquiline nose gives decision to his otherwise delicate profile. His aspect is sedate and courteous: his mein [sic] erect, and his demeanor dignified. His dress and horse furniture become his rank and the costume of his time, but they are not particularly showy. His "*gipon*," or short cassoc, is of yellow fustian, with a high straight collar. His ruff is narrow, and his breeches are of the same stuff as his "gipon." His boots are of grayish olive-coloured leather. His bonnet is of a dark purple silk, with loose lappets falling behind. He wears a cloak of the same fabric and colour, but so very short, that it must have been worn more for fashion than for use.

I have already remarked, that he is in the same oblique line with the Franklein, yet he rides a little apart from him; just so much so that, although the Reve is somewhat less forward, the forehead of his gray stallion is seen advancing between the two. It will be perceived from this, that this rank is neither formal nor encumbered. The circumstance last mentioned breaks the uniformity of the line, and gives a loose, agreeable negligence to the several members of the group.

He is mounted upon a Charger, the companion of former victories; aged, but of a commanding figure: his chest powerful, his neck lofty, with a tinge of gray upon its conspicuous arch. He moves with a grave and stately pace, as if proud of past services, and conscious of his master's rank. Excepting a spot of white upon the nose, his coat is of a dark, rich colour, having the force of black; but mellower, warmer, more transparent; opposing a vigorous shadowy mass to a well-diffused breadth of light, and giving additional brilliancy to the surrounding assemblage of harmonious and glowing hues.

THE REVE.

Owing to his being the length of a horse's neck less advanced on the road, this character is seen close behind the Knight, although he rides on his off side, as already noted. He was a Steward; and his riding apart; joined to his dress and look, may be supposed to mark his inferior station in life. His hanging back from the rest of the company is recorded:

> Ever he rode the *hindermost* of the rout.

From a strict adherence to the letter of this passage, the Painter, with the due license of his art, has deviated. He has partially detached the Reve from the others, but he has placed his figure where it is most advantageous to the composition. Forming a contrast, so close to the Knight and Squire, his uncouth aspect and homely apparel serve to set off the courtly dignity of the one, and the youthful grace of the other. He also prevents a naked space in the centre of the picture, gives fulness to the rear of the first group, and forms an important link in connecting it with the second. At the same time it is to be observed, that there is no farcical introduction, no attempt to extort laughter by strained humour, nothing mean or offensive, in his appearance. The merit of the character is a simple following of individual nature.

His long "*surcote*" of "*perse*" is of mixed colours, a pale blue and dull red; the hood wholly of the latter. His figure is tall, stiff, and slender; his chin and head are shaved, excepting a thin circle of gray hair over his ears. His neck is bare and scraggy. His features are rigid. His colouring is bilious, and his eye bent in splenetic austerity upon the Master of the Ceremonies. This is a close but masterly copy of the Poet's description, as may be seen by the following partial extract:-

> The Reve was a slendre colerike man;
> His berd was shave as neighe as ever he can,
> His here was by his eres round yshorne;
> His top was docked like a preest beforne.

THE YOUNG SQUIRE.

The Poet has exerted his utmost power in describing this character. His figure, age, dress, genius, temper, accomplishments, bodily and mental endowments, are all distinctly marked. The picture is painted with an *attention to detail* equal to that of *Miravelt*[16] or *Janssens*:[17] with a sweetness and spirit which rivals the delicacy of Vandyck, in his happiest productions. In the whole range of our language it would be difficult to produce a more highly-finished portrait.

It is not a little remarkable, that *poetry* and *painting* are enumerated among his other polite accomplishments. Of the latter, from the low state of the Art at that period, it is difficult to form any notion. The very mention of Painting in England in the fourteenth century, must excite a smile of incredulity or derision. Even in the country of her resurrection, she had not yet shook off the lethargy of the tomb, not burst from the gothic cerements, in which she had for ages slumbered. *Chaucer*, when in *Italy*, was introduced to *Petrarch*, the friend of contemporary Art. But whether the British Bard ever took up the pencil, or acquired any interest in the works of others, is a question.

Nevertheless, on reading Chaucer's life, a supposition arises, that, with a few points of exception, he drew the character of the Squire from what he was himself when he wrote his "*Court of Love.*"[18] He was then under twenty years of age; gay, handsome, and admired, as the accomplished favorite of his Sovereign. The surmise has no other foundation but general likeness, corroborated by the frequency of the practice among Painters and Poets. Paul Veronese painted himself, in the *Marriage of Cana*, and in many more of his sacred and profane compositions. Raphael gave his own countenance a place in the *Baptism of Constantine*. Rubens more reprehensibly introduced his portrait into his capital picture of *Christ bearing the Cross*. Horace has left a bold but unfinished sketch of his person, in the conclusion of the first book of his *Epistles*. Spenser, Swift, Pope, Goldsmith, Smollet, Fielding, and many more of our best writers, delighted to perpetuate, either avowedly or otherwise, their own resemblances, in their works. –The following is the character from Chaucer:-

> With him there was his sone, a yonge Squier,
> A *lover*, and a lusty bacheler;
> With lockes, crull [curled] as they were laide in presse.
> Of twenty yere of age he was I gesse:
> Of his stature he was of even lengthe;
> And wonderly deliver [agile], and grete of strengthe.
> And he hadde be, sometime, in chevachie,
> In Flaundres, in Artois, and in Picardie,
> And borne him wel, as of so litel space [time],
> In hope to stonden in his ladies grace.
> Embrouded [embroidered] was he, as it were a mede,
> Alle ful of freshe floures, white and rede.
> Singing he was, or floyting [playing the flute], alle the day:
> He was as freshe as in the moneth of May.

Short was his goune, with sleves long and wide.
Wel coude he sitte on hors, and fayre ride[.]
He coude songes make, and wel endite;
Juste and eke dance, and wel pourtraie and write:
So hote he loved, that by nightertale,
He slept no more than doth the nightingale.
Curteis he was, lowly, and servisable;
And carf before his fader at the table.
A *yeman* hadde he, and servantes no mo
At that time; for him luste to ride so.

We are told in Chaucer's Life, that "his gay disposition united to lively talents; the art of advancing at once, in exterior elegance and profound attainments, recommended him to the liberal and magnificent Edward the III. and procured for him a facile and inviting introduction at a brilliant Court."

Whether Chaucer drew from himself, or from some young Courtier whom he wished to compliment, it is obvious that the character was a favorite; and that he sought to render it conspicuous. Stothard has therefore given the young Squire a distinguished place in the Procession; and with great skill has done justice to the Author's conception. His person exhibits an union of youthful activity, strength, and symmetry. His fore-shortened profile is comely, and his complexion fair, embrowned by travel and manly exercises[.]

His apparel and all that belongs to him, are fashioned for a display of form, pride, and spirit. His strait well-shaped boots, short violet-coloured vest embroidered with flowers, his purple and yellow sash fluttering in airy negligence over his shoulders, the handsome form of his collar and high silk cap, with his dark chesnut hair waving in light curls; all mark the nice attentions of a courtly gallant in his twentieth year, anxious

To stonden in his ladies grace.

His spurs and stirrups are of silver. The long full tail of his steed is carefully dressed and bound across the middle, so as to give a picturesque show and form to that natural ornament. In that "age of chivalry," the pride of horsemanship was a prevailing passion. He had served in the Cavalry, and had "borne him wel' in Flaunders, in Artois, and in Picardie;"-The Poet, in a line already quoted, expressly, vaunts

Wel coude he sitte *on hors, and fayre ride.*-

This point of personal accomplishment admitted of an advantageous display upon canvas. The Painter has therefore mounted him upon a spirited white horse, of a noble figure from the *manege*. He leans back in the saddle, touching the animal with his spur, to exhibit his address and figure, to the fair Pilgrims behind.

> While his left heel, insiduously aside,
> Provokes the caper which he seems to chide.[iv/19]

This stroke of character is perfectly natural in a military equestrian, an admirer of the Ladies, of whom we are told,

> So hote he loved that by nightertale,
> He slep no more than doth the nightingale.

It has also a fine effect. The horse's head is thrown back: he rears on his hind feet, and his rider, sitting with the fiery grace of a young soldier, forms an imposing object on a most conspicuous part of the fore-ground. Together they introduce a bold variety of outline and action in the leading group; they give it an air of martial consequence, and create an animated interest, in place of that uniform movement, which must have otherwise injured this part of the composition.

THE MASS OF LIGHT

in this group, spreads in an irregular form, but with an unbroken diffusion over the drapery of the Serjeant at Law, the Franklein, the Merchant, the Knight, and the Young Squire. The faces of the two former partake of the brightness. From the person of the latter it extends to the bold breadth of white formed by his horse near the centre of the fore-ground, which acts as the high and commanding light of the picture.

In its receding part, this mass is extended in a lower tone, but with great lustre, by the face and body of the bright bay horse on which the Franklein rides. From this it passes in a still descending but glowing tone, over the more distant bays on which the Serjeant at Law and Merchant are mounted. Passing from them, it is insensibly lost in the brown shades of the farthest horse and mellow hues of the ground.

The transitions in this mass are lively and delicate. They range in the following order:—The Squire's horse, white; his drapery pale violet; the Knight's yellow; the Franklein's pale violet; the Serjeant at Law's and the Merchant's tender mixed blue; the horses of the three latter, bright bay in different gradations. Of these, the cool tints, the violets and blues, harmonize with the blue of the sky. The yellows and other warm gradations unite with the ochrey shadows of the ground, with the rich burnt *terra-sienna* colour of the Host's horse, and with the scarlet of his cloak.

The breadth of white on the rearing horse serves to unite the warm and cool gradations in the mass of *light*, as it agrees well with either.

The bold dark mass formed by the Knight's charger being partly inclined to gray, and partly to a burnt-umber hue, is equally successful in giving brilliancy to the light, and uniting the cool and warm shadows.

The subordinate lights, which play round this main mass, are managed with great chastity. They prevent it from appearing spotty or partial, by connecting it with the other main lights of the picture. The bright carnations of the Host's face and hand, with the alternately warm and silvery tints of the Miller and his Dogs, conduce to this effect in front. The Doctor's face operates as a low gradation. Behind the group, the sober hues of the Reve's head and drapery, with the shadowy lustre gleaming on the back-ground near him, and the grey forehead of the horse on which the Nun's Priest rides, have a similar tendency.

The gray forehead of this last horse, although in the second rank, approaches close to the light upon the Young Squire's hind shoulder, as it is thrown back by the rearing of his steed. By this close approach, the lights of the first and second group are insensibly connected.

The effect of this mass is brilliant and harmonious, yet it is not produced by any unfair sacrifice. The light is not suppressed in one part to give a false value to a favorite light or character elsewhere. The day shines in every part of the picture. Nor does it owe any of its vivid aspect to undue introductions of *neutral tint*.[v]   So far from that being the case, it is admitted, that simplicity of execution and truth of local colour are among its distinguishing features.

The principle upon which it is painted is *opposition of colour*. On the one side the dark shadows of the yellow road, over which the procession moves, form a ground into which all the other shadows subside. Opposed to this, the broad blue of the sky serves as a ground to give force and brightness to all the local colours of the scenery and figures. To subdue the violent contrast of these two discordant masses, it was necessary to create a third compounded of the two, and, occasionally, borrowing its prevailing tinge from either. This is produced by the tender green of the intermediate landscape, which, in the receding distances, fades into the deep tone of the sky, and, in the nearer grounds, exhibits the warm and dewy effect of sunshine on a fine *May* morning.

Upon this principle, the distribution of colours is conducted through all the groups. The charm with which the *Procession of the Pilgrims* instantly fixes the eye, is not produced by neutralized tints, and the extinction of local colour. It owes nothing to monotony. On the contrary, its first powerful impression is the result of bold bright colours, opposed, balanced, and toned, into a rich and sparkling character of harmony.

THE COLOURING

is so admirably managed, that any change must be for the worse.

If we were to take away the blue of that serene sky, and to change it to the grayer, and less decided character of a sober, clouded morning, the tone would assimilate too nearly to that of the middle and fore-grounds. The change would be fatal. The flesh tints must lose their lustre. The enchanting vivacity of all the other local colours must fade, and become flat in proportion. The consequence would be somewhat like that which follows the plucking of a cluster of flowers in full blow. Their heads droop, their brilliant hues expire, and their glory is for ever extinguished.

If, on the other hand, we were to change the yellow ochre of the road, over which the Pilgrims are in motion, into a stony gray, or to cover it with verdure, the consequences would be as injurious. The cold hues would become predominant, and the change create discord and insurrection among the remaining colours. Many of the celebrated old Masters painted on *gold*[vi] *grounds*. That yellow ochre is the *gold ground* of the Procession, and like the fabled Pactolus,[20] it communicates a golden value to whatever it touches. That gold ground enabled the Artist to clothe his figures in the richest scarlets, without producing any tendency to a gaudy appearance. They have an agency like that of the scarlet on the *Murderer*, in Titian's[vii] *Martyrdom* of St[.] Peter *the Dominican*. By the accession of their brightness, Stothard succeeded in giving so rich a hue to his flesh tints and to all his other colours, without over-stepping the modesty of nature.

The consequence of changing the gold or ochrey ground to a gray or silver, would be, that the carnations would flare; the violets grow cold; the yellow draperies and burnt *terra-sienna* tints become hard, and the scarlets have the effect of an offensive crudity. The characters depend so much upon costume, and the costume upon colour, that I am warranted in averring, the colouring, as it now stands, has grown out of the subject; forms an important portion of its veracity; and is, in fact, the proper element of the characters.

THE YEOMAN.

As Mr. Stothard has drawn the Yeoman immediately behind the Young Squire, the spectator must suppose that the Artist designed him to appear as his attendant. That very eminent authority, Mr. Tyrwhitt, however, declares "The late editions call this character the *Squire's Yeoman*, but improperly: the *pronoun* HE *relates to the Knight*, Chaucer would *never have given the Son an attendant, when his Father had none*."[21]

I am sorry that I see no reason to agree with Mr. Tyrwhitt in this point. To join in his opinion, we must suppose that the pronoun "he" has no relation to the several cases of the pronoun ("he," "his," "him,") which occur fifteen times in the twenty-two lines immediately preceding it. I refer the reader to the line,

A *Yeman* hadde he, and servantes no mo.

which I have inserted under the description of the *Young Squire*, exactly in the same order as it stands in Chaucer's Prologue.

We must still further suppose, that the same pronoun "he" has no relation to the "*Yonge Squier*," of which, in these fifteen instances, the several cases of the pronoun ("he" "his," "him,") are the unquestionable relatives. If we thus overlook the positive construction of the passage, and violate the laws of our language, we must proceed still beyond these twenty-two lines, in order to connect the same pronoun "he" with the "veray parfit gentil Knight," who is nine lines further removed.-To read the text backwards in this fashion would, I fear, furnish occasion for a new version of the old complaint, that

-learned Commentators view
In Homer, more than Homer knew.[22]

I will now venture to explain why I cannot approve of Mr. Tyrwhitt's assigned reason for his opinion; "Chaucer would *never have given the Son an atten-dant, when his Father had none.*" This is, in effect, to say I disbelieve Chaucer's own words; because, if I believe them, I must conclude that the Poet fell into an error or inconsistency. But it does not appear to me to be any inconsistency or error, to have given the Son a servant when his Father had none. At his time of life we may suppose that the latter retained little of the vanity of show in his own person. There is a conscious dignity in dispensing with parade, which forms a noble trait in the Knight. Chaucer's description warrants this belief,

But for to telen you of his arraie,
His hors was good, but he ne was not gaie.
Of fustian he wered a gipon,
All besmotred with his habergeon.

Here is nothing ostentatious either in his horse or person. His "gipon," or cassoc, is even soiled by his armour. It appears to me to be a fine stroke of character, and a high compliment to both Father and Son, that the Knight went without a servant himself, with a paternal pride of being respected in his Son's appearance. A Father, who had experienced filial neglect, would have taken care to guard against a repetition of it. We may, therefore, infer, that the Knight in going unattended, was assured of being treated with respect and affectionate attention by his Son and his Son's Yeoman.

There is also an additional strong reason in the *youth of the Yeoman* for believing him to be the Young Squire's attendant. From the parity of their years, we may suppose him to have been his foster-brother, or early play-mate. On the contrary, if the Knight had brought a servant, it is probable that he would have been an old tried one, the faithful attendant of his former life. For this opinion we have the coincident example of a great authority on our side. The Painter has mounted the Knight on the *aged Charger*, which had borne him in the field. This is painting the heart. Whoever studies this Picture attentively, will confess, that the Master who composed it, has merits beyond an ordinary conception. From the discrimination with which he has marked the characters, it is plain that he has used the world as his library, and studied man as his book.

I have not seen any of the late editions alluded to by Mr. Tyrwhitt: but I think that there is another reason for adhering to their opinion on this point. The Young Squire is vain of his person, fond of show, and spruced out from the crown of his head to the tail of his horse. It would be a contradiction in character, to send a gay Gallant, like him, riding forth upon a journey, without a servant.

Even if it were an error to have assigned the servant to the son, still I conceive such an admission could be of no weight against *the text* in favor of Mr. *Tyrwhitt's* opinion, unless we are to suppose that *Chaucer was above error* in the design or invention of his characters. His late Editor's good sense and fine taste secured him from the dominion of so vulgar a prejudice. But I have known in many others, the wish to see nothing but beauties in the Ancients, frequently accompanied by something like a resolution to discover nothing in the Moderns but defects. Chaucer's acknowledged judgment, and his rich invention, did not lift him[viii] above the commission of error and oversight in composition. Great beauties, not an exemption from faults, constitute the glory of superior Genius. The characteristics of a sterile writer are care and diligence, polish, jingle, and verbal nicety; the opposites of neglect. His works are not condemned so much for their *errors* as for their *wants*.

I have already observed, that Mr. Stothard's Yeoman rides behind the Young Squire. His face is seen in three quarter view. He is a soldierly stout figure, of the Squire's age. His complexion is a clear healthy brown. He appears to have all his attention roused by the rearing of his master's steed. The good effect of introducing that spirited incident is here again obvious. To escape the shock, he reins in his nag, and the head of the animal is turned round in obedience to the check of the bridle. This view varies considerably from that of the Squire's horse, which is nearly a side view; and still more from that of the Shipman's rouncey, which follows.

The Yeoman's appearance conveys some idea of that which is generally formed of one of Robin Hood's bold archers. His round face, short hair, and rustic visage, are faithfully described. He is coated in Forester's green, with a hood and cap of the same colour. His breeches are of a dusky orange, and his boots of dark olive leather. The "*cristofe of silver shene*" hangs by a chain on his breast. His sword and leathern buckler are belted at his side. His "mighty bow" gleams in his grasp. There is an earnestness in his look, and a spirit in his action, as he leans back in his saddle, that throw life into the effect, and give a spur to the interests of the spectator.

Excepting a white streak down the nose, and some fleshy tints about the mouth, the entire body, limbs, and head of the horse, are of a strong dark mouse colour, in some parts inclining to an iron-gray. This hue agrees with the near white, and makes a good gradation between the ochrey hues of the ground and the green drapery. It is still further mellowed by reflexions, by the gleaming yellow of his bow, the warm hues of the flesh, and some parts of his dress, already noted.

The horse and the rider form a broad mass which is spread, below, by the ground; and, behind, by the dark dove-coloured cloak of the Lady Eglentine, with which it is connected. This dark breadth gives a bold relief to the white horse of the Squire, and is itself well relieved, behind, from the light drapery and gray neck of the horse on which the Prioress rides.

The composition here is well managed. This horse acts as a link to connect the first group or rank with the second. It accounts for the characters of the latter not riding formally close to the preceding, and prevents an unsightly chasm, which would have otherwise occurred in this part of the picture.

THE SECOND GROUP

is composed of the old PLOUGHMAN, the good PARSON, the NUN'S PRIEST, the NUN, the LADY PRIORESS, and the SHIPMAN. The five first Pilgrims ride side by side in somewhat of a diagonal direction like that of the preceding group. The reader will form a correct idea of their order, by conceiving a second rank, irregularly advancing after the first, at just distance enough for one person (the Yeoman) to ride between.

The old Ploughman is the farthest figure, or *pivot-man*, of the second line, and most advanced on the road. His person is seen no lower than the breast, the remainder being intercepted from view by the nearer figures. Although he rides more in the middle ground, and is apart from the Squire and Yeoman, yet, from their oblique direction, he occupies a space between the two, but much nearer the latter.

The dry, simple character of aged rusticity is well expressed in his lean and colourless profile. A few remaining white hairs, "the blossoms of the grave," hang upon his temples, and a thin gray down is barely visible upon his withered chin. This is a sort of grandsire face which nothing but nature could furnish. It reminds me of a class of heads, which that fine Artist, Greuze, in his best time, introduced into his domestic subjects from village life.[23] The russet coat, and flat-crowned broad-brimmed hat of the same colour, form a good variety in the dresses of the company. His head, and figure as far as it is seen, relieve, as a low mellow tone of light, from the shadowy verdure of the distant hill.

THE GOOD PARSON,

who is brother to the Ploughman, rides next to him, in three-quarter view. Being in the middle ground, his head, one of his shoulders, and part of an arm, are seen directly above the Yeoman, so that his white beard gives force and value to the sun-burnt hue of the latter. All the rest of his figure is intercepted from our eye. His cloak of sanguine purple has a rich effect opposed to the drapery of Forester's green immediately before it. The hood is drawn up round his face; which, with his long white beard, already noted, and mild meditative aspect, forms a striking contrast to the

NUN'S PRIEST,

whose shaven, uncovered pate, and jutting, double chin, appear close beside him. His rubicond, jolly profile, hooked nose, pampered look, and small twinkling eye, betray few marks of fasting and mortification. He wears a light gray coat, inclining to blue, buttoned close up to his neck. But his person is almost wholly concealed from our view by the interesting

NUN,

who rides close on this side of him. Her face and the upper part of her figure are seen in front, somewhat inclined back, in conversation with her superior, the Lady Eglentine. The latter is a little less advanced upon the road, on the side next to the spectator.

There is a chaste, retiring grace in her countenance and costume. Her expression is that of cheerful innocence, and her cheeks glow with the bloom of youth, rendered more fresh and lovely by the nimble air of a bright morning.

The arrangements of her dress and her whole appearance, inspire an idea of native modesty. There is nothing of studied decoration about her person . It is evident that she does not seek to attract the eye of others; nor does she notice the gay figure of the Young Squire, or the rearing of his steed.

Her cloak, of dark dove-colour, is drawn over her bosom and neck, and tied under her chin. Her hood is brought forward so close round her face, that only the edge of her wimple is seen. Her being painted without hair, that natural ornament of which Beauty is so proud, adds to the simplicity of her appearance. The spectator cannot help regretting that the fatal scissars have been employed

to sever
Her lovely locks, for ever and for ever.[24]

THE LADY PRIORESS,

on the contrary, allows herself more license. Although her neck, chin, and bosom, are carefully veiled by her wimple of fine linen, her dark dove-coloured cloak is thrown open, and the upper part of her delicate form is seen. Her gown is of a pale carnation colour; and her coral beads hang from her arm, ornamented with a "broche of gold."

She appears to be in the flower of life. Her profile is pleasing. Her complexion fair; but the tints of her cheek show more of the paleness of the lily than the lustre of the rose. This circumstance gives her somewhat of a pensive character. There is a happy affectation, a sort of demure elegance, in her downcast look and action, which perfectly agrees with the Poet's description of one who

> Peined hire to contrefeten chere
> Of court, and ben estatelich of mannere,
> And to ben holden digne of reverence.

The Yeoman and his nag conceal the head and fore part of her horse. The upper arch, only, of his gray neck is seen. A portion of his chest is covered by the skirt of her light-coloured gown; and his body by the spreading folds of her dark cloak. His hinder parts are intercepted from view by the following Pilgrim. Her favorite dog appears beneath her horse, kept down in strong half shadow.

THE SHIPMAN.

This sturdy figure is the nearest in the second rank, or group, although he appears somewhat detached from the line. He wears a red cap and wide buff pantaloons. His rough gown hangs loose upon him. It is of yellowish brown falding, somewhat deeper in colour than the bright bay of the little rouncey, on which he is mounted. His belt appears across his shoulders, and his dagger hangs under his arm.

The roving son of the waves pays no attention to the voice of Harry Baillie, the Host, or to the reserved Beauties of the Cloister, beside him. He has discovered "metal more attractive"[25] in the company behind. His back is turned to the spectator, and a glimpse of his face (bearing some resemblance to *Cooke*[26] the actor) is seen. It is in foreshortened profile; his head being turned round, and his eye fixed on the Wife of Bath, who follows near him.

This characteristic action produces another fortunate variation from the uniform march of the procession. It also enriches the form and extends the line of the group, with material advantage to the general effect. Instead of tamely sideling by the Prioress, his beautiful little animal is foreshortened; the head is directed towards the flank of her horse, and the hind feet form the termination of the second rank, on the foreground.

THE LIGHT ON THE SECOND GROUP

is less in quantity, and more scattered, than that on the first. This, considering the Procession as a spectacle, serves to keep up the attraction of the leading rank of the Pilgrims. The subordination, however, is produced with most perfect simplicity. It does not arise from an *undue* introduction of cold neutral hues, nor from any *false* shadows. It is effected solely by the sober hues of the principal draperies, which divide and narrow the lights, and in their shadows harmonize, as neutral or middle tints, between the blue sky and the warm colours of the picture. It is to be noticed also, that these sober hues were not created for the purpose of keeping this group back; they were absolutely necessary for a correct exhibition of the costume.

All that appears of the Ploughman, with the face and beard of the good Priest, forms the receding portion of this light. In the upper part it relieves from the shadowy verdure of the distant hill; below, it subsides into the gleaming brightness of the nearer grounds. The next portion is the head and a bit of light gray drapery on the breast of the Nun's Priest. The portion still nearer, is the face of the Nun and the edge of her wimple. The skirt of the Abbess's light carnation gown spread upon her horse's shoulders, the gray arch of her horse's neck, her face, and the upper part of her figure, form the main and near portion of this light.

It will be seen, that these portions are confined and separated. They have also less warm tones than the main light of the first group, and the cool are more inclined to gray, sober, and neutral hues. But none of the lights are toned lower than their relative value. They possess all their clearness and truth. The group enjoys the broad beam of day, as well as the preceding rank. The beard of the good Priest, the wimple and face of the Prioress, are left bright and spirited, but not so as to attract the eye, at the expence of the two main masses of light in the composition.

As there are no touches of light upon the Shipman and his horse, they form altogether a bold extent of rich yellow and brown hues, in various shadowy gradations. There is no great depth of shade on his figure. It relieves principally by breadth, and opposition of colour, from the mellow diffusion of light formed by the third group. The head and body of his little bay horse relieve from the vigorous shadows of the ground, and from the Nun's dark drapery. But the parts, just mentioned, being of a very deep tone, and the remainder of the animal strongly tinted down, it altogether unites with the surrounding shadows in giving value to the lights of this group.

I have already shewed, that the first group is connected with the second by the figure of the Yeoman. Here, the Shipman and his horse form a connecting link between the second group and the figures of CHAUCER, the MANCIPLE, and the OXFORD SCHOLAR, who are in

THE THIRD GROUP.

These three Pilgrims ride together, more in the middle ground, immediately after the good Parson, the Nun's Priest, and the Nun. But they are so placed, that the Shipman and his horse intervene, partially, between them and the foreground.

THE OXFORD SCHOLAR,

the farthest figure of this group, is nearly half a horse's length advanced before the other two. He is in the middle ground, apart from the Lady Abbess and Shipman; but, from their oblique position, is seen between them. His vest is of a salmon colour, with a low open collar. His linen cap is of scanty and ordinary form, with blue and white stripes. He rides straight on, but his eye is fixed in abstraction. His countenance is seen in three-quarter view; it is thin and pale; and appears still more so from its being directly opposed to the scarlet of the Shipman's cap. His neck is bare, and his person emaciated. There is an appearance of poverty and neglect about him, which well agrees with the Poet's description.

> A clerk ther was of Oxenforde also,
> That unto logike hadde long ygo.
> As lene was his hors as is a rake,
> And he was not right fat, I undertake;
> But loked holwe, and therto soberly.
> Full thredbare was his overest courtepy [short overcoat],
> For he hadde geten him yet no benefice.

THE MANCIPLE

was a Purveyor to one of the Inns of Court. The Poet has not described the face or person of this character. The Painter has also nearly kept both out of view. They are intercepted by the figures of Chaucer and the Shipman. The part of his features which is seen, shews that his complexion is dingy and sallow, and his form meagre. His vest is of a pale blue, and his cap brown and yellow. His head is turned back, and the spectator discovers that he is looking behind on the buxom figure of the Wife of Bath, who is the main object of attraction, in this part of the composition.

CHAUCER.

The vest or "gipon" of the Poet is of pale lilach colour. His cap is of the same, with lappets falling on his shoulders, like those of the Knight. His person is of middle stature, and his mien courtly. His complexion is fair; his features are mild, regular, and delicate. His face is seen in three-quarter view, and is turned aside to catch the sprightly conversation of the laughter-loving dame behind.

The countenance of Chaucer is designed from that in the British Museum, *painted* by Thomas Occleve, who was the Poet's scholar.[27] I think that I have somewhere read the life of this Thomas Occleve. But *I had sent, to a distant part of the kingdom, all my books and works of art, some days before I thought of commencing this essay.* I have now nothing to refer to but the Bible, Johnson's Dictionary, Montgomery's Poems,[28] and Chaucer's Works: the two former are fixtures in my lodgings; the latter are borrowed, and I have not been able to discover any mention of this Painter or Picture in Chaucer. Although the few other references in this work are from memory, here I dare not trust to recollection. It appears to me, however, an interesting question: Who taught Thomas Occleve to paint?

THE LIGHT ON THE THIRD GROUP.

Nearly the whole of these figures, that is, all which is not intercepted from view, may be said to act in the general effect, as a well diffused and undivided mass of low, rich, and, I must add, lovely light. It is composed of the following delicious gradations: the pale face of the Oxford Scholar and his vest of salmon colour; the small portion of tender sweet blue on the shoulder and breast of the Manciple's coat; Chaucer's face with his cap and "gipon," or "cassoc," of pearly lilach. Of these, the first unites with the warm hues of the other groups, and of the ground; the second partakes of the sky blue; the latter harmonizes with every bright hue in the picture.

There is but a small degree of shadow on any of these figures. They are made out with a little more than half tints, and the few dark touches are only just strong enough to relieve them from the back ground, but not to bring them forward and make them stick against the nearer figures.

Some slight folds in his cap and a small tuft of hair, tenderly marked, are the only dark touches which bear out the Manciple's figure from the back ground. All that we see of his face is kept down in broad half tint.

Perhaps there is here something like a management which makes us *think of the Artist.* From the Manciple's situation in the middle ground, an inexperienced eye might have expected somewhat more light on his face, a little more making out of details, and more *strength* of shadow on some parts. But, if this conception were founded in truth and had been here followed, the light on the Lady Prioress and on the Wife of Bath would have found a rival in this mass and have lost a portion of its value. The general repose required the keeping down of this head. It is particularly turned from the light, and the effect is mellow and masterly. So far from implying a doubt, I am sensible of the consummate skill with which it is conducted, and I consider it, from its relative importance, to be one of the most seductive passages to a scientific examiner. If there be any part where Art, for an instant, drops her veil, it is here; but the grace and beauty, which we behold in that momentary glance, amply repay us for her appearance.

The subordination of the second group to the first is produced by the light being less in quantity and more divided; and the shadows of a sober retiring nature, in the second. But the subordination of the third group to the second is effected by the quiet tone of the light and by the faintness of the shadows. In the second the light being scattered, is, in parts, left bright and bold to bring the figures duly forward. In the third the light, being connected and broader, is kept down still lower, in due gradation, which prevents it from taking off the eye from the main groups. But, again I must repeat, although it is kept down in fine subordination, it retains a pearly and transparent brightness, from its rich opposition to the verdure of the landscape and the charming blue of the sky.

The warm hues of the Oxford Scholar are prevented from having a harsh effect against the sky, by the blue of his cap. As there is no shadow on his figure, the dark collar was necessary to bring it up from the ground. The salmon colour of his vest mellows the scarlet of the Shipman's cap on one side; the tender blue and pearly lilach of the Manciple's and Chaucer's draperies oppose that scarlet on the other. In front, the cool, delicate and charming hues of the two Pilgrims last mentioned, acquire singular brilliancy from the warm brown mass formed by the Shipman and his rouncey.

Over head, silvery clouds stream upon the horizon, and, with the deep-toned blue of the sky, give sweetness and lustre to the warm, and harmonize with the cool tints in this mass. Behind Chaucer, the mellow gleams of sunny green in the middle landscape have an inconceivable beauty. They, at once, set off the mass of light in this group by their admirable subordination, and exhibit the brightness of morning on the scenery. The gray and white cottages on the distant hill spread the light in a chaste gradation, and form a simple embellishment of the prospect.

THE FOURTH GROUP

is composed of the WIFE of BATH, the PARDONERE, the MONK, the FRIAR, and the SOMPNOUR. No chasm in the composition occurs between this and the preceding group. The chain is still connected. The leading Dame follows so closely, that her horse's head appears above the hinder part of the

Shipman's rouncey; and intercepts from view the hinder part of Chaucer's horse. The raised fore-leg of her's also touches the hind leg of the Shipman's. The reader will judge from this, of the order and fullness of the groups, and will perceive that they are so diversified as to exhibit the several characters to the best advantage.

THE WIFE OF BATH.

My readers, who are acquainted with Chaucer's works, must be, at once, sensible of the extreme difficulty of painting this female latitudinarian. To exhibit a decorous view of an indecorous character, is a task of which very few Artists have ever been capable.

Yet I think, that every person, who examines the picture, will, without hesitation, agree with me, that the Wife of Bath is the *chef d'œuvre* of the Artist.

She is mounted on a delicate Ambler, of most beautiful shape. His body is of a transparent murrey colour, and the yellow main flows proudly over the raised arch of his neck. The outline and anatomical details are drawn and marked with a lightness and slender elegance, which would do honour to Vandyck. Without affecting to draw a parallel, I may be allowed to mention that this reminds me of the noble horse upon which Charles the First is mounted in the picture with the Duke D'Epernon, in Warwick Castle. It also brings to my recollection the superb animal upon which Rubens has elevated the Queen in the Luxemburgh Gallery at Paris. I do not mean to imply a particular resemblance between these three superior objects. I simply convey an idea that, although there are some main essentials of form and character in which they differ, there are certain beauties in which they agree.

The face of the fair Dame is seen in three-quarter view, her figure in front. The Artist has taken a very allowable license in her age. Notwithstanding her repeated vows at the Altar of Hymen, she does not appear to be more than eight-and-twenty or thirty years old. This is perhaps a dozen years younger than Chaucer has represented her.

Although she appears without a cloak, there is nothing of levity or exposure in her dress. It is selected with taste, and fashioned to shew an alluring form, but adjusted with a due attention to decorum. She wears a close short gown of scarlet silk, and a foot-mantle of tender rose colour. Her hair is nearly concealed. Not a ringlet is permitted to wanton over her forehead. Her gown and kerchief shame the freedom of modern fashion. They wholly cover her bosom without hiding its shape. Her broad black hat is worn with an appearance of unstudied elegance. It serves to shew off the rich assemblage of bright colours about her person, with great brilliancy of effect. She sits her horse with easy freedom, and as she looks back, dealing out her "quips and cranks" to the Pardonere, Monk, and Friar, a smile of peculiar archness sports

upon her vermillion lip. There is I know not what of vivacity, an inexpress-
ible something in her look, which the eye is sensible of, but which language
cannot define correctly. The round voluptuous turn of her neck and person,
the sparkling gaiety of her features, the dimple on her cheeks, and the brilliant
glow of her sanguine complexion, exhibit, altogether, a character of very prevailing attraction. The most fastidious Moralist forgets his severity on a view
of her aspect, although it conveys the full idea which the Poet sought to
impress upon the Reader.

THE PARDONERE

follows next. He rides on the further side of her, but so far less advanced on
the road, that his person is seen, down to the middle, immediately after her in
the composition. His horse is intercepted from view by her's, and by that of
the Friar. He wears a sky-blue vest and morone silk cap, on which the
Vernicle is placed. He appears to be a sort of jointless, nerveless, compound
of youth and imbecility, half-made and loosely-put-together; a limber, her-
ring-backed "Popinjay, " fashioned to provoke risibility. The Artist has used
no neutral tints here. With a glance of the eye our opinion of the character is
decided. It is a sort of a link in the human species which I know not how to name.

His yellow hair hangs dishevelled on his shoulders, which are narrow, and
grow to a point, "fine by degrees, and beautifully less."[29] His long slender
neck, conical forehead, beardless chin, and hatchet face, compose a ludicrous
species of effeminacy. The comic effect of his figure is heightened by the
strange roll of his large gogling eye. His hands are laid upon his wallet full
of pardons, and he looks with a whifling simper at the wife of five husbands,
as if sure of meeting with one who stood in need of a pardon in her.

THE SOMPNOUR

was the ancient title of the Criers of the Court. The girlish whey-faced *profile* of the Pardonere presents a rich contrast to the rat[t]ling, roaring, fiery
aspect of this boisterous Son of Bacchus, who is seen close behind *in three-
quarter view*. The roughness, the redness, the whelks and carbuncles, of his
broad visage, answer the description of his coarse gluttonous character.
"*Epicuri de grege porcus.*"[30] The small half-shut eye, puffed out cheeks, and
open laughing mouth, exhibit him in the act of singing out

> a stiff burdoun
> Was never trompe of half so gret a soun.

The hair and beard, of this lover of garlic and onions, are black, short and
stubbed. He is dressed in white, without a hat, and, like a true disciple of the

Jolly God, wears a green garland on his brows. The spirit with which this fine head is conceived and coloured, is worthy of the pencil of Rubens himself. The face rises just above the horizon, and opposed to the deep blue of the sky, appears to flame like a beacon upon the top of the distant hill.

THE MONK,

"full, fat, and in good point, " next attracts notice. He is nearer the foreground than the Wife of Bath, but the Friar rides between him and her, although this latter is so much less advanced upon the road, that the upper part of his horse's head and neck intercepts the hinder part of the gay wife's ambler from view.

The Monk himself is half a horse's length less advanced on the road than the Bath Lady. His steed is of a noble shape, full of spirit, and fit to bear a warrior in the field. His indignation of the curb is well expressed, by the haughty bend of his neck, the bearing in of his head upon his chest, and the action of champing the bit impatiently as he moves. His coat is of deep bay or reddish berry brown. His bridle is decorated with bells. The Monk's love of show in this particular, is recorded by the Poet:

> When he rode, men mighte his bridel here
> Gingeling, in a whistling wind, as clere
> And eke as loud as dothe the chapell belle:

He wears the gray habit of his order. The hood is thrown back, and his head is seen in profile uncovered. His chin and crown are shaven, and the circle of hair left by the tonsor on his temples and the back of his head, is black, silvered by age. But if we are to judge from appearances, time has not wholly subdued his wordly propensities. On looking at him and the Friar, we cannot help repeating the Poet of Twickenham's highly censured lines;

> The soul subsides, and wickedly inclines
> To seem but mortal, even in sound divines.[31]

In Pope's time it was deemed a crime to ridicule the ministers of the Church. In Chaucer's age, it was, by some, deemed a merit. At present, we admit the Monks and Friars of Spain, as Buonaparte's enemies, to be a very good sort of christians.

It is to be remembered, that Chaucer was a disciple of *Wickliff*,[32] and as such he discharged the shafts of his satire against the religious orders. Stothard has followed the text, and given a new edge to the keen weapons of the Bard. In the head of the Monk he may be said to have personified Sensuality. His twinkling swinish eye, double chin, and rosy jowls, betray a certain cast of character, which, with the leer upon his features, may induce a supposition, that his conversation with the Bath Beauty, has more in it of the pleasures of this world than the punishments of the next.

THE FRIAR.

"The wanton and merry" old Huberd is seen in three-quarter view, between the Monk and the Pardonere. He is mounted on a fawn-coloured horse, and wears a dark gray habit similar to the former: the cowl is also thrown back, and his shaven poll uncovered. His broad, jovial, high-coloured face, agrees with the Poet's description:-

> -he strong was as a champioun,
> And knew wel the tavernes in every toun,
> And every hosteler and gay tapstere,
> Better than a lazar or a beggere[.]

His eyes, also, are directed, with a jesting expression, to the main object of attraction, the gay Lady wife; and the carnal smile upon his lip may be likened to smoke rising from consumed embers. It reminds the spectator of fires extinguished by Time.

THE LIGHT ON THE FOURTH GROUP.

The main objects upon which this light falls are the Wife of Bath and her horse. The Painter evidently designed this dame to be the most attractive personage in the composition. He has, accordingly, placed her more detached from the rivalship of other figures; and given her the most vivid colours, with the brightest lights, supported by the force of the only positive black in the picture. The principal portion of light on her figure is composed of the large wimple of fine linen which surrounds her face, of the florid carnations of her face and neck, and the linen coverchief on her bosom. This light is spread behind her shoulders by the folds of her wimple. It also acquires a predominant brilliancy from the strong effect of her black hat, which, itself, possesses a commanding power over the eye, from the particular circumstances of its paramount force, and there being no dark colours near to abate its power.

The scarlet body and sleeves of her gown relieve her figure, with very vivid effect, from the golden verdure of the landscape behind. This relief is produced by opposition and lustre of colour; for, excepting a touch of dark purple riband on her breast, the shades are so very faintly indicated, as not to disturb the purity of the red. The Artist was solicitous to preserve it as pure as possible; and, near to her arm next the Sompnour, the gray, darkish manes of her horse and of the Pardonere's, form a cool sober mass, which adds to its relief and brightness.

The second portion of light is diffused over her footmantle, or riding petticoat, which is of a tender warm rose colour. This part of her dress is of an ample breadth. It descends with a few flowing and simple folds below her stirrup, and covers the body of her horse. To the left, this light is spread by the yellow mane over the arch of her horse's neck and his forehead. To the right it is continued by the head and neck of the Friar's horse, which are of a clear fawn colour, and by the hands and white wallet of the Pardonere.

The remaining portion of light is spread by the white coat of the Sompnour, and the face and yellow hair of the Pardonere. In the general effect, the head of the former, and those of the Monk and Friar, act as fine gradations to this light.

It is to be noticed, that the light on her horse's forehead approaches so near to Chaucer, as to be connected with the broad but low-toned gradations of light formed by the group to which he belongs. This is balanced, on her other side, by the light formed by the Sompnour and Pardonere. These, with the lights on and round her footmantle, are connected in the *general effect*, and compose a form somewhat like an ample, but irregular, crescent. In the centre of this, she rises as the *Queen of Pilgrims*, without any rival to detain the eye, and with every surrounding object in subordination to render her conspicuous.

The white upon her drapery is not, in itself, more bright than that on the coverchief of the Lady Prioress, or the beard of the good Priest, in the second group; but, on these latter, the white is less in quantity, and inferior in relative value, from its being kept down by the cool retiring shades with which it is connected.

On the contrary, the white drapery on the Wife of Bath possesses a great relative value. The reader may form some idea of the rich tone of verdure behind her, when I state, that it acts as a light ground to the clear scarlet of her gown, and as shade to the lights on her face and person. It will be easily understood, that there is little more than a tender half tint upon these parts. All about her is transparent and sparkling, and the brilliancy is almost wholly kept up by judicious oppositions of colour. The linen acquires the sprightly effect of virgin white touched upon deep colours, from the vivid contrasts with which it is every where surrounded. It appears to strike with a spirited sharpness upon the scarlet of her gown, on the golden verdure of the landscape, and the shining black of her hat, the predominant depth of which has been already noticed.

The single figure in the Procession which can for a moment be supposed to stand in competition with her is that of the Young Squire. But his face is in fore-shortened profile, of a brown hue, and the touches of light upon it are not so bright as to render it equally conspicuous. In point of quantity the white of his horse forms the commanding light, but it is not so immediately connected with brilliant colours, and, from the relative causes already mentioned, the white drapery, and vivid colours on the Wife of Bath, appear to possess a greater purity and power to catch the eye.

Although the scarlet of the host's cloak is greater in quantity, yet it does not possess so much relative force as the scarlet gown of the Wife of Bath. It has fewer and less immediate oppositions of colour. It is also rendered less catching to the eye by the warm hues of the advancing horses, and its main brightness subsides in the burnt-terra-sienna shades of the roadster on which he is mounted. In addition to this, its preponderance in the effect is further prevented by the want of any touches of bright light on the horse, or rider, excepting the carnations of the latter.

But, in painting the Wife of Bath, the Artist has not subdued the force of her scarlet, by the immediate assimilation of any dark reddish hues. The greens of the back-ground oppose it; and it has no near friendly shade to *subside into*, or unite with. On the contrary, it is *brought forward* by the mass of warm light hues on her footmantle. Owing to this, it instantly catches the eye as a particular and detached portion of vivid colour, committed in a contest for brilliancy with the sprightly blue of the Pardonere's vest. The latter, from the Artist's judicious management, strikes the spectator's eye at the same moment, but only with a sufficient power to display the main object, the Lady, with greater effect.

The light, which is diffused over the warm and brilliant hues of her face and person, is set off by sufficient counterpoises. It derives great value from the subordination of the deep local colours on the foreground objects immediately near; although many of them are sufficiently bright to act as gradations between it and the most vigorous shadows. The cool murrey shades of her horse acquire singular transparency from being surrounded by warm hues. The broad mass of browns, formed by the entire of the Shipman and his rouncey, obtains great relative force from these cool murrey shades, and unites with them in giving force and beauty to the lights on the animal and his mistress. The dark lead-coloured cloaks of the Monk and Friar, the deep "berry-brown" horse of the former, and the strong dark horse of the near citizen, the shadows of his drapery, those of his companions and their horses, and of the cook and his horse, all unite with different degrees of force, to set off the brightness of the fair Bath Pilgrim. The whole of these shadowy masses are mellowed and embodied by the commanding breadth of shade which stretches under the procession in one bold sweep along the fore-ground.

Behind her the tone of the sky deepens. The shadows of the extreme distance partake of its hue, and their forms, to the right, melt indistinctly into one blue mass upon the horizon. In the midst of this, the gray towers of Westminster Abbey, like specks afar off upon the ocean, are barely distinguishable. The landscape receives an additional splendor from the deepened tone of the sky. I have called it a golden verdure, but the words poorly convey an idea of its shadowy brightness. It is the effect of the sun upon young grass-lands, in the middle distance. I have seen something of this sunny effect in the scenery of Breughell,[33] combined with the small historical compositions of Rottenhammer; [34] in Landscapes painted by Paul Brill,[35] subordinate to the figures of Annibal Carracci;[36] and I have also seen somewhat like it in backgrounds, painted by Van Uden,[37] to cabinet subjects by Rubens. But I have seen nothing lately, in a small-sized picture, so bright, and yet in so low and lovely a tone of keeping, as the landscape by Stothard, in this part of the picture.

Not only is the gay Wife thus made a principal figure, but she is also rendered conspicuous by the sympathies of her fellow Pilgrims. To her countenance we behold the eye of the Shipman turned back. To her gay conversation the ear of the Poet Chaucer is inclined. The sickly-looking Manciple strains himself round to catch a refreshing glimpse of her features. She is at once the burden of the Sompnour's song, and of the Pardonere's expectations. The Monk and Friar appear to grow warm in the beam of her eye. And from the countenances and expression of the five citizens behind, we may suppose that she is the theme of their conversation.

THE FIFTH GROUP.

The figures next in the Procession, are the GOLDSMITH, the WEAVER, the HABERDASHER, the DYER, and the TAPESTRY MERCHANT. As Citizens of London, of one class, they appear in nearly the same costume. The Poet declares

> They were alle ycolthed in o livere
> Of a solempne and grete fraternite.

They each wear a long cloak of light warm purple, or deep lilach. This colour is kept in perfect subordination to the preceding group. It also relieves admirably from the sunny verdure of the adjacent landscape, and harmonizes well with the bright flesh tints on their faces.

The nearest to the fore-ground, of these Pilgrims, is seen in foreshortened profile, mounted on a dark stout horse of ordinary figure. He rides so close to the preceding group, that the breast of his horse is intercepted from view by the tail of the Monk's. His hood and cap are of a shadowy green; and the latter is something in the form of a turban, but of inferior size.

The Citizen, who rides on the off side of him, is seen, somewhat more advanced on the road, in a three-quarter view. He wears a cap of the same fashion, but of transparent brown, striped with yellow. His tippet is of straw colour, which, with his lilach drapery, gives a very brilliant tone to the carnations of his head. His countenance is comely, and his eyes are directed to the Wife of Bath, with a look of sleek opulent importance.

The Citizen who rides on the off side of the preceding, is seen in something more than profile. His horse is a dark brown; his hood of the same colour as his cloak; his hat a dark beaver, and low-crowned, with a brim to the fore part only, somewhat like our modern hunting-caps. His figure is that of a pains-taking Trader, from whose countenance the cares attendant on money-getting appear to have obliterated every other trait.

Of the person, who rides beside the latter, little more can be seen than his red cap. But he appears to be in conversation with the farthest of this group, whose round face is turned back with a look of unmeaning jollity upon him.

There is something of Scarron's *Ragotin*[38] in the little fat pursy form of the Cook, who closes the procession immediately after the preceding figures. The stew-pan and ladles are fastened upon his saddle behind. A cap and hood of dingy reddish brown, a short vest of muddy green, with gray, soiled sleeves, a red cloth tied round his middle, a sort of greasy buff breeches, and shapeless boots, constitute the ornaments of his person. The Poet informs us, that "Wel coude he know a draft of London ale;" and he takes care not to let that species of knowledge be lost in dry theory. We behold him raised in the stirrups, with one hand resting on the saddle, while the other holds up a flask to his mouth, the contents of which he appears to discuss, with no small degree of eagerness and satisfaction.

The gray and fleshy hues upon the faces of the Citizens' horses, with a small portion of the fawn-coloured horse of the Friar, group together immediately behind the latter and the Monk. This mass is low in tone, and only just sufficient in quantity to relieve the figures, and prevent the lights on the preceding group from appearing partial. A fold of gray lining of the near Citizen's cloak acts as a gradation to this. The effect is enlivened by a sharp touch of white upon the edge of the next Citizen's tippet, and by a similar sprightly touch on the narrow neck bandage of the farthest. These touches have more spirit from their being the only whites upon the group, or in any part of the picture, from the Sompnour to its termination behind the Cook, which is nearly one-fourth of the composition. The warm gray, upon the horses' fetlocks, bears out the figures, below. The mellow tone of keeping on the Cook, and the rich colour of his head, are singularly excellent.

The broad light upon this last group is spread on the faces and lilach cloaks of four of the Citizens. The deep-toned brightness of the landscape behind, and of the sky immediately above them, produces a rich opposition to the living flesh tints of their finely painted heads.

Setting the discrimination of character out of the question, there is no part of the picture, which does more honor to the executive skill of the Artist than this. The scarlet and blue, which sparkle against each other along the whole line of the Pilgrims, are here reconciled. On the Bath Wife and the Pardonere, they are committed in direct opposition; but in the dark lead-coloured habits of the Monk and Friar, and in the light purple drapery of the Citizens, they are blended together. Placed between the sky and the dark lead-colour, the purple appears sufficiently warm to maintain a due importance: but, upon the golden verdure behind, it lies cool and quiet. The long strife of the yellow and blue, here, subsides into green and olive shades. All the other hues here, also, melt and mingle, and flow together in sweetness. There is a richness and sobriety in these passages, which a Painter only can duly appreciate. The fourth group attracts the spectator by the sparkling purity of virgin tints; the fifth by the lustre of vivid tints subdued. Their beauties are of a different order, but relative and auxiliary. The spirit and brightness of the one is rendered more brilliant; the union and repose of the other more mellow, by their proximity.

From this point we look back along the whole line of the Procession, and are struck with a combination of beauties[ix] which we do not often meet in one picture. Force and transparency, subordination and truth of local colour, opposition and harmony, are distinguished merits in the general effect. The design exhibits an union of humour and decorum, contrast and simplicity, diversity of character and lively discrimination. The composition displays several groups, so detached from each other, that each maintains a due relative importance; and yet so judiciously connected, that, altogether, they form one great and well-ordered group, in motion for the attainment of a common goal. The subject does not afford a wide scope for fancy, but the invention is that of a master. The scenery is appropriate, and marked with the verity of a prospect. The two main interests, that of the Host's proposition, and the Wife of Bath's admirers, are well balanced. The drawing is correct. In all representations of public spectacle, where no story is unfolded, whatever adds to the splendor becomes an important instrument. The time, therefore, is well chosen, as it adds the brightness of morning to the gay dresses of the Pilgrims. The execution is light but firm, and the eye is charmed with suavities of tone and blandishments of pencil, to which I am sorry I have not ability[x] to do justice. It appears to me, that the Artist commenced with an exertion of his best powers, kindled as he proceeded, and reached a climax of excellence in the shadowy splendor of his close.

THE ENGRAVING OF THE PILGRIMS.

When the World was deprived of that admirable Artist, SCHIAVONETTI,[39] apprehensions were entertained that the task of proceeding with the plate from STOTHARD'S fine picture, might fall into hands incapable of doing justice to his beginning. But we may rejoice that his bold etching and the spirited delicacy of the Senior HEATH'S[40] finishing have been united. Having had the painting so long in my possession, when writing the Critical Description, in 1808, its beauties of composition, character, colouring, and penciling were, at the end of nine years, imprinted on my memory; and, on receiving my print, as a *Subscriber*, I was surprised by the spirit and fidelity of the resemblance. I instantly recognized the sottish stupor of the Miller and cheerful pleasantry of the Host. My eye, as speedily, caught the dry abstraction of the Doctor of Physic, the shrewd speculation of the Merchant, and the well-fed importance of the Franklein, contrasted, on the one side, by the pale cast of acute intelligence in the Serjeant at Law, and, on the other, by the courtly suavity of the Knight. The gay vanity of the Young Squire, flourishing his amorous bravery before the Ladies, on his curveting steed; and the bold rusticity of his Yeoman, with the splenetic austerity of the Reeve, were fresh in my memory. In the second group, the modest serenity of the Nun and demure elegance of the Lady Abbess are as admirably transcribed. The Ploughman, the Good Parson and Nun's Priest furnished as lively recollections as the Shipman, Chaucer and his two companions. Although much of the Wife of Bath's beauty depended upon colour in the picture, Mr. HEATH'S graver has lost none of her allurements. The gogling simper of the limberhammed Pardonere, the roaring jollity of the Sompnour, the leer of the Monk and carnal smile of the Friar, are copied with great felicity. The heads of the Merchants, and fat pursy Cook who closes the rear, are not less accurate. Taking a view of the several groups along the whole line of this interesting procession, the drawing, characters, and expression are transferred from the painting to the print, with a happy combination of fidelity and spirit, delicacy and vigor, which does ample justice to the feeling, grace, and playful humour of STOTHARD'S invention.

To give the middle-tints their due value, that is, a sufficient strength to support the shadows, without making them so dark as to diminish the transparency and breadth of the lights, is one of the great difficulties of the graphic art. Some degree of variation in the gradations, is inseparable from the process, especially in engraving after a picture, like STOTHARD'S Pilgrims, in which so much of its charm lies in the exquisite transitions of light and colour. There are, perhaps, few Masters living, whose works are, in so eminent a degree, the result of feeling. This is not only visible in his conception of his story, in his characters, action, forms, drapery and all his accessaries [sic]; but in the use of his materials. There is an airy elegance in his penciling, a blended negligence and sweetness, which no pen can describe. Grace and loveliness glide from his hand, as if, without effort. A soul full of gentle sensibility is in all his works, and let him touch what subject he will, he is sure to cast a spell over the spectator. Both SCHIAVONETTI and HEATH have been eminently successful, in giving the fine feeling of his Pilgrims. The masses of the grounds are not, perhaps, as insensible in all their transitions as in the picture, especially in some parts of the distances. But these variations took place, no doubt, under the direction of STOTHARD, and the print has acquired a great accession of force. The taste, spirit, brilliancy and beauty of the execution can only be fairly estimated by comparison with other masterpieces; and I am happy to own that this splendid performance has not been surpassed by any productions of the burine in this country, since the admirable print of the "Battle of La Hogue,"[41] by WOOLLET,[42] which spread the fame of the British pencil and graver over the civilized world.

Notes

[i]   *It is but justice to note, that we are indebted to Mr. Cromek for the first intention of employing Mr. Stothard to paint the picture of the* Procession of Chaucer's Pilgrims. *The same spirit conceived the idea of employing that extraordinary Artist,* Blake, *to compose his* grand designs *for* [Robert] Blair's Grave [1808]. *We owe also to Mr. Cromek's honest ardour, the rescue of an additional volume of the Poet* Burn[s]'s *literary remains from destruction-The reader will be pleased to remember, that this is written without a communication with any individual. I would say more, but Mr. Cromek is to be the publisher of this little Essay.*

[ii] *I am aware, that in thus barely doing justice to a* living *Artist, I shall give a shock to the prejudices of some of my amateur friends. Their opinion of my taste and judgment will perhaps be lowered. I do not wish to produce this change; but the apprehension of it is not a reason of sufficient force to prevent me from frankly speaking that which I strongly feel.*

[iii] *From this defect the friezes of Polidore Carravaggio are exempt. I instance his* Rape of the Sabines; *his* Departure of the Israelites; *his* Naval Combats; *and, above all, that summary of classic beauty, the* Niobe, *etched by Galestruzzi.*[1] *As the prints are not uncommon, the mass of common place collectors pass them with neglect, to hunt for the* Bathers *by* Rembrandt, *or the drunken mummeries of Van Vliet!*[2] *Yet, after having once beheld the noble productions of Polidore, is there a true lover of Art, whose breast does not palpitate, and his eye kindle, at the recollection?* [1.Giovan Battista Galestruzzi (b. 1618 d. 1661) was an Italian engraver known for his engravings of Caravaggio. 2.Jan Joris van Vliet (b. 1610 d. 1635) was a Dutch etcher known to have worked with Rembrandt in Amsterdam].

[iv] *Prologue by Sheridan.*

[v]   *"Neutral tint,"-"no colour,"-"a safe and* expeditious method of producing effect"-*are favorite terms. The best principles may be pushed into extremes. The rage for "no colour," and "neutral tint," has given birth to* colourless landscapes *and historical compositions* of neutral character. *The "safe and expeditious mode of producing effect," or in other words, the* receipt-in-full for making good pictures, *has, after all, only led its rapid and industrious partisans into something very like the* tea-tray *practice and high prices of* Birmingham.
      The two systems, that of neutral tint, and opposition of colour, are, in their extremes, the Scylla and Charybdis *of art. The muddy, disgusting monotony of the one, and the raw, glaring crudity of the other, offer only a choice of errors. A good taste will select the golden mean.*
      On an examination of the Giorgiones[3] *and the* Titians, *in the Marquis of Stafford's gallery, in Blenheim House and Hamilton Palace, it will be found, that their deep toned harmony was not produced by either of these extremes: but by the most powerful colours judiciously opposed and subdued into union. There are no* dead *tints in them: their deepest shadows are endued with* life. *Their colours* burn.

With respect to the boasted "spirit of pencil," and "quickness of hand," I shall venture one or two remarks. The analogies of nature and art are, in this respect, perfect: and the descriptive characteristics, rapidly produced, feeble in construction, short-lived, apply equally to both. It may be necessary for a traveller to ride post *sometimes. But woe to the Poet or Painter who hopes to arrive at the goal of celebrity by* writing *or* painting post *through poems and pictures!*

Mannered system, mechanic facility, audacity of hand, marked the decline and fall of Art in all the Schools. When the Muse of Painting lost her chastity, she was compelled to become bold and meretricious. As Invention sunk, Ostentation was called in; and where the spectator's mind starved, his eye was fed. Witness the names of Vasari,[4] D'Arpino [5] and Palma, [6] of Pietro da Cortona [7] and Luca Giordano,[8] of Carlo Vanloo [9] and Boucher.[10] Expedition and dash of pencil form no part of the merits of Raphael and Correggio. Yet these are almost the only recommendations of the Rosa da Tivolies,[11] and Antonio Pellegrinies [12] of every country! [3.Giorgione or Giorgio Da Castelfranco (b. circa 1477 d. 1510) was a Venetian painter of the High Renaissance known for the evocative mood of his work. 4.Giorgio Vasari (b. 1511 d. 1574) was an Italian painter, architect, and biographer. His best known paintings are a group of frescoes in Florence's Palazzo Vecchio, and he designed the Uffizi in Florence. Yet his reputation stands on his *Le Vite de' Più Eccellenti Architetti, Pittori, et Scultori Italiani* (1550). 5.Cavaliere D'Arpino (b. *circa* 1568 d. 1649) was an Italian Mannerist painter. 6.Jacopo Palma (b. *circa* 1480 d. 1528) was a High Renaissance Venetian painter known for his *sacra conversazione*. 7.Pietro da Cortona (b. 1596 d. 1669) was an Italian Baroque painter and architect. 8.Luca Giordano (b. 1632 d. 1705) was a Neopolitan painter known for the range of his work as well as his speed in completing it. 9.Charles-André Van Loo (b. 1705 d. 1765) was a French Rococo painter. 10.François Boucher (b. 1703 d. 1770) was a French Rococo painter and engraver, appointed as "first painter" to Louis XV. 11.Philipp Peter Roos, also Rosa da Tivoli (b. 1657 d. 1706) was a painter from the Rhine region who studied in Italy and was known for his interest in animals. 12.Giovanni Antonio Pellegrini (b. 1675 d. 1741) was a Venetian history painter].

vi   *The Bellini, Ghirlandaio,[13] Verrocchio, Pietro Perugino,[14] Raphel, and their scholars, often painted on* gold *grounds, to heighten their colours. M. Schoen,[15] Albert Durer, and the early Germans, occasionally, employed the same expedient. I recently saw in a private collection, a head of Chrsit painted upon a* gold ground *by Lionardo da Vinci. The face is a front view, and in all probability, is one of the many studies, which he painted for the principal character in his Last Supper.*

It is wholly free from green or violet tints in the flesh; the predominance of which sullied Sir William Hamilton's *head of Francis the First, attributed to this Artist. In depth and force of colour it equals any of the Venetian Masters, and it reminded me of the powerful tone of his* Leda, *in the possession of the* Earl of Pembroke. *The drapery is broad and unfinished: the head perfect. There is a celestial beauty in the features. It is a beauty mingled with a cast of sadness; a brightness clouded; but more moving and ineffable than if it broke in full effulgence on the view. Shakspeare's exquisite thought "the tender eye of day," faintly conveys the idea. It is not a smile, which gives sweetness to the mouth; nor is it a look of command, which displays the majestic character of the Deity on the forehead. The authority, with which it is invested is that of impassioned sentiment obeyed and reverenced by the heart. The love and compassion of the Redeemer are blended with an expression of Omnipotence. In* Mr. Ackerman's [16] *fine head of Christ, by Carlo Dolce,[17] the* Man of Sorrow *is painted with great excellence: but it is the sorrow of a* mortal *only. I have never seen the majesty of the Divine Nature, and the meekness of the Son of Mary, so admirably united as in the Florentine picture, which is the subject of this note.*

It is the prerogative of Poetry and Painting to excite the emotions. This picture possesses that power in a high degree. What then must be the feelings of the Stranger, who in the same apartment beholds one of the most admirable productions of Art, and one of the living ornaments of society. [13.Domenico Ghirlandaio (b. 1448-49 d. 1494) was a Florentine painter known for his religious works. 14.Pietro di Cristofor Vannucci or Perugino (b. 1450 d. 1523) was an Italian painter who worked mainly in Perugia. 15.Martin Schongauer, also Schoen (b. *circa* 1435 d. 1491), was a German painter and engraver from the Rhine region. 16.Rudolph Ackermann (b. 1764 d. 1834) was an English publisher, dealer, and supporter of the arts. 17.Carlo Dolce or Dolci (b.1616 d.1687) was a Florentine Late Baroque painter].

vii *In the* San Pietro, *and many other of his most powerfully toned pictures,* Titian *painted his carnations of such an astonishing force, that, if unchecked, they must have offended by an appearance of too violent exaggeration. To mitigate this, he introduced a portion of scarlet drapery, which enabled him to give the utmost vigour to his other colours. Opposed to shadows of a midnight depth, his scarlet gleams with the intense brightness of live fuel. As the eye passes from this fiery brilliancy to the flesh tints, they appear to lose their fierceness, and the spectator is charmed with an union of the deepest tone and the most glowing tenderness of nature.*

On the contrary, Vandyck sought by the introduction of blue and purple draperies, to give value to his flesh tints: placed near these hues, his sober carnations appear sufficiently warm. Dignity and truth, breadth and detail, spirit and sweetness, degrees of excellence the most opposite, give body and soul, and every thing but motion, to his resemblances-I have examined some of his prime works lately[.] There is a solemn, silvery tone; a pensive moonlight grace, in his portraits at Warwick Castle, *and in the select specimens at* Wilton House, *which being once seen, can never be forgotten. Titian was less firm in his outline, less correct in the* detail of forms, *but he saw nature in a magnifying mirror, and breathed a loftier inspiration. Instead of sinking History to the littleness of Portrait, he gave to Portait an historical elevation. Grandeur was his element. His light a sun beam-His colour gold.*

The Art of Vandyck may be likened to Modesty, which charms the spectator while retiring from his view; that of Titian, to Beauty and Majesty, conscious of their powers, and commanding homage at first sight.

viii *The fancy of him, who gathers cockle-shells, cannot ascend upon the wings of inspiration to the throne of light. Nor can the Poet, whose eye is intent upon the Heavens count the pebbles at his feet. There is no great Artist, whose Pictures exhibit so many neglects, and so much incorrectness as those of Rubens. But before we have leisure to scan his failures, or utter our censures, his gigantic Genius rushes upon us with irresistible force, beats down our objections, and hurries us along with his impassioned Agents to the catastrophe which he is about to unfold. I do not know any Painter who exercises so lawless a dominion. Even some time after we have viewed his pictures, their impression remains; and the movement of our feelings may be compared to the swell and agitation of the waves after the winds have ceased.*

I have ever fancied some great features of resemblance in the genius of Rubens and that of Shakespeare. There are lesser shades and important points in which they differ: but richness of combination, unexampled energy of colour, and fertility of invention; a dauntless bravery in overleaping established forms; a promptitude to offend, and, at the same moment, a power to take captive the senses, and make men advocate their faults, are distinguished characteristics of the Prince of the Flemish School, and the great British Dramatic Poet.

What Rowe is to Shakespeare, Vleughells [18] is to Rubens. There are shining strokes, pathetic passages, and correctly drawn characters in Rowe's Dramas. There are pretty parts, scattered graces, and a warm fancy in Vleughell's Paintings. We read the one and examine the other with a degree of calm pleasure. Whatever can be taught in the schools, decorum, propriety, correctness, all the "negative successes," are there. The ear is lulled. The eye is caught. But no stormy messenger forces a passage to the heart. The interest which they excite is feeble, and soon forgotten. [18.Nicolas Vleughels (b. 1668 d. 1737) was a French painter influenced by Rubens].

ix *I was present when a lady delivered her opinion of this picture to one, who appeared to be, in every sense, her sister. Her lively feeling of its beauties proved that a good taste, like a mirror, is ever a faithful representative of its object. The justness of her sentiments, and her happy turn of expression, bespoke a rare union of talents and acquirements. I was struck with the polish of high life in her manner, and with those easy graces in her person, which nature, alone, can bestow, and a pure heart, only, can retain in the midst of fashionable society. On her departure I learned her name, and the commercial respectability of her husband. The enquiry placed in my hands the two little volumes, which, in the bloom of life, and in the possession of opulence, the maternal affection of this exemplary woman has consecrated to the instruction and happiness of her child. How poor are other distinctions compared with the nobility of such a mind! At once imprest with the ascendancy of genius, and the loveliness of domestic virtue, I hastened to place her* Poetical Selections, *as an invaluable present, in the hands of my wife, for the improvement of my children.*

x *Albert Durer and Chaucer described minutely. In this attempt to follow the exact details of the Poet, in Stothard's picture; I fear that, like other translators, I have often mistaken my author's meaning. The Artist will, however, excuse much, when he learns, that from my beginning it, there existed a necessity that each hour should bring the work to a close; that a part of the first sheet, was written from transient glimpses of the picture, and that I had not time for revising, as each sheet was in the hands of the printer before the succeeding was composed.*

---

1 Gaius Mucius Scaevola, the Roman hero of myth, was believed to have saved the city of Rome from conquest by the Etruscan King Lars Porsena c. 509 BC. Scaevola's attempt to assassinate Porsena failed, but his courage demonstrated in captivity earned his freedom from Porsena's camp and it is believed was responsible for Porsena's withdrawal.

2 Under a commission from Louis XIV, Charles Le Brun (b. 1619, d. 1690), the influential 17th century French painter, created a series of paintings based on the life of Alexander the Great. Louis XIV much admired Alexander and believed himself a newer version of the magnificent Greek.

3 Francis Douce (b. 1757, d. 1834) was an English antiquarian and collector. His *Illustrations of Shakespeare and Ancient Manners,* a collection of early Shakespeare illustrations, was published in London in 1807.

4 John Hoppner (b. 1758, d.1810) was an English painter most widely successful in the field of portraiture. His works are in the collections at the Tate and Saint James' Palace, London.

5 Charles Antoine Coypel (b. 1694, d. 1752) was a French history painter who received a commisssion in 1716 to complete a series based on Cervantes' *Don Quixote.*

6 Rosinante is the name of Don Quixote's horse just as Dapple is the name of Sancho Panza's donkey in *El Ingenioso Hidalgo Don Quijote De La Mancha,* the Spanish classic by Miguel de Cervantes, published in 1605 and 1615, Parts I and II respectively.

[7] David Teniers (b. 1582, d. 1649) was an Antwerp history painter, known for his altarpieces.

[8] Thomas Major (b. 1714, or 1720 d. 1799) was an English engraver who studied in Paris under Jacques-Philippe Lebas.

[9] Jacques-Philippe Lebas (b. 1707, d. 1783) was a French engraver whose highly successful studio often produced work collectively.

[10] Philips Wouwerman, also Philippus Wouwermans (b. 1619, d. 1668), was a Dutch painter and apprentice of Frans Hals.

[11] Nicolaes Pietersz Berchem, also Berghem, Berighem, and Berrighem (b. 1620, d. 1683), was a Dutch painter and etcher. Known as a "Dutch Italianate," he created over 850 paintings, many of Mediterranean scenes.

[12] Pieter van Laer (b. 1599, d. 1642) was a Dutch painter who worked in Rome.

[13] A Sheffield Wittle is an unusually large knife.

[14] Pietro Santi Bartoli (b. 1615, d. 1700) was an Italian engraver and painter, a student of Poussin.

[15] This quotation is from Alexander Pope's *Moral Essays*, Epistle I.

[16] Michiel van Mierevelt (b. 1567, d. 1641) was a Dutch portrait painter who was appointed as the official portraitist to the House of Orange Nassau.

[17] Jan Janssens (b. 1590, d. 1650) was a Flemish painter highly influenced by Caravaggio.

[18] "The Court of Love" is one of Chaucer's earliest known works. Scholars date this poem that concerns a Clerk of Cambridge who is summoned to the Court of Love to about 1346, when Chaucer would have been 18.

[19] Richard Brinsley Sheridan (b. 1751, d. 1816), was the Dublin-born dramatist and Whig politician. This quotation is from Sheridan's "Prologue to *The Miniature Picture* [by the Countess of Craven]," though it appears Carey has changed the "off heel" to "left heel."

[20] The Pactolus is a small river in Asia Minor once believed to have produced gold.

[21] Thomas Tyrwhitt (b. 1730, d. 1786) was the widely respected English scholar, noted for his work on Geoffrey Chaucer in particular, though he also published a translation of Aristotle's *Poetics* in 1794. His five-volume edition of the *Canterbury Tales*, published from 1775-1778, was valued for its explanation for modern audiences of Chaucer's poetic conventions and historical contexts.

[22] This quotation is from Jonathan Swift's (b. 1667, d. 1745) "On Poetry" (1733).

[23] Jean-Baptiste Greuze (b.1725, d.1805) was a French painter well known for his sentimentalization of subject in genre paintings.

[24] This quotation is from Alexander Pope's *The Rape of the Lock*, Part 3, although Carey has changed his version from Pope's original, "that sacred Hair dissever/ From the fair Head, for ever and for ever."

[25] This quotation is from Shakespeare's *Hamlet*, 3.2.109-110.

[26] George Frederick Cooke (b.1756, d.1811) was the preeminent English stage actor of the late 18th and early 19th centuries. He performed in New York and Philadelphia in 1810. Thomas Sulley's 1811 portrait of Cooke as Richard III is in the Pennsylvania Academy of Fine Arts in Philadelphia.

[27] Thomas Hoccleve, also Occleve (b. 1368/69, d.*circa* 1450), was a contemporary of Chaucer. His *De regimine principum* (*The Regiment of Princes*) includes a portrait of Chaucer in the manuscript.

[28] James Montgomery (b.1771, d. 1854) was a Scottish poet well respected for his *Psalms*.

[29] This quotation is from Matthew Prior's (b.1664, d.1721) *Henry and Emma*.

[30] Horace, Quintus Horatius Flaccus (b 65 BC., d. 8 BC), was a Roman writer. This quotation translates, "a pig from the herd of Epicure." It is a famously mocking use of "pig" or "porcus." Horace joins an animal with a reputation for undiscriminating gluttony with Epicureans, those known to enjoy luxurious and refined libations and comestibles. This quotation comes from the final line of his *Epistle 1.4*.

[31] Alexander Pope, the "Poet of Twickenham" (b. 1688, d. 1744), was the English Roman Catholic poet who moved to his villa on the Thames outside of London at Twickenham in 1719. This quotation is from Pope's *Second Satire of the Second Book of Horace*, lines 79-80.

[32] John Wycliffe (b. 1324, d. 1384) was a 14th century English critic of the Church. His questioning of the abuses of the Church presaged the Reformation by two centuries.

[33] Jan Breughel the elder (b. 1568, d. 1625) was a citizen of Antwerp and court painter, famous for his renderings of historical subjects. He was the father of Jan Breughel the younger and son of Pieter Breughel.

[34] Hans [Johann] Rottenhammer (b. 1564/65, d. 1625) was a German painter, highly influenced by Venetian contemporaries. He worked in Rome, where he is known to have met Paul Bril and Jan Breughel. Some critics suggest he perhaps even collaborated with Bril.

[35] Paul Brill, also Paulus Bril (b. 1554, d. 1626), was a Flemish landscape painter who worked largely in Rome. Several of his frescoes remain visible in Vatican City.

[36] Annibale Carracci (b. 1560, d. 1609) was an Italian painter known for his classical style in the traditions of the High Italian Renaissance. His landscapes were influential in the stylistic development of subsequent fresco painting.

[37] Lucas van Uden (b. 1595, d. 1672), a Flemish painter and engraver, was best known for his landscapes and the great specificity and care for detail in his work.

38 Paul Scarron (b. 1610, d. 1660) was a French writer most remembered for his *Le Roman comique* (*The Comic Novel*), published in 3 volumes from 1651-1659. The novel is among those written in the picaresque tradition. Ragotin is one of the burlesque characters in this work.

39 Luigi Schiavonetti (b. 1765, d. 1810) was from the famed Italian family of publishers and engravers. He was engaged to engrave a plate of Stothard's *Canterbury Pilgrims* but died before he could complete the task. Cromek had commissioned him previously to etch William Blake's illustrations for Robert Blair's *The Grave* in 1808. Carey mentions this work in one of his original notes (note i, above). William Paulet Carey admired Schiavonetti's work and wrote a generous appraisal of Schiavonetti published in the *New Monthly Magazine* in December 1815.

40 James Heath (b. 1757, d. 1834) was an English engraver. He was commissioned to complete the *Canterbury Pilgrims* engraving of Luigi Schiavonetti upon Schiavonetti's death. Heath was a friend of Stothard and frequently engraved Stothard's work for publication in *Harrison's Novelists Magazine* between 1780 and 1786.

41 The Battle of La Hogue refers to a series of engagements between the British, their Dutch allies, and France in May 1692.

42 William Woollett (b. 1735, d. 1785) was an English engraver and printmaker.

Appendix 3

Chaucer at Home:
The Canterbury Pilgrims at Georgian Court

William K. Finley

As interior decoration, murals and friezes date back to early Greek, Roman, and Egyptian civilizations, which achieved a high degree of artistic expression in this form. From that time to today, a variety of subjects and themes have decorated both public buildings and private homes. In the nineteenth century, mural painting in the United States (given prominence initially by renowned artists such as John La Farge and William Morris Hunt) reached a high artistic level.

In the decades after the Civil War, wealthy Americans vied with one another to build magnificent mansions to rival the stately homes of England and Europe. As a prominent feature of interior decoration, it was not at all uncommon for wealthy individuals to commission murals or frescoes for the walls of the parlors, dining rooms, and halls of their palatial homes. As subjects, both classical and mediaeval themes were popular for both public and private commissions. Several impressive examples survive to show that Chaucer's *Canterbury Tales* has been popular as a subject for murals from the late nineteenth century through the twentieth century.

That the Library of Congress should celebrate one of the great works of English literature in its interior decoration is not so surprising. On the west and east walls of the North Reading Room of the John Adams Building is a mural of the *Canterbury Tales*, completed by the formal opening of the building in 1939. The work of artist Ezra Winter, the mural depicts the Pilgrims in essentially the order in which Chaucer presents them (the main exception being Chaucer's appearance in the very middle of the group): Miller, Harry Bailey, Knight, Squire, Yeoman, Doctor of Physic, Chaucer, Clerk, Manciple, Sailor, Prioress,

Nun, Nun's Priests, Merchant, Friar, Monk, Franklin, Wife of Bath, Parson, Ploughman, Guildsmen, Cook, Summoner, Pardoner, and Reeve. High on the walls of the North Reading Room, Chaucer's Pilgrims are depicted nearly life-size.

At least two hostelries in the United States named for the *Canterbury Tales* have utilized the Pilgrimage for interior decoration. The Best Western Canterbury Hotel in San Francisco not only has a copy of the *Canterbury Tales* in every one of its 255 guest rooms, but each room displays a vignette from seven large Canterbury Tales murals painted for the hotel's public room in 1934 by Jo Moran. Further east, the Canterbury Bookseller Café Inn in Madison, Wisconsin, decorates each guest room with a hand-painted mural of a scene from Chaucer's masterpiece.

Private residences too have used the *Canterbury Tales* as decoration. At Stan Hywet, the Akron, Ohio mansion of F. A. Seiberling, co-founder of Goodyear Tire and Rubber Company, a large mural of the Canterbury pilgrims dominates the walls of the dining room.

The most impressive mural of the Canterbury pilgrimage ever to be designed for a private home in the United States was painted for George Gould, the son of nineteenth-century robber baron Jay Gould. When Georgian Court, Gould's impressive mansion of more than fifty rooms at Lakeside, New Jersey, was completed in 1897, Gould spared no expense for its interior decoration. As befitting a man of wealth and social position, the furnishings were of the finest materials and construction. As the centerpiece for the imposing entrance hall, Gould commissioned New York muralist Robert van Vorst Sewell (1860-1924) to paint a huge mural of the Canterbury pilgrims.

The Canterbury mural dominates three of the walls of the 48′x 18′ entrance hall at the second-story level. The fourth wall has a balcony and gallery that puts the viewer at eye-level with the mural. Lighted primarily by a ten-foot crystal chandelier, the mural features twenty-four life-size pilgrims from the *Canterbury Tales*. The colorful images of pilgrims and horses are seven feet in height and stretch around the three walls for a total of eighty-four feet.

Although Sewell himself had a fondness for depicting great works of English literature (including a series of murals of Tennyson's *Idylls of the King* in several buildings at Choate Rosemary Hall) and was especially enamored of the *Canterbury Tales*, there is no evidence that George Gould was attracted to Chaucer or his masterpiece.

It is more likely that Gould, who owned a huge stable at Georgian Court, was drawn to the equestrian nature of the mural. As M. Christina Geis, author of a history of Georgian Court estate, has stated, "As a sportsman, George Gould delighted in a subject that would allow for many steeds."[1]

Indeed, horses and riders vie for attention in the Canterbury mural at Georgian Court. Although Chaucer gives little attention to the pilgrims' mounts, Sewell depicts the steeds in varying sizes and colors: brown, black, white, and dappled; the Miller and the Cook ride asses. The pilgrims and their horses stand out against a background of a low white wall with wide double gates, presumably Sewell's interpretation of the Tabard Inn. Unlike the Ezra White frieze at the Library of Congress, Sewell's mural does not adhere to Chaucer's order of presentation of the pilgrims, as can be seen in Sewell's accompanying description. Although Sewell is generally faithful to Chaucer's description of the pilgrims in the Prologue, there are noticeable differences, some undoubtedly created for artistic effect. On the west wall, Madame Eglantyne is given central prominence, both by her position in the foreground of this grouping of six pilgrims and by the highlighting of her bright red stockings and the corresponding red trappings of her white horse, colors which Chaucer omits. For visual effect, Sewell adds red to the clothing and trappings of many pilgrims, sometimes inappropriately, even when Chaucer omits such color. Thus Sewell's Pardoner is dressed in scarlet robe and hat; while in addition to the Wife of Bath and the Physician wearing red as the Prologue indicates, the Merchant, Haberdasher, Sergeant-at-Law, Maniciple, and Cook also have noticeable elements of red in their clothing, never mentioned by Chaucer.

Chaucer's physical description of many pilgrims is meager, and Sewell thus often had to supply his own interpretation of pilgrim and steed. The depiction of such pilgrims as the Parson, the Second Nun, the Maniciple, Harry Bailey, and the Poet himself is more Sewell than Chaucer. In keeping with Chaucer's depiction of the Parson as a benign, simple man, Sewell clothes him in a monk's habit and puts him astride a meek, unadorned brown horse. With little physical description of the Maniciple to go by, Sewell dresses this pilgrim in a green coat with red trim and places a small flask of wine in his hand. Sewell's Chaucer, placed directly in front of the double gates of the inn and looking straight ahead with a serious air, is simply dressed in an untrimmed brown cloak and holds a symbolic white flower in his right hand.

Sewell's mural omits ten of the total of thirty-four pilgrims (including two that join the assemblage en route) that Chaucer identifies. Excluded are the Franklin and the Ploughman, along with the three priests who accompany Madame Eglantyne, four of the five tradesmen (represented only by the Haberdasher), and the Canon and his Yeoman who join the pilgrimage. An interesting addition to the Georgian Court frieze is the character identified as a "Humble Wayfarer," who accompanies the Knight, Squire, and Yeoman and carries the Knight's spear (a weapon not specified by Chaucer). This figure is ambiguous, but Sewell's comment that he has "attached himself to the party" may indicate that he is actually Chaucer's Canon's Yeoman.

In the accompanying description of this mural, published by the American Art Galleries in New York at an unspecified date (perhaps before the turn of the century; certainly before Sewell's death in 1924), Sewell in his introduction says little of the *Canterbury Tales* mural specifically except that he has "endeavored to portray a mediaeval scene in a modern way"; yet his "List of Characters" shows clearly the passages from the Prologue on which he based his mural.

George Gould's Georgian Court mansion is today the centerpiece of Georgian Court College, a small Catholic college for women. Sewell's magnificent Canterbury mural is still perfectly preserved, a testimonial to a literary masterpiece that has inspired numerous impressive artistic interpretations.

The Canterbury Pilgrimage:
A Decorative Frieze

Portraying all the principal characters in Chaucer's great poem

by

Robert van Vorst Sewell[2]

American Art Galleries
Madison Square South
New York

Introductory

In the production of this work I have endeavored to portray a medi-aeval scene in a modern way, and to apply the principles of the "plein-air" school to the production of a decoration.

The full range of tone from black to white and the entire gamut of pigment have been used. I have eschewed producing by any conventionalities of tone or color the qualities commonly called "mural," as I am of the opinion that the real mural quality is a matter of design, and that in the enrichment of design it is legitimate to employ, if we wish, the full resources which these enlightened times afford, chief among which I hold to be "plein-airism," the most important contribution of this cycle to art.

In taking this stand I anticipate and desire to face the criticism which my attitude will be sure to provoke. The theory has been advanced, and by many accepted, that extreme modern naturalism, though legitimate and even necessary in pictorial art, is out of place in decorative work—a theory with which I cannot concur.

The history of decoration points to the fact that, in the past, any new discovery in the direction of naturalism was quickly adopted by the men who left their mark upon their period as decorators. Before the discovery of perspective its laws were continually violated by artists who, notwithstanding, produced very beautiful works. For us to affect their ignorance in order to produce an appearance of archaism or primitive "naïfté" would be not only to stultify our own age, but to furnish a strong argument to those who desire to prove that civilization has in this century developed the germ of degeneration and decline.

The artists of the early Renaissance were not so wedded to the stiff and flat portrayal of the human figure that they were unable to quickly profit by the examples of grace and naturalism afforded by the discovery of the Greek statues. Had they been as great admirers of pre-Raphaelism, Primativism, and archaic conventionality as many are to-day we may be quite safe in saying that there would have been no Renaissance in art; and had the same indifference to new thought extended to all other branches of knowledge, the dark ages would still be with us.

Robert Van Vorst Sewell

Fig. 1 - Robert van Vorst Sewell's murals at Georgian Court

List of Characters in the Frieze, beginning with the Rearmost Horseman

FIRST PANEL [Figure 1]

1. THE REEVE, OR BAILIFF, OF A MANOR HOUSE.

> "Full longé were his leggés and full lean,
> All like a staff, there was no calf yseen.
> Well could he keep a garner and a bin;
> There was no auditor could on him win.
> Tucked he was, as is a friar, about,
> And ever he rode the hindmost of the rout."

2. THE COUNTRY PARSON.

> "A good man was there of religioun,
> Which was a pooré Parson of a toun;
> But rich he was of holy thought and work
> He was also a learned man, a clerk.
> This noble ensample to his sheep he gave,
> That first he wrought, and after that he taught,

Out of the gospel he the wordès caught,
And this figure he added yet thereto,
That if gold rusté, what must iron do?
He waited for ne pomp ne reverence,
Nor makéd him a spiced conscience,
But Christe's lore and his apostles twelve,
He taught, and first he followed it himself."

3. THE PRIORESS.

"There was also a nun, a Prioress,
That of her smiling was full simple and coy;
Her greatest oath was but by Saint Eloy;
And she was clepèd Madame Eglantine.
Full well she sang the servicé divine,
Entuned in her nose full seemely;
And French she spake full fair and fetisly,
After the school of Stratford atteé Bow,
For French of Paris was to her unknowe."

4. THE SECOND NUN.
(The narrator of the tale of Saint Cecilia.)

5. THE MONK.

"A manly man, to be an abbot able.
Full many a dainty-horse had he in stable.

This ilké monk let oldé thingés pace,
And held after the newé world the trace.

I saw his sleeves purfilèd at the hand
With gris, and that the finest in the land.
And for to fasten his hood under his chin
He had of gold ywrought a curious pin."

6. THE MILLER.

"The miller was a stout carle for the nónès,
Full big he was of brawn, and eke of bónès;
A baggèpipè could he blow and soune,
And therewithal he brought us out of towne."

SMALL PANEL[3]

7. THE PARDONER.

> "He had a cross of laton full as stones,
> And in a glass he haddé piggès bones.
> But with these relics, whenne that he found
> A pooré parson dwelling upon lond,
> Upon a day he got him more monéy
> Than that the parson got in monthes three."

8. THE CANON (Astrologer).

> "In clothes black,
> And under that he had a white surplice.
>
> .   .   .   .
>
> All light for summer rode this worthy man,
> And in mine hartè, wondering I began
> What that he was, till that I understood
> How that his cloak was sewed unto his hood.
> For which, when I had long advisèd me,
> I deemèd him some Canon for to be."

CENTRAL PANEL [Figure 2]

9. THE FRIAR.

> "A Frere there was, a wanton and a merry,
> A limitour, a full solemnè man—
> Full sweetèly heard he confessïon,
> And pleasant was his absolütion.
> He was an easy man to give penánce
> There as he wist to have a good pittánce."

10. THE WIFE OF BATH

> "A good wife was there of beside Bath,
> But she was somewhat deaf, and that was scáthe.
>
> Upon an ambler easily she sat,
> Wimpled full well, and on her head a hat
> As broad as is a buckler or a targe,
> A foot-mantél about her hippès large;

Fig. 2 - Robert van Vorst Sewell's murals at Georgian Court

> And on her feet a pair of spurres sharp.
> In fellowship well could she laugh and carp
> Of remedies of love she knew perchance,
> For of that art she knew the oldè dance."

11. THE SQUIRE.

> "A lover, and a lusty bachelor . . .
> Embroidered was he, as it were a meade
> All full of freshé floweres, white and rede.
> Singing he was, or fluting, all the day;
> He was as fresh as was the month of May.
> Short was his gown, with sleevès long and wide.
> Well could he sit on horse, and fairè ride.
>
> Courteous he was, lowly, and serviceable,
> and carved before his father at the table."

12. THE KNIGHT.

> "A knight there was, and that a worthy man,
> That from the timè that he first began

To riden out, he lovèd chivalry,
Truth and honóur, freedom, and courtesy.

And evermore he had his sovereigns praise.
For though that he was worthy he was wise,
And of his port, as meek as is a maid.
He never yet no villainy ne said
In all his life unto no meaner wight.
He was a very parfait gentil knight.
But for to tellen you of his array,
His horse was good, but he ne was wrought gay.
Of fustian he weared a gipon
All besmotted with his habergeon,
For he was latè comen from his viáge,
And wentè for to do his pilgrimage."

13. THE YEOMAN.

"He was clad in coat and hood of green,
A sheaf of peacock arrows bright and keen
Under his belt he bare full thriftily.
Well could he dress his tackle yeomanly;
His arrows droopéd not with feathers low,
And in his hand he bare a mighty bow.

A Christopher on his breast of silver sheen

A forester was he smoothly, as I guess."

14. AN HUMBLE WAYFARER.

(A wayfaring acquaintance of the yeoman, who has attached himself to the party, and is carrying the knight's spear.)

15. THE DOCTOR OF PHYSIC.

"In all the world ne was there none him like
To speak of physic and of surgery;
For he was grounded in astronomy.
He kept his patient wonderfully well
In hourès by his magick naturelle.

Full ready had he his apothecaries,
To send him druggès and electuaries,
For each of them made other for to win;
Their friendship was not newè to begin.

Of his diet measurable was he,
For it was of no superfluity,
But of great nourishing and digestible.
His study was but little on the Bible.
In sanguine and in perse he clad was all,
Lined with taffeta and eke sendàl.
And yet he was but easy in dispense;
He keptè what he won in pestilence.
For gold in physick is a cordïal;
Therefore he loved gold in special."

16. THE SHIPMAN.

"Certainly he was a good fellawe.
Full many a draught of wine he haddé draw
From Bordeaux ward, while that the chapmen sleep.
Of nicè conscience tookè he no keep.
If that he fought, and had the higher hand,
By water he sent them home to every land."

17. THE HABERDASHER.

"Clothed in a livery,
Of a solémne and great fraternity."

Both the haberdasher and the merchant are garbed in the uniform of
their trade guilds.

18. THE MERCHANT.

"A merchant was there with a forkéd beard,
In motley, and high on horse he sat,
Upon his head a Flandrish beaver hat;
His bootès claspèd fair and fetisly.
His reasons spakè he full solemnèly,
Sounding always the increase of his winning.

This worthy man so well his wit beset;
There wistè no man that he was in debt."

19. THE SERGEANT AT LAW. [Figure 3]

"Discreet he was, and of great reverence;
He seemèd such, his wordés were so wise,
Justice he was full often at assize,

For his science, and for his high renown,
Of fees and robès had he many a óne.
So great a prosecutor was no where none.
All was fee simple to him in effect,
His purchasing might not be suspect.

20. THE CLERK OF OXENFORD.

"A clerk there was of Oxenford also,
That unto logic haddè long ygo.
As leanè was his horse as is a rake,
And he was not right fat, I undertake;
But lookèd hollow, and thereto soberly.
Full treadbare was his overest courtepy,
He had not getten him yet a benefice,
He was nought worldly to have an office.
For him was leever have at his beds head
A twenty bookès, clothed in black and red,
Of Aristotle and his philosophy,
Than robès rich, or fiddle, or psaltery.
But although that he were a philosópher,
Yet hadde he but littel gold in coffer;

Fig. 3 - Robert van Vorst Sewell's murals at Georgian Court

But all that he might get, and friends sent
On bookès and on learning he it spent,
And busily gan for the soulès pray
Of them that gave him wherewith to scholay.

Sounding in moral virtue was his speech,
And gladly would he learn, and gladly teach."

21. HARRY BAILEY THE HOST.

"A seemely man our hostè was withal
For to have been a marshal in a hall;
A largé man was he with eyen steep,
A fairer burgess is there none in Cheap:
Bold of his speech, and wise and well ytaught,
And of manhood lacked him righte naught.
Eke thereto he was right a merry man."

22. THE POET CHAUCER.

"When that Aprille with his showres sweet
the drought of March hath pierced at the root,
And bathed every vein with such licour,
Of which vertue engendered is the fleure;—

And smalle fowlès makén melody,
That sleepen all the night with open eye.

Then longeth folk to go on pilgrimages,
Befel that, in that season on a day
In Southwark at the Tabard as I lay,
Ready to wenden on my pilgrimage
To Canterbury with full devout couráge,
At night was come into that hostelry
Well nine and twenty in a company,
Of sundry folk by ádventure yfall
In fellowship, and pilgrims were they all,
That toward Canterbury woulden ride."

23. THE MANCIPLE (Purveyor to an inn at Court).

"I have here in a gourd
A draught of wine, yea of a ripè grape.
And right anon ye shall see a good jápe.
This cook shall drinkè thereof, if I may;
On pain of death he will not say me nay."

24. THE COOK.

> "A cook they hadden with them for the nonce,
> To boile chickens and the marrow bones
>
> He coulde roastè, seethè, broil, and fry,
> Make mortrewes, and well bake a pie.
> Bur great harm was it, as it thoughté me,
> That on his shin a normal [sic] haddié he;
> For blancmanger he madè with the best."

American Art Association,

Managers.

Notes

[1] M. Christina Geis, R.S.M, *Georgian Court: An Estate of the Gilded Age* (Philadelphia: The Art Alliance Press; London and Toronto: Associated University Presses, 1982), 164.

[2] The accompanying illustrations to Sewell's text and color plate 43, photographs by Vincent Hart, originally appeared in M. Christina Geis, *Georgian Court: An Estate of the Gilded Age* and are reproduced here through the courtesy of M. Christina Geis and Georgian Court College.

[3] I am uncertain about Sewell's reference to this "small panel." The arrangement of the pilgrims on the west (left) wall of the entrance hall matches Sewell's grouping of six pilgrims in his "first panel": Reeve, Parson, Prioress, Second Nun, Monk, and Miller. The grouping on the north (center) wall includes the two pilgrims— Pardoner and Canon— that Sewell places in his "small panel" and adds the first ten pilgrims of Sewell's "central panel." The east (right) wall depicts the final six pilgrims (from Sergeant-at-Law to the Cook) in Sewell's description.

Index